MW00527339

Introduction to Business Data Mining

THE MCGRAW-HILL/IRWIN SERIES
Operations and Decision Sciences

OPERATIONS MANAGEMENT

Bowersox, Closs and Cooper, **Supply Chain Logistics Management**, *Second Edition*,

Burt, Dobler and Starling, **Purchasing and Supply Management**, *Seventh Edition*

Chase, Jacobs and Aquilano, **Operations Management for Competitive Advantage,** *Eleventh Edition*

Davis and Heineke, **Operations Management: Integrating Manufacturing and Services**, *Fifth Edition*

Davis and Heineke, **Managing Services**, *First Edition*

Finch, **Operations Now**, *Second Edition*

Flaherty, **Global Operations Management**, *First Edition*

Fitzsimmons and Fitzsimmons, **Service Management**, *Fifth Edition*

Gehrlein, **Operations Management Cases**, *First Edition*

Gray and Larson, **Project Management,** *Third Edition*

Harrison and Samson, **Technology Management,** *First Edition*

Hill, **Manufacturing Strategy: Text & Cases,** *Third Edition*

Hopp and Spearman, **Factory Physics**, *Second Edition*

Jacobs and Whybark, **Why ERP?,** *First Edition*

Knod and Schonberger, **Operations Management,** *Seventh Edition*

Lambert and Stock, **Strategic Logistics Management**, *Third Edition*

Leenders, Johnson, Flynn, and Fearon, **Purchasing and Supply Chain Management,** *Thirteenth Edition*

Melnyk and Swink, **Value-Driven Operations Management,** *First Edition*

Moses, Seshadri and Yakir, **HOM Operations Management Software,** *First Edition*

Nahmias, **Production and Operations Analysis,** *Fifth Edition*

Nicholas, **Competitive Manufacturing Management**, *First Edition*

Olson, **Introduction to Information Systems Project Management,** *Second Edition*

Pinto and Parente, **SimProject: A Project Management Simulation for Classroom Instruction,** *First Edition*

Schroeder, **Operations Management: Contemporary Concepts and Cases,** *Third Edition*

Seppanen, Kumar and Chandra, **Process Analysis and Improvement**, *First Edition*

Simchi-Levi, Kaminsky and Simchi-Levi, **Designing and Managing the Supply Chain,** *Second Edition*

Stevenson, **Operations Management,** *Eighth Edition*

Vollmann, Berry, Whybark, and Jacobs, **Manufacturing Planning & Control Systems,** *Fifth Edition*

BUSINESS STATISTICS

Aczel and Sounderpandian, **Complete Business Statistics,** *Sixth Edition*

ALEKS Corporation, **ALEKS for Business Statistics,** *First Edition*

Alwan, **Statistical Process Analysis,** *First Edition*

Bowerman and O'Connell, **Business Statistics in Practice,** *Fourth Edition*

Bowerman, O'Connell and Orris, **Essentials of Business Statistics,** *First Edition*

Bryant and Smith, **Practical Data Analysis: Case Studies in Business Statistics, Volumes I, II, and III**

Cooper and Schindler, **Business Research Methods,** *Ninth Edition*

Doane and Seward, **Applied Statistics in Business and Economics,** *First Edition*

Delurgio, **Forecasting Principles and Applications,** *First Edition*

Doane, **LearningStats CD Rom**, *Second Edition, 2.0*

Doane, Mathieson, and Tracy, **Visual Statistics,** *Second Edition, 2.0*

Gitlow, Oppenheim, Oppenheim, and Levine, **Quality Management,** *Third Edition*

Lind, Marchal and Wathen, **Basic Statistics for Business and Economics,** *Fifh Edition*

Lind, Marchal and Wathen, **Statistical Techniques in Business and Economics,** *Twelfth Edition*

Merchant, Goffinet and Koehler, **Basic Statistics Using Excel for Office XP,** *Third Edition*

Kutner, Nachtsheim, Neter and Li, **Applied Linear Statistical Models,** *Fifth Edition*

Kutner, Nachtsheim and Neter, **Applied Linear Regression Models,** *Fourth Edition*

Siegel, **Practical Business Statistics,** *Fifth Edition*

Wilson, Keating and John Galt Solutions, Inc., **Business Forecasting,** *Fourth Edition*

Zagorsky, **Business Information**, *First Edition*

Introduction to Business Data Mining

David Olson
University of Nebraska–Lincoln

Yong Shi
*Graduate University of the
Chinese Academy of Sciences
University of Nebraska–Omaha*

**McGraw-Hill
Irwin**

Boston   Burr Ridge, IL   Dubuque, IA   Madison, WI   New York   San Francisco   St. Louis
Bangkok   Bogotá   Caracas   Kuala Lumpur   Lisbon   London   Madrid   Mexico City
Milan   Montreal   New Delhi   Santiago   Seoul   Singapore   Sydney   Taipei   Toronto

McGraw-Hill
Irwin

INTRODUCTION TO BUSINESS DATA MINING

Published by McGraw-Hill/Irwin, a business unit of The McGraw-Hill Companies, Inc., 1221 Avenue of the Americas, New York, NY, 10020. Copyright © 2007 by The McGraw-Hill Companies, Inc. All rights reserved. No part of this publication may be reproduced or distributed in any form or by any means, or stored in a database or retrieval system, without the prior written consent of The McGraw-Hill Companies, Inc., including, but not limited to, in any network or other electronic storage or transmission, or broadcast for distance learning.

Some ancillaries, including electronic and print components, may not be available to customers outside the United States.

This book is printed on acid-free paper.

1 2 3 4 5 6 7 8 9 0 CCW/CCW 0 9 8 7 6 5

ISBN-13: 978-0-07-295971-0
ISBN-10: 0-07-295971-1

Editorial director: *Brent Gordon*
Executive editor: *Scott Isenberg*
Editorial coordinator: *Lee Stone*
Senior marketing manager: *Douglas Reiner*
Senior media producer: *Victor Chiu*
Project manager: *Harvey Yep*
Senior production supervisor: *Sesha Bolisetty*
Designer: *Cara David*
Lead media project manager: *Brian Nacik*
Cover design: *Chris Bowyer*
Typeface: *10/12 Palatino*
Compositor: *International Typesetting & Composition*
Printer: *Courier Westford*

Library of Congress Cataloging-in-Publication Data

Olson, David Louis.
    Introduction to business data mining / David Olson, Yong Shi.
       p. cm.
    Includes index.
    ISBN-13: 978-0-07-295971-0 (alk. paper)
    ISBN-10: 0-07-295971-1 (alk. paper)
    1. Data mining. 2. Business—Data processing. I. Shi, Yong, 1956– II. Title.
HF5548.2.O46 2007
006.3'12—dc22   2005044525

www.mhhe.com

To my family.

David Olson

This book is dedicated to my parents,
Li Guihua and Shi Yuanqing for their constant
support and understanding of my
academic career.

Yong Shi

About the Authors

David L. Olson
University of Nebraska–Lincoln

David Olson is the James & H. K. Stuart Professor in MIS and Othmer Professor at the University of Nebraska. He received his Ph.D. in Business from the University of Nebraska in 1981. He has published research in over eighty refereed journal articles, primarily on the topic of multiple objective decision making. He teaches in the management information systems, management science, and operations management areas. He has authored the books *Decision Aids for Selection Problems, Introduction to Information Systems Project Management*, and *Managerial Issues of Enterprise Resource Planning Systems*, and co-authored the books *Decision Support Models and Expert Systems; Introduction to Management Science; Introduction to Simulation and Risk Analysis; Business Statistics: Quality Information for Decision Analysis; Statistics, Decision Analysis, and Decision Modeling; Multiple Criteria Analysis in Strategic Siting Problems;* and *Introduction to Business Data Mining*. He has made over one hundred presentations at international and national conferences on research topics. He is a member of the Association for Information Systems, the Decision Sciences Institute, the Institute for Operations Research and Management Sciences, and the Multiple Criteria Decision-Making Society. He has coordinated the Decision Sciences Institute Dissertation Competition and the Innovative Education Competition, chaired the Doctoral Affairs Committee, and served as nationally elected vice president three times and as National Program Chair. He was with Texas A&M University from 1981 through 2001—the last two years as Lowry Mays Professor of Business in the Department of Information and Operations Management. He received a Research Fellow Award from the College of Business and Graduate School of Business at Texas A&M University and held the Business Analysis Faculty Excellence Fellowship for two years. He is a Fellow of the Decision Sciences Institute.

Yong Shi
Graduate University of the Chinese Academy of Sciences
University of Nebraska–Omaha

Professor Yong Shi currently is the director of Chinese Academy of Sciences Research Center on Data Technology & Knowledge Economy and Assistant President of the Graduate University of Chinese Academy of Sciences. He has been the Charles W. and Margre H. Durham Distinguished Professor of Information Technology, College of Information Science and Technology, University of Nebraska at Omaha since 1999. Dr. Shi's research interests cover data mining, information overload, multiple criteria decision making, and telecommunications management. He has published seven books, more than sixty papers in various journals, and numerous conferences/proceedings papers. He is the Editor-in-Chief of *International Journal of Information Technology and Decision Making (SCI),* an Area Editor of *International Journal of Operations and*

Quantitative Management, and an Editorial Board Member for a number of academic journals. Dr. Shi has received many distinguished awards including Outstanding Young Scientist Award, National Natural Science Foundation of China, 2001; Member of Overseas Assessor for the Chinese Academy of Sciences, May 2000; and Speaker of Distinguished Visitors Program (DVP) for 1997–2000, IEEE Computer Society. He has consulted for a number of famous companies in data mining and knowledge management projects.

Preface

The intent of this book is to serve advanced undergraduate and graduate classes presenting data mining. Data mining is a very useful topic, applying quantitative analysis to large-scale data made available through recently developed information technology. Each of us has taught such material, and we both have extensive experience in quantitative analysis in business. Yong Shi also has extensive real experience in commercial data mining analysis. We want to take this opportunity to acknowledge the graduate students at the University of Nebraska at Omaha, Gang Kou, Nian Yan, and Wei Zhuang, who helped us prepare the data mining reports by using computer software for this book.

Book Concept

Our intent is to cover the fundamental concepts of data mining, to demonstrate the potential of gathering large sets of data and analyzing these data sets to gain useful business understanding. We have organized the material into four parts. Part I introduces concepts. Part II describes and demonstrates basic data mining algorithms. Part III focuses on business applications of data mining. Part IV presents developing areas, including web mining, text mining, and ethical aspects of data mining. Part I is overview material. Part II contains chapters on a number of different techniques often used in data mining. Not all of these chapters need to be covered, and their sequence can be varied according to instructor need. Part III covers applications, and while we feel that these chapters contain the most interesting and important material, instructors who wish to focus on techniques might not wish to cover these chapters. Conversely, instructors more interested in business applications can cover Part III before reviewing content as needed in Part II. This approach would work especially well if data mining software is available to do the modeling. Part IV contains material we feel is important now and is growing in importance. However, again, coverage and sequence is up to the instructor.

The book includes short vignettes of how specific concepts have been applied in real business. A series of representative data sets are generated to demonstrate specific methods and concepts. References to data mining software and sites such as www.kdnuggets.com are provided.

Supplements accompanying this text include (1) an instructor's CD-ROM, containing a solutions guide, PowerPoint slides, and the data set; (2) a student's CD-ROM, containing PowerPoint slides and the data set; and (3) an online learning center.

Part I: Introduction

Chapter 1 gives an overview of data mining and provides a description of the data mining process. An overview of useful business applications is provided. Chapter 2 presents the data mining process in more detail. It demonstrates this process with a typical set of data. Visualization of data through data mining software is addressed. Chapter 3 presents database support to data mining. Different software tools are described, from data warehouse products through data marts to online analytic processing. Data quality is addressed. Again, different concepts are demonstrated through prototypical data.

Part II: Data Mining Methods as Tools

Chapter 4 provides an overview of data mining techniques and functions. Chapter 5 describes and demonstrates clustering algorithms. Software product support available is reviewed. Chapter 6 reviews various forms of regression tools to identify the best fit over given data sets. Chapter 7 discusses neural networks, a popular application of artificial intelligence suitable for many data mining applications. Chapter 8 reviews decision tree algorithms. The basic algorithm is described, along with descriptions of tree structure, machine learning, and fuzzy set aspects of decision trees. Software products are reviewed, and See5 is demonstrated. Chapter 9 presents linear programming-based methods of fitting data. Real data mining applications are described and demonstrated.

Part III: Business Applications

Chapter 10 reviews the major applications of data mining in business, focusing on the value of these analyses to business decision making. This includes the important topics of customer relationship management. The concept of lift is described. The development of market segmentation by Fingerhut Inc. is reviewed. Chapter 11 describes market-basket analysis, a more qualitative data mining technique. This methodology is described through an example reported in the practitioner literature, and the fundamental data mining concepts of actionability, affinity positioning, and cross-selling are described.

Part IV: Developing Issues

Chapter 12 presents text and web mining. Chapter 13 discusses ethical issues related to data mining.

David L. Olson, University of Nebraska–Lincoln

Yong Shi, University of Nebraska–Omaha

Brief Table

Contents

PART ONE

Introduction

CHAPTER ONE

Initial Description of Data Mining in Business

This chapter:

- Introduces data mining concepts
- Presents typical business data mining applications
- Explains the meaning of key concepts
- Gives a brief overview of data mining tools
- Outlines the remaining chapters of the book

Our culture has developed the ability to generate masses of data. Computer systems expand much faster than the human ability to absorb. Furthermore, Internet connections make it possible to share data in real time on a global basis.

Recent political events emphasize the existence of data to predict. Some blame the system when terrorist strikes are not prevented, because if you dig deep enough, you can always find some data or a memo that pointed to the coming occurrence of these events. However, you would also find a great deal more data predicting things that didn't happen. Obviously, there's a clear need for many organizations to be able to process data faster and more reliably. Data mining involves the use of analysis to detect patterns and allow predictions. Though it's not a perfect science, the intent of data mining is to gain small advantages, because perfect predictions are impossible. These small advantages can be extremely profitable to business. For instance, retail sales organizations have developed sophisticated customer segmentation models to save them from sending sales materials to consumers who likely won't purchase their products, focusing instead on those segments with a higher probability of sales. Banks and other organizations have developed sophisticated customer relationship management programs (supported by data mining) that can predict the value of specific types of customers to that organization, and predict repayment of loans as well. Insurance companies have long applied statistical analysis, which has been extended by data mining tools to aid in the prediction of fraudulent claims. These are only three of many important data mining applications to business.

This book seeks to describe some business applications of data mining. It also will describe the general process of data mining, those database tools needed to support data mining, and the techniques available for data mining.

Introduction

Data mining refers to the analysis of the large quantities of data that are stored in computers. For example, grocery stores have large amounts of data generated by our purchases. Bar coding has made checking out very convenient for us, and provides retail establishments with masses of data. Grocery stores and other retail stores are able to quickly process our purchases, and use computers to accurately determine product prices. These same computers can help the stores with their inventory management, by instantaneously determining the quantity of items of each product on hand. They are also able to apply computer technology to contact their vendors so they don't run out of the things that we want to purchase. Computers allow the store's accounting system to more accurately measure costs, and determine the profit that store stockholders are concerned about. All of this information is available based upon the bar code information attached to each product. Along with many other sources of information, data gathered through bar coding can be used for data mining analysis.

Data mining is not limited to business. Both major parties in the 2004 U.S. election utilized data mining of potential voters.[1] Data mining has been heavily used in the medical field, to include patient diagnosis records to help identify best practices.[2] The Mayo Clinic worked with IBM to develop an online computer system to identify how that last 100 Mayo patients with the same gender, age, and medical history responded to particular treatments.[3]

Business use of data mining is also impressive. Toyota used the data mining of its **data warehouse** to determine more efficient transportation routes, reducing the time to deliver cars to customers by an average of 19 days. Data warehouses (to be discussed in Chapter 3) are enormous database systems capable of systematically storing all transactional data generated by a business organization, such as WalMart. Toyota also was able to identify sales trends faster, and identify the best locations for new dealerships. Benefits were estimated to be $30 million per year in North America.[4]

Data mining is widely used by banking firms in soliciting credit card customers,[5] by insurance and telecommunication companies in detecting fraud,[6] by manufacturing firms in quality control,[7] and many other applications. Data mining is being applied to improve food product safety,[8] criminal detection,[9] and tourism.[10] Fingerhut has become very successful in **micromarketing,** targeting small groups of highly responsive customers. Media companies such as R. R. Donnelly & Sons provide consumer and life-style data, as well as customized individual publications to firms that use data mining for catalog marketing.

Data mining involves statistical and/or artificial intelligence analysis, usually applied to large-scale data sets. Traditional statistical analysis involves an approach that is usually directed, in that a specific set of expected outcomes exists. This approach is referred to as supervised. However, there is more to data mining than the technical tools used. Data mining involves a spirit of **knowledge discovery** (learning new and useful things), which is referred to as unsupervised. Much of this can be accomplished through automatic means, as we will see in decision tree analysis, for example. But data mining is not limited to automated analysis. Knowledge discovery by humans can be enhanced by graphical tools and the identification of unexpected patterns through a combination of human and computer interaction.

Data mining can be used by businesses in many ways. Three examples are

- **Customer profiling**   Identifying those subsets of customers that are most profitable to the business
- **Targeting**   Determining the characteristics of profitable customers who have been captured by competitors
- **Market-basket analysis**   Determining product purchases by consumers, which can be used for product positioning and for cross-selling.

These are not the only applications of data mining, but they are three of the most important to businesses. Customer profiling is a key part of customer relationship management (CRM), which will be elaborated upon in Chapter 10. Targeting is a key concept in managing **churn,** or customer turnover, also discussed in Chapter 10. Market-basket analysis is an interesting use of data mining that we discuss in Chapter 11.

What Is Needed to Do Data Mining?

Data mining requires the identification of a problem, along with collection of data that can lead to a better understanding of the market, and computer models to provide statistical or other means of analysis. There are two general types of data mining studies. **Hypothesis testing** involves expressing a theory about the relationship between actions and outcomes. In a simple form, it can be hypothesized that advertising will yield greater profit. This relationship has long been studied by retailing firms in the context of their specific operations. Data mining is applied to identifying relationships based on large quantities of data, which could include testing the response rates to various types of advertising on the sales and profitability of specific product lines. The second form of data mining study is knowledge discovery. In this form of analysis, a preconceived notion may not be present, but rather relationships can be identified by looking at the data. This may be supported by visualization tools that display data, or through fundamental statistical analysis, such as correlation analysis.

A variety of analytic computer models have been used in data mining. Chapters 5 through 9 of this book will discuss various types of these models. Also required is access to data. Quite often, systems including data warehouses and data marts are used to manage large quantities of data (see Chapter 3). Other data mining analyses are done with smaller sets of data, such as can be organized in online analytic processing systems.

Data Mining

Data mining has been called exploratory data analysis, among other things. Masses of data generated from cash registers, from scanning, and from topic-specific databases throughout the company are explored, analyzed, reduced, and reused. Searches are performed across different models proposed for predicting sales, marketing response, and profit. Classical statistical approaches are fundamental to data mining. Automated AI methods are also used. However, systematic exploration through classical statistical methods is still the basis of data mining. Some of the tools developed by the field of statistical analysis are harnessed through automatic control (with some key human guidance) in dealing with data.

Data mining tools need to be versatile, scalable, capable of accurately predicting responses between actions and results, and capable of automatic implementation. **Versatile** refers to the ability of the tool to apply a wide variety of models. **Scalable** tools imply that if the tools work on a small data set, they should also work on larger data sets. Automation is useful, but its application is relative. Some analytic functions are often automated, but human setup prior to implementing procedures is required. In fact, analyst judgment is critical to successful implementation of data mining. Proper selection of data to include in searches is critical. Data transformation also is often required. Too many variables produce too much output, while too few can overlook key relationships in the data. Herb Edelstein of Two Crows Corporation was quoted: "To think you can do data mining without a statistical or mining background is mind-boggling."[11]

Data mining is expanding rapidly, with many benefits to business. Two of the most profitable application areas have been the use of customer segmentation by marketing organizations to identify those with marginally greater probabilities of responding to different forms of marketing media, and banks using data mining to more accurately predict the likelihood of people to respond to offers of different services offered. Many companies are using this technology to identify their blue-chip customers so they can provide them the service needed to retain them.

First National Bank of North Dakota found that only 10 percent of its customers were providing almost all of the bank's profitability.[12] Bank of America in San Francisco also found that a small portion of its customers, 20 percent, determined bank profitability. Bank of America develops profiles of its top accounts to target services. They also are able to assess the likelihood that particular customers are likely to take their business to a competitor, or churn, in telephone business terminology.

The casino business has also adopted data warehousing and data mining. Historically, casinos have wanted to know everything about their customers.[13] Harrah's Entertainment Inc. is one of many casino organizations who use incentive programs.[14] About 8 million customers hold Total Gold cards, which are used whenever the customer plays at the casino, or eats, or stays, or spends money in other ways. Points accumulated can be used for complementary meals and lodging. More points are awarded for activities which provide Harrah's with more profit. The information obtained is sent to the firm's corporate database, where it's retained for several years. Trump's Taj Card is used in a similar fashion. Recently, high competition has led to the use of data mining. Instead of advertising the loosest slots in town, Bellagio and Mandelay Bay have developed the strategy of promoting luxury visits. Data mining is used to identify high rollers so that these valued customers can be cultivated. Data warehouses enable casinos to estimate the lifetime value of players. Incentive travel programs, in-house promotions, corporate business, and customer follow-up are tools used to maintain the most profitable customers. Casino gaming is one of the richest data sets available. Very specific individual profiles can be developed. Some customers are identified as those who should be encouraged to play longer. Other customers are identified as those who are discouraged from playing. Harrah's found that 26 percent of its gamblers generated 82 percent of its revenues. They also found that their best customers were not high rollers, but rather middle-aged and senior adults who were former professionals. Harrah's developed a quantitative model to predict individual spending over the long run, and set up a program to invite back $1,000-per-month customers who had not visited in three months. If a customer lost in a prior visit, she/he would be invited back to a special event.[15]

Data mining has even been applied in the business of delivering the arts.[16] Applications include identification of potential consumers for particular shows. Software programs to manage shows are available that operate much as airline seating chart software. Moving to computerized box offices has led to the generation of high volumes of data, which can be imported into data warehouses.

Focused Marketing

Fingerhut Companies, founded in 1948, has been a leader in the field of focused marketing. In recent years, it has sent out about 130 different catalogs to over 65 million customers, and the firm currently has a 6-terabyte data warehouse. Data mining analysis focuses on 3,000 variables related to their 12 million most active customers, with over 300 predictive models reportedly in use at this time.[17] Federated Department Stores purchased Fingerhut Companies for $1.7 billion in February 1999 to acquire their database.[18] Fingerhut had a $1.6 to $2 billion business per year, targeting lower-income households.[19] At its peak, it could mail 340 million catalogs per year to 7 million active customers.[20] Fingerhut operated through specialty catalogs (400 million per year)[21] sent to data-mined customers expected to be interested in one of the many types of products that Fingerhut markets. Each product line had its own catalog. Target customers were identified as the small subset of people with a marginally higher probability of purchasing (the concept of **lift** in marketing terminology—see Chapter 10). Federated Department Stores was expected to transfer Fingerhut's technology to their Macy's and Bloomingdale's stores.

Fingerhut used segmentation, decision tree, regression analysis, and neural modeling tools from SAS for regression analysis tools and SPSS Inc. for neural network tools. When one of Fingerhut's 7 million active customers ordered a product (toys, games, household items, many others), transaction, demographic, and psychographic data were stored in the firm's relational database. There were up to 3,000 potential data items per customer. The firm had a staff dedicated to the data warehouse.[22] One of their roles was training other Fingerhut personnel in the use of the warehouse.

The segmentation model combined order and basic demographic data with Fingerhut's product offerings. This enabled Fingerhut to create new mailings targeted at customers with the greatest potential payoff. Fingerhut analysts determined that customers who recently had moved tripled their purchasing in the 12 weeks after the move.[23] Fingerhut therefore created a catalog containing products that those who were moving would likely be interested in, such as furniture, telephones, and decorations, while deleting products such as jewelry or home electronics.

A second application was mailstream optimization. This model showed which customers were most likely to respond to existing catalog mailings. Fingerhut estimated savings of nearly $3 million per year through mailstream optimizing.[24] This system enabled Fingerhut to go against the trend of the catalog sales industry in 1998 and reduce mailings by 20 percent while increasing net earnings to over $37 million.[25]

Neural network models, a common type of data mining tool (covered in Chapter 7), have been used to identify overlaps in mailing patterns and order-filling telephone call orders. This enabled Fingerhut to more efficiently staff their telephones and enabled them to handle heavy order loads.

Business Data Mining

Data mining has been very effective in many business venues. The key is to find **actionable** information, or information that can be utilized in a concrete way to improve profitability. Some of the earliest applications were in retailing, especially in the form of market-basket analysis. Table 1.1 shows the general application areas we will be discussing. Note that they are meant to be representative rather than comprehensive.

Retailing

Data mining offers retailers (in general) and grocery stores (specifically) valuable predictive information from mountains of data. **Affinity positioning** is based upon the identification of products that the same customer is likely to want. For instance, if you are interested in cold medicine, you probably are interested in tissues. Thus, it would make marketing sense to locate both items within easy reach of the other. **Cross-selling** is a related concept. The knowledge of products that go together can be used by marketing the complementary product. Grocery stores do that through position product shelf location. Retail stores relying upon advertising can send ads for sales on shirts and ties to those who have recently purchased suits. These strategies have long been employed by wise retailers. However, data mining provides the ability to identify less expected product affinities and cross-selling opportunities.

Grocery stores generate mountains of cash register data that require automated tools for analysis. Software is marketed to service a spectrum of users. In the past, it was assumed that cash register data was so massive that it couldn't be quickly analyzed. However, current technology enables grocers to look at customers who have defected from a store, their purchase history, and characteristics of other potential defectors. Tom Rubel of Price Waterhouse Management Consulting viewed the greatest data mining potential to come from retailers and manufacturers sharing data.[26] Targeted marketing programs are beginning to be successfully used by grocers. Single store operations may be able to operate with PC software for as little as $4,000. Free Internet software is emerging as well. Most larger chain operations have to spend up to $750,000 for data mining operations.

TABLE 1.1 Data Mining Application Areas

Application Area	Applications	Specifics
Retailing	Affinity positioning	Position products effectively
	Cross-selling	Find more products for customers
Banking	Customer relationship management	Identify customer value, develop programs to maximize revenue
Credit Card Management	Lift	Identify effective market segments
	Churn	Identify likely customer turnover
Insurance	Fraud detection	Identify claims meriting investigation
Telecommunications	Churn	Identify likely customer turnover
Telemarketing	Online information	Aid telemarketers with easy data access
Human Resource Management	Churn	Identify potential employee turnover

Banking

The banking industry was one of the first users of data mining.[27] Banks have turned to technology to find out what motivates their customers, and what will keep their business **(customer relationship management—CRM).**[28] CRM involves the application of technology to monitor customer service, a function that's enhanced through data mining support. Understanding the value a customer provides the firm makes it possible to rationally evaluate whether extra expenditure is appropriate in order to keep the customer. There are many opportunities for data mining in banking. Deloitte Consulting found that only 31 percent of senior bank executives were confident that their current distribution mix anticipated customer needs. Kathleen Khirallah, an analyst at The Tower Group, predicted that spending by U.S. banks on CRM would grow at 11 percent per year.

Dhar dismissed the view that data mining is an undirected data dredging expedition where machine learning algorithms automatically produce interesting patterns.[29] Rather, the exercise is an iterative updating of an existing framework of knowledge. Data mining applications in finance include predicting the prices of equities involving a dynamic environment with surprise information, some of which might be inaccurate and some of which might be too complex to comprehend and reconcile with intuition. Some customers are more profitable to banks than others. Only 3 percent of the customers at Norwest (who recently merged with Wells Fargo) provided 44 percent of their profits.[30] Bank of America utilized a program to cultivate ties to the top 10 percent of their customers. CRM products enable banks to define and identify customer and household relationships. This is the first step of the process, which must then be disseminated throughout the banking organization so that it can be taken advantage of through better product design and greater attention to key customers.

Fleet Financial Group has blended product- and customer-based approaches. Information is being used to provide customer focus within a product-based organization rather than reorganizing around customer groups, as other financial institutions have done. Fleet has invested about $30 million in a data warehouse to support the entire organization. They also hired about 60 database marketers and statistical/quantitative analysts, as well as specialists in decision support and other areas. They expect to add an extra $100 million in profit.

First Union has concentrated on the contact-point end of CRM. The bank previously had very focused product groups with little coordination. It created marketing customer information files, which integrated information across products through an enterprisewide data warehouse and marketing-based data mart. Their CRM structure uses SAS tools to develop offers for customers, and for modeling and statistical analysis.

Data mining provides a way for banks to identify patterns. This is valuable in assessing loan applications, as well as in target marketing. Credit unions use data mining to track member profitability, as well as to monitor the effectiveness of marketing programs and sales representatives. They also are used for member care, seeking to identify what credit union customers want in the way of services.

Credit Card Management

The credit card industry has proven very profitable. It has attracted many card issuers, and many customers carry four or five cards. Balance surfing is a common practice, where the card user pays an old balance with a new card. These are not considered attractive customers, and one of the uses of data warehousing and data mining is to identify balance surfers. The profitability of the industry has also attracted those who wish to push the edge of credit risk, both from the customer and the card issuer perspective. Michael Eichorst, vice president of analytics for Chase Manhattan Bank, claims that card issuers have no choice but to maintain database marketing as a core competency.[31] Whether this is true or not, database marketing provides credit card issuers with a valuable tool to give them a clearer picture of their operations. Bank credit card marketing promotions typically generate 1,000 responses to mailed solicitations—a response rate of about 1 percent. This rate is improved significantly through data mining analysis.[32]

Data mining tools used by banks include credit scoring,[33] which is a quantified analysis of credit applicants with respect to predictions of on-time loan repayment. The key is a consolidated data warehouse, covering all products, including demand deposits, savings, loans, credit cards, insurance, annuities, retirement programs, securities underwriting, and every other product banks provide. Credit scoring provides a number for each applicant by multiplying a set of weighted numbers determined by the data mining analysis multiplied by the ratings for that applicant. These credit scores can be used to accept/reject recommendations, as well as to establish the size of a credit line. Credit scoring used to be conducted by bank loan officers, who considered a few tested variables, such as employment, income, age, assets, debt, and loan history. Data mining makes it possible to include many more variables, with greater accuracy.

Data mining provides a means to predict what customers might use. Once this information is obtained, it can be implemented to improve operations. New methods of reaching customers are developed every day. ATM machines could be rigged up with electronic sales pitches for products that a particular customer is likely to be interested in. If a database indicates a new address for a customer with high credit scores, this customer may have traded up to a new, larger house, and may be a prime target for an increased credit line, a higher-end credit card, or a home improvement loan, which could be offered in a card statement mailing. Databases can also be used to support telephone representatives when customers call. The representative's computer screen can indicate the customer's characteristics as well as products the customer may be interested in.

The new wave of technology is broadening the application of database use and targeted marketing strategies. In the early 1990s, nearly all credit card issuers were mass-marketing to expand their cardholder bases.[34] However, with so many cards available, broad-based marketing campaigns have not been as effective as they initially were. Card issuers are more carefully examining the expected net present value of each customer. Data warehouses provide the information giving issuers the ability to try to more accurately predict what the customer is interested in, as well as their potential value to the issuer. Desktop campaign management software is used by the more advanced credit card issuers, utilizing data mining tools such as neural networks to recognize customer behavior patterns in order to predict their future relationship with the bank.

Insurance

The insurance industry utilizes data mining for marketing, just as retailing and banking organizations do.[35] But they also have specialty applications. Farmers Insurance Group has developed a system for underwriting that generates millions of dollars in higher revenues and lower claims. The system allows the firm to better understand narrow market niches, and to predict losses for specific lines of insurance. One discovery was that it could lower its rates on sports cars, which increased their market share for this product line significantly. Farmers uses seven databases and 35 million records.

Unfortunately, our complex society leads to some inappropriate business operations, including insurance fraud. Specialists in this underground industry often use multiple personas to bilk insurance companies, especially in the automobile insurance environment. InfoGlide specializes in products to identify insurance fraud.[36] InfoGlide's Fraud-Investigator system uses a similarity search engine, analyzing information in company claims for similarities. By linking names, telephone numbers, streets, birthdays, and other information with slight variations, patterns can be identified indicating fraud. The similarity search engine has been found to be able to identify up to seven times more fraud than exact-match systems.

Alta Analytics' NetMap for Claims searches for suspicious data using an industrywide database from the National Insurance Crime Board. Consolidating data internal and external to the insurance company creates a data mart that can be used for expanded searches. Other patterns this type of software can identify are unusual activities for specific chiropractors or attorneys. HNC Insurance Solutions focuses on workers' compensation fraud. Their VeriComp software is predictive, comparing claims to what is normally the pattern. VeriComp uses a neural network on historical claims data. This system was credited with saving the State of Utah over $2 million, and is used by the Province of British Columbia.[37]

Telecommunications

Deregulation of the telephone industry has led to widespread competition. Telephone service carriers fight hard for customers. The problem is that once a customer is obtained, it's attacked by competitors, and retention of customers is very difficult. The phenomenon of a customer switching carriers is referred to as **churn,** a fundamental concept in telemarketing as well as in other fields.

A director of product marketing for a communications company considered that one-third of churn is due to poor call quality, and up to one-half is due to poor equipment. That firm has a wireless telephone performance monitor tracking telephones with poor performances.[38] This system reduced churn by an estimated 61 percent, amounting to about 3 percent of the firm's overall subscribers over the course of a year. Given an average business volume of $150 per month, this churn reduction was estimated to be worth $580,000 a year in revenue. The firm's cellular fraud prevention system monitors traffic to spot problems with faulty telephones. When a telephone begins to go bad, telemarketing personnel are alerted to contact the customer and suggest bringing the equipment in for service.

Metapath markets a Communications Enterprise Operating System to help identify telephone customer problems.[39] Dropped calls, mobility patterns, and demographic data are recorded. This allows the firm to target specific customers. Further, customers with faulty service can be contacted before they complain, allowing the firm to offer a solution before the customer switches servers.

Another way to reduce churn is to protect customers from subscription and cloning fraud. Cloning has been estimated to have cost the wireless industry $650 million in 1996.[40] A number of fraud prevention systems are marketed. These systems provide verification that is transparent to legitimate subscribers. Subscription fraud has been estimated to have an economic impact of $1.1 billion. Deadbeat accounts and service shutoffs are used to screen potentially fraudulent applicants. Churn Prophet and ChurnAlert are tools that apply data mining to predict the characteristics of subscribers who have canceled service in the past. Arbor/Mobile is a set of products that includes churn analysis. A number of other products exist to perform this service for telephone providers.

Churn is a concept that's used by many retail marketing operations. Banks widely use churn information to drive their promotions.[41] Once data mining identifies customers by characteristic, direct mailing and telemarketing are used to present the bank's promotional program. The mortgage market saw massive refinancing in the early 1990s. Banks were quick to recognize that they needed to keep their mortgage customers happy if they wanted to retain their business. This has led to banks contacting current customers if those customers hold a mortgage at a rate significantly above the market rate. While they may cut their own lucrative financial packages, banks realize that if they don't offer a better service to borrowers, a competitor will. By utilizing data mining and telemarketing, Crestar Mortgage reported increasing its retention rate from 8 percent to over 20 percent in one year.

Telemarketing

Telephone providers obviously are among the many marketing operations utilizing telemarketing. MCI Communications has utilized a strategy of **data marts,** extracting data on prospective customers from a data warehouse. Data marts are often used for temporary data mining studies. In MCI's case, this data is typically applied in a two-month program, after which the data mart is shut down. Use of the data along with data mining analysis was credited with a 20-percent improvement in the quality of sales leads.[42] The data system required a multimillion dollar investment in data marts and parallel hardware to support it. The operation is staffed by 45 people.

The ability to utilize comprehensive databases provides telemarketers the ability to custom design their pitches for each specific customer. The Australian Tourist Commission has been a proactive user of telemarketing, utilizing detailed knowledge of prospective customers.[43] The commission has maintained a database since 1992, capturing all responses to travel inquiries on tour operators, hotels, airlines, travel agents, and consumers. Data mining is used to determine which travel agents and consumers are responding to promotional efforts by advertising media. The Australian Tourist Commission estimated their sales closure rate at 10 percent and up. Travel and tourism students from Australia have been hired by the data warehouse provider for 12 to 18 months, providing insider perspective to consumers. Lead lists are faxed weekly to productive travel agents.

Segmentation involves grouping data with common characteristics, such as the set of customers who respond to new promotions, the set of customers that respond to discounts, or the set of customers that respond to new product offers. This information is used to determine the group of customers to be offered a new service, or to predict the set of customers most likely to commit fraud. Data mining can be used to determine segments. Once segments have been defined, **online analytic processing (OLAP)** tools can be used to explore them in greater depth.

The MCI system has been used for trend spotting. If a prospect turns down one frequent-flier pitch enough times, the program can suggest a different approach, such as switching airlines. On the data mart, data can be updated by the user. Data marts for a specific application are designed to include only the information needed for the specific promotion. However, it's important that all required information be included, so initial design of the data mart is crucial. Too much data slows the system, while too little causes problems requiring additional data.

Human Resource Management

Business intelligence is a way to truly understand markets, competitors, and processes. Software technology such as data warehouses, data marts, online analytical processing (OLAP), and data mining make it possible to sift through data in order to spot trends and patterns that can be used by the firm to improve profitability. In the human resources field, this analysis can lead to the identification of individuals who are liable to leave the company unless additional compensation or benefits are provided.[44]

Data mining can be used to expand upon things that are already known. A firm might realize that 20 percent of its employees use 80 percent of the services offered, but it may not know which particular individuals are in that 20 percent. Business intelligence provides a means of identifying segments so that programs can be devised to cut costs and increase productivity.[45] Data mining can also be used to examine the way in which an organization uses its people. The question might be whether the most talented people are working for those business units with the highest priority, or where they will have the greatest impact on profit.[46]

Companies are seeking to stay in business with fewer people. Sound human resource management would identify the right people so that organizations could treat them well and retain them (reduce churn). This requires tracking key performance indicators, and gathering data on talents, company needs, and competitor requirements. An example data warehouse of this type is the State of Mississippi's MERLIN network. This system includes data from 30 databases on finances, payroll, personnel, and capital projects, and is set be expanded to incorporate more agencies. Lotus Notes is used as a PC user interface. The Cognos Impromptu system is used behind Lotus Notes to provide a suite of analytical tools. As of this writing, MERLIN has 230 users, including analysts and executives.

Data Mining Tools

Many statistical and analytic software tools are available to provide data mining. *Computerworld* reported over 25 vendors used by the 77 companies he surveyed, with no single vendor being used by more than eight of the companies.[47] Many good data mining software products are being used, including the well-established (and expensive) Enterprise Miner by SAS and Intelligent Miner by IBM, CLEMENTINE by SPSS (a little more accessible by students), PolyAnalyst by Megaputer, and many others in a growing and dynamic industry.

These products use one or more of a number of analytic approaches, often as complementary tools that might involve initial cluster analysis to identify relationships and visual analysis to try to understand why data clustered as it did, followed by various prediction models. The major categories of methods applied are regression, decision trees, neural networks, cluster detection, and market-basket analysis.

PNC Bank is using data mining software to strengthen its target marketing.[48] The system is designed to provide the ability to better exploit customer contacts for more effective marketing and promotions. Modeling is expedited through wizards and a booster. Modules include a response model, a customer segmentation module, a module to evaluate customer value, and a cross-selling support module.

Many data mining products exist, some of which suffer from short shelf life. These specialty products cover just about every possible profitable business application. (A good source to view current products is www.KDNuggets.com.) The UCI Machine Learning Repository is a source of very good data mining datasets at http://www.ics.uci.edu/~mlearn/MLOther.html.[49] That site also includes references of other good data mining sites. Vendors selling data access tools include IBM, SAS Institute Inc., Microsoft, Brio Technology Inc., Oracle, and others. IBM's Intelligent Mining Toolkit has a set of algorithms available for data mining to identify hidden relationships, trends, and patterns. SAS's System for Information Delivery integrates executive information systems, statistical tools for data analysis, and neural network tools.

Summary

This chapter has introduced the topic of data mining, focusing on business applications. Data mining has proven to be extremely effective in improving many business operations. The process of data mining relies heavily on information technology in the form of data storage support (data warehouses, data marts, and/or online analytic processing tools) as well as software to analyze the data (data mining software). However, the process of data mining is far more than simply applying these data mining software tools to a firm's data. Intelligence is required on the part of the analyst in the selection of model types, in the selection and transformation of the data relating to the specific problem, and in interpreting results.

This chapter gave a broad overview of the methods used in data mining, as demonstrated with typical applications.[50] Chapter 2 will discuss the process of data mining. Chapter 3 reviews database tools supporting data mining operations. Part II discusses data mining methods, including an overview in Chapter 4, with specific demonstrations of different models in Chapters 5 through 9. Each of these chapters will include discussions of the types of problems for which that method works best, and an evaluation of that method's strengths and weaknesses. Part III discusses important business applications, such as in Chapter 10, which describes customer relationship marketing and segmentation. Chapter 11 covers market-basket analysis. Part IV discusses developing issues, presenting web and text mining in Chapter 12, and ethical considerations in data mining in Chapter 13. Note that these parts can be covered in any order desired. For instance, you may want to start with applications in Part III, or you may want to start with ethical considerations as explored in Chapter 13. The chapters are reasonably modular, allowing coverage without the need to follow a rigid order.

Glossary

actionable   Information that can be used to make more effective business decisions (make more profit).

affinity positioning   Laying out retail stores to place complementary products together.

churn   Turnover in customers, especially loss of customers in the telephone industry.

cross-selling   Marketing products to a customer that are related to other products the customer has purchased.

customer profiling   Identification of good customers.

customer relationship management (CRM)   Use of data mining to identify details about a customer, to include the customer's value to the organization, and the characteristics that the customer is looking for in products.

data mart   A database system used to extract a subset of data from a data warehouse so it can be used for a data mining application.

data warehouse   A large-scale data storage system designed to contain complete and clean data that can be accessed efficiently.

hypothesis testing   Developing a theory, and conducting a test to statistically validate or reject the theory.

knowledge discovery   Looking for patterns in data without a reliance on preconceived theories.

lift   The marginal difference in a segment's proportion of response to a promotion and the average rate of response.

market-basket analysis   Analysis of the tendency for purchase of items by the same consumer at the same time.

micromarketing   Focused marketing directed at a small subset of the total population. This subset is expected to contain a much higher proportion of product purchasers than the general population.

online analytic processing (OLAP)   Tools for accessing databases with the intent of providing users with the multidimensional display of information.

scalable   The ability to efficiently analyze very large data sets.

targeting   Determination of characteristics of customers who have left for competitors.

versatile   Providing a wide variety of data mining tools.

Exercises

1. How is micromarketing different than marketing based on Superbowl advertising?
2. What is the relationship of data mining to classical statistical analysis?
3. Describe the difference between customer profiling and targeting.
4. Discuss the difference between hypothesis testing and knowledge discovery.
5. Describe the difference between versatile and scalable tools.
6. Churn is a concept originating in the telephone industry. How can the same concept apply to banking? To human resources?
7. How is focused marketing different than mass marketing, such as network television? What is a television media analogy to focused marketing?
8. Describe the concept of actionable information.
9. Go to the Internet, find a data mining product. Provide a report of the kind of problems for which the product is useful, and the type of input required. Also report on any successful applications reported.
10. Go to the Internet and find a data warehouse product. Provide a report discussing the product's value to a firm, its relative cost and operational requirements, and if possible, a discussion of its value to a firm.
11. Go to the Internet and find a data mining application. Report the decision problem involved, the type of input available, and the value contributed to the organization that used it. If possible, report on the software products used to conduct the analysis.
12. Search the library (electronic if possible) and find a recent application of data mining in finance.
13. Search the library (electronic if possible) and find a recent application of data mining in banking.

14. Search the library (electronic if possible) and find a recent application of data mining in insurance.

15. Search the library (electronic if possible) and find a recent application of data mining in retail

Endnotes

1. L. Grossman, V. Novak, and E. Roston, "What Your Party Knows about You," *Time*, volume 164, issue 16, October 18, 2004, pp. 38–39.

2. J. Morris, "Beyond Clinical Documentation: Using the EMR as a Quality Tool," *Health Management Technology*, volume 25, issue 11, November 2004, pp. 20, 22–24.

3. N. Swartz, "IBM, Mayo Clinic to Mine Medical Data," *The Information Management Journal*, volume 38, issue 6, November/December 2004, p. 8.

4. L. Dignan, M. Duvall, and J. McCormick, "Triumphs and Trip-Ups in 2004," *Baseline*, volume 38, December 2004, pp. 20, 22.

5. Anonymous, "Managing your Customer Resources Through Data Mining," *Community Banker*, volume 12, number 4, 2003, pp. 10–12.

6. L. Chordas, "Data-Mining Information Helps MetLife Detect Fraud," *Best's Review*, volume 104, issue 3, 2003, pp. 109–111; D. West. "Data Mining Helps Underwriters Unearth Gems," *National Underwriter/Property & Casualty Risk & Benefits*, volume 108, issue 36, September 27, 2004, pp. 20, 22; C. Dorn, "Data Mining Technology Helps Insurers Detect Health Care Fraud," *National Underwriter/Life & Health Financial Series*, volume 108, issue 39, October 18, 2004, pp. 34, 39.

7. R. Whiting, "Automakers Rev Up Data-Mining Efforts," *InformationWeek*, issue 933, March 31, 2003, p. 32.

8. Anonymous, "Improving Product Safety Through Data Mining," *FDA Consumer*, volume 37, issue 4, 2003, p. 5.

9. B. Rothke, "Investigation Data Mining For Security And Criminal Detection," *Security Management*, volume 47, issue 7, 2003, pp. 160–161.

10. C. Petropoulos, A. Patelis, K. Metaxiotis, K. Nikolopoulos, and V. Assimakopoulos, "SFTIS: A Decision Support System for Tourism Demand Analysis and Forecasting," *Journal of Computer Information Systems*, volume 44, issue 1, 2003, pp. 21–32.

11. S. Deck, "Mining Your Business," *Computerworld*, volume 33, number 20 May 17, 1999, pp. 94–98.

12. R. Whiting, "Automakers Rev Up Data-Mining Efforts," *InformationWeek*, issue 933, March, 31, 2003, p. 32.

13. R. McKim, "Betting on Loyalty Marketing," *Zip/Target Marketing*, volume 22, number 3, March 1999, pp. 42–43+.

14. R. Whiting, "Automakers Rev Up Data-Mining Efforts," *InformationWeek*, issue 933, March 31, 2003, p. 32.

15. S. Thelen, S. Mottner, and B. Berman, "Data Mining: On the Trail to Marketing Gold," *Business Horizons*, volume 47, issue 6, November/December 2004, pp. 25–32.

16. C. Murphy, "Captive Audiences," *Marketing*, January 28, 1999, p. 33.

17. J. Lach, "Data Mining Digs In," *American Demographics*, volume 21, number 7, July 1999, pp. 38–45.

18. G. Rosenberg, "The E-Tailing Phenomenon: Wall Street Helps Retailers' Mad Dash to the Internet," *Investment Dealers Digest*, May 31, 1999, pp. 18–22.

19. R. Whiting, "Automakers Rev Up Data-Mining Efforts," *InformationWeek*, issue 933, March 31, 2003, p. 32.

20. D. Campbell, R. Erdahl, D. Johnson, E. Bibelnieks, M. Haydock, M. Bullock, and H. Crowder, "Optimizing Customer Mail Streams at Fingerhut," *Interfaces*, volume 31, number 1, 2001, pp. 77–90.

21. S. Deck, "Mining Your Business," *Computerworld*, volume 33, number 20, May 17, 1999, pp. 94–98.

22. D. Pearson, "Marketing for Survival," *CIO*, volume 11, number 13, section 1, April 15, 1998, pp. 44–48.

23. S. Deck, "Mining Your Business," *Computerworld*, volume 33, number 20, May 17, 1999, pp. 94–98.

24. Ibid.

25. S. Chiger, "Bragging Rights," *Catalog Age*, volume 15, number 9, August 1998, pp. 1, 66+.

26. S. Weinstein, "Tackling Technology," *Progressive Grocer*, volume 78, number 2, February 1999, pp. 43–49.

27. Anonymous, "Managing Your Customer Resources Through Data Mining," *Community Banker*, volume 12, number 4, 2003, pp. 28–30.

28. K. Kiesnoski, "Customer Relationship Management," *Bank Systems & Technology*, volume 36, number 2, February 1999, pp. 30–34; L. Ryals, "Creating Profitable Customers Through the Magic of Data Mining," *Journal of Targeting, Measurement, & Analysis for Marketing*, volume 11, issue 4, 2003, pp. 343–349.

29. V. Dhar, "Data Mining in Finance: Using Counterfactuals to Generate Knowledge from Organizational Information Systems," *Information Systems*, volume 23, number 7, 1998, pp. 423–437.

30. K. Kiesnoski, "Customer Relationship Management," *Bank Systems & Technology*, volume 36, number 2, February 1999, pp. 30–34; L. Ryals, "Creating Profitable Customers Through the Magic of Data Mining," *Journal of Targeting, Measurement, & Analysis for Marketing*, volume 11, issue 4, 2003, pp. 343–349.

31. P. Demery, "The Decade of Marketing," *Credit Card Management*, volume 11, number 11, February 1999, pp. 74–84.

32. Ibid.

33. A. Levinsohn, "Modern Miners Plumb for Gold," *ABA Banking Journal*, volume 90, number 12, December 1998, pp. 52–55.

34. P. Demery, "The Decade of Marketing," *Credit Card Management*, volume 11, number 11, February 1999, pp. 74–84.

35. T. Hoffman, "Finding a Rich Niche," *Computerworld*, volume 33, number 6, February 8, 1999, p. 44.

36. T. Goveia, "Short Circuiting Crime," *Canadian Insurance*, volume 104, number 5, May 1999, pp. 16–17+.

37. Ibid.

38. B. Reeves, "All in the Family," *Wireless Review*, volume 15, number 7, April 1, 1998, pp. 42–50.

39. Ibid.

40. Ibid.

41. M. McGarity, "Keeping Your Borrowers," *Mortgage Banking*, volume 58, number, June 1998, pp. 12–23.

42. T. Hoffman, "MCI Connects with Disposable Marts," *Computerworld,* volume 31, number 50, December 15, 1997, pp. 67–70.

43. R. Robinson, "1:1 Marketing: An Integrated Strategy to Reach Customers," *Telemarketing,* volume 15, number 11, May 1997, pp. 66–74.

44. H. Min and A. Emam, "Developing the Profiles of Truck Drivers for Their Successful Recruitment and Retention: A Data Mining Approach," *Journal of Physical Distribution & Logistics Management,* volume 33, issue 2, 2003, pp. 149–162.

45. S. Greengard, "Mine Your Corporate Data with Business Intelligence," *Workforce,* volume 78, number 1, January 1999, pp. 103–104.

46. B. Roberts, "HR's Link to the Corporate Big Picture," *HRMagazine,* volume 44, number 4, April 1999, pp. 103–110.

47. J. M. Connolly, "Fast facts," *Computerworld*, volume 33, number 20, May 17, 1999, p. 98.

48. K. Kiesnoski, "PNC Add GUI-Based Modeling Solution," *Bank Systems & Technology,* volume 36, number 4, April 1999, p. 18.

49. C. J. Merz and P. M. Murphy, *UCI Repository of Machine Learning Databases,* http://www.ics.uci.edu/~mlearn/MLOther.html Irvine, CA: University of California, Department of Information and Computer Science.

50. Other sources for applications include M. J. A. Berry and G. Linoff, *Data Mining Techniques* (New York: John Wiley & Sons, 1997). Specific applications in finance are provided by V. Dhar, "Data Mining in Finance: Using Counterfactuals to Generate Knowledge from Organizational Information Systems," *Information Systems,* volume 23, number 7, 1998, pp. 423–437; and marketing applications in P. R. Peacock, "Data Mining in Marketing: Part I," *Marketing Management,* volume 6, number 4, Winter 1998, pp. 8–18; and D. Pearson, "Marketing for Survival," *CIO,* volume 11, number 13, section 1, April 15, 1998, pp. 44–48.

CHAPTER TWO

Data Mining Processes and Knowledge Discovery

This chapter:

- Describes the Cross-Industry Standard Process for Data Mining (CRISP-DM), a set of phases that can be used in data mining studies
- Discusses each phase in detail
- Gives an example illustration
- Discusses a knowledge discovery process

When faced with masses of data, businesses (and other organizations) would benefit by a systematic process to try to make sense of these data sets. For instance, a business providing services to many customers encounters some delinquency in the payment of bills. There are trade-offs in how delinquency should be treated. If service is terminated at the first sign of delinquency, there is some motivation to customers to pay on time. However, there also is some motivation to picket the service provider. If a telephone provider terminated service the day after a bill wasn't paid, it would lose a lot of customers, which would negatively affect profitability. On the other hand, there's no need to waste money tracking accounts that haven't been paid in five years. It isn't easy to answer the question of just how late bills should be before they're written off. In fact, some types of accounts might be treated differently than others. Data mining can provide a tool that helps identify the impact of different policies, thus enabling a more rational and sound business policy.

In order to conduct data mining analyses, a general process is useful. This chapter describes an industry standard process that's often used, consisting of a sequence of steps that are usually involved in a data mining study. While each step isn't needed in every analysis, this process provides a good coverage of the steps needed, starting with data exploration, data collection, data processing, analysis, inferences drawn, and implementation.

CRISP-DM

There is a Cross-Industry Standard Process for Data Mining (CRISP-DM) widely used by industry members. This model consists of six phases intended as a cyclical process:

- **Business understanding**   Business understanding includes determining business objectives, assessing the current situation, establishing data mining goals, and developing a project plan.

- **Data understanding**   Once business objectives and the project plan are established, data understanding considers data requirements. This step can include initial data collection, data description, data exploration, and the verification of data quality. Data exploration such as viewing summary statistics (which includes the visual display of categorical variables) can occur at the end of this phase. Models such as cluster analysis can also be applied during this phase, with the intent of identifying patterns in the data.

- **Data preparation**   Once the data resources available are identified, they need to be selected, cleaned, built into the form desired, and formatted. Data cleaning and data transformation in preparation of data modeling needs to occur in this phase. Data exploration at a greater depth can be applied during this phase, and additional models utilized, again providing the opportunity to see patterns based on business understanding.

- **Modeling**   Data mining software tools such as visualization (plotting data and establishing relationships) and cluster analysis (to identify which variables go well together) are useful for initial analysis. Tools such as generalized rule induction can develop initial association rules. Once greater data understanding is gained (often through pattern recognition triggered by viewing model output), more detailed models appropriate to the data type can be applied. The division of data into training and test sets is also needed for modeling.

- **Evaluation**   Model results should be evaluated in the context of the business objectives established in the first phase (business understanding). This will lead to the identification of other needs (often through pattern recognition), frequently reverting to prior phases of CRISP-DM. Gaining business understanding is an iterative procedure in data mining, where the results of various visualization, statistical, and artificial intelligence tools show the user new relationships that provide a deeper understanding of organizational operations.

- **Deployment**   Data mining can be used to both verify previously held hypotheses, or for knowledge discovery (identification of unexpected and useful relationships). Through the knowledge discovered in the earlier phases of the CRISP-DM process, sound models can be obtained that may then be applied to business operations for many purposes, including prediction or identification of key situations. These models need to be monitored for changes in operating conditions, because what might be true today may not be true a year from now. If significant changes do occur, the model should be redone. It's also wise to record the results of data mining projects so documented evidence is available for future studies.

Figure 2.1 outlines this process. This six-phase process is not a rigid, by-the-numbers procedure. There's usually a great deal of backtracking. Additionally, experienced analysts may not need to apply each phase for every study. But CRISP-DM provides a useful framework for data mining.

FIGURE 2.1
The CRISP-DM
Data Mining
Process

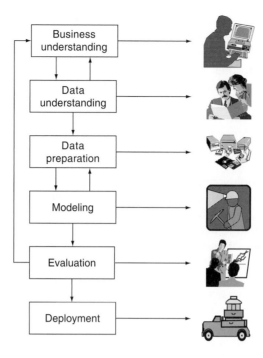

Business Understanding

The key element of a data mining study is knowing what the study is for. This begins with a managerial need for new knowledge, and an expression of the business objective regarding the study to be undertaken. Goals in terms of things such as "What types of customers are interested in each of our products?" or "What are typical profiles of our customers, and how much value do each of them provide to us?" are needed. Then a plan for finding such knowledge needs to be developed, in terms of those responsible for collecting data, analyzing data, and reporting. At this stage, a budget to support the study should be established, at least in preliminary terms.

In customer segmentation models, such as Fingerhut's retail catalog business, the identification of a business purpose meant identifying the type of customer that would be expected to yield a profitable return. The same analysis is useful to credit card distributors. For business purposes, grocery stores often try to identify which items tend to be purchased together so it can be used for affinity positioning within the store, or to intelligently guide promotional campaigns. Data mining has many useful business applications, some of which will be presented throughout the course of the book.

Data Understanding

Since data mining is task-oriented, different business tasks require different sets of data. The first stage of the data mining process is to select the related data from many available databases to correctly describe a given business task. There are at least three issues to be considered in the data selection. The first issue is to set up a concise and clear description of the problem. For example, a retail data-mining project may seek to identify spending behaviors of female shoppers who purchase seasonal clothes. Another example may seek to identify bankruptcy patterns of credit card holders. The second issue would be to identify the relevant data for the problem description. Most demographical, credit card transactional, and financial data could be relevant to both retail and credit card bankruptcy projects. However, gender data may be prohibited for use by law for the latter, but be legal and prove important for the former. The third issue is that selected variables for the relevant data should be independent of each other. Variable independence means that the variables do not contain overlapping information. A careful selection of independent variables can make it easier for data mining algorithms to quickly discover useful knowledge patterns.

Data sources for data selection can vary. Normally, types of data sources for business applications include **demographic data** (such as income, education, number of households, and age), **socio-graphic data** (such as hobby, club membership, and entertainment), **transactional data** (sales record, credit card spending, issued checks), and so on. The data type can be categorized as quantitative and qualitative data. **Quantitative data** are measurable using numerical values. They can be either discrete (such as integers) or continuous (such as real numbers). **Qualitative data,** also known as categorical data, contain both nominal and ordinal data. Nominal data have finite non-ordered values, such as gender data which have two values: male and female. Ordinal data have finite ordered values. For example, customer credit ratings are considered ordinal data since the ratings can be excellent, fair, and bad. Quantitative data can be readily represented by some sort of probability distribution. A probability distribution describes how the data are dispersed and shaped. For instance, normally distributed data are symmetric, and are commonly referred to as bell-shaped. Qualitative data may be first coded to numbers and then be described by frequency distributions. Once relevant data are selected according to the data mining business objective, data preprocessing should be pursued.

Data Preparation

The purpose of data preprocessing is to clean selected data for better quality. Some selected data may have different formats because they are chosen from different data sources. If selected data are from flat files, voice message, and web text, they should be converted to a consistent electronic format. In general, data cleaning means to filter, aggregate, and fill in missing values **(imputation).** By filtering data, the selected data are examined for outliers and redundancies. Outliers differ greatly from the majority of data, or data that are clearly out of range of the selected data groups. For example, if the income of a customer included in the middle class is $250,000, it is an error and should be taken out from the data mining project that examines the various aspects of the middle class. Outliers may be caused by many reasons, such as human errors or technical errors, or may naturally occur in a data set due to extreme events. Suppose the age of a credit card holder is recorded as "12." This is likely a human error. However, there might actually be an independently wealthy pre-teen with important purchasing habits. Arbitrarily deleting this outlier could dismiss valuable information.

Redundant data are the same information recorded in several different ways. Daily sales of a particular product are redundant to seasonal sales of the same product, because we can derive the sales from either daily data or seasonal data. By aggregating data, data dimensions are reduced to obtain aggregated information. Note that although an aggregated data set has a small volume, the information will remain. If a marketing promotion for furniture sales is considered in the next three or four years, then the available daily sales data can be aggregated as annual sales data. The size of sales data is dramatically reduced. By smoothing data, missing values of the selected data are found and new or reasonable values then added. These added values could be the average number of the variable (mean) or the mode. A missing value often causes no solution when a data-mining algorithm is applied to discover the knowledge patterns.

Data can be expressed in a number of different forms. For instance, in CLEMENTINE, the following data types can be used.

- **RANGE** Numeric values (integer, real, or date/time)
- **FLAG** Binary—Yes/No, 0/1, or other data with two outcomes (text, integer, real number, or date/time)
- **SET** Data with distinct multiple values (numeric, string, or date/time)
- **TYPELESS** For other types of data

Usually we think of data as real numbers, such as age in years or annual income in dollars (we would use RANGE in those cases). Sometimes variables occur as either/or types, such as having a driver's license or not, or an insurance claim being fraudulent or not. This case could be dealt with using real numeric values (for instance, 0 or 1). But it's more efficient to treat them as FLAG variables. Often, it's more appropriate to deal with categorical data, such as age in terms of the set {young, middle-aged, elderly}, or income in the set {low, middle, high}. In that case, we could group the data and assign the appropriate category in terms of a string, using a set. The most complete form is RANGE, but sometimes data do not come in that form so analysts are forced to use SET or FLAG types. Sometimes it may actually be more accurate to deal with SET data types than RANGE data types.

As another example, PolyAnalyst has the following data types available:

- **Numerical** Continuous values
- **Integer** Integer values
- **Yes/no** Binary data
- **Category** A finite set of possible values
- **Date**
- **String**
- **Text**

Each software tool will have a different data scheme, but the primary types of data dealt with are represented in these two lists.

There are many statistical methods and visualization tools that can be used to preprocess the selected data. Common statistics, such as max, min, mean, and mode can be readily used to aggregate or smooth the data, while scatter plots and box plots are usually used to filter outliers. More advanced techniques (including regression analyses, cluster analysis, decision tree, or hierarchical analysis) may be applied in data preprocessing depending on the requirements for the quality of the selected data. Because data preprocessing is detailed and tedious, it demands a great deal of time. In some cases, data preprocessing could take over 50 percent of the time of the entire data mining process. Shortening data processing time can reduce much of the total computation time in data mining. The simple and standard data format resulting from data preprocessing can provide an environment of information sharing across different computer systems, which creates the flexibility to implement various data mining algorithms or tools.

As an important component of data preparation, data transformation is to use simple mathematical formulations or learning curves to convert different measurements of selected, and clean, data into a unified numerical scale for the purpose of data analysis. Many available statistics measurements, such as mean, median, mode, and variance can readily be used to transform the data. In terms of the representation of data, data transformation may be used to (1) transform from numerical to numerical scales, and (2) recode categorical data to numerical scales. For numerical to numerical scales, we can use a mathematical transformation to "shrink" or "enlarge" the given data. One reason for transformation is to eliminate differences in variable scales. For example, if the attribute "salary" ranges from "$20,000" to "$100,000," we can use the formula $S = (x - min)/(max - min)$ to "shrink" any known salary value, say $50,000 to 0.6, a number in [0.0, 1.0]. If the mean of salary is given as $45,000, and standard deviation is given as $15,000, the $50,000 can be normalized as 0.33. Transforming data from the metric system (e.g., meter, kilometer) to the English system (e.g., foot and mile) is another example. For categorical to numerical scales, we have to assign an appropriate numerical number to a categorical value according to needs. Categorical variables can be ordinal (such as less, moderate, and strong) and nominal (such as red, yellow, blue, and green). For example, a binary variable {yes, no} can be transformed into "1 = yes and 0 = no." Note that transforming a numerical value to an ordinal value means transformation with order, while transforming to a nominal value is a less rigid transformation. We need to be careful not to introduce more precision than is present in the original data. For instance, Likert scales often represent ordinal information with coded numbers (1 to 7, 1 to 5, and so on). However, these numbers usually don't imply a common scale of difference. An object rated as 4 may not be meant to be twice as strong on some measure as an object rated as 2. Sometimes, we can apply values to represent a block of numbers or a range of categorical variables. For example, we may use "1" to represent the monetary values from "$0" to "$20,000," and use "2" for "$20,001 to $40,000," and so on. We can use "0001" to represent "two-store house" and "0002" for "one-and-half-store house." All kinds of "quick-and-dirty" methods could be used to transform data. There is no unique procedure and the only criterion is to transform the data for convenience of use during the data mining stage.

Modeling

Data modeling is where the data mining software is used to generate results for various situations. A cluster analysis and visual exploration of the data are usually applied first. Depending upon the type of data, various models might then be applied. If the task is to group data, and the groups are given, discriminant analysis might be appropriate. If the purpose is estimation, regression is appropriate if the data are continuous (and logistic regression if not). Neural networks could be applied for both tasks.

Decision trees is yet another tool to classify data. Other modeling tools are available as well. We'll cover these different models in greater detail in subsequent chapters. The point of data mining software is to allow the user to work with the data to gain understanding. This is often fostered by the iterative use of multiple models.

Data Treatment

Data mining is essentially the analysis of statistical data, usually using enormous data sets. The standard process of data mining is to take this large set of data and divide it, using a portion of the data (the **training set**) for development of the model (no matter what modeling technique is used), and reserving a portion of the data (the **test set**) for testing the model that's built. The principle is that if you build a model on a particular set of data, it will of course test quite well. By dividing the data and using part of it for model development, and testing it on a separate set of data, a more convincing test of model accuracy is obtained.

This idea of splitting the data into components is often carried to additional levels in the practice of data mining. Further portions of the data can be used to refine the model.

Data Mining Techniques

Data mining can be achieved by Association, Classification, Clustering, Predictions, Sequential Patterns, and Similar Time Sequences.[1]

In **Association,** the relationship of a particular item in a data transaction on other items in the same transaction is used to predict patterns. For example, if a customer purchases a laptop PC (X), then he or she also buys a mouse (Y) in 60 percent of the cases. This pattern occurs in 5.6 percent of laptop PC purchases. An association rule in this situation can be "X implies Y, where 60 percent is the confidence factor and 5.6 percent is the support factor." When the confidence factor and support factor are represented by linguistic variables "high" and "low," respectively, the association rule can be written in the fuzzy logic form, such as: "where the support factor is low, X implies Y is high."[2] In the case of many qualitative variables, fuzzy association is a necessary and promising technique in data mining.

In **Classification,** the methods are intended for learning different functions that map each item of the selected data into one of a predefined set of classes. Given the set of predefined classes, a number of attributes, and a "learning (or training) set," the classification methods can automatically predict the class of other unclassified data of the learning set. Two key research problems related to classification results are the evaluation of misclassification and prediction power. Mathematical techniques that are often used to construct classification methods are binary decision trees, neural networks, linear programming, and statistics. By using binary decision trees, a tree induction model with a "Yes-No" format can be built to split data into different classes according to their attributes. Models fit to data can be measured by either statistical estimation[3] or information entropy.[4] However, the classification obtained from tree induction may not produce an optimal solution where prediction power is limited. By using neural networks, a neural induction model can be built. In this approach, the attributes become input layers in the neural network while the classes associated with data are output layers. Between input layers and output layers, there are a larger number of hidden layers processing the accuracy of the classification. Although the neural induction model often yields better results in many cases of data mining, since the relationships involve complex nonlinear relationships, implementing this method is difficult when there's a large set of attributes. In linear programming approaches, the classification problem is viewed as a special form of linear program.[5] Given a set of classes and a set of attribute variables, one can define a cutoff limit (or boundary) separating the classes. Then each class is represented by a group of constraints with respect to a boundary in the linear program. The objective function in the linear programming model can minimize the overlapping rate across classes and maximize the distance between classes.[6] The linear programming approach results in an optimal classification. It's also very feasible to construct an effective separation in multiclass problems. However, the computation time required may exceed that of statistical approaches. Various statistical methods, such as linear discriminant regression, quadratic discriminant regression, and logistic discriminant regression are very popular and are commonly used in real business classifications. Even though statistical software has been developed to handle a large amount of data, statistical approaches have a disadvantage in efficiently separating multiclass problems in which a pair-wise comparison (that is, one class versus the rest of the classes) has to be adopted.

Clustering analysis takes ungrouped data and uses automatic techniques to put this data into groups. Clustering is unsupervised, and does not require a learning set. It shares a common methodological ground with Classification. In other words, most of the mathematical models mentioned earlier in regards to Classification can be applied to Clustering Analysis as well. Clustering analysis is described in Chapter 5.

Prediction Analysis is related to regression techniques. The key idea of Prediction Analysis is to discover the relationship between the dependent and independent variables, the relationship between the independent variables (one versus another, one versus the rest, and so on). For example, if sales is an independent variable, then profit may be a dependent variable. By using historical data from both sales and profit, either linear or nonlinear regression techniques can produce a fitted regression curve that can be used for profit prediction in the future.

Sequential pattern analysis seeks to find similar patterns in data transaction over a business period. These patterns can be used by business analysts to identify relationships among data. The mathematical models behind Sequential Patterns are logic rules, fuzzy logic, and so on. As an extension of Sequential Patterns, **Similar Time Sequences** are applied to discover sequences similar to a known sequence over both past and current business periods. In the data mining stage, several similar sequences can be studied to identify future trends in transaction development. This approach is useful in dealing with databases that have time-series characteristics.

Evaluation

The data interpretation stage is very critical. It assimilates knowledge from mined data. Two issues are essential. One is how to recognize the business value from knowledge patterns discovered in the data mining stage. Another issue is which visualization tool should be used to show the data mining results. Determining the business value from discovered knowledge patterns is similar to playing "puzzles." The mined data is a puzzle that needs to be put together for a business purpose. This operation depends on the interaction between data analysts, business analysts and decision makers (such as managers or CEOs). Because data analysts may not be fully aware of the purpose of the data mining goal or objective, and while business analysts may not understand the results of sophisticated mathematical solutions, interaction between them is necessary. In order to properly interpret knowledge patterns, it's important to choose an appropriate visualization tool. Many visualization packages and tools are available, including pie charts, histograms, box plots, scatter plots, and distributions. Good interpretation leads to productive business decisions, while poor interpretation analysis may miss useful information. Normally, the simpler the graphical interpretation, the easier it is for end users to understand.

Deployment

The results of the data mining study need to be reported back to project sponsors. The data mining study has uncovered new knowledge, which needs to be tied to the original data mining project goals. Management will then be in a position to apply this new understanding of their business environment.

It is important that the knowledge gained from a particular data mining study be monitored for change. Customer behavior changes over time, and what was true during the period when the data were collected may have already changed. If fundamental changes occur, the knowledge uncovered is no longer true. Therefore, it's critical that the domain of interest be monitored during its period of deployment.

Knowledge Discovery Process

A recent data mining study in insurance applied a knowledge discovery process.[7] This process involved iteratively applying the steps that we covered in CRISP-DM, and demonstrating how the methodology can work in practice.

Stage 1. Business Understanding: A model was needed to predict which customers would be insolvent early enough for the firm to take preventive measures (or measures to avert losing good customers). This goal included minimizing the misclassification of legitimate customers.

In this case, the billing period was two months. Customers used their phone for four weeks, and received bills about one week later. Payment was due a month after the date of billing. In the industry, companies typically gave customers about two weeks after the due date before taking action, at which time the phone was disconnected if the unpaid bill was greater than a set amount. Bills were sent every month for another six months, during which period the late customer could make payment arrangements. If no payment was received at the end of this six-month period, the unpaid balance was transferred to the uncollectible category.

This study hypothesized that insolvent customers would change their calling habits and phone usage during a critical period before and immediately after termination of the billing period. Changes in calling habits, combined with paying patterns were tested for their ability to provide sound predictions of future insolvencies.

Stage 2. Data Understanding: Static customer information was available from customer files. Time-dependent data were available on bills, payments, and usage. Data came from several databases, but all of these databases were internal to the company. A data warehouse was built to gather and organize this data. The data were coded to protect customer privacy. Data included customer information, phone usage from switching centers, billing information, payment reports by customer, phone disconnections due to a failure to pay, phone reconnections after payment, and reports of permanent contract nullifications.

Data were selected for 100,000 customers covering a 17-month period, and were collected from one rural/agricultural region of customers, a semi-rural touring area, and an urban/industrial area in order to assure representative cross-sections of the company's customer base. The data warehouse used over 10 gigabytes of storage for raw data.

Stage 3. Data Preparation: The data were tested for quality, and data that weren't useful for the study were filtered out. Heterogeneous data items were interrelated. As examples, it was clear that inexpensive calls had little impact on the study. This allowed a 50-percent reduction in the total volume of data. The low percentage of fraudulent cases made it necessary to clean the data from missing or erroneous values due to different recording practices within the organization and the dispersion of data sources. Thus it was necessary to cross-check data such as phone disconnections. The lagged data required synchronization of different data elements.

Data synchronization revealed a number of insolvent customers with missing information that had to be deleted from the data set. It was thus necessary to reduce and project data, so information was grouped by account to make data manipulation easier, and customer data were aggregated by two-week periods. Statistics were applied to find characteristics that were discriminant factors for solvent versus insolvent customers. Data included the following:

- Telephone account category (23 categories, such as payphone, business, and so on).
- Average amount owed was calculated for all solvent and insolvent customers. Insolvent customers had significantly higher averages across all categories of accounts.
- Extra charges on bills were identified by comparing total charges for phone usage for the period as opposed to balances carried forward or purchases of hardware or other services. This also proved to be statistically significant across the two outcome categories.
- Payment by installments was investigated. However, this variable was not found to be statistically significant.

Stage 4. Modeling: The prediction problem was classification, with two classes: most possibly solvent (99.3 percent of the cases) and most possibly insolvent (0.7 percent of the cases). Thus, the count of insolvent cases was very small in a given billing period. The costs of error varied widely in the two categories. This has been noted by many as a very difficult classification problem.

A new dataset was created through stratified sampling for solvent customers, altering the distribution of customers to be 90-percent solvent and 10-percent insolvent. All of the insolvent cases were retained, while care was taken to maintain a proportional representation of the geographic area, type of phone connection, and groups of phone accounts for the solvent set of data. A dataset of 2,066 total cases was developed.

A critical period for each phone account was established. For those accounts that were nullified, this critical period was the last 15 two-week periods prior to service interruption. For accounts that remained active, the critical period was set as a similar period to possible disruption. There were six possible disruption dates per year. For the active accounts, one of these six dates was selected at random.

For each account, variables were defined by counting the appropriate measure for every two-week period in the critical period for that observation. At the end of this phase, new variables were created to describe phone usage by account compared to a moving average of four previous two-week periods. At this stage, there were 46 variables as candidate discriminating factors. These variables included 40 variables measured as call habits over 15 two-week periods, as well as variables concerning the type of customer, whether or not a customer was new, and four variables relating to customer bill payment.

Discriminant analysis, decision trees and neural network algorithms were used to test hypotheses over the reduced data set of 2,066 cases measured over 46 variables. Discriminant analysis yielded a linear model, the neural network came out as a nonlinear model, and the decision tree was a rule-based classifier.

Stage 5. Evaluation: Experiments were conducted to test and compare performance. The data set was divided into a training set (about two-thirds of the 2,066 cases) and test set (the remaining cases). Classification errors are commonly displayed in **coincidence matrices** (called confusion matrices by some). A coincidence matrix shows the count of cases correctly classified, as well as the count of cases classified in each incorrect category. But in many data mining studies, the model may be very good at classifying one category, while very poor at classifying another category. The primary value of the coincidence matrix is that it identifies what kinds of errors are made. It may be much more important to avoid one kind of error than another. For instance, a bank loan officer suffers a great deal more from giving a loan to someone who's expected to repay and does not than making the mistake of not giving a loan to an applicant who actually would have paid. Both instances would be classification errors, but in data mining, often one category of error is much more important than another. Coincidence matrices provide a means of focusing on what kinds of errors particular models tend to make.

A way to reflect relative error importance is through cost. This is a relatively simple idea, allowing the user to assign relative costs by type of error. For instance, if our model predicted that an account was insolvent, that might involve an average write-off of $200. On the other hand, waiting for an account that ultimately was repaid might involve a cost of $10. Thus, there would be a major difference in the cost of errors in this case. Treating a case that turned out to be repaid as a dead account would risk the loss of $190, in addition to alienating the customer (which may or may not have future profitability implications). Conversely, treating an account that was never going to be repaid may involve carrying the account on the books longer than needed, at an additional cost of $10. Here, a **cost function** for the coincidence matrix could be:

$$\$190 \times \text{(closing good account)} + \$10 \times \text{(keeping bad account open)}$$

(Note that we used our own dollar costs for purposes of demonstration, and these were not based on the real case.) This measure (like the **correct classification rate**) can be used to compare alternative models.

SPSS was used for discriminant analysis, including a stepwise forward selection procedure. The best model included 17 of the available 46 variables. Using equal misclassification costs yielded the coincidence matrix shown in Table 2.1.

Overall classification accuracy is obtained by dividing the correct number of classifications (50 + 578 = 628) by the total number of cases (718). Thus, the test

TABLE 2.1
The Coincidence Matrix—Equal Misclassification Costs

Telephone Bill	Model Insolvent	Model Solvent	
Actual Insolvent	50	14	64
Actual Solvent	76	578	654
	126	592	718

TABLE 2.2
The Coincidence
Matrix—Unequal
Misclassification
Costs

Telephone Bill	Model Insolvent	Model Solvent	
Actual Insolvent	36	28	64
Actual Solvent	22	632	654
	58	660	718

data was correctly classified in 87.5 percent of the cases. The cost function value here was:

$$\$190 \times 76 + \$10 \times 14 = \$14,580$$

The high proportion of actually solvent cases classified as insolvent was judged to be unacceptable, because it would chase away too many good customers. The experiment was reconducted using a-priori probabilities. This improved output significantly, as shown in the coincidence matrix in Table 2.2.

Thus, the test data was correctly classified in 93.0 percent of the cases. For the training data, this figure was 93.6 percent. Models usually fit training data a little better than test data, but that's because they were built on training data. Independent test data provides a much better test. The accuracy for insolvent customers, which is very important because it costs so much more, decreased from 78 percent in the training data to 56 percent in the test data. The cost function value here was the following:

$$\$190 \times 22 + \$10 \times 28 = \$4,460$$

From a total cost perspective, the model utilizing unequal misclassification costs (using real costs) was considered more useful.

The 17 variables identified in the discriminant analysis were used for the other two models. The same training and test sets were employed. The training set was used to build a rule-based classifier model. The coincidence matrix for the test set is shown in Table 2.3.

Thus the test data was correctly classified in 95.26 percent of the cases. For the training data, this figure was 95.3 percent. The cost function value here was

$$\$190 \times 8 + \$10 \times 26 = \$1,780$$

This was an improvement over the discriminant analysis model.

A number of experiments were conducted with a neural network model using the same 17 variables and training set. The resulting coincidence matrix over the test data is shown in Table 2.4.

Thus, the test data was correctly classified in 92.9 percent of the cases. For the training data, this figure was 94.1 percent. The cost function value here was

$$\$190 \times 11 + \$10 \times 40 = \$2,490$$

However, these results were inferior to that of the decision tree model.

TABLE 2.3
The Coincidence
Matrix—The
Rule-Based Model

Telephone Bill	Model Insolvent	Model Solvent	
Actual Insolvent	38	26	64
Actual Solvent	8	646	654
	46	672	718

TABLE 2.4
The Coincidence
Matrix—The Neural
Network Model

Telephone Bill	Model Insolvent	Model Solvent	
Actual Insolvent	24	40	64
Actual Solvent	11	643	654
	35	683	718

TABLE 2.5
The Coincidence
Matrix—Combined
Models

Telephone Bill	Model Insolvent	Model Solvent	Unclassified	Total
Actual Insolvent	19	17	28	64
Actual Solvent	1	626	27	654
	20	643	91	718

The first objective was to maximize accuracy of predicting insolvent customers. The decision tree classifier appeared to be best at doing that. The second objective was to minimize the error rate for solvent customers. The neural network model was close to the performance of the decision tree model. It was decided to use all three models on a case-by-case basis.

Stage 6. Deployment: Every customer was examined using all three algorithms. If all three agreed on classification, that result was adopted. If there was disagreement in the model results, the customer was categorized as unclassified. Using this scheme over the test set yielded the coincidence matrix shown in Table 2.5.

Thus, the test data was correctly classified in 89.8 percent of the cases. But only one actually solvent customer would have been disconnected without further analysis. The cost function value here was

$$\$190 \times 1 + \$10 \times 17 = \$360$$

The steps used in this application match the six stages we have presented. Data Selection relates to Learning the application domain and Creating a target dataset. Data Preprocessing involves Data Cleaning and preprocessing. Data Transformation involves Data Reduction and projection. Data Mining was expanded in the earlier application to include (1) choosing the function of data mining, (2) choosing the data mining algorithms, and (3) data mining. Data Interpretation involves the interpretation and use of discovered knowledge.

Summary

The industry-standard CRISP-DM data mining process has six stages: (1) Business Understanding, (2) Data Understanding, (3) Data Preparation, (4) Modeling, (5) Evaluation, and (6) Deployment. Data selection and understanding, preparation, and model interpretation require teamwork between data mining analysts and business analysts, while data transformation and data mining are conducted by data mining analysts alone. Each stage is a preparation for the next stage. In the remaining chapters of this book, we'll discuss details regarding this process from a different perspective, such as data mining tools and applications. This will provide the reader with a better understanding as to why the correct process sometimes is even more important than the correct performance of the methodology.

Glossary

association Data mining function identifying correlation patterns

classification Analysis assigning cases to different classes

clustering Analysis grouping data into classes

coincidence matrix Table displaying actual counts with model predictions

correct classification rate Ratio of correct assignments of test cases to total opportunities

cost function Sum of test case errors multiplied by expected cost by type of error

demographic data Data relating to population characteristics

imputation Filling in missing data with values consistent with adjacent data

prediction analysis Analysis of the relationship between case values and the values of explanatory variables

qualitative data Data not measured numerically

quantitative data Data measured numerically

sequential pattern analysis Search for patterns of similarity

similar time sequences Search for sequences in data

socio-graphic data Data related to cultural activities

test set Portion of the data available that's used to test the data mining model

training set Portion of the data available that's used to build the data mining model

transactional data Data related to business activities at the basic level

Exercises

1. Discuss three issues involved in selecting data for data mining analysis.
2. Contrast differences between demographic, socio-graphic, and transactional data.
3. What is the difference between quantitative data and qualitative data?
4. What is redundant data?
5. Why can't one type of data mining software support all types of data mining analysis?
6. Does data mining software eliminate the need for users to understand statistics?
7. Is it good statistical form to test the accuracy of a model on data used to build the model?
8. Transform the following numeric data concerning client ages into categories of young (under 40), middle-aged (40 to 60), and elderly (over 60).

Client	Age
Fred	46
Herman	52
George	36
Frieda	39
Hermione	28

9. Transform the following salaries to numerical scales with $20,000 equal to 0, $220,000 equal to 1.0, and everything else linearly related between 0 and 1.

Client	Salary
Fred	$120,000
Herman	$200,000

George	$50,000
Frieda	$65,000
Hermione	$35,000

10. Why should nominal data not be converted to numeric scales?

11. Given the following data, alternative data mining models have been applied on a test set of data. What appears to be the best model?

Subject	Actual	Regression	Clustering	Neural Net	Rule-Based
Fred	good	good	good	good	good
Herman	bad	good	bad	good	bad
George	good	good	bad	bad	bad
Frieda	good	good	good	good	bad
Hermione	bad	good	bad	bad	good

12. Do the coincidence matrix for each of the four models in problem 11.

13. In problem 12, the regression and neural net models had the same number of errors. Why might the results of one model be considered better than the results of the other?

14. In problem 11, given relative error costs of the model calling an actually good outcome bad to be $100 and calling an actually bad outcome good to be $500, what is the total cost of errors for each of the four models?

Endnotes

1. P. Cabena, P. Hadjinian, R. Stadler, J. Verhees, and A. Zanasi, *Discovering Data Mining from Concepts to Implementation* (Upper Saddle River, NJ: Prentice Hall, 1997).

2. J.-S. R. Jang, C.-T. Sun, and E. Mizutani, *Neuro-Fuzzy and Soft Computing* (Upper Saddle River, NJ: Prentice Hall, 1997).

3. L. Breiman, J. Friedman, R. Olshen, and C. Stone, *Classification and Regression Trees* (Belmont: Wadsworth, 1984).

4. J. Quinlan, "Induction of decision trees," *Machine Learning*, volume 1 (1986), pp. 81–106.

5. N. Freed and F. Glover, "Simple but Powerful Goal Programming Models for Discriminant Problems," *European Journal of Operational Research*, volume 7 (1981), pp. 44–60; Y. Shi and P. L. Yu, "Goal Setting and Compromise Solutions," in *Multiple Criteria Decision Making and Risk Analysis Using Microcomputers*, edited by B. Karpak and S. Zionts (Berling: Springer-Verlag, 1989), pp. 165–204.

6. Y. Shi, "Multiple Criteria Decision Making in Credit Card Portfolio Management," (the College of Information and Technology, the University of Nebraska at Omaha, 1998).

7. S. Daskalaki, I. Kopanas, M. Goudara, and N. Avouris, "Data Mining for Decision Support on Customer Insolvency in the Telecommunications Business," European Journal of Operational Research, volume 145 (2003), pp. 239–255.

CHAPTER THREE

Database Support to Data Mining

This chapter:

- Describes data warehousing and related database systems
- Discusses features of data found in data warehouses
- Describes how data warehouses are typically implemented and operated
- Defines metadata in the context of data warehouses
- Shows how different data systems are typically used in data mining
- Provides real examples of database systems used in data mining
- Discusses the concept of data quality
- Reviews the database software market

Retail organizations generate masses of data from their cash registers. This information requires very advanced data storage systems. An example is Wal-Mart, which has relied upon modern data management to gain a competitive advantage in supply chain and inventory management, making it one of the most profitable business organizations in the 20th Century (and this century as well). Wal-Mart has invested in one of the largest private data warehouse systems in the world.

Many organizations utilize internal data (such as that generated through their cash register systems) as the basis for control of their operations. This can include a number of analytic tools such as optimization. Summers Rubber Company tied their data storage system to algorithms that enabled them to schedule production in a way that optimized use of resources.

The manipulation of data is a key element in the data mining process. Before data mining can be conducted, access to appropriate data needs to be gained. Data mining and other forms of analysis can draw upon data collected in internal systems as well as gather data from external sources. This chapter discusses a variety of data storage tools that are available for use in support of data mining (as well as other applications).

Access to data is an important requirement for data mining. While data warehouses are not requirements to do data mining, data warehouses store massive amounts of data that can be used for data mining. Data mining analyses are also often accomplished using smaller sets of data that can be organized in online analytic processing systems or in data marts. This unit discusses the major data storage tools useful in data mining.

Data needs to be consolidated in order to maximize its usefulness. First National Bank North Dakota used to have a separate computer system for each division of the bank.[1] This led to problems, such as one division of the bank bouncing a check for one account of a customer who had a trust fund worth several million dollars in another division.

There are many database products. Database software is available to support individuals, allowing them to record information that they consider personally important. They can extract information provided by repetitive organizational reports, such as sales by region within their area of responsibility, and regularly add external data such as industrywide sales, as well as keep records of detailed information such as sales representative expense account expenditure. Users can also find pertinent data on the Web, which they can store on their personal database system. However, most data used for data mining comes from larger database storage systems. A step up in the hierarchy of database products is **online analytical processing (OLAP),** which provides access to report generators and graphical support. Data marts are more powerful database products, followed in size by data warehouses. All of these products can be the source of data used in data mining.

Data Warehousing

Data mining is possible because of the existence of large quantities of data. This data must be stored in a structured and reliable form. Data warehousing is an orderly and accessible repository of known facts and related data that is used as a basis for making better management decisions.[2] Data warehouses provide ready access to information about a company's business, products, and customers. This data can be from both internal and external sources. **Data warehouses** are used to store massive quantities of data in a manner that can be easily updated and allow quick retrieval of specific types of data.

Data warehouses often integrate information from a variety of sources. Data needs to be identified and obtained, cleaned, catalogued, and stored in a fashion that expedites organizational decision making. Three general data warehouse processes exist. (1) Warehouse generation is the process of designing the warehouse and loading data. (2) **Data management** is the process of storing the data. (3) Information analysis is the process of using the data to support organizational decision making.

Data warehousing provides the following benefits[3]:

- Providing business users with views of data appropriate to mission accomplishment
- Eliminating barriers between business elements by consolidating and reconciling data
- Providing macro views of critically important aspects of the organization
- Providing more timely and detailed access to information
- Making specific information available to particular groups, such as customers
- Providing the ability to identify trends

Within data warehouses, data is classified and organized around subjects meaningful to the company. These subjects can be critical success factors, such as customers, employees, or products. The data is gathered from operational systems (bar code readers at cash registers, information from e-commerce, daily reports, and so on) and external data sources (industry volumes, economic data, and so on). Data from different sources (shipping, marketing, billing) are integrated into a common format. Data is transformed to be organized by time elements and the focus of managerial decision making. Transformation also includes filtering data to eliminate unnecessary details, cleaning the data to eliminate incorrect data or duplications, and consolidating data from multiple sources. This transformation, part of the data warehouse management rather than the data mining process, makes accessing data more efficient.

Designing a data warehouse tends to start from the analysis of existing aspects of organizational performance, using it later to decide how this data can be collected. Data warehouses should be organic, in that they have the capacity to hold growing data-input streams. A data warehouse is a central aggregation of data, intended as a permanent storage facility with normalized, formatted data. This data, once stored, is usually not changed without a compelling reason. Normalized implies the use of small, stable data structures within the database. For example, a personnel record may contain many bits of information, some relating to pay, some to experience, some to expertise, and so on. In total, this can be very large. Normalized data would group data elements by category, making it possible to apply relational principles for efficiency in data updating. This is accomplished by assigning data attributes to specific tables.

One of the most important aspects of data warehouses is **scalability.** Scalability refers to the ability to easily change the size or configuration to suit changing conditions. This implies that the data warehouse system can handle a wide variety of data and large data sets. Indeed, scalability is important in all parts of the data warehousing/data mining system.

Data Marts

In order to apply data mining, an intermediate storage form is used. **Data marts** are sometimes used to extract specific items of information for data mining analysis. Terminology in this field is dynamic, and definitions have evolved as new products have entered the market. Originally, many data marts were marketed as preliminary data warehouses. Inmon differentiated dependent data marts (whose source is exclusively a data warehouse) from independent data marts (whose source is typically a legacy application).[4] Currently, many data marts are used in conjunction with data warehouses rather than as competitive products. But there are also many data marts that are being used independently in order to take advantage of lower-priced software and hardware.

Data marts are usually used as repositories of data gathered to serve a particular set of users, providing data extracted from data warehouses and/or other sources. Designing a data mart tends to begin with the analysis of user needs. The information that pertains to the issue at hand is relevant. This may involve a specific time frame and specific products, people, and locations.

Data marts are available for data miners to transform information to create new variables (such as ratios, or coded data suitable for a specific application). In addition, only that information expected to be pertinent to the specific data mining analysis is extracted. This vastly reduces the computer time required to process the data, as data marts are expected to contain small subsets of the data warehouse's contents. Data marts are also expected to have ample space available to generate additional data by transformation.

Granularity refers to the level of data detail. Data warehouses tend to focus on data that is close to raw form. It is necessary to clean data, because it should be accurate, complete, and in the proper format. Ideally, once data is cleaned, it should be entered into the data warehouse permanently. For decision making, data usually needs to be aggregated. But it is never known beforehand what data is going to be needed. The data warehouse contains the data in its finest level of granularity. Part of the data mart's function is to extract the desired data, and to aggregate it in the form desired for decision making. What might be desired are sales of all vehicle products for each region during the period 1999 through 2002, on a quarterly basis. This data is aggregated quite a bit from the granular data of each specific sale in each specific outlet each day over the history of the firm (or at least since they've kept this level of records).

Another difference between data warehouses and data marts is ownership. Data warehouses are owned by the organization, a truly corporate effort. They are permanent repositories of granular data. Data marts, on the other hand, are owned by the groups that use them. What they contain depends upon user requirements.

Online Analytic Processing

Online analytic processing (OLAP) is a multidimensional spreadsheet approach to shared data storage designed to allow users to extract data and generate reports on the dimensions important to them. Data is segregated into different dimensions and organized in a hierarchical manner. There are many variants and extensions generated by the OLAP vendor industry.

A typical procedure is for OLAP products to take data from relational databases and store them in multidimensional form, often called a **hypercube,** to reflect the OLAP ability to access data on these multiple dimensions. Data can be analyzed locally within this structure. One function of OLAP is standard report generation, including financial performance analysis on selected dimensions (such as by department, geographical region, product, salesperson, time, or other dimensions desired by the analyst). Planning and forecasting are supported through spreadsheet analytic tools. Budgeting calculations can be included through spreadsheet tools as well. Usually, pattern analysis tools are also available. An OLAP product is part of a system including a data warehouse, an OLAP server, and a client server, often on a local area network. Client users are connected. Information is retrieved from the data warehouse by the OLAP server, which then processes the information and sends it on to the main server. Users access this information through the Web or through spreadsheet packages.

Web sites providing significant information on OLAP include the following:

- www.knowledgecenters.org
- www.olapreport.com
- www.olapcouncil.org

OLAP functioning requires multidimensional data views, the ability to conduct calculation-intensive operations, and time intelligence. The multidimensional capability gives managers the ability to look at data from a number of different perspectives. Different levels of aggregation can be selected as well as dimensions. Aggregation along a hierarchy is accomplished through OLAP calculations, as well as calculations of market share, or allocations by department. Complex calculation support also gives the ability to obtain key performance indicators and trend forecasting. **Time intelligence** refers to the ability to specify a variety of time dimensions for reporting, including such things as reports of performance for specific months, or reports per month over a particular time frame, and other time aspects.

FIGURE 3.1
Possible
Relationships of
Database Products
and Data Mining

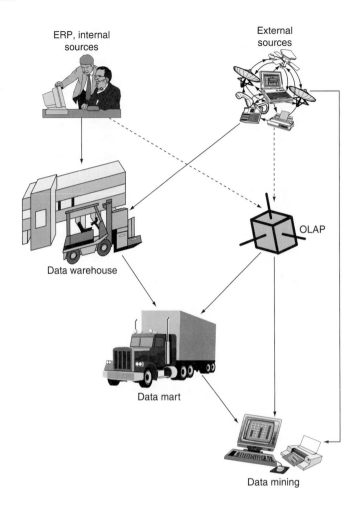

Almost every leading data storage producer has OLAP products. Sales growth began to slow in 1999 because rapid growth of this nature is difficult to maintain. Also, there was a degree of market saturation, and a reduction in price (thus reducing the market dollar value even with increased unit sales). While data warehouses focus on efficiently storing vast quantities of data, OLAP systems are designed to make it easy to analyze data.

Figure 3.1 demonstrates the relationship of database products to data mining. Data warehouses are not required for data mining, nor are OLAP systems. However, the existence of either presents many opportunities to data mine.

Data Warehouse Implementation

Data warehouses create the opportunity to provide much better information than what was available in the past. Data are often not understood, giving them a different meaning to different people.[5] Since systems are frequently developed independently, data needs are often focused on local problems. Therefore, one part of the organization may collect one aspect of data, while other parts of the organization may measure basically the same operation in an entirely different way. This can lead to inconsistent views of events and inconsistent reports, which in turn lead to lack of trust in reports. If misunderstanding is generated through these different views of the same events, a natural reluctance to sharing data arises, and gaps in important measures occur over time. This state of affairs often leads to views of "dirty" data. From an organizational perspective, dirty data are unreliable and untrustworthy.

Data warehouses can mitigate this state of affairs by providing a reliable, comprehensive source of clean data. From a technical perspective, dirty data are inaccurate, incomplete, or in the wrong format. Clean data are not only accurate, but also complete, and in the correct format. By centralizing data and taking care to acquire and retain reliable and accurate data, more consistent reports can be obtained, along with clearer communication throughout the organization.

The three primary processes related to implementing a data warehouse system include the following:

- System development
- Data acquisition
- Data extraction for use

All of these processes involve a degree of continuity since data warehousing is a dynamic environment.

Data warehouse systems can take on a variety of forms. One of these is to have a suite of software tools to extract data from sources and move it to the data warehouse itself, as well as a suite of tools (possibly data marts) that provides user access to this information.

Data acquisition is supported by **data warehouse generation,** the process of extracting data from sources, transforming and cleansing this data, and loading the data into the data warehouse. Significant effort is required for data warehouse generation. Sixty to eighty percent of data warehouse effort has been estimated to occur in warehouse generation.[6] Extraction programs are executed periodically to obtain the appropriate data. Data extraction routines interpret data formats, identify changed records, and copy the information to an intermediate file. Transformation programs then accomplish final data preparation, which includes the following tasks:

- The consolidation of data from multiple sources
- Filtering data to eliminate unnecessary details
- Cleaning data to eliminate incorrect entries or duplications
- Converting and translating data into the format established for the data warehouse
- The aggregation of data

Data management involves retrieving information from the data warehouse. Extraction programs are periodically run to generate repetitive reports, and to serve specific needs as they arise. Data marts and OLAP products support the data management process.

Data warehouse systems are complex and comprehensive. Thus, not all attempts to implement them have been successful. Some comprehensive data warehousing projects fail because of a lack of sound planning and design. Projects that take too long often miss the useful time window due to changing business needs. This problem can be averted by focusing on organizational needs. Another reason for failure is due to an attempt to collect all information, rather than identify the information that is needed by the organization. Specific problems encountered in a recent study included the following:[7]

- The required data were not available.
- The initial data warehouse scope was too broad.
- Insufficient time was allocated for prototyping, or for the analysis of needs.
- Senior management did not provide sufficient direction, resulting in a variance between data needs and data collection.

Data warehouses should therefore be driven by a specific need. Data warehouse architecture should be flexible enough to allow for changes in organizational needs. Flexibility needs to be incorporated within the three data warehouse components of data acquisition, data storage, and data delivery. This can often be accomplished through modular system designs. Incremental systems development is also a useful approach in data warehouse development. Finally, management of user expectations is important. There will always be a need to balance data quality and system complexity. (Greater complexity translates to greater costs.) Managers and other users need to be kept informed throughout the project life about data availability and system access features. Prototype systems are useful in explaining data issues, in gaining consensus support, and in developing the overall system more efficiently.

Data storage product development has been rapid, and it has been instrumental in the development of data mining. A number of publications are available that explain more about data warehouses.[8] A great deal of information can also be found at www.datawarehouse.com. Alternate web sites were listed earlier for OLAP products.

Metadata

Data warehouse management differs from data management. Data management concerns the management of all of the enterprise's data. Data warehouse management, on the other hand, refers to the design and operation of the data warehouse through all phases of its life cycle. This life cycle includes the following operations:

- Managing metadata
- Designing the data warehouse
- Ensuring data quality
- Managing the system during operations

Metadata is the set of references to keep track of data, and is used to describe the organization of the warehouse. A data catalog provides users with the ability to see specifically what the data warehouse contains. The content of the data warehouse is defined by metadata, which also provides business views of data (for use by information access tools) and technical views (for use by warehouse generation tools). Business metadata includes the following:

- Available data
- The source of each data element
- The frequency of data update
- The location of specific data
- Predefined reports and queries
- Methods of data access

Technical metadata is available to data warehouse administrators and can include

- Data sources, internal or external
- Data preparation features, including transformation and aggregation rules
- The logical structure of data
- The physical structure and content of the data warehouse
- Data ownership
- Security aspects, such as who has access rights and restrictions on data use
- System information, including the date of the last update, retention policy information, and data usage

Metadata is key to the technical operation of the data warehouse. It consists of references important to business operations and provides data warehouse administrators with a view of what they provide users. Metadata also offers technical operations, supplying information needed to make the computer system function.

System Demonstrations

To demonstrate these concepts, consider a dealer wholesaling mass volumes of objects suitable for the young of mind. These items are obtained from all over the world and are sold through differing media, including the Internet.

Data Warehouse

The data warehouse would deal with granular data, information at its rawest form. Within the data warehouse each transaction may be recorded. A small portion for the first 10 shipments a year might be listed as in Table 3.1.

In this case, the key represents a specific order for a particular type of toy. The date is month, day, and year (year represented by only a single digit, as in 10 years the owner plans to be living on an island she will purchase in the south Pacific). The product is the type of toy sold wholesale (by cases), and each product has an item number. The database includes the client by name. Suppliers are identified, as well as the shipper for each case of material. The last three columns represent the number of cases in each order by type of toy, revenue generated, and profit generated.

Note that data warehouses are normalized into relational form. This means that the data is organized into a series of tables connected by keys. Thus, you may not

TABLE 3.1 Data Warehouse Extract

Key	Date	Product	Item#	Client	Supp	Ship	Cases	Rev	Profit
7332	1061	Jacks	A001	Finn	Inter	Downs	1	350	50
7333	1061	Comp	C370	Finn	Cuba	Tiger	1	5863	958
7334	1081	Hoops	A011	Gold	Matl	Bear	1	702	132
7335	1081	Slink	A799	Gold	Matl	Ups	2	1386	256
7336	1081	Game	B235	Gold	Cuba	Tiger	1	2810	459
7337	1131	Jacks	A001	Hart	Matl	Ups	3	1050	150
7338	1131	Video	C314	Orr	Inter	Downs	4	23340	3932
7339	1151	Bow	A596	Jones	Inter	Lion	2	1242	202
7340	1151	Farm	B231	Lima	Inter	Bear	1	2805	433
7341	1151	AntF	D986	Lima	Inter	Bear	2	20018	4692

find a complete flat file like that shown in Table 3.1 with all the information relating to a particular transaction. However, all the information shown in Table 3.1 is efficiently stored within the data warehouse and can, just as efficiently, be recovered as needed.

Data Mart

A data mart is interested in data relating to a question under study. For instance, the firm might be interested in examining the characteristics of customers who buy their products. They would be interested in response to advertising by mail, advertising by Internet, or advertising by print media. They also would be interested in the profitability by product, and the effectiveness of advertising in increasing sales by product. The data warehouse would contain much useful information related to these questions. But it would not necessarily include all of the information needed. Analysts have choices to make about manipulating currently available information, generating additional information, or purchasing information from vendors. Information available from the data warehouse could include, of course, sales volume and profitability figures by time and region. Data marts could extract this data, and aggregate it in a form useful for data mining, keeping only that information important for the study at hand, and possibly specifying a specific time frame. But the data warehouse might not include the advertising media that triggered sales. This information would have to be generated by survey. Survey results could then be added to the data mart. For observations where survey information is not obtained, the observation might be deleted, or might be retained with a code for missing data. Additional observations or variable information might be available by purchase from information vendors. Table 3.2 shows entries that might be found in a data mart, extracting information on product D428 over the course of two years in the data warehouse, and adding survey data.

Survey results identifying media are appended within the data mart from an external source. The data warehouse provided the first nine columns of data shown, and survey data were used to supplement the data warehouse results.

OLAP

An OLAP application would be focused more on analyzing trends or other aspects of organizational operations. It may obtain much of its information from

TABLE 3.2   Data Mart Entries for Cases of Construction Sets Sold

Key	Client	Mo	Year	Shipper	Cases	Revenue	Profit	Source	Media
M071	Gold	May	1	Lion	3	29,508	6,759	Iran	TV
M076	Que	May	1	Bear	1	9,836	2,253	Iran	Print
M098	Lima	Jun	1	Ups	3	29,508	6,759	Inter	Internet
M124	Que	Aug	1	Ups	3	29,508	6,759	Iran	TV
M148	Que	Sep	1	Lion	3	29,508	6,759	Inter	Internet
M173	Lima	Nov	1	Lion	3	29,508	6,759	Matl	Mail
M178	Ross	Nov	1	Fedy	1	9,836	2,253	Lucas	Mail
M278	Que	Mar	2	Downs	1	9,836	2,253	Inter	Internet
M357	Orr	Aug	2	Downs	3	29,508	6,759	Matl	Mail
M391	Que	Sep	2	Bear	4	39,344	9,012	Matl	Word
M455	Ross	Dec	2	Lion	3	29,508	6,759	Inter	Internet
M475	Orr	Dec	2	Lion	3	29,508	6,759	Inter	Internet

TABLE 3.3 An OLAP Report of Cases Sold by Quarter

Category	Q IV Year 1	Q I	Q II	Q III	Q IV	Revenue Year 2	Profit Year 2	Return on Rev
Small	74	46	66	27	99	138,539	23,795	0.172
Personal	55	24	20	36	52	372,582	59,765	0.160
Electronic	19	22	26	42	76	1,004,613	168,688	0.168
Advanced	50	30	30	25	55	1,419,547	342,546	0.241
Totals	**198**	**122**	**142**	**130**	**282**	**2,935,281**	**594,794**	**0.203**

the data warehouse, but extracts granular information that is of interest to the users being supported. It then aggregates this information and makes it easily accessible in a number of ways. This information could be accessed to make a report by product category, as shown in Table 3.3.

In this case, sales of electronics seem to have increased significantly compared to the same quarter from last year. Personal toy products, on the other hand, actually declined from last year, at least as measured by cases sold. Rates of return are healthy for all products, but are healthiest for more complex (Advanced) toy products.

One type of special study that a data mart might support is evaluating the value of each client to the firm. This would involve tapping the data warehouse for pertinent raw data, which would be stored on the data mart. This data can then be aggregated within the data mart, or on an OLAP system. In this case, the resulting aggregated content by client is shown in Table 3.4.

This report enables management to identify the value of each client to the firm not only by year, but also by ratio of profit to revenue.

Another useful report might organize volume according to the shipper. Pertinent raw data could be downloaded from the data warehouse to a data mart. Most data mart software includes the ability to manipulate data to generate reports in the needed format. An OLAP could also be used to organize data by shipper. Table 3.5 displays the results of cases by shipper per quarter.

This shows management the volume of traffic by quarter for each shipper.

TABLE 3.4 Profit per Client by Year

Client	Year 1 Rev	Year 1 Profit	Ratio	Year 2 Rev	Year 2 Profit	Ratio
Que	509,088	123,252	0.242	635,426	150,801	0.237
Ross	369,091	90,606	0.245	420,710	104,712	0.249
Orr	465,277	92,568	0.199	480,203	87,703	0.183
Finn	278,665	56,882	0.204	453,155	86,546	0.191
Lima	242,036	45,156	0.187	332,546	63,623	0.191
Putt	96,279	16,470	0.171	188,765	31,415	0.166
Gold	150,095	26,221	0.175	190,166	31,326	0.165
Hart	61,934	10,436	0.169	65,954	10,905	0.165
Moon	181,372	29,159	0.161	67,421	10,755	0.16
Nunn	26,033	4,200	0.161	54,173	8,860	0.164
Jones	21,489	3,503	0.163	26,525	4,658	0.176
Klein	8,656	1,446	0.167	20,237	3,490	0.172
Totals	**2,410,015**	**499,899**	**0.207**	**2,935,281**	**594,794**	**0.203**

TABLE 3.5 Shipper Volume in Cases by Time Period

Shipper	QI-1	QII-1	QIII-1	QIV-1	QI-2	QII-2	QIII-2	QIV-2	Total
Bear	38	72	32	72	49	25	47	86	421
Downs	24	25	21	35	19	20	33	36	213
Lion	34	16	13	25	7	26	16	65	202
Fedy	14	10	17	27	21	12	5	31	137
USP	17	10	8	19	18	21	16	11	120
Ups	9	5	11	12	8	14	9	42	110
Tiger	5	3	17	8	0	24	4	11	72
Totals	141	141	119	198	122	142	130	282	1275

Data Quality

Data warehouse projects can fail for a number of reasons. One of the most common is the refusal of users to accept the validity of data obtained from a data warehouse.[9] This is an issue of data integrity. Such problems can arise because of one or more of the following:

- The corruption of data or missing data from the original sources
- Failure of the software transferring data into or out of the data warehouse
- Failure of the data-cleansing process to resolve data inconsistencies

In the initial stages of data warehouse use, it's critical that data prove to be reliable. Once a reputation is lost, it's very difficult to recover it. The information system staff operating the data warehouse must verify the integrity of data, ensuring that when data is loaded into the data warehouse, it is stored as planned. It's also necessary that the systems used to extract data from the data warehouse function properly.

Data integrity requires that meaningless, corrupt, or redundant data not be entered into the data warehouse. Controls can be implemented prior to loading data, in the data migration, cleansing, transforming, and loading processes. This is the most efficient stage to prevent meaningless, corrupt, or redundant data from entering the system.

An example of multiple variations for the variable Client in the example data warehouse is shown in Table 3.6.

In this case, the Client variable includes three variations of the same customer. The second is a misspelling. The third is correctly spelled but includes a more complete definition. The process of developing unique variable values is **data standardization.**

TABLE 3.6 An Example of Multiple Variations

Key	Date	Product	Item#	Client	Supp	Ship	Cases	Rev	Profit
7521	1085	Gboy	C336	Putt	Iran	Lion	1	6532	1138
7555	1125	Walk	C361	Putz	King	Bear	4	24404	4128
7574	1158	Gboy	C336	Putt	Matl	Lion	2	13064	2276
7603	1226	Chess	C389	Putt	Matl	Bear	4	28420	5012
7667	1315	Gboy	C336	CJ Putt	Matl	Fedy	1	6532	1138
7668	1315	Comp	C370	CJ Putt	Inter	Bear	2	11726	1916

Matching involves associating variables. It's necessary for efficient data warehouse operation that the database contain the minimum number of consistent entries for each variable. As discussed earlier, one name entry for "CJ Putt" needs to be identified. Thus, the overall system needs to be adjusted to reflect these choices. Software used to introduce new data into the data warehouse needs to check that the appropriate spellings and entry values are used. This also includes matching companies with addresses, an obvious opportunity for variety. Care needs to be taken to keep up with changes, such as telephone area code changes, or new ZIP codes. Personnel turnover makes maintaining proper contact names an interesting challenge.

Means to guarantee data quality begin with assuring that the data extraction process operates correctly. A framework for error identification and correction as well as reconciliation needs to be operating when the data warehouse is created. Data validation and testing tools are needed to monitor data quality and resolve problems as they arise.

Various data quality software tools are available. Some of these are full-function tools that perform data matching, data standardization, and data validation. However, most comprehensive tools are designed and priced for more expensive data warehouse systems. Software for specific functions, though, is available at more popular prices. Some of the functions of this class of software include the following:

- The analysis of data for type
- The construction of standardization schemes
- The identification of redundant data
- The adjustment of matching criteria to achieve selected levels of discrimination
- The transformation of data into designed format

Once data are stored in the data warehouse, controls can be applied to detect accuracy and completeness. Quick reviews should be performed soon after data is loaded to make sure that the correct numbers of records were entered. It's useful to check aggregate totals as a means of verifying a degree of accuracy. More detailed validation efforts are often performed during data warehouse implementation. Ownership and accountability for particular data are assigned to a specific person or organization. Detailed validation checks whether data are complete and correct, whether business rules are followed, and whether the transformation processes of consolidation, filtering, cleaning, and aggregating are done properly. Validation also checks to make sure that data was loaded correctly. Data also are checked to make sure that entries are within tolerance levels. Any errors detected should be investigated to determine cause, so that appropriate changes can be made to the overall system.

Software Products

Vendor support to the overall database market is complex, with many specialist products performing specific tasks such as data cleansing. Table 3.7 provides an overview of major vendors by product category.

This table is, of course, vastly incomplete, and it covers a constantly changing field. There also are many vendors in the data mart market, as well as in specialty utility functions such as data cleansing. The table is presented to give a quick

TABLE 3.7 Representative Vendors by Product Category

Warehouse Generation Vendors	OLAP Data Management Vendors	Data Access Tool Vendors
IBM	Gentia	Brio
Informatics	Hyperion Solutions	Cognos
Platinum Technology	IBM	Hummingbird Communications
Praxis International	Oracle	IQ Software
Prism Solutions	Platinum Technology	Platinum Technology
Sagent Technology	Red Brick Systems	Seagate Software

overview of an important industry. In no way is this presentation intended to indicate relative time in the field, or relative market share.

Real Examples

We conclude this chapter with a review of reports on two actual data warehousing implementations.

Wal-Mart's Data Warehouse System

Wal-Mart was founded in 1962. In 40 years, it has come to dominate the retail market. One of the primary reasons for this dominance has been the use of information technology, used in great part to support Wal-Mart's core competency of supply chain distribution throughout its 2,900 outlets. Wal-Mart uses a data warehouse consisting of 101 terabytes, believed to be the world's largest commercial database.[10] The investment for this data warehouse operation totaled over $4 billion.

The initial Wal-Mart data warehouse was stocked with point-of-sale and shipment data. This was then supplemented with inventory, forecast, demographic, markdown, return, and market-basket information. Data about competition are also included. The system processes 65 million transactions per week. Data warehouses are subject-oriented, integrated, time-variant, and contain non-volatile data. They include 65 weeks of data by item, by store, and by day.

The purpose of this information is to support decision making. Buyers, merchandisers, logistics personnel, and forecasters have direct access to the data warehouse, as do 3,500 vendor partners. The system can handle up to 35,000 queries per week. The benefits of this operation were estimated to be over $12,000 per query. A few power users were running about 1,000 queries per day.

Summers Rubber Company Data Storage Design

Firms have developed the ability to collect and store data within their transaction-processing systems on an enormous scale. Traditionally, data-driven querying and reporting systems needed extraction programs to gather and format information as required. Extraction programs would read from transaction-based files and create output files. The complexity of growing reporting systems that were not integrated led to a major problem of computer support capacity. An extreme example of a typical problem was a case where a query to extract manufacturing defect data by shift and by day took over a week to generate, making it less than useful for decision making, and also bogging down the computer system.[11] Data warehouses provide an integrated means of supporting this need for reports based on accurate, timely data.

In order to provide stable, efficient data support, data warehouses are designed to provide subject-oriented data by time period. This requires a different focus than was appropriate for traditional transactional data systems. Data warehouses need to be carefully designed as permanent repositories that can be relied upon to contain key organizational data. Data warehouse operation requires data integration and the ability to support anticipated user requests and output reports. Key design considerations include data granularity, which determines storage volumes and the type of queries that can be supported. The more detailed the granularity of the data, the greater the cost in terms of storage space required, data distribution and transmission costs, query costs, and report costs.

Summers Rubber Company is a distribution firm with seven operating locations. Summers stocked about 10,000 items and has over 3,000 customers. Tribute software was used to support online transaction-processing, which could generate reports, extract data, and maintain databases. These databases were both transactional and summarized, and data was stored in a number of locations. Users had to learn a complex system in order to know what data was available and how it could be accessed.

Summers decided to improve reporting and analysis capabilities through adoption of a data storage system. The system selected was built in-house and based on personal computers. Access was used as the database engine. Front-end and query language system components were generated using Visual Basic 4.0 and Excel, while laptops and desktop computers were used for the hardware platform.

To move data from transactional databases to the new data system involved extracting data from the Tribute software program into the Access database. An iterative approach was used to design the data warehouse, beginning with a very small prototype and obtaining feedback from users. This approach was useful in identifying the appropriate level of data granularity. Primary data tables were identified based upon system intent and user feedback from prototypes. Data marts were then used to reduce the average data system size. Because data came from many sources within the Summers organization, data integrity was a major design issue. Scrubbing data involves reformatting data from various sources and molding this data into a common format (such as time units, scales, and currency measures, and employing consistent treatment to a variety of data forms).

A distributed data system was applied. The data server accumulated and built data required to update distributed data storage sites, and coordinated the update process. The data warehouse server also controlled queries and managed resources such as CPU time, input-output volume, connect time, and memory use. While the distributed data system worked well for Summers, it was noted that there was an incremental cost added for each element of decentralization, which could become prohibitive for large organizations.

The Summers data system contained critical information that needed protection from competitor access. The decentralized nature of the Summers data system increased the risk that data could be stolen. Password protections provided some security, but not from internal personnel who could leave the organization. Therefore, Summers used data marts with very scaled-down versions of the central database as a means to limit risk. This security measure increased the cost of queries in terms of time. It was alleviated in part by adopting Windows NT and using system operating security features to limit access by type of data.

Summers personnel reported a number of negative features of their distributed data warehouse system. They used too much disk space on user local drives, and were often difficult to understand and use. Updating multiple data sites was slow,

TABLE 3.8 A Comparison of Major Database Products Supporting Data Mining

Product	Use	Duration	Granularity
Data warehouse	Repository	Permanent	Finest
Data mart	Specific study	Temporary	Aggregate
OLAP	Report and Analysis	Repetitive	Summary
Database	Personal	Any desired	Any desired

limiting access to current data. Only the transaction-processing system contained current information. Summary data was often useless in answering specific questions. Users wanted data mining tools, which were infeasible with the aggregated data stored in the data system. There also were problems with missing, incomplete, or incorrect data, which required additional scrubbing.

However, in general, users were positive about the system. Exception reporting and other features were credited that enabled management to better identify trends and access important data hidden in the older detail-level reports. Sales personnel appreciated having data mart information available on laptops to answer customer questions in real time.

Summary

Data warehouses are capable of storing vast quantities of data. How these warehouses are implemented is of paramount importance. Missing and miscoded data have to be cleaned up. Additionally, it must be taken into account that variables often come in a variety of types, such as nominal data with no numeric content, dates, counts, averages, and many other forms. Data marts are products designed to select particular data from data warehouses (as well as from external sources) to be used for analysis, especially in data mining. OLAP products come in a variety of product forms, but all are intended to give users the ability to design reports that give them insight into their operational environment.

Table 3.8 compares the three data products discussed in broad terms.

Each of these products can do other things, but all are instrumental in supporting data mining. Metadata is necessary for the efficient technical operation of data warehouse systems.

The data-warehousing market has undergone tremendous growth and development. It will continue to grow, as organizations learn to use the constantly developing technology. The industry will probably grow rapidly in areas integrating data warehousing capabilities within enterprise resource planning systems, and in web operations.

Data quality is very important in assuring the accuracy needed for successful system use. Data need to be checked for accuracy before entry into the data warehouse. In an ideal system, if accurate data is entered, there should be little problem during subsequent operations. Realistically, there are many required changes to data, which makes the administration of a data warehouse challenging.

Glossary

data integrity The elimination of meaningless, corrupt, or redundant data.

data management Retrieving information from the data warehouse.

data mart A database system used to extract a subset of data from a data warehouse so that it can be used for a data mining application.

data standardization   The process of developing unique variable values.

data warehouse   A large-scale data storage system designed to contain complete and clean data that can be accessed efficiently.

data warehouse generation   The process of extracting data from sources, and then transform and cleanse this data before loading it into the data warehouse.

granularity   The level of data detail.

hypercube   Term used to describe the multidimensional capabilities of OLAP systems.

matching   Associating variables.

metadata   The set of references needed to keep track of data.

online analytic processing (OLAP)   Tools for accessing databases with the intent of providing users with a multidimensional display of information.

scalable   The ability to efficiently analyze very large data sets.

time intelligence   The ability to specify a variety of time dimensions for reporting.

Exercises

1. Compare and contrast database software packages, online analytical processing software, data marts, and data warehouses.
2. What is the relationship between data warehouses and data mining?
3. How does a data warehouse differ from a data mart?
4. How does scalability impact the database systems discussed?
5. What does the transformation of data prior to entry into the data warehouse include?
6. Discuss the relative granularity of data in data warehouses and online analytical processing systems.
7. Data in data warehouses should be normalized, formatted, and stable. What does this mean?
8. What functions does online analytic processing support?
9. Describe "clean" data in the context of data warehouses.
10. What does metadata do for a data storage system?
11. Describe data integrity and its importance in data warehouse systems.
12. How are different systems typically used to gather data for a specific data mining study? What sources are usually used?
13. What typical problems arise in implementing data warehouse systems?
14. Visit web sites to identify software currently sold in the following categories:
    a. Data warehouses
    b. Data marts
    c. OLAP

Endnotes

1. R. Whiting and J. Sweat, "Profitable Customers," *InformationWeek*, March 29, 1999, pp. 44–56.
2. E. Berg and M. Katz, ed., *Price Waterhouse Technology Forecast: 1999*, Menlo Park, CA: Price Waterhouse World Technology Centre, October 1998.
3. Ibid.
4. W. Inmon, "Data Mart Does Not Equal Data Warehouse," *DM Review*, www.datawarehouse.com, May 1998.

5. S. Adelman and L. Moss, "Data Warehouse Goals and Objectives (Parts 1, 2, and 3)," *DM Review*, www.datawarehouse.com, July 18, 2000, August 7, 2000, and August 14, 2000.

6. Berg and Katz, ed., op. cit.

7. B. C. Gaskin, "Realizing the Strategic Value of Data Warehousing," *DM Review*, www.datawarehouse.com, July 18, 2000.

8. W. Inmon and R. Hackathorn, *Using the Data Warehouse*, New York: John Wiley & Sons, 1994; R. Kimball, *The Data Warehouse Toolkit: Practical Techniques for Building Dimension Data Warehouses*, New York: John Wiley & Sons, 1996; W. H. Inmon, *Building the Data Warehouse*, 2nd Edition, New York: Wiley & Sons, 1996; E. Berg and M. Katz, ed., *Price Waterhouse Technology Forecast: 1999*, Menlo Park, CA: Price Waterhouse World Technology Centre, October 1998; M. Corey, M. Abbey, I. Abramson, L. Barnes, B. Taub, and R. Venkitachalam, *Data Warehousing*, New York: Osborne, 1999.

9. J. Wu, "Ensuring Data Integrity (Parts 1, 2, and 3)," *DM Review*, www.datawarehouse.com, July 18, 2000, August 7, 2000, and August 14, 2000.

10. P. S. Foote and M. Krishnamurthi, "Forecasting Using Data Warehousing Model: Wal-Mart's Experience," *The Journal of Business Forecasting*, Fall 2001, pp. 13–17.

11. N. Gorla and S. Krehbiel, "Summers Rubber Company Designs Its Data Warehouse," *Interfaces*, volume 29, number 2, 1999, pp. 104–117.

PART TWO

Data Mining Methods as Tools

CHAPTER FOUR

Overview of Data Mining Techniques

This chapter:

- Reviews data mining tools
- Compares data mining perspectives
- Discusses data mining functions
- Presents four sets of data used to demonstrate tools in subsequent chapters
- Shows the Enterprise Miner structure for data mining analysis in the appendix

Data useful to business come in many forms. For instance, an automobile insurance company, faced with millions of accident claims, realizes that not all claims are legitimate. If they are extremely tough and investigate each claim thoroughly, they would spend more money on investigation than they would pay out in claims. They would also find that they're unable to sell any new policies. If they were as understanding and trusting as their television ads imply, they would reduce their investigation costs to zero, and leave themselves vulnerable to fraudulent claims. Insurance firms have developed ways to profile claims, considering many variables along the way, and so provide an early indication of cases that probably merit expending funds for investigation. This has the effect of reducing overall policy expenses, because it discourages fraud, while minimizing the imposition on valid claims. The same approach is used by the Internal Revenue Service in processing individual tax returns. Fraud detection has become a viable data mining industry, with a large number of software vendors. This is typical of many applications of data mining.

Data mining can be conducted in many business contexts. This chapter presents four data sets that will be utilized to demonstrate the techniques to be covered in Part II of the book. In addition to insurance fraud, files have been generated reflecting other common business applications, such as loan evaluation and customer segmentation. The same concepts can be applied to other applications, such as the evaluation of employees.

So far, we've described data mining, its process, and the data storage systems that make it possible. The next section of the book explores data mining methods. Data mining tools have been categorized by the tasks of classification, **estimation, clustering,** and **summarization.** Classification and estimation are predictive, while clustering and summarization are descriptive.[1] Not all methods will be presented, but those most commonly used will be. We'll demonstrate each of these methods with small example data sets intended to show how methods work. We don't intend to give the impression that these data sets are anywhere near the scale of real data mining applications. But they do represent micro-versions of real applications, and are much more convenient for demonstrating concepts.

This chapter is intended as an overview for the next section of the book, which presents a variety of modeling techniques. We provide an overview of these techniques here. Then we'll present four data sets that will be used throughout the modeling section to demonstrate techniques on representative data sets. These data sets were fabricated to reflect common data mining applications. As with real data sets, they include information that can be used for good or bad. The appendix at the end of this chapter provides a quick view of data mining software, Enterprise Miner. This appendix shows some of the ability of data mining software to provide visualization tools.

Data Mining Models

Data mining uses a variety of modeling tools for a variety of purposes. Various authors have viewed these purposes along with available tools (see Table 4.1). Radding (1997) gave seven major algorithms for data mining market-oriented data.[2] Peacock (1998) provided a view of data mining functions.[3] These methods come from both classical statistics as well as from artificial intelligence. Statistical techniques have strong diagnostic tools that can be used for the development of confidence intervals on parameter estimates, hypothesis testing, and other things. **Artificial intelligence** techniques require less assumptions about the data, and are generally more automatic.

Regression comes in a variety of forms, to include ordinary least squares regression, logistic regression (widely used in data mining when outcomes are binary), and discriminant analysis (used when outcomes are categorical and predetermined). Least absolute value regression is accomplished through linear programming. We cover multiple criteria linear programming methods in Chapter 9. Neural networks can be used for a variety of tasks as well. Association rules can be used for classification, as well as description in the case of some market-basket analysis. Genetic algorithms are specialized tools that can be used to boost performance of a number of other algorithms. Link analysis is a form of identification of relationships especially useful in fraud detection or detection of other problems. Finally, there are many ways in which query tools (such as

TABLE 4.1 Data Mining Modeling Tools

Radding Algorithms	Peacock Functions	Basis	Task	Coverage
Cluster detection	Cluster analysis	Statistics	Classification	Chapter 5
	Regression models	Statistics	Estimation	Chapter 6
	Logistic regression	Statistics	Classification	Chapter 6
	Discriminant analysis	Statistics	Classification	Chapter 6
Neural networks	Neural networks	AI	Classification	Chapter 7
	Kohonen nets	AI	Cluster	Chapter 7
Decision trees	Association rules	AI	Classification	Chapter 8
Rule induction	Association rules	AI	Description	Chapter 8
Link analysis			Description	Chapter 10
	Query tools		Description	
	Descriptive statistics	Statistics	Description	
	Visualization tools	Statistics	Description	

OLAP, covered in Chapter 3), descriptive **statistics,** and visualization support data mining analysis.

The point of data mining is to have a variety of tools available to assist the analyst and user in better understanding what the data consists of. Each method does something different, and usually this implies that a specific problem is best treated with a particular algorithm type. However, sometimes different algorithm types can be used for the same problem. Most involve setting parameters, which can be important when it comes to the effectiveness of the method. Further, output needs to be interpreted.

There are a number of overlaps. Cluster analysis helps data miners visualize the relationship among customer purchases, and is supported by visualization techniques that provide a different perspective. Link analysis helps identify connections between variables, often displayed through graphs as a means of visualization. An example of link analysis application can be seen in telephony, where calls are represented by the linkage between caller and receiver.[4] Another example of linkage is physician referral patterns. Patients may visit their regular doctor, who detects something that they don't know a lot about. They refer to their network of acquaintances to identify a reliable specialist who does. Clinics are collections of physician specialists, and might be referred to for especially difficult cases.

Data Mining Perspectives

Methods can be viewed from different perspectives. From the perspective of statistics and operations research, data mining methods include the following:[5]

- Cluster analysis (Chapter 5)
- Regression of various forms (best fit methods; Chapter 6)
- Discriminant analysis (use of regression for classification; Chapter 6)
- Line fitting through the operations research tool of multiple objective linear programming (Chapter 9).

From the perspective of artificial intelligence, these methods include

- Neural networks (best fit methods; Chapter 7)
- Rule induction (decision trees; Chapter 8)
- Genetic algorithms (often used to supplement other methods)

In this book, we combine regression and neural network approaches as best fit methods, because they usually are applied together. Regression tends to have advantages with linear data, while neural network models do very well with irregular data. Software usually allows the user to apply variants of each, and lets the analyst select the model that fits best. Cluster analysis, discriminant analysis, and case-based reasoning seek to assign new cases to the closest cluster of past observations. Rule induction is the basis of decision tree methods of data mining. Genetic algorithms apply to special forms of data, and often are used to boost or improve the operation of other techniques.

The ability of some of these techniques to deal with common data mining characteristics is compared in Table 4.2. This table demonstrates that there are different tools for different types of problems. If the data is especially noisy, this can lead to difficulties for classical statistical methods such as regression, cluster analysis, and discriminant analysis. The methods using rule induction and case-based reasoning can deal with such problems, but if the noise was false information, this

TABLE 4.2   **General Ability of Data Mining Techniques to Deal with Data Features**

Data Characteristic	Rule Induction	Neural Networks	Case-Based Reasoning	Genetic Algorithms
Handle noisy data	Good	Very good	Good	Very good
Handle missing data	Good	Good	Very good	Good
Process large data sets	Very good	Poor	Good	Good
Process different data types	Good	Transform to numerical	Very good	Transformation needed
Predictive accuracy	High	Very high	High	High
Explanation capability	Very good	Poor	Very good	Good
Ease of integration	Good	Good	Good	Very good
Ease of operation	Easy	Difficult	Easy	Difficult

Extracted from Bose and Mahapatra (2001)

can lead to rules concluding the wrong things. Neural networks and genetic algorithms have proven useful relative to classical methods in environments where there are complexities in the data, including interactions among variables that are nonlinear.

Neural networks have relative disadvantages when dealing with enormous numbers of variables since the computational complexity increases dramatically. Genetic algorithms require a specific data structure for genetic algorithms to operate, and it's not always easy to transform data to accommodate this requirement.

Another negative feature of neural networks is their hidden nature. Due to the large number of node connections, it's impractical to print out and analyze a large neural network model. This makes it difficult to take a model that was built using one system and then transport it to another system. Therefore, new data must be entered on the system where the neural network model was built in order to apply it to new cases. This makes it nearly impossible to apply neural network models outside of the system upon which they were built.

Data Mining Functions

Bose and Mahapatra[6] also provided an extensive list of applications by area, technique, and problem type. Published research was surveyed as the source. Problem types fell into four categories:

- **Classification**   Uses a training data set to identify classes or clusters, which are then used to categorize data. Typical applications include categorizing risk and return characteristics of investments, and the credit risk of loan applicants.
- **Prediction**   Identifies key attributes from data to develop a formula for the prediction of future cases, as in regression models.
- **Association**   Identifies rules that determine the relationships among entities, such as in market-basket analysis, or the association of symptoms with diseases.
- **Detection**   Determines anomalies and irregularities; valuable in fraud detection.

Table 4.3 extracts information from Bose and Mahapatra[7] to demonstrate the types of applications according to their data mining technique.

Table 4.3 demonstrates the wide variety of applications of data mining techniques to many functional areas. Many of these applications combine techniques, including visualization and statistical analysis. The point is that there are many

TABLE 4.3   Data Mining Applications by Method

Area	Technique	Application	Problem Type
Finance	Neural network	Forecast stock price	Prediction
	Neural network	Forecast bankruptcy	Prediction
	Rule induction	Forecast price index futures	Prediction
		Fraud detection	Detection
	Neural network	Forecast interest rates	Prediction
	Case-based reasoning		
	Neural network	Delinquent bank loan detection	Detection
	Visualization		
	Rule induction	Forecast defaulting loans	Prediction
		Credit assessment	Prediction
		Portfolio management	Prediction
		Risk classification	Classification
		Financial customer classification	Classification
	Rule induction	Corporate bond rating	Prediction
	Case-based reasoning		
	Rule induction, visualization	Loan approval	Prediction
Telecom	Neural network	Forecast network behavior	Prediction
	Rule induction		
	Rule induction	Churn management	Classification
		Fraud detection	Detection
	Case-based reasoning	Call tracking	Classification
Marketing	Rule induction	Market segmentation	Classification
		Cross-selling improvement	Association
	Rule induction	Lifestyle behavior analysis	Classification
	Visualization	Product performance analysis	Association
	Rule induction	Customer reaction to promotion	Prediction
	Genetic algorithm		
	Visualization		
	Case-based reasoning	Online sales support	Classification
Web	Rule induction	User browsing similarity analysis	Classification
	Visualization		Association
	Rule-based heuristics	Web page content similarity	Association
Others	Neural network	Software cost estimation	Detection
	Neural network	Litigation assessment	Prediction
	Rule induction		
	Rule induction	Insurance fraud detection	Detection
		Healthcare exception reporting	Detection
	Case-based reasoning	Insurance claim estimation	Prediction
		Software quality control	Classification
	Genetic algorithms	Budget expenditure	Classification

data mining tools available for a variety of functional purposes, spanning almost every area of human endeavor (including business). This section of the book seeks to demonstrate how these primary data mining tools work.

Demonstration Data Sets

In this section, we'll use some simple models to demonstrate concepts. These data sets were generated by the authors and reflect important business applications. The first model includes loan applicants, with 20 observations for building data,

TABLE 4.4 Loan Application Training Data Set

Age	Income	Assets	Debts	Want	Risk	Credit	Result
20 (young)	17,152 (low)	11,090	20,455	400	high	Green	On-time
23 (young)	25,862 (low)	24,756	30,083	2,300	high	Green	On-time
28 (young)	26,169 (low)	47,355	49,341	3,100	high	Yellow	Late
23 (young)	21,117 (low)	21,242	30,278	300	high	Red	Default
22 (young)	7,127 (low)	23,903	17,231	900	low	Yellow	On-time
26 (young)	42,083 (average)	35,726	41,421	300	high	Red	Late
24 (young)	55,557 (average)	27,040	48,191	1,500	high	Green	On-time
27 (young)	34,843 (average)	0	21,031	2,100	high	Red	On-time
29 (young)	74,295 (average)	88,827	100,599	100	high	Yellow	On-time
23 (young)	38,887 (average)	6,260	33,635	9,400	low	Green	On-time
28 (young)	31,758 (average)	58,492	49,268	1,000	low	Green	On-time
25 (young)	80,180 (high)	31,696	69,529	1,000	high	Green	Late
33 (middle)	40,921 (average)	91,111	90,076	2,900	average	Yellow	Late
36 (middle)	63,124 (average)	164,631	144,697	300	low	Green	On-time
39 (middle)	59,006 (average)	195,759	161,750	600	low	Green	On-time
39 (middle)	125,713 (high)	382,180	315,396	5,200	low	Yellow	On-time
55 (middle)	80,149 (high)	511,937	21,923	1,000	low	Green	On-time
62 (old)	101,291 (high)	783,164	23,052	1,800	low	Green	On-time
71 (old)	81,723 (high)	776,344	20,277	900	low	Green	On-time
63 (old)	99,522 (high)	783,491	24,643	200	low	Green	On-time

and 10 applicants serving as a test data set. The second data set represents job applicants. Here 10 observations with known outcomes serve as the training set, with five additional cases in the test set. A third data set of insurance claims has 10 known outcomes for training and five observations in the test set. All three data sets will be applied to new cases.

Larger data sets for each of these three cases will be provided, as well as a data set on expenditure data. These larger data sets will be used in various chapters to demonstrate methods.

Loan Application Data

This data set (shown in Table 4.4) consists of information on applicants for appliance loans. The full data set involves 650 past observations. Applicant information

TABLE 4.5 Loan Application Test Data

Age	Income	Assets	Debts	Want	Risk	Credit	Result
37 (middle)	37,214 (average)	123,420	106,241	4,100	Low	Green	On-time
45 (middle)	57,391 (average)	250,410	191,879	5,800	Low	Green	On-time
45 (middle)	36,692 (average)	175,037	137,800	3,400	Low	Green	On-time
25 (young)	67,808 (average)	25,174	61,271	3,100	High	Yellow	On-time
36 (middle)	102,143 (high)	246,148	231,334	600	Low	Green	On-time
29 (young)	34,579 (average)	49,387	59,412	4,600	High	Red	On-time
26 (young)	22,958 (low)	29,878	36,508	400	High	Yellow	Late
34 (middle)	42,526 (average)	109,934	92,494	3,700	Low	Green	On-time
28 (young)	80,019 (high)	78,632	100,957	12,800	High	Green	On-time
32 (middle)	57,407 (average)	117,062	101,967	100	Low	Green	On-time

TABLE 4.6
New Appliance
Loan Applications

Age	Income	Assets	Debts	Want	Credit
25	28,650	9,824	2,000	10,000	green
30	35,760	12,974	32,634	4,000	yellow
32	41,862	625,321	428,643	3,000	red
36	36,843	80,431	120,643	12,006	green
37	62,743	421,753	321,845	5,000	yellow
37	53,869	286,375	302,958	4,380	green
37	70,120	484,264	303,958	6,000	green
38	60,429	296,843	185,769	5,250	green
39	65,826	321,959	392,817	12,070	green
40	90,426	142,098	25,426	1,280	yellow
40	70,256	528,493	283,745	3,280	green
42	58,326	328,457	120,849	4,870	green
42	61,242	525,673	184,762	3,300	green
42	39,676	326,346	421,094	1,290	red
43	102,496	823,532	175,932	3,370	green
43	80,376	753,256	239,845	5,150	yellow
44	74,623	584,234	398,456	1,525	green
45	91,672	436,854	275,632	5,800	green
52	120,721	921,482	128,573	2,500	yellow
63	86,521	241,689	5,326	30,000	green

on age, income, assets, debts, and credit rating (from a credit bureau, with red for bad credit, yellow for some credit problems, and green for clean credit record) is assumed available from loan applications. Variable Want is the amount requested in the appliance loan application. For past observations, variable On-time is 1 if all payments were received on time, and 0 if not (Late or Default). The majority of past loans were paid on time. Data were transformed to obtain categorical data for some of the techniques. Age was grouped into less than 30 (young), 60 and over (old), and in between (middle aged). Income was grouped as less than or equal to $30,000 per year and lower (low income), $80,000 per year or more (high income), and average or in between. Asset, debt, and loan amount (variable Want) were used to generate categorical variable risk. Risk was categorized as high if debts exceeded assets, as low if assets exceeded the sum of debts plus the borrowing amount requested, and average if in between.

Table 4.5 offers a test set of data.

The model can be applied to the new applicants, as shown in Table 4.6.

Job Application Data

The second data set involves 500 past job applicants. Variables include the following:

Age	integer, 20 to 65	
State	State of origin	
Degree	Cert	Professional Certification
	UG	Undergraduate degree
	MBA	Masters in Business Administration
	MS	Masters of Science
	PhD	Doctorate

Major	none	
	Engr	Engineering
	Sci	Science or Math
	Csci	Computer Science
	BusAd	Business Administration
	IS	Information Systems
Experience	integer	years of experience in this field
Outcome	ordinal	Unacceptable
		Minimal
		Adequate
		Excellent

Table 4.7 shows the ten observations in the learning set.

Notice that some of these variables are quantitative and others are nominal. State, degree, and major are nominal. There's no information content intended by state or major. State isn't expected to have a specific order prior to analysis, nor is major. (The analysis may conclude that there is a relationship between state, major, and outcome, however.) Degree is ordinal, in that MS and MBA are higher degrees than BS. However, as with state and major, the analysis may find a reverse relationship with outcome. Table 4.8 shows the test data set for this case.

Table 4.9 provides a set of new job applicants to be classified by predicted job performance.

Insurance Fraud Data

The third data set involves insurance claims. The full data set includes 5,000 past claims with known outcomes. Variables include claimant age, gender, amount of the insurance claim, the number of traffic tickets currently on record (less than three years old), the number of prior accident claims of the type insured, and attorney (if any). Table 4.10 shows the training data set.

The test set is shown in Table 4.11.

A set of new claims is shown in Table 4.12.

TABLE 4.7 Job Applicant Training Data Set

Record	Age	State	Degree	Major	Experience	Outcome
1	27	CA	BS	Engineering	2 years	Excellent
2	33	NV	MBA	Business Administration	5 years	Adequate
3	30	CA	MS	Computer Science	0	Adequate
4	22	CA	BS	Information Systems	0	Unacceptable
5	28	CA	BS	Information Systems	2 years	Minimal
6	26	CA	MS	Business Administration	0	Excellent
7	25	CA	BS	Engineering	3 years	Adequate
8	28	OR	MS	Computer Science	2 years	Adequate
9	25	CA	BS	Information Systems	2 years	Minimal
10	24	CA	BS	Information Systems	1 year	Adequate

TABLE 4.8 Job Applicant Test Data Set

Record	Age	State	Degree	Major	Experience	Outcome
11	36	CA	MS	Information Systems	0	Minimal
12	28	OR	BS	Computer Science	5 years	Unacceptable
13	24	NV	BS	Information Systems	0	Excellent
14	33	CA	BS	Engineering	2 years	Adequate
15	26	CA	BS	Business Administration	3 years	Minimal

TABLE 4.9
New Job
Applicant Set

Age	State	Degree	Major	Experience
28	CA	MBA	Engr	0
26	NM	UG	Sci	3
33	TX	MS	Engr	6
21	CA	Cert	none	0
26	OR	Cert	none	5
25	CA	UG	BusAd	0
32	AR	UG	Engr	8
41	PA	MBA	BusAd	2
29	CA	UG	Sci	6
28	WA	UG	Csci	3

TABLE 4.10
Training Data Set—
Insurance Claims

Claimant Age	Gender	Claim Amount	Tickets	Prior Claims	Attorney	Outcome
52	Male	2000	0	1	Jones	OK
38	Male	1800	0	0	None	OK
21	Female	5600	1	2	Smith	Fraudulent
36	Female	3800	0	1	None	OK
19	Male	600	2	2	Adams	OK
41	Male	4200	1	2	Smith	Fraudulent
38	Male	2700	0	0	None	OK
33	Female	2500	0	1	None	Fraudulent
18	Female	1300	0	0	None	OK
26	Male	2600	2	0	None	OK

TABLE 4.11
Test Data Set—
Insurance Claims

Claimant Age	Gender	Claim Amount	Tickets	Prior Claims	Attorney	Outcome
23	Male	2800	1	0	None	OK
31	Female	1400	0	0	None	OK
28	Male	4200	2	3	Smith	Fraudulent
19	Male	2800	0	1	None	OK
41	Male	1600	0	0	Henry	OK

TABLE 4.12
New Insurance
Claims

Claimant Age	Gender	Claim Amount	Tickets	Prior Claims	Attorney
23	Male	1800	1	1	None
32	Female	2100	0	0	None
20	Female	1600	0	0	None
18	Female	3300	2	0	None
55	Male	4000	0	0	Smith
41	Male	2600	1	1	None
38	Female	3100	0	0	None
21	Male	2500	1	0	None
16	Female	4500	1	2	Gold
24	Male	2600	1	1	None

Expenditure Data

This data set represents consumer data for a community gathered by a hypothetical market research company in a medium-sized city. Ten thousand observations have been gathered using the following variables:

DEMOGRAPHIC	Age	integer, 16 and up
	Gender	0-female, 1-male
	Marital Status	0-single, 0.5, divorced, 1-married
	Dependents	Number of dependents
	Income	Annual income in dollars
	Job yrs	Years in current job (integer)
	Town yrs	Years in this community
	Yrs Ed	Years of education completed
	Dri Lic	Drivers License (0-no, 1-yes)
	Own Home	0-no, 1-yes
	# Cred C	number of credit cards
CONSUMER	Churn	Number of credit card balances cancelled last year
	ProGroc	Proportion of income spent at grocery stores
	ProRest	Proportion of income spent at restaurants
	ProHous	Proportion of income spent on housing
	ProUtil	Proportion of income spent on utilities
	ProAuto	Proportion of income spent on automobiles (own & operate)
	ProCloth	Proportion of income spent on clothing
	ProEnt	Proportion of income spent on entertainment

This data set can be used for a number of studies, such as:

What types of customers are most likely to eat at restaurants?
What is the market for home furnishings?
What types of customers are most likely to be interested in the following?:

Clothing
Entertainment

What is the relationship of spending to demographic variables?

The book comes with the expanded versions of the data set used in Chapter 3 as well as all three of the data sets used in this chapter, which are available for data mining and are supported by software. All of these data sets can be used by multiple algorithms.

Appendix

Enterprise Miner Demonstration on Expenditure Data Set

This appendix is presented to give an overview of a data mining software. It includes many details related to methods that we'll cover in the next section of the book. It's presented here to show where we're going.

Enterprise Miner, produced by SAS, is one of the most commonly used data mining software products. In this appendix, we demonstrate its use in the process of data mining.

In the Expenditure data set, described in this chapter, we're interested in the question: "What types of customers are most likely to seek restaurants?"

In Enterprise Miner, we first access the file BIGOUT, which contains the Expenditure data set. To answer the question, we need to modify the data by coding SAS. We create another variable, called Inc-ProRest which means income is multiplied by ProRest. This variable will be our target to answer the research question. (Income _ ProRest = Inc-ProRest: Target). Figure 4A.1 shows the flow of control within Enterprise Miner.

DATA PARTITIONING

This section offers an overview of the Enterprise Miner stream of a data mining study. These elements will be shown in more detail in the following figures. The first step is to enter the data. This can be a challenge, because data often comes from a variety of sources. Data mining software is built to accommodate most common data sources, but if data comes from a source not on the menu, it usually works to save a file in the form of CSV comma delimited. Figure 4A.2 shows the Enterprise Miner screen where you can select the file. Note that it contains 10,000 rows and 23 columns. The tabs at the top allow you to view the variables.

Once data is entered, we use data partitioning to work with it. The next operation could be to select the target variable. Figure 4A.3 demonstrates this, with target

FIGURE 4A.1
Enterprise Miner
Control Screen

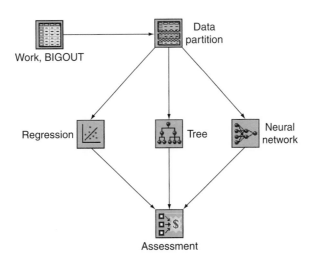

FIGURE 4A.2
Enterprise Miner
Screen to Open
Data File

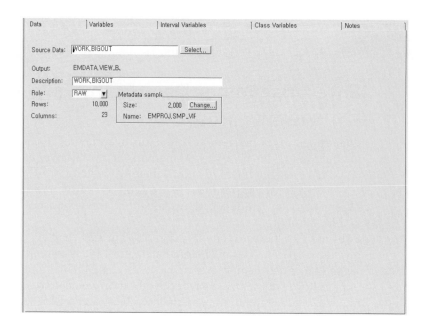

variable INC_PROREST representing the transformed variable that is the product of observation income times the observation proportion of income spent on restaurants.

In this case, the proportion of income spent on restaurants was selected. The user might then apply various data mining models. Here, three modeling types are available: regression, decision trees, and neural networks.

REGRESSION MODELING

In Figure 4A.4, clicking the Regression icon opens the dialogue for modeling with that tool.

FIGURE 4A.3
Enterprise Miner
Screen for Setting
Target Variable

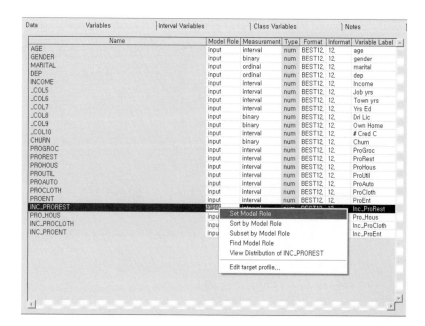

FIGURE 4A.4
The Enterprise
Miner Control
Screen

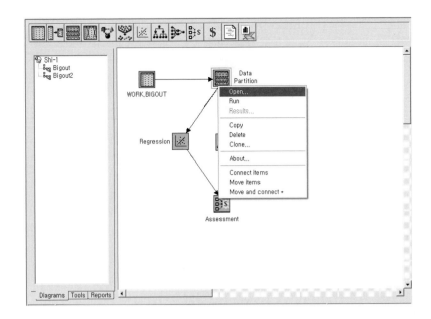

The next screen (Figure 4A.5) gives the user the ability to control how many observations are used for training, validation, and testing, as well as other control parameters.

In this case, 40 percent of the data (4,000 observations) are allocated to training, 30 percent (3,000 observations) to the validation of the model, and 30 percent (3,000 observations) to testing. Other parameters allow the control of how particular observations are assigned to each of these categories. We use the default "Simple Random" for random assignment. The stratified method would be used if significant differences were expected in different parts of the data set. The random number seed can be used to assure that future runs of this model yield the same random assignment of observations. This is a valuable means of assuring stability in model output.

FIGURE 4A.5
The Enterprise
Miner Screen for
Data Control

FIGURE 4A.6
The Enterprise
Miner Screen for
Model Results

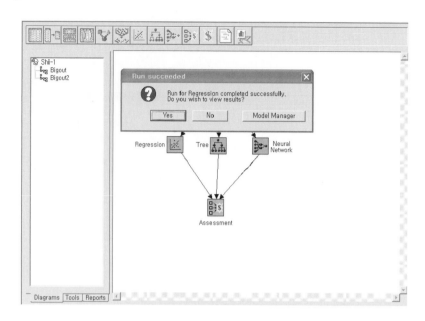

Figure 4A.6 shows the Enterprise Miner screen for a successful model run. If errors had occurred in the input, they would be displayed at this time.

By clicking Yes, Enterprise Miner provides a great deal of useful visual output. Figure 4A.7 shows a graphic of regression variable T-scores. Figure 4A.8 plots the model predictions against actual results.

The dependent variable, actual Inc_ProRest (money spent on restaurants by observation), is plotted on the X-axis, against the model prediction on the Y-axis. There clearly is a great deal of correspondence, with some error. Obviously, it's more difficult to predict the amount spent on restaurants for those with higher incomes. Actual T-scores (using those displayed in Figure 4A.7) are shown in Table 4A.1.

FIGURE 4A.7
Enterprise Miner
Output for
Regression Model
T-scores

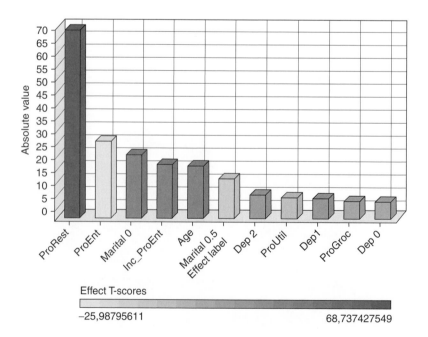

FIGURE 4A.8
Enterprise Miner
Regression Results

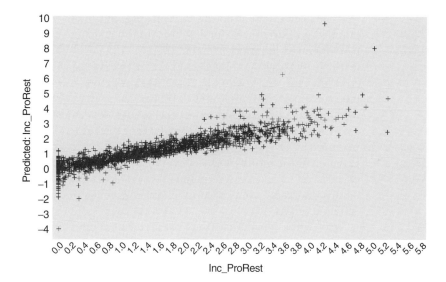

TABLE 4A.1
Regression Model
Estimates, T-Scores,
and Significance
Probabilities

Parameter	Estimate	T-Value	Pr > |t|
Intercept	−0.3110	−2.01	0.0444
Age	0.0094	16.70	<0.0001
Churn	−0.0021	−0.16	0.8767
Dep 0 (no dependents)	0.2617	2.90	0.0037
Dep 1	0.3037	4.02	<0.0001
Dep 2	0.3326	5.56	<0.0001
Dep 3	0.0956	1.80	0.0714
Dep 4	0.0368	0.56	0.5741
Dep 5	−0.2321	−2.34	0.0191
Dep 6	−0.2731	−1.75	0.0800
Gender	−0.0066	−0.81	0.4201
Marital 0 (single)	0.3376	20.84	<0.0001
Marital 0.5 (divorced)	−0.1654	−11.57	<0.0001
ProAuto	−0.7741	−1.90	0.0572
ProCloth	0.5099	1.86	0.0623
ProEnt	−10.8093	−25.99	<0.0001
ProGroc	1.1478	3.16	0.0016
ProHous	−0.6405	−1.95	0.0517
ProRest	26.9854	68.74	<0.0001
ProUtil	−1.8023	−4.35	<0.0001
Income	−0.0021	−1.41	0.1584
Job Years	−0.0012	−0.66	0.5115
Town Years	0.0002	0.24	0.8119
Years Education	−0.00144	−0.35	0.7233
Drivers License	−0.0268	−1.36	0.1734
Own Home	−0.220	−1.14	0.2538
Number Credit Cards	−0.0016	−0.59	0.5546
ProHousing	0.0263	2.49	0.0129
Inc_ProCloth	0.0107	1.15	0.2488
Inc+ProEnt	0.2873	16.97	<0.0001

Note how much easier it is to interpret Figure 4A.7 than Table 4A.1. However, detailed work requires detailed information, such as that given in the table. A feature of regression models is that there is some error. Figure 4A.8 shows that at the lower levels, the model yielded some negative expenditures on restaurants. This couldn't happen, of course. Sometimes regression models can be constrained to take on specific kinds of values (here greater than or equal to zero would probably have been appropriate, but the model nevertheless provides useful output). Enterprise Miner provides the analysis of variance and the analysis of effects output (not shown here). Model fitting information is also provided. In this case, the R^2 value of the model was 0.8031, which is fairly good, although with the number of variables available, it remains relatively unimpressive. The adjusted R^2 value of 0.8016 indicates that adding extra variables does not introduce significant unwanted bias.

The regression model (the parameter estimates in Table 4A.1) can be applied within Enterprise Miner to new observations described by their variable values. The parameter estimates in turn can be entered into a spreadsheet or other system to apply this model externally as well.

DECISION TREE MODELING

A decision tree model can be selected from Figure 4A.1. Successful decision tree output for the Expenditure data set is shown in Figure 4A.9.

The table in the upper-left quadrant of Figure 4A.9 shows that 4,000 observations were used in the training, with an average error of 1.39 (R^2 equivalent of 0.942). The validation phase obtained an average error of 1.396 (R^2 equivalent of 0.920). There were 56 leaves on the resulting decision tree, which is graphically displayed in the circular figure, thus showing how these 56 leaves partitioned the data. The average squared error rates for the training and validation data are displayed at the lower right, showing the progress in each leaf in reducing unexplained variance in the data. This output can be obtained from Enterprise Miner

FIGURE 4A.9
The Enterprise
Miner Control
Screen for the Tree
Model

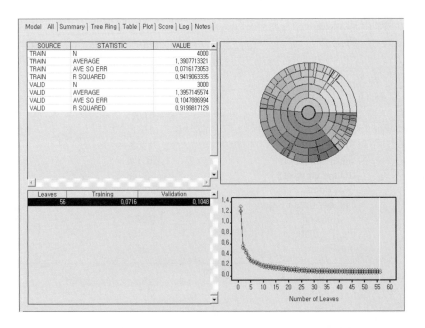

FIGURE 4A.10

Enterprise Miner
Decision Tree
Partitioning

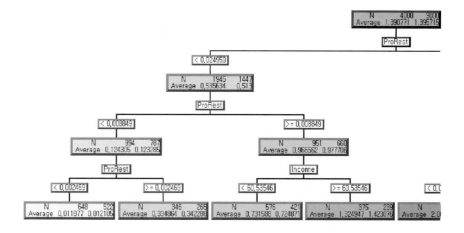

windows by selecting View, followed by Tree, and placing a check in the Tree Statistics box. Figure 4A.10 gives a partial view of the output, thus providing details of data partitioning.

NEURAL NETWORK MODELING

Neural network modeling is activated from the Neural Network icon displayed in Figure 4A.1. Options are available to define the number of neurons and hidden layers, but we used the default settings. Each software package will have help guidance to refine the models. Figure 4A.11 shows output from the model for each of the three data set elements: training, validation, and testing.

This output provides model fit statistics. The average squared error is the most illuminating. As expected, the training data had the best fit. Here the test fit is comparable to that obtained from the decision tree, with an average squared error of 0.0701 compared to the decision tree model's 0.0701. Neural networks provide a model, but it's relatively complex. Figure 4A.12 shows the Enterprise Miner neural network model output, giving the weight on each of the arcs displayed. Here, input variable weights to hidden nodes H11 and H12 are shown. But there are many other arcs in the full model. This is why neural network models are difficult to transport outside of the software system where they were built.

Figure 4A.13 shows the progress of the neural network model in terms of the average error reduction for the training, and the validation sets by the number of iterations.

FIGURE 4A.11

Enterprise Miner
Neural Network
Output for
Expenditure Data

	Fit Statistic	Training	Validation	Test
1	[TARGET=INC_PROREST]	.	.	.
2	Average Error	0,0689388108	0,0701896323	0,0700979678
3	Average Squared Error	0,0689388108	0,0701896323	0,0700979678
4	Sum of Squared Errors	275,75524329	210,56889704	210,29390349
5	Root Average Squared Error	0,2625620133	0,2649332602	0,2647602082
6	Root Final Prediction Error	0,26673045	.	.
7	Root Mean Squared Error	0,2646544386	0,2649332602	0,2647602082
8	Error Function	275,75524329	210,56889704	210,29390349
9	Mean Squared Error	0,0700419719	0,0701896323	0,0700979678
10	Maximum Absolute Error	2,551499182	2,3812649461	2,4462288552
11	Final Prediction Error	0,0711451329	.	.
12	Divisor for ASE	4000	3000	3000
13	Model Degrees of Freedom	63	.	.
14	Degrees of Freedom for Error	3937	.	.
15	Total Degrees of Freedom	4000	.	.
16	Sum of Frequencies	4000	3000	3000
17	Sum Case Weights + Frequencies	4000	3000	3000
18	Akaike's Information Criterion	-10572,14387	.	.
19	Schwarz's Baysian Criterion	-10175,61874	.	.

FIGURE 4A.12
Part of the
Enterprise Miner
Neural Network
Model for
Enterprise Data

	From	To	Weight
1	AGE	H11	0.0021419077
2	INCOME	H11	0.3523466907
3	INC_PROCLOTH	H11	-0.290979301
4	INC_PROENT	H11	-0.096327711
5	PROAUTO	H11	0.0914633133
6	PROCLOTH	H11	-0.632313489
7	PROENT	H11	0.2256242347
8	PROGROC	H11	0.7709558936
9	PROHOUS	H11	0.389614804
10	PROREST	H11	-1.315138917
11	PROUTIL	H11	0.0682432474
12	PRO_HOUS	H11	-0.367622024
13	_COL10	H11	-0.002805201
14	_COL5	H11	-0.001089506
15	_COL6	H11	0.0005898156
16	_COL7	H11	-0.003997827
17	AGE	H12	0.0114381967
18	INCOME	H12	0.1932173174
19	INC_PROCLOTH	H12	0.0367003793
20	INC_PROENT	H12	0.4231122142
21	PROAUTO	H12	-0.02472552
22	PROCLOTH	H12	-0.962203365
23	PROENT	H12	-0.9889621
24	PROGROC	H12	0.3414809832
25	PROHOUS	H12	0.0987301935
26	PROREST	H12	1.738845653
27	PROUTIL	H12	0.0244076813
28	PRO_HOUS	H12	-0.116079188

FIGURE 4A.13
Enterprise Miner
Neural Network
Progress for
Expenditure Data

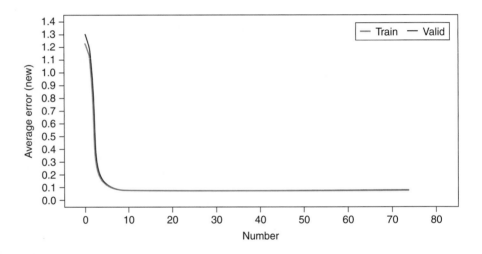

Summary

Many tools are available for data mining and can accomplish a number of functions. The tools come from areas of statistics, operations research, and artificial intelligence, and provide techniques useful in accomplishing a variety of analytic functions, such as cluster identification, discriminant analysis, and development of association rules. Data mining software provides a powerful means of applying these tools to large sets of data, giving organizational management a means of coping with an overwhelming glut of data and converting some of it into useful knowledge.

This chapter begins with an overview of tools and functions. It also previews four data sets that are used in subsequent chapters. These data sets are small, but provide readers with views of the type of data typically encountered in some data mining studies.

The preceding appendix gives a quick view of the types of tools and information available from Enterprise Miner, a leading data mining software product. The basic initial data views and analytic models are demonstrated, with some model output.

Glossary

artificial intelligence   Use of machine learning to reach conclusions; in the context of data mining, use of neural networks, case-based reasoning, genetic algorithms, or other artificial intelligence tools.

Association   Set of rules used to express relationships among data.

Classification   Method to sort data into classes of outcomes.

clustering   Initial analytic tool to identify general groupings in data.

detection   Identification of anomalies and irregularities, as in fraud detection.

Estimation   Method to predict an outcome.

Prediction   Model used to take explanatory variable inputs and convert through a formula to predict an outcome variable.

statistics   In the context of data mining tools, the use of algorithms based on traditional statistical methods, such as regression.

summarization   Descriptive statistical and graphical analysis to show variable features to data mining analysts.

Exercises

1. What sources generate large-scale data sets for a business?
2. What is the difference between statistically based data mining methods and data mining methods based on artificial intelligence?
3. Describe the difference between classifying and predicting.
4. In the file Loan Applications, what would your prior expectations (meaning prior to data mining analysis) be of the characteristics of loans that would not be paid on time?
5. With no other information on the loan applications given in Table 4.6, to which segment would you grant a loan?
6. In the file Job Applicants, what would your prior expectations (meaning prior to data mining analysis) be of the characteristics covered by the data set for unacceptable and excellent job performance?
7. Of the Job Applicants shown in Table 4.9, which would be the one you would hire? If you could hire any number of applicants, which would you hire?
8. In the file Insurance Claims, what would your prior expectations (meaning prior to data mining analysis) be of the characteristics covered by the data set for fraudulent applications?
9. Of the insurance claims given in Table 4.12, which would you be willing to spend $2,000 to investigate? Which would you be willing to spend $20,000 to investigate?
10. In the file Expenditure Data, what would your prior expectations (meaning prior to data mining analysis) be of the characteristics of those who would spend over $10,000 per year in restaurants?
11. In the file Expenditure Data, what type of people would you expect to spend significant portions of their income on home furnishings?
12. In the file Expenditure Data, what type of people would you expect to spend significant portions of their income on clothing?
13. In the file Expenditure Data, what type of people would you expect to spend significant portions of their income on entertainment?
14. In the file Expenditure Data, what type of people would you expect to spend significant portions of their income on owning and operating automobiles?
15. In the file Expenditure Data, what type of people would you expect to have credit card account cancellations?

Endnotes

1. M. Y. Kiang and A. Kumar, "An Evaluation of Self-Organizing Map Networks as a Robust Alternative to Factor Analysis in Data Mining Applications," *Information Systems Research,* volume 12, number 2, 2001, pp. 177–194.

2. A. Radding, "Unpacking the Mystery of the Black Box," *Software Magazine,* Data Mining Primer Supplement, December 1997, pp. S8–S9.

3. P. R. Peacock, "Data Mining in Marketing: Part I," *Marketing Management,* 6:4, Winter 1998, pp. 8–18.

4. M. J. A. Berry and G. Linoff, *Data Mining Techniques,* New York: John Wiley & Sons, 1997.

5. I. Bose and R. K. Mahapatra, "Business Data Mining—A Machine Learning Perspective," *Information & Management,* volume 39, 2001, pp. 211–225.

6. Ibid.

7. Ibid.

CHAPTER FIVE

Cluster Analysis

This chapter:

- Describes the concept of clustering
- Demonstrates representative clustering algorithms on simple cases
- Reviews real applications of clustering models
- Shows the application of clustering models to larger data sets
- Demonstrates web plots through Clementine in an appendix

Credit cards have become endemic to life in the 21st Century. While 40 years ago credit card use was rare, today it's hard to imagine doing business without them. The use of credit is what makes an economy work, and the overall system (whether a physical card is used or not) now ties in to Internet business, allowing us to buy things from around the world in real time.

As with telephone accounts (discussed in Chapter 2), there is a need for credit card companies to monitor their accounts for repayment. Nonpayment of an account on the day due is a bad thing, but does not mean that the business granting credit should terminate the account. It makes far more business sense to extend credit (continuing to charge interest) than to close the account. Credit companies in fact have a variety of methods available, usually used in order of politeness. If an account is late, a friendly e-mail might be sent reminding the delinquent account holder that payment was due but not received. This in fact may be due to some misunderstanding, or the check may really have been delayed in the mail. Credit granting institutions make a great deal of money on late payments, because they usually charge premium rates of interest. If they could be assured that they ultimately would receive payment, the most profitable case for them would be to revolve credit to those who are unable to repay on time. However, on some accounts no payment is received for extended periods of time. In such cases, telephone calls might be the next step (first using softer female voices, and then relying on harsher male voices). That could be followed up by severe letters, and ultimately cases could be turned over to collection agencies, or in instances of large accounts, to attorneys for court settlement. The more severe measures usually cost more, and additionally risk alienating valuable customers. Careful analysis of the impact of various options is needed. Data mining provides a tool enabling credit granting institutions to measure the expected impact of these alternative policies.

Cluster analysis is usually used as an initial analytic tool, giving data mining analysts the ability to identify general groupings in the data. It often follows the initial graphical display of data, and provides a numeric means to describe underlying patterns. This can include patterns in credit card account repayment, as described in one of this chapter's real applications. Cluster analysis is thus a type of model, but one that is usually applied in the process of data understanding.

Clustering involves the identification of groups of observations measured over variables. Here we distinguish between discriminant analysis (where the groups are given as part of the data, and the point is to predict group membership) and cluster analysis (where the clusters are based on the data, and thus not predetermined—the point being to find items that belong together rather than to predict group membership). Cluster analysis is an unsupervised technique, where data are examined without reference to a response variable. It's thus an example of machine learning, where the value of clustering models is in their ability to capture interesting data groupings. The technique requires a large enough data set to establish statistical significance, but conversely suffers from the curse of dimensionality in that the more variables and values these variables take on, the more difficult the computational task. A typical use is to initially apply clustering models to identify segments of the data that are used in subsequent predictive analyses. There are a number of techniques used for cluster analysis.

Cluster Analysis

The most general form of clustering analysis allows the algorithm to determine the number of clusters. At the other extreme, the number of clusters may be pre-specified. Partitioning is used to define new categorical variables that divide the data into a fixed number of regions (k means clustering, for example). A common practice is to apply factor analysis as a preprocessing technique to get a reasonable idea of the number of clusters, as well as to give managers a view of which types of items go together.[1] Given a particular number (k) of centers, data observations are assigned to that center with the minimum distance to the observation. A variety of distance measures are available, although conventionally the centroid (a centroid has the average value—mean, median, and so on—for each variable) of each cluster is used as the center, and the squared distance is minimized. This is the most widely used form of cluster analysis in data mining.

Cluster analysis is often the initial technique applied in a data mining study, and has been used by data miners to segment customers, allowing customer service representatives to apply unique treatment to each segment.[2] It has also been applied to home equity loans by banks.[3] One bank discovered that one cluster accounted for about one-quarter of their customers. Further analysis of this cluster showed that these customers also had business accounts. Through clustering, the bank identified a key segment of customers who took out home equity loans to start their own businesses. This information was used to redirect the bank's marketing efforts. Berry and Linoff (1997) gave a detailed example of cluster analysis of the brightness and temperature of stars.[4] Three clusters were found: the majority of stars converting hydrogen to helium, red giants which expand after their hydrogen is used up, and white dwarfs that cool. Measures of brightness and star temperature can be used to classify new stars into these three categories. Berry and Linoff also gave an example of the U.S. Army using cluster analysis to rationally identify sizes needed for female soldiers, enabling the Army to identify an economic number of size combinations appropriate for new female soldiers.

Description of Cluster Analysis

The idea of cluster analysis is to identify the average characteristics of available measures for data in groups, or clusters. New data can then be measured by their distance from each of the cluster averages. If the data are totally independent, there would be as many clusters as there are observations. If the data were totally dependent, there would be one cluster. Most data are, of course, in between. That leads to the problem of selecting the number of clusters. For the Berry and Linoff star example, this was rather easy since there were three known distinct types of stars. (That problem could grow complex for more detailed study of stars.) The Army had a number of options for clusters. They could not custom-tailor uniforms for each female soldier (n clusters, or one for each observation), because it would be too expensive. At the other extreme, the Army was once famous for its "one-size fits all" clothing policy, essentially using one cluster. The number of clusters may be determined by the decision problem. A bank is interested in two broad classes of loan applicants—those who pay and those who don't. This could be expanded to include a third cluster for those who may be late sometimes, but still pay. Most problems involve ambiguity relative to the number of clusters associated with known outcomes.

A Clustering Algorithm

The following is a simple k-means algorithm:[5]

1. Select the desired number of clusters k (or iterate from 2 to the maximum number of clusters desired).
2. Select k initial observations as seeds (could be arbitrary, but the algorithm would work better if these seed values were as far apart as possible).
3. Calculate average cluster values over each variable (for the initial iteration, this will simply be the initial seed observations).
4. Assign each of the other training observations to the closest cluster, as measured by squared distance (other metrics could be used, but squared distance is conventional).
5. Recalculate cluster averages based on the assignments from step 4.
6. Iterate between steps 4 and 5 until the same set of assignments are obtained.

Note that this algorithm does not guarantee the same result no matter what the initial seeds are. However, it is a relatively straightforward procedure. The problem of how to determine k can be dealt with by applying the procedure for two clusters, then for three, and so forth until the maximum desired number of clusters is reached. Selecting from among these alternatives may be relatively obvious in some cases, but can be a source of uncertainty in others.

There are some drawbacks to **k-means clustering.** The data needs to be put in standardized form to get rid of the differences in scale. However, even this approach assumes that all variables are equally important. If there are some variables more important than others, weights can be used in the distance calculation, but determining these weights is another source of uncertainty.

Insurance Fraud Data

We can apply the k-means procedure to the insurance fraud data set (Tables 4.10 and 4.11). Table 5.1 gives the standardized data for each of the 10 test cases using the following transformations:

Age < 20	score = 0.0
Age 20 to 40	score = (Age − 20)/20
Age 40 to 60	score = 1.0
Age 60 to 70	score = 1.0 − (Age − 60)/10
Age 70 and up	score = 0.0

TABLE 5.1
Standardized
Insurance Fraud
Training Data

Case	Age	Gender	Claim	Tickets	Prior Claims	Attorney	Outcome
1	1	1	0.6	1	0.5	0	OK
2	0.9	1	0.64	1	1	1	OK
3	0.05	0	0	0.6	0	0	Fraudulent
4	0.8	0	0.24	1	0.5	1	OK
5	0	1	0.88	0	0	0	OK
6	1	1	0.16	0.6	0	0	Fraudulent
7	0.9	1	0.46	1	1	1	OK
8	0.65	0	0.5	1	0.5	1	Fraudulent
9	0	0	0.74	1	1	1	OK
10	0.3	1	0.48	0	1	1	OK

TABLE 5.2
Cluster Averages
for Insurance
Fraud Data

Cluster	Age	Gender	Claim	Tickets	Prior	Atty	Outcome
Cluster 1	1.0	1.0	0.6	1.0	0.5	0.0	0.0
Cluster 2	0.05	0.0	0.0	0.6	0.0	0.0	1.0

TABLE 5.3
Sum of Squared
Distances of Fraud
Training Cases to
Clusters

Training Case	Cluster 1	Cluster 2	Outcome
1	0	2.673	Cluster 1
2	1.262	4.292	Cluster 1
3	2.673	0	Cluster 2
4	2.170	2.030	Cluster 2
5	2.328	2.137	Cluster 2
6	0.604	1.928	Cluster 1
7	1.280	4.094	Cluster 1
8	2.133	2.020	Cluster 2
9	3.270	2.710	Cluster 2
10	2.754	3.653	Cluster 1

TABLE 5.4
Second Iteration
Cluster Averages
for Insurance
Fraud Data

Cluster	Age	Gender	Claim	Tickets	Prior	Atty	Outcome
Cluster 1	0.820	1	0.468	0.720	0.7	0.6	0.2
Cluster 2	0.300	0.2	0.472	0.720	0.4	0.6	0.4

TABLE 5.5
Sum of Squared
Distances of Fraud
Training Cases to
Clusters (Second
Iteration)

Training Case	Cluster 1	Cluster 2	Outcome
1	0.528	1.595	Cluster 1
2	0.364	1.627	Cluster 1
3	2.676	0.860	Cluster 2
4	1.331	0.592	Cluster 2
5	2.211	1.935	Cluster 2
6	0.992	1.762	Cluster 1
7	0.335	1.599	Cluster 1
8	1.308	0.412	Cluster 2
9	2.075	0.800	Cluster 2
10	1.039	1.678	Cluster 1

Gender is a categorical variable, where arbitrarily the Female score is 0 and the Male score is 1.

Claim amount is transformed by the formula: score = MAX(1 – Claim/5000, 0)

Number of tickets is transformed categorically:

0 Tickets	score = 1.0
1 Ticket	score = 0.6
2 or more Tickets	score = 0

Number of prior claims is transformed categorically:

0 Prior Claims	score = 1.0
1 Prior Claims	score = 0.5
2 or more Prior Claims	score = 0

The presence of an attorney is scored 1 for None, and 0 otherwise.

We can select the first test observation with each outcome (OK and Fraudulent) for our seeds. This would be Cases 1 and 3 from Table 5.1, giving cluster averages (means) as shown in Table 5.2.

Step 3 of the k-means algorithm calculates the ordinary least squares distance to these cluster averages, as shown in Table 5.3. This calculation for training Case 2 to Cluster 1 would be

$$(0.9 - 1)^2 + (1 - 1)^2 + (0.64 - 0.6)^2 + (1 - 1)^2 + (1 - 0.5)^2 + (1 - 0)^2 = 1.2616$$

The distance to Cluster 2 is

$$(0.9 - 0.05)^2 + (1 - 0)^2 + (0.64 - 0)^2 + (1 - 0.6)^2 + (1 - 0)^2 + (1 - 0)^2 = 4.2921$$

Because the distance to Cluster 1 (1.2616) is closer than to Cluster 2 (4.2921), the algorithm would assign Case 2 to Cluster 1.

This yields new cluster averages, as shown in Table 5.4.

This yields the assignments shown in Table 5.5.

Since this yields the same assignments encountered in the prior iteration, the algorithm stops. The final cluster means are as shown in Table 5.4. Clustering is not meant to be predictive, but rather descriptive of the data. The final clusters may not be associated with any particular outcome, although it is of great interest to see the relationship of clusters to outcomes. Here the clusters differ from most of our prior claims, with a lot of difference in the variables age, gender, and prior claims. Age seems to make some difference, with those with higher scores (middle-aged) more represented in the first cluster. Gender is a big difference, with those in Cluster 1 being all male and those in Cluster 2 mostly female. There are minor or no differences in claim amounts, tickets, and the presence of an attorney. There is little difference in the number of prior claims. Cluster 1 had less fraud experience than Cluster 2, but this is a small sample for demonstration purposes so no inferences should be drawn. Users need to be sure that they have a valid legal basis for using variables. In insurance, this is clearly specified by State regulation. If these variables were all valid for the purpose of the analysis, the clustering model would indicate a difference in that Cluster 1 is older is more male,

TABLE 5.6
Insurance Fraud Test Set Scores

Case	Age	Gender	Claim	Tickets	Prior Claims	Attorney	Outcome
1	0.15	1	0.44	0.6	1	1	OK
2	0.55	0	0.72	1	1	1	OK
3	0.4	1	0.16	0	0	0	Fraudulent
4	0	1	0.44	1	0.5	1	OK
5	1	1	0.68	1	1	0	OK

TABLE 5.7 Weighted Distance Calculation

Variable	Train #2	Cluster #1	Distance	Cluster #2	Distance
Age	0.9	1	$0.01*(0.9-1)^2 = 0.0001$	0.05	$0.01*(0.9-0.05)^2 = 0.0072$
Gender	1	1	$0.2*(1-1)^2 = 0.0000$	0	$0.2*(1-0)^2 = 0.2000$
Claim	0.64	0.6	$0.2*(0.64-0.6)^2 = 0.0003$	0	$0.2*(0.64-0)^2 = 0.0819$
Tickets	1	1	$0.1*(1-1)^2 = 0.0000$	0.6	$0.1*(1-0.6)^2 = 0.0016$
Prior	1	0.5	$0.29*(1-0.5)^2 = 0.0725$	0	$0.29*(1-0)^2 = 0.2900$
Attorney	1	0	$0.2*(1-0)^2 = 0.2000$	0	$0.2*(1-0)^2 = 0.2000$
Sum			0.2729		0.7951

TABLE 5.8
Weighted Sum of Squared Distances of Fraud Training Cases to Clusters

Training Case	Cluster 1	Cluster 2	Outcome
1	0	0.370	Cluster 1
2	0.273	0.795	Cluster 1
3	0.370	0	Cluster 2
4	0.426	0.306	Cluster 2
5	0.198	0.391	Cluster 1
6	0.127	0.214	Cluster 1
7	0.277	0.756	Cluster 1
8	0.403	0.342	Cluster 2
9	0.486	0.616	Cluster 1
10	0.380	0.773	Cluster 1

TABLE 5.9
Second Iteration Cluster Averages for Weighted Insurance Fraud Data

Cluster	Age	Gender	Claim	Tickets	Prior	Atty	Outcome
Cluster 1	0.586	0.857	0.566	0.657	0.643	0.571	0.143
Cluster 2	0.5	0	0.247	0.867	0.333	0.667	0.667

TABLE 5.10
Weighted Squared Distances of Fraud Training Cases to Clusters (Second Iteration)

Training Case	Cluster 1	Cluster 2	Outcome
1	0.089	0.326	Cluster 1
2	0.092	0.385	Cluster 1
3	0.399	0.142	Cluster 2
4	0.223	0.033	Cluster 2
5	0.256	0.479	Cluster 1
6	0.224	0.332	Cluster 1
7	0.093	0.364	Cluster 1
8	0.202	0.045	Cluster 2
9	0.242	0.204	Cluster 2
10	0.123	0.438	Cluster 1

is more likely to have an attorney, and to have prior claims. Table 5.6 gives the transformed scores for the five test cases.

We calculate the squared distance from both cluster averages to each test case. The distance from Cluster 1 to Test Case 1 would be

$$(0.82 - 0.15)^2 + (1 - 1)^2 + (0.468 - 0.44)^2 + (0.72 - 0.6)^2 \\ + (0.7 - 1)^2 + (0.6 - 1)^2 = 0.714$$

The distance from Cluster 2 to Test Case 1 is

$$(0.3 - 0.15)^2 + (0.2 - 1)^2 + (0.472 - 0.44)^2 + (0.72 - 0.6)^2 \\ + (0.4 - 1)^2 + (0.6 - 1)^2 = 1.198.$$

Test Case 1 is thus closer to Cluster 1. Test Cases 1, 3, 4, and 5 were all closer to Cluster 1. Three of these were accurately predicted, but Test Case 3 was actually fraudulent. Test Case 2 was closer to Cluster 2 (distance 1.465 to Cluster 1, distance 0.762 to Cluster 2), and had the outcome OK.

Weighted Distance Cluster Model

Some of the variables may be expected to be more important than others. It is easy to reflect differential importance through weights. Using a set of weights of 0.01 for Age, 0.2 for Gender, 0.2 for Claim Amount, 0.1 for Tickets, 0.29 for Prior Claims, and 0.2 for Attorney, identical results were obtained. Cluster averages initially were as in Table 5.2. The calculation for training observation 1 is shown in Table 5.7.

Training Observation 1's weighted distance is closer to Cluster 1. Applying the weights to all ten training observations gives the results shown in Table 5.8.

This yields new cluster averages, as shown in Table 5.9.

The next iteration yields the assignments shown in Table 5.10.

This set of clusters is slightly different, with Training Case 9 reassigned to Cluster 2. The new cluster averages are the same as those found in Table 5.4, and yield the same cluster assignments as given in Table 5.5. While the weights yielded the same clusters in this small example (albeit by a different path), they can provide a useful means to emphasize variables known to be more important.

Varying the Number of Clusters

In the examples we've looked at so far, the number of clusters were established by the context of the problem (either by given classes, as with the Job Applicant data using discriminant analysis, or by binary outcome, as with the Insurance Fraud data). Cluster analysis usually assumes the general situation of an unknown optimal number of clusters. We use the expenditure data set to examine the proportion of money spent on groceries, with the target variable being the proportion ranges. This could be a simple binary division, or it could divide expenditure proportions into as many groups as there are observations. The best fit would be with the largest number of divisions, but that would not provide useful or actionable information. We use the first 10 observations of the data set for training, as shown in Table 5.11.

TABLE 5.11
Training Data from the Expenditure Data Set

Case	1	2	3	4	5	6	7	8	9	10
Age	87	64	23	48	56	27	54	53	56	65
Gender	F	F	F	F	M	M	M	M	F	F
Marital	Div	Mar	Sing	Mar	Mar	Mar	Mar	Mar	Mar	Mar
Dependents	0	0	0	1	0	1	0	2	0	0
Income	80054	51253	41426	59073	57397	29203	41541	43321	31082	58995
Years–Job	5	4	7	13	21	6	15	3	10	12
Yrs–Town	0	0	23	0	18	0	15	9	2	8
Yrs–Educ.	13	11	11	13	13	12	18	11	11	13
Driv. Lic.	No	Yes	Yes	Yes	Yes	Yes	Yes	No	Yes	Yes
Own Home	No	No	No	Yes	Yes	Yes	No	No	No	Yes
Credit Cards	1	13	1	4	9	2	12	0	6	3
Churn	0	1	0	0	1	0	1	0	1	0
PropGroc	0.031	0.044	0.000	0.073	0.037	0.140	0.052	0.059	0.069	0.036

This data need to be transformed to 0–1 values prior to the calculation of distances. Table 5.12 gives such a transformation, using the following:

Age	MAX(0,MIN(1,(Age-20)/50))
Gender	F=0, M=1
Marital	Single = 0, Divorced = 0.5, Married = 1.0
Dependents	=IF(dependents>4,1,dependents/5)
Income	=MIN(1,income/100000)
Job Years	=MIN(1,job years/10)
Town Years	=MIN(1,town years/20)
Years Education	=IF(YrsEd<12,0,IF(YrsEd<14,.3,IF(YrsEd<16,.5,1)))
Driver's License	No = 0, Yes = 1
Own Home	No = 0, Yes = 1
Credit Cards	=IF(credit cards>4,1,credit cards/5)
Churn	No = 0, Yes = 1

The data could be divided into up to 10 different groups. We will demonstrate with two groups, and then with three groups. For the two-group case, seeds are

TABLE 5.12
Standardized Scores for the First 10 Observations of the Training Set

Case	1	2	3	4	5	6	7	8	9	10
Age	1.00	0.88	0.06	0.56	0.72	0.14	0.68	0.66	0.72	0.90
Gender	0	0	0	0	1	1	1	1	0	0
Marital	0.5	1	0	1	1	1	1	1	1	1
Dependents	0	0	0	0.2	0	0.2	0	0.4	0	0
Income	0.800	0.512	0.414	0.591	0.574	0.292	0.415	0.433	0.311	0.590
Years–Job	0.5	0.4	0.7	1.0	1.0	0.6	1.0	0.3	1.0	1.0
Yrs–Town	0	0	1.00	0	0.90	0	0.75	0.45	0.10	0.40
Yrs–Educ.	0.3	0	0	0.3	0.3	0.3	1.0	0	0	0.3
Driv. Lic.	0	1	1	1	1	1	1	0	1	1
Own Home	0	0	0	1	1	1	0	0	0	1
Credit Cards	0.2	1	0.2	0.8	1.0	0.4	1.0	0	1.0	0.6
Churn	0	1	0	0	1	0	1	0	1	0
ProGroceries	0.031	0.044	0.000	0.073	0.037	0.140	0.052	0.059	0.069	0.036

TABLE 5.13
First Iteration—Two
Clusters for Grocery
Expenditure

Variable	Cluster 1 Value	Cluster 2 Value
Age	0.06	0.14
Gender	0	1
Marital	0	1
Dependents	0	0.2
Income	0.414	0.292
Years–Job	0.700	0.6
Yrs–Town	1.00	0
Yrs–Educ.	0	0.3
Driv. Lic.	1	1
Own Home	0	1
Credit Cards	0.20	0.4
Churn	0	0

the third observation (for its abnormally low expenditure on groceries) and the sixth observation (for its high expenditure on groceries). Table 5.13 gives the first iteration for this data.

The squared distance for each of the 10 training cases is calculated to both clusters. Table 5.14 shows this calculation for Training Observation 1.

Since the distance from Training Observation 1 to Cluster 1 is 3.413, and the distance to Cluster 2 is 4.338, it is closer to Cluster 1 and so is assigned to that cluster. In this case, 3 of the 10 training observations were assigned to Cluster 1 (Cases 1, 2, and 3), and the remaining seven cases were assigned to Cluster 2. Cluster averages were calculated, yielding the values and results given in Table 5.15.

There is some difference from the first iteration, with Observation 8 shifting to Cluster 1. The third iteration cluster averages are shown in Table 5.16.

Case 2 was switched to Cluster 2. Now the first cluster contains cases 1, 3, and 8, while the second cluster contains cases 2, 4, 5, 6, 7, 9, and 10. The fourth iteration averages are given in Table 5.17.

In this case, the same cluster groupings were obtained, so the algorithm would stop. Cluster 1 (Cases 1, 3, and 8) averaged grocery expenditures of 0.030, while Cluster 2 (Cases 2, 4, 5, 6, 7, 9, and 10) averaged grocery expenditures of 0.158. Clearly, Cluster 1 spends less on groceries. Radically different features are that Cluster 1 has a much lower married status, fewer years on the job, fewer years of education, a much lower driver's license score, and much lower credit card use and churn. None of the cases in Cluster 1 owned their home.

TABLE 5.14
Distance Calculation
for Training
Observation 1

Variable	Training 1	Cluster 1	Distance	Cluster 2	Distance
Age	1.0	0.06	$(1 - 0.06)^2 = 0.884$	0.14	$(1 - 0.14)^2 = 0.740$
Gender	0	0	$(0 - 0)^2 = 0.000$	1	$(0 - 1)^2 = 1.000$
Marital	0.5	0	$(0.5 - 0)^2 = 0.250$	1	$(0.5 - 1)^2 = 0.250$
Dependents	0	0	$(0 - 0)^2 = 0.000$	0.2	$(0 - 0.2)^2 = 0.040$
Income	0.8	0.414	$(0.8 - 0.414)^2 = 0.149$	0.292	$(0.8 - 0.292)^2 = 0.258$
Years–Job	0.5	0.700	$(0.5 - 0.7)^2 = 0.040$	0.6	$(0.5 - 0.6)^2 = 0.010$
Yrs–Town	0	1	$(0 - 1)^2 = 1.000$	0	$(0 - 0)^2 = 0.000$
Yrs–Educ.	0.3	0	$(0.3 - 0)^2 = 0.090$	0.3	$(0.3 - 0.3)^2 = 0.000$
Driv. Lic.	0	1	$(0 - 1)^2 = 1.000$	1	$(0 - 1)^2 = 1.000$
Own Home	0	0	$(0 - 0)^2 = 0.000$	1	$(0 - 1)^2 = 1.000$
Credit Cards	0.2	0.20	$(0.2 - 0.2)^2 = 0.000$	0.4	$(0.2 - 0.4)^2 = 0.040$
Churn	0	0	$(0 - 0)^2 = 0.000$	0	$(0 - 0)^2 = 0.000$
			3.413		4.338

TABLE 5.15
Second Iteration—
Two Clusters for
Grocery
Expenditure

Variable	Cluster 1: 1,2,3 Cluster 1 Value	Cluster 2: 4,5,6,7,8,9,10 Cluster 2 Value
Age	0.647	0.626
Gender	0	0.571
Marital	0.5	1
Dependents	0	0.114
Income	0.575	0.458
Years–Job	0.533	0.843
Yrs–Town	0.333	0.371
Yrs–Educ.	0.1	0.314
Driv. Lic.	0.667	0.857
Own Home	0	0.571
Credit Cards	0.467	0.686
Churn	0.333	0.429

TABLE 5.16
Third Iteration—
Two Clusters for
Grocery
Expenditure

Variable	Cluster 1: 1,2,3,8 Cluster 1 Value	Cluster 2: 4,5,6,7,9,10 Cluster 2 Value
Age	0.65	0.62
Gender	0.25	0.5
Marital	0.625	1
Dependents	0.1	0.067
Income	0.540	0.462
Years–Job	0.475	0.933
Yrs–Town	0.363	0.358
Yrs–Educ.	0.075	0.367
Driv. Lic.	0.5	1
Own Home	0	0.667
Credit Cards	0.35	0.8
Churn	0.25	0.5

TABLE 5.17
Third Iteration—
Two Clusters for
Grocery
Expenditure

Variable	Cluster 1: 1, 3, 8 Cluster 1 Value	Cluster 2: 2, 4, 5, 6, 7, 9, 10 Cluster 2 Value
Age	0.573	0.657
Gender	0.333	0.429
Marital	0.5	1
Dependents	0.133	0.057
Income	0.549	0.469
Years–Job	0.5	0.857
Yrs–Town	0.483	0.307
Yrs–Educ.	0.1	0.314
Driv. Lic.	0.333	1
Own Home	0	0.571
Credit Cards	0.133	0.829
Churn	0	0.571

TABLE 5.18
Cluster Means for
Grocery
Expenditures—
Three Cluster,
Iteration 1

Variable	Cluster 1: 1 Cluster 1 Value	Cluster 2: 5, 6, 7, 8 Cluster 2 Value	Cluster 3: 1, 2, 4, 9, 10 Cluster 3 Value
Age	0.06	0.55	0.812
Gender	0	1	0
Marital	0	1	0.9
Dependents	0	0.15	0.04
Income	0.414	0.429	0.561
Years–Job	0.7	0.725	0.78
Yrs–Town	1	0.525	0.1
Yrs–Educ.	0	0.4	0.18
Driv. Lic.	1	0.75	0.8
Own Home	0	0.5	0.4
Credit Cards	0.2	0.6	0.72
Churn	0	0.5	0.4

TABLE 5.19
Distance
Calculations for the
Three-Cluster
Model

Case	Distance-C1	Distance-C2	Distance-D3	Cluster Assigned
1	3.413	3.382	1.727	3
2	4.412	2.372	0.791	3
3	0.000	3.582	3.017	1
4	4.141	2.023	0.758	3
5	5.291	0.991	2.509	2
6	4.801	1.123	2.202	2
7	5.177	1.218	2.779	2
8	4.863	2.473	4.022	2
9	3.986	2.174	0.749	3
10	3.916	1.965	0.759	3

The Three-Cluster Model

We'll use three seeds for this model, Case 3 for the low grocery expenditure case, Case 6 for the high grocery expenditure case, and Case 4 with a grocery expenditure that's about in the middle of the two extremes. We then identify the squared distance for the first 10 observations in the data set (which we arbitrarily select as our training set). Table 5.18 shows the means for the 11 variables for the three clusters.

The average grocery expenditure for Cluster 1 was 0, for Cluster 2 0.155, and for Cluster 3 0.115. The second iteration yielded squared distances as shown in Table 5.19.

The cluster assignments were identical to the first iteration, so the algorithm stops. The proportion of expenditures on groceries for each cluster was 0 for Cluster 1, 0.072 for Cluster 2, and 0.051 for Cluster 3.

Applications of Cluster Analysis

Here we present two short descriptions of the use of cluster analysis in data mining. The first is a compared pattern search with traditional cluster analysis in the mining of credit account repayment, demonstrating the use of data mining to monitor accounts for difficulties in repayment. The second is applied knowledge discovery using cluster analysis as part of a data mining analysis of insurance fraud detection and customer retention. Decision trees and neural network algorithms were also used in this study.

Monitoring Credit Card Accounts

Credit scoring is key to data mining in the credit-granting business. Application scoring uses past records of loan applicants to develop a model that predicts payback, which is applied to new applications providing the required input data. Behavioral scoring monitors the use of credit mechanisms with the intent of monitoring account status to provide early warning of trouble.

A large British credit card company was interested in the performance of revolving loans.[6] These loans required minimum payments each month. A large dataset of monthly account status for over 90,000 customers was obtained for a year of operations. The primary variable of observation was state, which was an integer value reporting the months of cumulative missed monthly repayments. The greatest state value in the data was eight months. The data included some cases where there were anomalous changes (errors or missing data), which were eliminated, thus providing an example of data cleansing to improve data quality. A biased sample of 10,000 observations was gathered. The bias was induced by requiring initial states to be zero. The proportion of initial observations in state 0 was 73 percent, reflecting both customers that had zero balance and those who paid at least the minimum payment level.

The study compared clustering approaches with an approach using pattern detection. The clustering method used **medians** to center data rather than centroids. Medians were selected as more stable than means. This approach partitioned the entire data sample to assign each object to one and only one group. The **pattern search** approach sought local clusterings, identifying profile neighborhoods of objects that had unexpectedly high numbers of data points. The pattern search method did not partition the entire dataset, but identified a few groups with unusual behavior. The **clustering** approach was useful to describe the general behavior of **customer profiles.** This was useful for market segmentation. The pattern search method was useful to identify customers with unusual behavior, which was useful to identify credit accounts in trouble.

Data Mining of Insurance Claims

This study reported data mining in a large insurance company.[7] This firm had a large data warehouse containing records of all of their financial transactions and claims. Customer retention modeling was very important to the firm, and data mining in the form of decision trees, regression, and neural networks were used for this very structured activity. Analysis of claim patterns was also important to the firm, but a much less structured problem. Clustering was used to analyze claim patterns.

Because claims analysis is open-ended, an approach more exploratory and undirected was required. Data needed to be examined for hidden trends and patterns. The firm had experienced recent growth in the number of policy holders, which resulted in decreased profitability.

Insurance risk is typically assessed by the statistical behavior of similar insured clients. Claim arrivals were assumed to follow Poisson processes, which depend upon the characteristics of policy holders as well as environmental factors. Claim sizes were described by known distributions, usually log-normal. Models depend upon distribution assumptions and the predetermined category rating systems to estimate individual risk and premium.

This study used **undirected knowledge discovery** in the form of cluster analysis to identify risk categories. Thus the approach was data-driven rather than predetermined. Data were extracted from the data warehouse for all premium-paying policy holders for the years 1996 through 1998. Quarterly data contained information on individual characteristics as well as claim behavior for the prior 12-month period. The contribution of each policy holder to profit was also included. There were over 100,000 samples available. Descriptive statistics found heavy growth in business with young people, and with expensive automobiles. Data were transformed to **normalize** data and remove **outliers.**

As with any cluster analysis, the number of clusters to include is an important strategic question. Too few clusters provide inadequate discrimination among subjects, while too many clusters yield particular clusters with too few observations. Experiments were conducted to determine the best number of clusters, which turned out to be 50. A k-means algorithm was used with a criterion to minimize the least-squared error.

The analysis identified a few clusters that had very high claims frequency and unprofitability. Key ratios reflecting these variables were identified by comparing 1998 data with 1996 data, seeking trends. The model was used to predict new policy holder performance. This in turn was the basis for the pricing of new policies.

Clustering Methods Used in Software

The most widely used clustering methods are hierarchical clustering, Bayesian clustering, k-means clustering, and self-organizing maps.[8] Hierarchical clustering algorithms do not require specification of the number of clusters prior to analysis. However, they only consider local neighbors at each stage, and cannot always separate overlapping clusters.[9] The TwoStep method is a form of hierarchical clustering, while Bayesian clustering is based on probabilities.[10] Bayesian networks are constructed with nodes representing outcomes, and decision trees constructed at each node. k-means clustering involves increasing the number of clusters as demonstrated earlier. **Self-organizing map** networks utilize neural network technology to convert many dimensions into a small number of dimensions, which has the benefit of eliminating possible data flaws such as noise (spurious relationships), outliers, or missing values.[11] k-means methods have been combined with self-organizing maps as well as with genetic algorithms to improve clustering performance.[12]

Two-step clustering first compresses data into subclusters, and then applies a statistical clustering method to merge subclusters into larger clusters until the desired number of clusters is reached. Thus, the optimal number of clusters for the training set will be obtained. Bayesian clustering also is statistically based. For further information, see endnote 9.

k-means algorithms work by defining a fixed number of clusters, and iteratively assigning records to clusters. In each iteration, the cluster centers are redefined. The reassignment and recalculation of cluster centers continues until any changes are below a specified threshold. The methods demonstrated earlier in this chapter fall into this class of algorithm.

Kohonen self-organizing maps (SOM, or Kohonen networks) are neural network applications to clustering. Input observations are connected to a set of output layers, with each connection having a strength (weight). A general four-step process is applied:[13]

1. **Initialize map**   A map with initialized reference vectors is created, and algorithm parameters such as neighborhood size and learning rate are set.
2. **Determine winning node**   For each input observation, select the best matching node by minimizing the distance to an input vector. The Euclidean norm is usually used.
3. **Update reference vectors**   Reference vectors and its neighborhood nodes are updated based upon the learning rule.
4. **Iterate** Return to step 2 until the selected number of epochs is reached, adjusting the neighborhood size.

Small maps (a few hundred nodes or less) are best. Large neighborhood sizes and learning rates are recommended initially, but can be decreased. With small maps, these parameters have not been found to be that important. Self-organizing maps are a useful tool for machine learning as applied to cluster analysis.

Application of Methods to Larger Data Sets

We'll now demonstrate clustering with the three larger data sets using Clementine software. Clementine has three clustering models. k-means clustering assigns records to a specified number of clusters by iteratively adjusting the cluster centers (much as described earlier in this chapter). Two-step clustering first compresses the data into subclusters, and then applies an algorithm to merge these subclusters until the minimum desired number of clusters is obtained. The optimal number of clusters is automatically selected. A third method, Kohonen networks, uses neural network technology for clustering. We'll now demonstrate k-means and TwoStep clustering.

Loan Application Data

The business purpose here is to identify the type of loan applicants least likely to have repayment problems. In the data set, an outcome of On-time is good, and Late is bad. We'll use 400 of the observations for cluster analysis. Transformation of data to a standardized form (between 0 and 1) is accomplished as follows:

Age	< 20	0
	20 to 50	(age-20)/30
	50 to 80	1 − (age-50)/30
	> 80	0
Income	< 0	0
	0 to $100,000	income/100000
	> $100,000	1
Risk	Max 1	assets/(debts + want)
Credit	Green	1
	Amber	0.3
	Red	0

We'll use these 400 observations for cluster analysis. The Excel model (a form of discriminant analysis in this case, which simply identifies the average attribute values for each given cluster) begins by sorting the 400 training cases into On-time and Late categories, and then identifying the average performance by variable for each group. These averages are shown in Table 5.20.

Cluster 1 included members that tended to be younger with worse risk measures and credit ratings. Income tended to be the same for both, although Cluster 1 members had slightly lower incomes.

Cluster analysis was applied using the k-means algorithm in Clementine. This procedure allows specification of the number of clusters. After entering the standardized data in the form of an Excel file saved as CSV comma delimited, and defining the outcome variable as output using a Type node, the k-means algorithm is applied specifying two clusters. We chose two clusters to compare results with the Excel model results, which minimize squared distance. By selecting the Execute button, we obtained the output given in Table 5.21.

Cluster 1 had more loans paid on-time. While the two clusters are similar in age, income, and risk, Cluster 1 has better credit ratings. This is similar to the results obtained from the TwoStep algorithm, but there is less difference in on-time repayment with the k-means output. Age and risk are less important in this second model, while credit rating is more important.

Both models were tested on the last 100 observations in the data set. Table 5.22 compares these results.

In this case, the Excel model was correct in 73 percent of the test cases while the k-means model was correct in 62 percent. Note that cluster models are intended to identify groups of observations, and usually are not limited to a specific number of outcomes.

Insurance Fraud Data

For the example in this section, the business purpose is to identify the characteristics of automobile insurance claims that are more likely to be fraudulent. This data set has 5,000 observations. We'll use 4,000 for training, and the last 1,000 for testing. The data are transformed as in Table 5.1. The 4,000 training observations were sorted by outcome, and averages were later obtained for each group. The results of the TwoStep Clementine model are shown in Table 5.23.

The difference in the clusters is apparent—those cases involving tickets, prior claims, or an attorney are in Cluster 2 (along with some others). Cluster 1 is older, with little difference in gender or claim amount. We then applied the k-means algorithm in Clementine, varying the number of clusters from two to five. Table 5.24 shows this model, comparing it with the TwoStep model.

The first cluster was very similar for both algorithms, but differences existed in Cluster 2 with respect to age, prior claims, and tickets. All of the cases involving attorneys were assigned to Cluster 2 by both algorithms, but the k-means algorithm concentrated these cases more. The point is that different algorithms yield slightly different results, yet often yield similar conclusions.

The number of clusters can be varied using the k-means algorithm. Table 5.25 shows the results for three clusters.

Here, all of the cases involving an attorney were assigned to the third cluster. This cluster had much higher prior claims, and tended to have higher late outcomes. Clusters 1 and 2 were very similar, except for age (Cluster 1 having lower age scores), with slightly higher tickets and prior claims.

TABLE 5.20
Group Standard
Score Averages for
Loan Application
Data

Cluster	On-Time	Age	Income	Risk	Credit
C1 (355 cases)	1	0.223	0.512	0.573	0.333
C2 (45 cases)	0	0.403	0.599	0.809	0.690

TABLE 5.21
Clementine
k-Means Clustering
Output for Loan
Training Data

Cluster	On-Time	Age	Income	Risk	Credit
C1 (224 cases)	0.960	0.384	0.590	0.804	1.000
C2 (176 cases)	0.795	0.382	0.588	0.756	0.205

TABLE 5.22
Cluster Algorithm
Performances

	Excel On-Time	Excel Late	k-means On-Time	k-means Late
Actual On-Time	69	25	58	36
Actual Late	2	4	2	4

TABLE 5.23
TwoStep Cluster
Analysis for Fraud
Data Training Set

	Cluster 1 (3126 cases)	Cluster 2 (874 cases)
Late Outcome	0	0.069
Age	0.727	0.471
Gender	0.499	0.485
Claim	0.609	0.589
Tickets	0.000	0.309
Prior Claims	0.000	0.425
Attorney	0.000	0.071

TABLE 5.24
Two Cluster Models
for the Fraud Data
Training Set

Variable	TwoStep C1	k-means C1	TwoStep C2	k-means C2
Cases	3126	3617	874	383
Late Outcome	0	0.012	0.069	0.042
Age	0.727	0.709	0.471	0.308
Gender	0.499	0.498	0.485	0.478
Claim	0.609	0.609	0.589	0.561
Tickets	0	0.061	0.309	0.133
Prior Claims	0	0.019	0.425	0.787
Attorney	0	0	0.071	0.162

TABLE 5.25
k-Means Cluster
Results for Fraud
Data—Three
Clusters

Variable	Cluster 1	Cluster 2	Cluster 3
Cases	1298	2477	225
Late Outcome	0.009	0.013	0.071
Age	0.204	0.935	0.458
Gender	0.508	0.493	0.462
Claim	0.614	0.607	0.521
Tickets	0.135	0.029	0.104
Prior claims	0.060	0.029	0.989
Attorney	0	0	0.276

TABLE 5.26
k-Means Cluster
Results for Fraud
Data—Four Clusters

Variable	Cluster 1	Cluster 2	Cluster 3	Cluster 4
Cases	739	1244	1954	63
Late Outcome	0.011	0.012	0.012	0.222
Age	0.210	0.942	0.681	0.406
Gender	0	0	1	0.492
Claim	0.615	0.611	0.608	0.266
Tickets	0.146	0.033	0.059	0.103
Prior Claims	0.118	0.057	0.077	1
Attorney	0	0	0	0.984

Table 5.26 shows the results for the four-cluster model.

Here, all of the cases involving an attorney were assigned to Cluster 4. This again involved much higher prior claims (indicating that prior claims and the presence of an attorney were positively correlated). Interestingly, the presence of an attorney also seems to be associated with lower claim amounts in these clusters, something that might call for further examination. Clusters 3 and 4 are very similar, except for gender. Cluster 1 is distinguished by a much younger average membership, along with higher ticket rates and higher prior claims, although the outcomes are quite good. Table 5.27 shows the results for the five-cluster model.

Here, those cases involving an attorney were found in Cluster 5, which had the worst outcome results. Cluster 1 had many males, tending to be younger with high ticket experience (but little fraudulent claim experience). Cluster 2 was differentiated from Cluster 1 by age (a much higher score, thus neither young nor old), all female, with very low ticket experience and low prior claims. Cluster 3 was all male, with many other characteristics shared with Cluster 2. Cluster 4 was all female, younger, and with low tickets. Each of the first four clusters had favorable experiences with respect to fraudulent claims. Cluster 5 had the worst experience with fraudulent claims, and also was characterized by low claim amounts, a high number of prior claims, and all had attorneys.

Varying the number of clusters allows the analyst to focus on more detail as the number of clusters is increased. This can provide clues as to the factors that seem to be associated with outcomes of interest.

Expenditure Data

Next, we'll apply cluster analysis to the Expenditure Data file. The business purpose is to identify who spends more on groceries. This yields the output given in Table 5.28.

TABLE 5.27
k-Means Cluster
Results for Fraud
Data—Five Clusters

Variable	Cluster 1	Cluster 2	Cluster 3	Cluster 4	Cluster 5
Cases	204	1243	1820	671	62
Late Outcome	0.005	0.012	0.012	0.013	0.210
Age	0.199	0.942	0.713	0.221	0.403
Gender	0.657	0	1	0	0.500
Claim	0.610	0.611	0.608	0.616	0.264
Tickets	0.811	0.033	0.010	0.058	0.105
Prior claims	0.125	0.058	0.075	0.114	1
Attorney	0	0	0	0	1

TABLE 5.28
Two Step Cluster
Results for
Expenditure Data

Variable	Cluster 1	Cluster 2	Cluster 3
Cases	2741	597	1662
Proportion—grocery	0.081	0.087	0.094
Age	0.319	0.489	0.359
Gender	0.570	0.593	0.639
Marital	0.768	0.804	0.904
Dependents	0.200	0.175	0.240
Income	0.401	0.506	0.584
Years on the Job	0.661	0.708	0.707
Years in Town	0.214	0.223	0.237
Years of Education	0.228	0.255	0.321
Driver's License	0.997	0.002	0.994
Own Home	0.009	0.395	0.887
Credit Cards	0.516	0.512	0.517
Churn	0.327	0.323	0.285

The strongest difference in the clusters seems to be the holding of a driver's license. Those without licenses are primarily assigned to Cluster 2. The other distinguishing characteristic of Cluster 2 is that it is older on average. Clusters 1 and 3 are quite similar, although Cluster 3 has a much higher rate of home ownership, while few in Cluster 1 do. Cluster 3 also has a higher rate of married people and dependents, higher income, more education, and a slightly higher rate of males relative to Cluster 1.

Correlation is a standard statistical procedure that measures the degree of relationship among variables. We use Excel's correlation tool to see the degree of relationships among the variables in this data set. We can compare the correlation matrix results in Table 5.29 with our earlier results.

Driver's license is not correlated well with anything but age (younger people tend to have a driver's license at a slightly higher rate than older people). Older people, meanwhile, tend to have worked longer at their current job, and have a higher income, both of which make sense. Males (gender code of 1) appear to have higher incomes. Married people have more dependents (again, an expected result),

TABLE 5.29 Correlation Matrix—Expenditure Data

	Age	Gen	Mar	Dep	Inc	YrJ	YrT	YrE	DL	OH	CC	Churn
Age	1.000											
Gen	0.010	1.000										
Mar	−0.109	−0.024	1.000									
Dep	−0.190	0.000	0.343	1.000								
Inc	0.219	0.142	−0.046	−0.018	1.000							
YrJ	0.235	0.060	−0.021	0.012	0.217	1.000						
YrT	−0.006	0.001	0.036	0.035	−0.008	0.016	1.000					
YrE	0.034	−0.001	−0.002	−0.020	0.160	0.055	0.008	1.000				
DL	−0.188	0.007	0.022	0.047	−0.059	−0.035	−0.002	0.008	1.000			
OH	0.067	0.065	0.194	0.058	0.355	0.083	0.021	0.042	−0.036	1.000		
CC	0.146	0.012	−0.039	0.001	0.034	0.106	−0.001	0.028	0.007	−0.005	1.000	
Churn	−0.024	0.006	0.029	0.030	−0.027	−0.007	0.001	−0.013	−0.008	−0.024	−0.003	1.000
ProGroc	0.000	0.022	−0.003	−0.002	−0.001	−0.023	−0.008	0.011	−0.002	0.016	0.012	−0.027

and are also more likely to own their own home. Those that own their own home tend to have higher incomes (probably the causation is reversed). Correlation matrices provide some insight into the data. However, cluster analysis provides different kinds of insight, leading to a better understanding of data grouping.

Software Products

Most (if not all) data mining products include clustering ability, because it is a fundamental initial analysis tool. SRA International's Mantas is a system designed to allow financial companies to sift through trading data to uncover trading patterns when trying to identify illegal trading and subsequent litigation risks in light of stricter Securities and Exchange Commission rules.[14] Clustering is one of the tools provided. Mantas looks for suspicious patterns, and alerts analysts of the detected pattern, along with suggested reasons.

There are alternative tools to initially explore data (in addition to graphical analysis, which is also supported by all data mining software). For instance, in addition to a Cluster algorithm, PolyAnalyst includes a Find Laws algorithm based on Symbolic Knowledge Acquisition Technology (SKAT) to search for hidden functional dependencies in data. PolyAnalyst also includes a Find Dependencies algorithm to show the strength of connections among attributes, guiding the analyst to explore these dependencies more thoroughly with other techniques.

Appendix

Clementine

Clementine (from SPSS) is a major data mining software. It is designed around streams of entities, as shown in Figure 5A.1. The intent of this appendix is to show

FIGURE 5A.1
Cluster Stream from SPSS Clementine

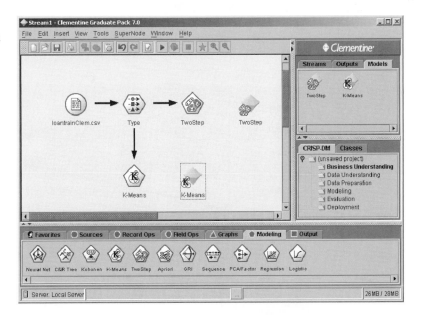

some of the Clementine output, especially the web plots, which supplement the understanding gained from cluster analysis. Almost all data mining software products provide such web plot tools.

The icon loantrain.Clem.csv accesses a data file (in this case, the loan training data). A "Type" icon defines variables as needed for particular analyses. The models for TwoStep and k-means are available for cluster analysis, as discussed in the chapter. Clementine also has a Kohonen self-organizing map algorithm that can be used for cluster analysis. Once each model is run, outputs are stored in the upper-right window of Clementine. These outputs provide cluster averages to the user.

WEB PLOT

Clementine provides a web plot tool. Using a "Type" node, all data must be defined as type "Set" with direction "Both." Figure 5A.2 gives the initial web plot, with a setting at 1. The variables are color coded, which shows up as shades of gray in Figure 5A.2. However, the primary point is still evident.

This web links all variables in the data set, and doesn't provide much information except that stronger relationships are shown in bold. Here, outcome 1 (On-time) seems to have a strong relationship with Average Income. The slider on the upper left can be moved to the right, and the web dynamically changes. Moving the slider increases the required degree of relationship among discrete variable outcomes, so as this required degree is increased, lines disappear and the more important lines remain. Figure 5A.3 shows a picture of relationships at the 100 setting.

At this stage, an On-time outcome is associated with young and middle aged applicants, with green credit ratings, low and high risk groups, and average income. This is useful when comparing it with cluster model results.

If more relationships are desired, the slider can be moved back. Figure 5A.4 shows such a web plot at the setting 25.

Outcome On-time here is connected with all variable outcomes except for old age and average risk. The strongest relationship is with average income. Outcome 0 (not

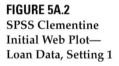

FIGURE 5A.2
SPSS Clementine
Initial Web Plot—
Loan Data, Setting 1

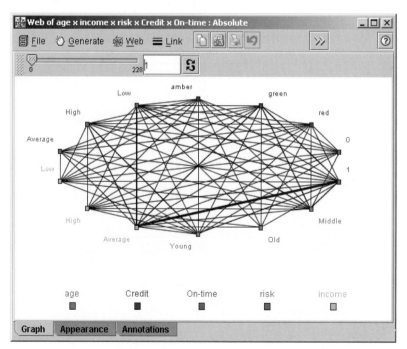

FIGURE 5A.3
SPSS Clementine
Web Plot of Loan
Data—Setting 100

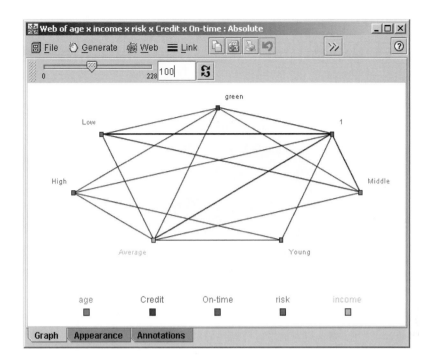

paid on-time) is associated with cases involving high risk, average income, and young age.

The same plot can be applied to the insurance fraud data. The initial plot (at a setting just above 0) is shown in Figure 5A.5.

It demonstrates what happens when data such as age is treated as having discrete outcomes. There are many variable values displayed. The same is true for the claim amount. It creates a mess.

FIGURE 5A.4
SPSS Clementine
Web Tool to Identify
Relationships—Loan
Data, Setting 25

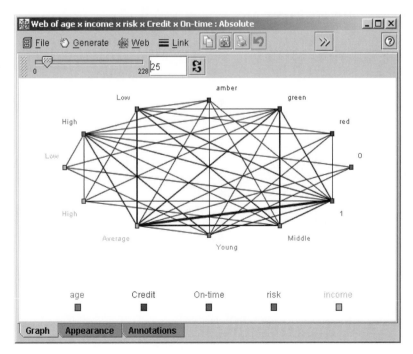

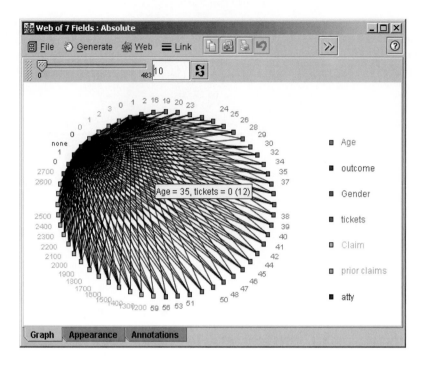

However, the mess can be cleared up by restricting the specification of relation-ships displayed. Moving the slider to 200 results in the screen shown in Figure 5A.6.

Here the relationships are much clearer. Nothing shows up for fraudulent claims, but OK claims are most strongly related to the absence of an attorney. There also are noted relationships to both genders (0 and 1), 0 tickets, and 0 prior claims.

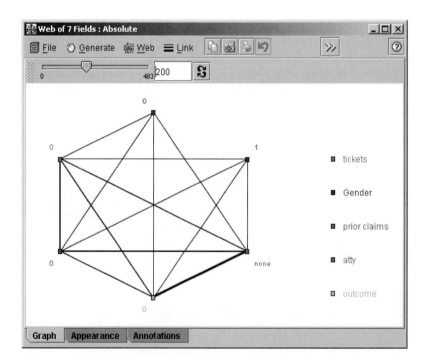

FIGURE 5A.7
SPSS Clementine
Job Applicant Data
Initial Web Plot

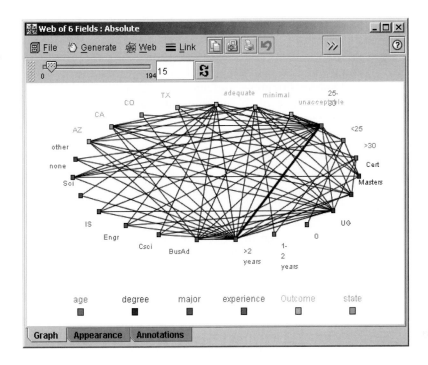

The web plot for the job applicant data set is shown in Figure 5A.7.

This data set was modified to include categorical data for age and experience. Note that it is cluttered but is much easier to decipher than Figure 5A.5. Processing the data to the best format for the particular analysis can be time-consuming, but it can also be very useful in helping users identify relationships.

Figure 5A.8 shows the same data at a setting of 50.

FIGURE 5A.8
SPSS Clementine
Job Applicant
Data Web Plot—
Setting 50

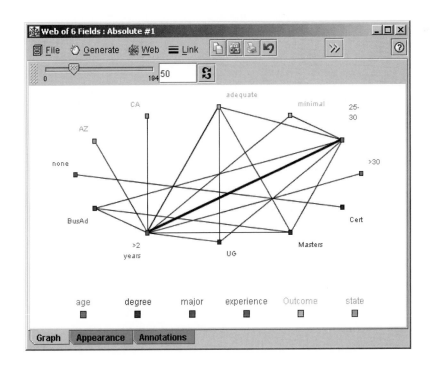

This shows the stronger relationships. There is a strong relationship between the age group 25 to 30 and over two years' experience. However, the business purpose is probably about identifying the relationship with outcome. Adequate outcome shows relationships with over two years' experience, both undergraduate and master's degrees, and age group 25 to 30. Minimal outcome has relationships shown for two of these same data categories (over two years' experience, age group 25 to 30).

Summary

Cluster analysis is a very attractive initial data examination tool. Once different clusters are identified, other methods are often used to discover rules and patterns.

Sometimes the median has been used rather than the mean as the basis for cluster centers, as the first real example did. That decision was made expecting the median to be more stable than the mean. This is because outlier observations (radically different from the norm) do not affect the median, but do influence the mean. It is very simple to implement the median rather than the mean in Excel (although not in packaged data mining software). In Excel, all one does is use the formula "=MEDIAN(range)" rather than "AVERAGE(range)".

Some problems may not have an obvious set of clusters (which is why modeling tools such as TwoStep in Clementine exist—to automatically identify the best number of clusters in terms of minimizing some error metric). A number of options exist for determining the number of clusters. Agglomeration is an approach where you start with the maximum number of clusters, and then merge clusters iteratively until there's only one cluster left. Then the cluster value that fits best is chosen. (The one that fits best is determined by whatever metric is selected, and based upon the need for correct prediction—fewer clusters are better, along with the need for the discrimination of difference—more clusters are better.) Commercial tools have a number of different parameters and methods. Some use probability density rather than distance measures, which tends to work better when clusters overlap. Coleman, et al. (1999) provided a detailed study of different methods.[15]

Glossary

cluster   A group of related objects, often defined by shared characteristics.

customer profile   A description of a case by values or categories for selected variables.

k-means clustering   A clustering technique where the number of clusters is predefined.

median   An average based on the midpoint value of each variable.

normalize   A statistical operation to subtract the mean and divide by the standard deviation in order to put data on a scale where dispersion is easy to detect.

outlier   A statistical observation with variable values that are quite different from the majority of other observations.

pattern search   A mathematical procedure to analyze data using a systematic pattern.

self-organizing map   A clustering algorithm based on neural network technology.

undirected knowledge discovery   An automatic data mining analysis where the computer software identifies relationships without user guidance.

Exercises

1. Apply the k-means algorithm to the Insurance Fraud data file using standardized scores of the six input variables. Set k to 2, reflecting the two outcomes. Use the first 1,000 observations as the training set, and apply it to the last 1,000 observations. Use the scoring scheme described for Table 5.1. Use data mining software if available, or Excel if not. Identify groups obtained and what they might reveal.

2. Apply the TwoStep algorithm to the Insurance Fraud data file, using standardized scores of the six input variables. Use the first 1,000 observations as the training set, and apply them to the last 1,000 observations. Employ the scoring scheme described for Table 5.1. Use data mining software if available, or Excel if not. Identify groups obtained and what they might reveal.

3. Apply the Kohonen neural network algorithm to the Insurance Fraud data file, using standardized scores of the six input variables. Use the first 1,000 observations as the training set, and apply it to the last 1,000 observations. Employ the scoring scheme described for Table 5.1. Use data mining software if available, or Excel if not. Identify groups obtained and what they might reveal.

4. Apply the k-means algorithm to the Loan Application data file using standardized scores of the five input variables: age, income, risk, credit rating, and the on-time variable (use the range option type). Set k to 2, representing the two known output values. Use the 650 observations as the training set. Use data mining software if available, or Excel if not. Identify groups obtained and what they might reveal.

5. Apply the TwoStep algorithm to the Loan Application data file using standardized scores of the five input variables: age, income, risk, credit rating, and the on-time variable (use the range option type). Employ the 650 observations as the training set. Use data mining software if available, or Excel if not. Identify groups obtained and what they might reveal.

6. Apply the Kohonen neural network algorithm to the Loan Application data file, using standardized scores of the five input variables: age, income, risk, credit rating, and the on-time variable (use the range option type). Employ the 650 observations as the training set. Use data mining software if available, or Excel if not. Identify groups obtained and what they might reveal.

7. Apply the k-means algorithm to the Job Application data file, using standardized scores of the four input variables: age, income, risk, and credit rating. Set k to 4, representing the four known output values. Use all 500 observations as the training set. Utilize data mining software if available, or Excel if not. Identify groups obtained and what they might reveal.

8. Apply the TwoStep algorithm to the Job Application data file, using standardized scores of the three input variables: age, income, and risk. Use all 500 observations as the training set. Use data mining software if available, or Excel if not. Identify groups obtained and what they might reveal.

9. Apply the Kohonen neural network algorithm to the Job Application data file using standardized scores of the three input variables: age, income, and risk. Use all 500 observations as the training set. Use data mining software if available, or Excel if not. Identify groups obtained and what they might reveal.

10. Apply the k-means algorithm to all 10,000 observations of the Expenditure data file using standardized scores given for the variables age through churn (12 variables). Set k to 5. Use data mining software if available, or Excel if not. Identify groups obtained and what they might reveal.

11. Apply the TwoStep algorithm to the Job Application data file using standardized scores of the three input variables: age, income, and risk. Use the 650 observations as the training set. Use data mining software if available, or Excel if not. Identify groups obtained and what they might reveal.

12. Apply the Kohonen neural network algorithm to the Job Application data file, using standardized scores of the three input variables: age, income, risk. Use the 500 observations as the training set. Use data mining software if available, or Excel if not. Identify groups obtained and what they might reveal.

Endnotes

1. M. Y. Kiang and A. Kumar, "An Evaluation of Self-Organizing Map Networks as a Robust Alternative to Factor Analysis in Data Mining Applications," *Information Systems Research,* volume 12, number 2, 2001, pp. 177–194.

2. P. Finerty, "Improving Customer Care Through Knowledge Management," *Cost & Management,* 71:9, November 1997, p. 33.

3. G. Linoff, "Which Way to the Mine?" *As/400 Systems Management,* 26:1, January 1998, pp. 42–44.

4. M. J. A. Berry and G. Linoff, *Data Mining Techniques,* New York: John Wiley & Sons, 1997.

5. R. A. Johnson and D. W. Wichern, *Applied Multivariate Statistical Analysis,* Upper Saddle River, NJ: Prentice Hall, 1998.

6. N. M. Adams, D. J. Hand, and R. J. Till, "Mining for Classes and Patterns in Behavioural Data," *The Journal of the Operational Research Society*, volume 52, number 9, 2001, pp. 1017–1024.

7. K. A. Smith, R. J. Willis, and M. Brooks, "An Analysis of Customer Retention and Insurance Claim Patterns Using Data Mining: A Case Study," *The Journal of the Operational Research Society,* volume 51, number 5, 2000, pp. 532–541.

8. S. Papadimitriou and K. Terzidis, "Growing Kernel-Based Self-Organized Maps Trained with Supervised Bias," *Intelligent Data Analysis,* 8, 2004, pp. 111–130.

9. C.-F. Tsai, C.-W. Tsai, H.-C. Wu, and T. Yang, "ACODF: A Novel Data Clustering Approach for Mining in Large Databases," *The Journal of Systems and Software,* 73, 2004, pp. 133–145.

10. N. Friedman, M. Linial, I. Nachman, and D'Peier, "Using Bayesian Networks to Analyze Expression Data," *Journal of Computational Biology,* 7, 2000, pp. 601–620.

11. M. Drobics, U. Bodenhofer, W. Winiwarter, "Mining Clusters and Corresponding Interpretable Descriptions—A Three-Stage Approach," *Expert Systems* 19(4), 2002, pp. 224–234.

12. C.-F. Tsai, C.-W. Tsai, H.-C. Wu, and T. Yang, "ACODF: A Novel Data Clustering Approach for Data Mining in Large Databases," *The Journal of Systems and Software,* 73, 2004, pp. 133–145.

13. T. Kohonen, *Self-Organizing Maps,* Berlin: Springer-Verlag, 1997.

14. J. Mateyaschuk, "Market Monitor," *InformationWeek,* issue 711, November 30, 1998, p. 135.

15. D. Coleman, X. Dong, J. Hardin, D. M. Rocke, and D. L. Woodruff, "Some Computational Issues in Cluster Analysis with No a Priori Metric," *Computational Statistics & Data Analysis,* 31, 1999, pp. 1–11.

CHAPTER SIX

Regression Algorithms in Data Mining

This chapter:

- Describes OLS regression and logistic regression
- Describes linear discriminant analysis and centroid discriminant analysis
- Demonstrates techniques on small data sets
- Reviews the real applications of each model
- Shows the application of models to larger data sets

Mobile technology has been a major development in our culture. The use of cellular telephones has become widespread all over the world, especially in countries such as South Korea and Finland. These pocket devices provide telephone service (of varying quality) in addition to high-quality access to games, and relatively reliable access to stock market quotations and other Internet access–related activities.

As with many other retail organizations, cellular telephone companies need to consider customer turnover (or churn). Telephone companies were one of the first service industries to worry about churn when the American Telephone and Telegraph (AT&T) monopoly was split up in the 1980s. High levels of competition were introduced into this industry, with MCI offering a "friends and family" program, seeking to draw all of those related to existing customers into their network. Competitive telephone services responded with programs of their own, and customers often were able to take advantage of attractive initial offerings by switching from one company to another over a period of months. Telephone companies soon learned that attracting new customers was not the answer to all of their problems. Keeping profitable customers was the key to their success.

In order to make rational decisions, these companies needed to better understand their customer base. This type of analysis is well supported by models, which can be applied to large sets of data that enable the profiling of customers into different segments, and then estimating the expected profit over the life of a customer's account. This can be tied to marketing programs that offer attractive packages of service to each customer profile. Some customer profiles will not be profitable at all. Knowing this enables service providers to avoid wasting marketing resources on these specific profiles of customers.

Regression is a basic statistical tool. In data mining, it's one of the basic tools for analysis, used in classification applications through logistic regression and discriminant analysis, as well as the prediction of continuous data through ordinary least squares (OLS) and other forms. As such, regression is often taught in one (or more) three-hour courses. We cannot hope to cover all of the basics of regression. However, we here present ways in which regression is used within the context of data mining.

Regression is used on a variety of data types. If the data represent a **time series,** output from regression models is often used for forecasting. Regression can be used to build predictive models for other types of data, and can be applied in a number of different forms. The class of regression models is a major class of tools available to support the Modeling phase of the data mining process.

Probably the most widely used data mining algorithms are data fitting, in the sense of regression. Regression is a fundamental tool for statistical analysis to characterize relationships between a dependent variable and one or more independent variables. **Regression** models can be used for many purposes, including explanation and prediction. Linear and **logistic regression** models are both primary tools in most general-purpose data mining software. Nonlinear data can sometimes be transformed into useful linear data and analyzed with linear regression. Some special forms of nonlinear regression also exist. **Neural network** models are also widely used for the same classes of models. Both regression and neural network models require that data be expressed numerically (or at least as 0–1 dummy variables). The primary operational difference between regression and neural networks is that regression provides a formula that has a strong body of theory behind it for application and interpretation. Neural networks generally do not provide models for interpretation, and are usually applied internally within the software that built the model. In this sense, neural networks appear to users as "black boxes" that classify or predict without explanation. There are, of course, models behind these classifications and predictions, but they tend to be so complex that they are neither printed out nor analyzed.

Regression Models

Ordinary least squares regression (OLS) is a model of the form:

$$Y = \beta_0 + \beta_1 X_1 + \beta_2 X_2 + \cdots + \beta_n X_n + \varepsilon$$

where

Y is the dependent variable (the one being forecast).

X_n are the n independent (explanatory) variables.

β_0 is the intercept term.

β_n are the n coefficients for the independent variables.

ε is the error term.

OLS regression is the straight line (with intercept and slope coefficients β_n), which minimizes the sum of squared error terms ε_i over all i observations. The idea is that you look at past data to determine the β coefficients which worked best. The model gives you the most likely future value of the dependent variable given knowledge of the X_n for future observations. This approach assumes a linear relationship, and error terms that are normally distributed around zero without patterns. While these assumptions are often unrealistic, regression is highly attractive because of the existence of widely available computer packages as well as highly developed statistical theory. Statistical packages provide the probability that estimated parameters differ from zero.

We can apply regression to the problem of extending a trend line. This is a very useful application of regression. For instance, you might be administering

TABLE 6.1
Time Series Data

Week	Requests	Week	Requests	Week	Requests	Week	Requests
1	10	11	62	21	92	31	160
2	3	12	68	22	110	32	173
3	5	13	56	23	123	33	168
4	15	14	84	24	126	34	164
5	22	15	67	25	136	35	182
6	38	16	87	26	130	36	175
7	34	17	100	27	134	37	190
8	49	18	88	28	140	38	192
9	45	19	101	29	157	39	199
10	59	20	98	30	150	40	204

a computer system with a help desk. The organization undergoes periods of growth, making it difficult to anticipate how many help desk personnel to provide. Assume data over the past 40 weeks are available. Over this period, the organization has gone from 30 employees to 300, in a fairly steady manner. The dependent variable (Y) is the number of requests for help. The independent variable (X) is time, an index of weeks beginning with 1 and ending at 40, the last available observation. The data are given in Table 6.1.

The number of requests has gone from 10 in the first week to 204 in week 40. A graph (Figure 6.1) provides a more complete understanding.

The number of requests has grown fairly steadily. The problem is the number of help personnel to assign. During the first few weeks, one person dealt with the demand quite easily. However, one person can only handle about 20 help requests per week (considering the average time required to solve a problem, and the irregular nature of request arrivals). By week 40, it was clear that ten people were required to staff the help facility. It was also clear that this would only satisfy current demand. Given the lead time for hiring and training, management would like a tool to help them predict demand at a period further out in the future (say 20 weeks).

A regression model would provide such a tool. Here the model is

$$Y = \beta_0 + \beta_1 X + \varepsilon$$

where Y is Requests and X is Week.

FIGURE 6.1
Graph of Time
Series Data

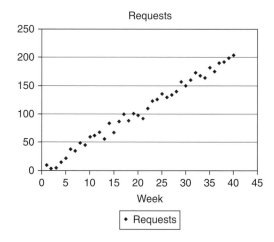

TABLE 6.2
Regression Output for Time Series Data

SUMMARY OUTPUT						
Regression Statistics						
Multiple *R*	0.993					
R Square	**0.987**					
Adjusted *R* Square	0.986					
Standard Error	6.971					
Observations	40					

ANOVA						
	df	SS	MS	F	Significance F	
Regression	1	137859.2	137859.2	2837.198	**2.59E-37**	
Residual	38	1846.416	48.5899			
Total	39	139705.6				

	Coefficients	Standard Error	t Stat	P-value	Lower 95%	Upper 95%
Intercept	**0.642**	2.246	0.286	0.7765	−3.905	5.190
Week	**5.086**	0.095	53.265	0.0000	4.892	5.279

The regression output for our data is shown in Table 6.2.

This output provides a great deal of information. We will discuss regression statistics, which measure the fit of the model to the data next. ANOVA information is an overall test of the model itself. The value for Significance F gives the probability that the model has no information about the dependent variable. Here, 2.59E-37 is practically zero (move the decimal place 37 digits to the left, which results in a lot of zeros). Finally, at the bottom of the report, is what we were after: the regression model.

$$\text{Requests} = 0.642 + 5.086 \times \text{Week}$$

This enables us predict the number of help requests expected in the future. It is tempting to extrapolate this model into the future, which violates the assumptions of the regression model. But extrapolation is the model's purpose in prediction. Still, the analyst needs to realize that the model error is expected to grow the further the model is projected beyond the data set that it was built upon. To forecast, multiply the week index by 5.086 and add 0.642. (Since we're really interested in integer values anyway, this is the same as adding zero in most cases.) The forecasts for weeks 41 through 60 are given in Table 6.3.

The graphical picture of this model is shown in Figure 6.2.

The actual data stop at week 40, and is seen to fluctuate a bit. The linear nature of the regression line is demonstrated by the model. You can see that the model fit the data very well in the past. If that same rate of increase held into the next 20 weeks, the model line would provide a forecast of the number of help requests (actual number of requests by week given in the prior table) that would be expected

TABLE 6.3
Time Series Forecasts from the Regression Model

Week	Requests	Week	Requests	Week	Requests	Week	Requests
41	209	46	234	51	260	56	285
42	214	47	239	52	265	57	290
43	219	48	244	53	270	58	295
44	224	49	249	54	275	59	300
45	229	50	254	55	280	60	305

FIGURE 6.2
A Graph of the
Time Series Model
and Its Forecasts

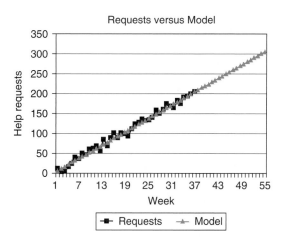

to have some error. This error would be expected to increase the further into the future a forecast was made.

Classical Tests of the Regression Model

The universal test for classification in data mining is the coincidence matrix. That focuses on the ability of the model to categorize data. For continuous regression, this requires identification of cutoffs between classes. Data mining software doesn't do that, but we will demonstrate how it can be done. There are many other aspects to accuracy, just as there are many applications of different models, especially regression. The classical tests of regression models are based on the assumption that errors are normally distributed around the mean, with no patterns. The basis of regression accuracy is the residuals, or the difference between the predicted and observed values. Residuals are then extended to a general measure of regression fit: r-squared.

SSE

The accuracy of any predictive or forecasting model can be assessed by calculating the **sum of squared errors (SSE).** In the regression we just completed, SSE is 1846.416. All that means is that you obtain a model which gives you a predictive or forecasting formula, then go back to the past observations and see what the model would have given you for the dependent variable for each past observation. (You can visualize this by comparing the actual requests with the model in the graph shown earlier.) Each observation's residual (error) is the difference between actual and predicted. The sign doesn't matter, because the next step is to square each of these errors. The more accurate the model is, the lower its SSE. An SSE doesn't mean much by itself, but it is a very good way of comparing alternative models, if there are equal opportunities for each model to have error.

R^2

SSE can be used to generate more information for a particular model. The statistic R^2 is the ratio of variance explained by the model over total variance in the data. Total squared values (139705.6, in our example) is explained using squared dependent variable values (137859.2, in this case) plus SSE (1846.416, in this instance). To obtain R^2, square the predicted or forecast values of the dependent variable values, add them up (yielding MSR), and divide MSR by (MSR + SSE). This gives the ratio of change in the dependent variable explained by the model

TABLE 6.4
Hiring Data
Training Set

Sales	Yrs Education	College GPA	Age	M/F	College Grad
123293	18	3.01	33	0	1
125930	16	2.78	25	1	1
0	18	3.15	26	1	1
103405	18	3.86	24	0	1
84671	16	2.58	25	0	1
33284	16	2.96	23	1	1
143290	17	3.56	35	1	1
81973	16	2.64	23	1	1
56062	18	3.43	32	0	1
140698	15	2.75	34	1	0
73211	13	2.95	28	1	0
108726	13	2.50	23	1	0
65850	16	2.86	24	1	1
112804	15	2.38	23	0	0
140956	16	3.47	27	0	1
82621	16	3.10	26	1	1
101628	13	2.98	21	1	0
158964	16	2.71	23	1	1
103562	13	2.95	20	0	0
53152	18	3.36	25	1	1

(137859.2/139705.6 = 0.986784, in our example). R^2 can range from a minimum of 0 (the model tells you absolutely nothing about the dependent variable) to 1.0 (the model is perfect).

$$R^2 = \frac{\text{SST} - \text{SSE}}{\text{SST}}$$

where SST is the sum of squared deviations of the dependent variable from its own mean, and SSE is the sum of the squared error (the difference between the actual dependent variable values and the predicted or forecast values).

Multiple Regression

You can include as many independent variables as you want. In traditional regression analysis, there are good reasons to limit the number of variables. The spirit of exploratory data mining, however, encourages examining a large number of independent variables. Here we are presenting very small models for demonstration purposes. In this case, we run the risk of having too many variables for the number of observations used. In data mining applications, however, the assumption is that you have very many observations so there's no technical limit on the number of independent variables.

To demonstrate, you may want to predict the success of salespeople in an organization. This would be valuable in hiring: the model could predict the volume of sales expected. Past data could be used to relate the characteristics of those being considered for a job with their expected sales performance in their first month after completing the firm's training program. Table 6.4 shows such data. The business purpose is to predict sales as a function of some set of the available independent variables.

The dependent variable, First Month Sales, is given first. Of the 20 past hires, one didn't pan out at all (zero sales). The best performance was sales of $158,964.

TABLE 6.5
Regression Results
for Hiring Data

SUMMARY OUTPUT						
Regression Statistics						
Multiple *R*		0.502				
R Square		**0.252**				
Adj *R* Square		**−0.015**				
Standard Error		40646.56				
Observations		20				

ANOVA						
	df	SS	MS	F	Significance F	
Regression	5	7.8E+09	1.56E+09	0.943944	0.483	
Residual	14	2.31E+10	1.65E+09			
Total	19	3.09E+10				

	Coefficients	Stand. Error	t Stat	P-value	Lower 95%	Upper 95%
Intercept	**269025.2**	150499.5	1.788	0.096	−53764	591814
Yrs Education	**−17148.4**	11997.8	−1.429	0.175	−42881	8584
College GPA	**−7171.9**	29553.1	−0.243	**0.812**	−70557	56213
Age	**4331.4**	2585.4	1.675	0.116	−1214	9877
M/F	**−23580.6**	20335.7	−1.160	0.266	−67196	20035
College Grad	**31001.1**	39847.4	0.778	**0.450**	−54463	116465

In this case, variables for sales (dependent variable), years of education, grade point average, and age are continuous variables. The last two variables are binary (can take on only one of two values, 0 or 1 in this case). The first of these indicates sex (0 for male, 1 for female). The second indicates whether or not the applicant had a college degree. The binary variables here are nominal, in that they describe a state and do not necessarily imply superior value. (The model beta coefficient will provide information about superior value.)

The regression model for this problem is obtained the same way as with the model with one independent variable. However, here the block of independent variables includes five columns instead of one. The resulting regression model is shown in Table 6.5.

Thus, the model is

```
Predicted First Month Sales = 269025.2
                   −      17,148.4 × Education
                   −       7,171.9 × GPA
                   +       4,331.4 × Age
                   −      23,580.6 × M/F
                   +      31,001.1 × Grad
```

For instance, if the firm were interviewing four new applicants, with the given characteristics, the predicted initial success at sales would be predicted by the model, as in Table 6.6.

The average for the initial data set was slightly over $94,000. Of the new applicants, the third appears the most promising. The first is also predicted to perform above average. The second and fourth applicants are not.

The fit of this model to the data is not as good as the simple regression we looked at earlier. The R^2 statistic is only 0.25, indicating that the model explains about one-fourth of the variance in first month sales. This is much lower than the

TABLE 6.6
Hiring Data Predictions for New Cases

Education	GPA	Age	M/F	Grad	Predicted
14	2.35	20	0	0	98721
21	3.35	32	0	1	54488
18	3.02	34	0	1	116963
16	2.86	22	1	1	76850

0.98 obtained through the regression with only one independent variable that we looked at earlier.

Adjusted R^2

Note that in the previous model, you were allowed an unlimited number of independent variables. The fact is that adding an independent variable to the model will always result in R^2 equal to or greater than R^2 without the last independent variable. This is true despite the probability that one or more of the independent variables have very little true relationships with the dependent variables. To get a truer picture of the worth of adding independent variables to the model, adjusted R^2 penalizes the R^2 calculation for having extra independent variables, as shown next.

$$\text{Adjusted } R^2 = 1 - \frac{\text{SSE } (n-1)}{\text{TSS } (n-k)}$$

where

SSE = sum of squared errors
MSR = sum of squared predicted values
TSS = SSE + MSR
n = number of observations
k = number of independent variables

Adjusted R^2 can be used to select more robust regression models. We can look at the regression output and see that the probability that the beta coefficient for

TABLE 6.7
Regression Output for a Subset of Hiring Data

SUMMARY OUTPUT

Regression Statistics

Multiple R	0.466
R Square	**0.218**
Adj R Square	**0.071**
Standard Error	38890.99
Observations	20

ANOVA

	df	SS	MS	F	Significance F
Regression	3	6.73E+09	2.24E+09	1.482637	0.256994
Residual	16	2.42E+10	1.51E+09		
Total	19	3.09E+10			

	Coeff	Standard Error	t Stat	P-value	Lower 95%	Upper 95%
Intercept	173284	88170	1.965	0.0670	−13627	360196
Yrs Education	−9991	5691	−1.756	**0.0983**	−22055	2072
Age	3537	2283	1.549	0.1409	−1303	8376
M/F	−18731	18568	−1.009	0.3281	−58094	20633

College GPA being significantly different than zero is 0.81, and for College Grad is 0.45, which are really quite high. We might get almost as much predictive accuracy without needing to gather these variables. Rerunning a simpler regression model, we get Table 6.7.

Here our adjusted R^2 is much better at 0.07. The R^2 itself drops to 0.22, as it must when variables are dropped from the model. If the data for College GPA and graduation is available, it would be expected to provide a slightly better prediction, but deleting that data would not be that important.

Logistic Regression

Some data of interest in a regression study may be ordinal or nominal. For instance, in our example job application model, sex and college degree are nominal. In the loan application data, the outcome is nominal, while credit rating is ordinal. Since regression analysis requires numerical data, we included them by *coding* the variables. Here, each of these variables is dichotomous; therefore, we can code them as either 0 or 1 (as we did in the regression model for loan applicants). For example, a male can be assigned a code of 0 while a female is assigned a code of 1. Employees with a college degree can be assigned a code of 1, and those without a code of 0.

The purpose of **logistic regression** is to classify cases into the most likely category. Logistic regression provides a set of β parameters for the intercept (or intercepts in the case of ordinal data with more than two categories) and independent variables, which can be applied to a logistic function to estimate the probability of belonging to a specified output class. The formula for probability of acceptance of a case i to a stated class j is

$$P_j = \frac{1}{1 + e^{(-\beta_0 - \Sigma \beta_i x_i)}}$$

where the β coefficients are obtained from logistic regression.

The regression model provides a continuous formula. A cutoff needs to be determined to divide the value obtained from this formula, given independent variable values, which will divide data into output categories in proportion to the population of cases.

Chapter 4 included a set of data for insurance claims, some of which were fraudulent. The independent variables included claimant age, gender, claim amount, number of traffic tickets on record, number of prior claims, and attorney. Here, we simplify the attorney data to focus on attorney Smith, making it a 0–1 variable. Table 6.8 provides 10 observations reflecting that data shown in Table 4.10.

A logistic regression model was developed for this data using SAS, which yielded the model shown in Table 6.9. This report gives the model in terms of coefficients for the intercept and each variable (the Estimate column) with the standard error of each estimate. Since the logistic regression is based on discrete values for some variables, a chi-squared test is conventional for the evaluation of each model coefficient (given in the Chi-Square column). The evaluation of these coefficients is easiest to understand by viewing the last column, which gives the probability of a random measure being greater than the chi-squared value. If this probability is high, the implication is that the coefficient is not very significant. If this probability is very low (or near zero), the implication is that the coefficient is significant.

TABLE 6.8
Insurance Claim Training Data

Age	Gender	Claim	Tickets	Prior	Attorney	Outcome
52	0	2000	0	1	0	OK
38	0	1800	0	0	0	OK
21	1	5600	1	2	1	Fraud
36	1	3800	0	1	0	OK
19	0	600	2	2	0	OK
41	0	4200	1	2	1	Fraud
38	0	2700	0	0	0	OK
33	1	2500	0	1	0	Fraud
18	1	1300	0	0	0	OK
26	0	2600	2	0	0	OK

TABLE 6.9
The Logistic Regression Model for Insurance Claim Data

Parameter	Estimate	Std. Error	Chi-Square	Pr > ChiSq
Intercept	81.624	309.3	0.0697	0.7918
Age	−2.778	10.4	0.0713	0.7894
Gender	−75.893	246.7	0.0946	0.7584
Claim	0.017	0.055	0.0959	0.7569
Tickets	−36.648	164.5	0.0496	0.8237
Prior	6.914	84.8	0.0067	0.9350
Smith?	−29.361	103.3	0.0809	0.7761

TABLE 6.10
The Logistic Regression Model Applied to Insurance—Fraud Test Cases

Age	Gender	Claim	Tickets	Prior	Attorney	Model	Prob	Predict	Actual
23	0	2800	1	0	0	28.958	1.0	OK	OK
31	1	1400	0	0	0	−56.453	0.0	Fraud	OK
28	0	4200	2	3	1	−6.261	0.002	Fraud	Fraud
19	0	2800	0	1	0	83.632	1.0	OK	OK
41	0	1600	0	0	0	−4.922	0.007	Fraud	OK

TABLE 6.11
The Coincidence Matrix for Insurance Fraud Data Using Logistic Regression

Actual	Fraud	OK	Total
Fraud	1	0	1
OK	2	2	4
Totals	3	2	0.60

TABLE 6.12
Standardized Training Data Set— Insurance Claims

Case	Age	Gender	Claim	Tickets	Prior	Attorney	Outcome
1	1	1	0.6	1	0.5	0	0
2	0.9	1	0.64	1	1	1	0
4	0.8	0	0.24	1	0.5	1	0
5	0	1	0.88	0	0	0	0
7	0.9	1	0.46	1	1	1	0
9	0	0	0.74	1	1	1	0
10	0.3	1	0.48	0	1	1	0
Means 0	**0.557**	**0.714**	**0.577**	**0.714**	**0.714**	**0.714**	**0**
3	0.05	0	0	1	0	0	1
6	1	1	0.16	1	0	0	1
8	0.65	0	0.5	1	0.5	1	1
Means 1	**0.567**	**0.333**	**0.220**	**1**	**0.167**	**0.333**	**1**

The Estimate column gives the model β coefficients. This model can be applied to the test data set given in Table 4.11 by using the probability formula noted earlier. Calculations are shown in Table 6.10.

The coincidence matrix for this set of data is shown in Table 6.11.

In this case, the model identified the one actually fraudulent case, at the expense of overpredicting fraud.

Linear Discriminant Analysis

Discriminant analysis groups objects defined by a set of variables into a predetermined set of outcome classes. One example of this type of analysis is classification of employees by their rated performance within an organization. The bank loan example could be divided into past cases sorted by two distinct categories of repayment or default. The technical analysis is thus determining the combination of variables that best predict membership in one of the given output categories.

A number of methods can be used for discriminant analysis, including regression. For the two-group case, this would require a cutoff between groups, and if a new set of data yielded a functional value below the cutoff, the prediction would be that group; or conversely, if the value was above the cutoff, the prediction would be the other group. However, other techniques can be used for discriminant analysis.[1] A discriminant function can be used in binary data to separate observations into two groups, with a cutoff limit used to divide the observations. We demonstrate this concept with the Loan Data.

Discriminant Function for Loan Data

Using the discriminant function method will identify the mean of each group's measures on each variable. This vector of means is referred to as a centroid. We then will assign test and new application cases to that centroid with the minimum distance. Again, we'll use the sum of squared distances as our metric. In order to eliminate differences in scale, observations over each variable will be standardized to a zero–one range using the formulas applied in Table 5.1. Table 6.12 offers these values as organized by outcome groups (not fraudulent 0, fraudulent 1).

Applying this model involves calculating the sum of squared distances from the set of Means 0 and the set of Means 1, and then selecting the minimum sum. For instance, the least square distance of Case 1 from Means 0 is 0.916, while the distance to Means 1 is 0.999.

$$(1-0.557)^2 + (1-0.714)^2 + (0.6-0.577)^2 + (1-0.714)^2 + (0.5-0.714)^2 + (0-0.714)^2 = 0.916$$

$$(1-0.567)^2 + (1-0.333)^2 + (0.6-0.220)^2 + (1-1)^2 + (0.5-0.167)^2 + (0-0.333)^2 = 0.999$$

Thus, the model would infer that Case 1 belonged to set 0 (no fraud). Table 6.13 shows the results for the test cases.

TABLE 6.13 Discriminant Analysis Based on the OLS Distance to Centroids

Case	Age	Gender	Claim	Tickets	Prior	Atty	Outcome	Dist(0)	Dist(1)	Model
1	0.15	1	0.44	1	1	1	0	0.511	1.805	0
2	0.55	0	0.72	1	1	1	0	0.776	1.500	0
3	0.40	1	0.16	0	0	0	1	1.811	1.615	1
4	0	1	0.44	1	0.5	1	0	0.620	1.370	0
5	1	1	0.68	1	1	0	0	0.962	1.649	0

TABLE 6.14
The Coincidence
Matrix for
Insurance Fraud
Test Cases—
Squared Distance
Metric

Actual	Fraudulent	OK	Total
Fraudulent	1	0	1
OK	0	4	4
Total	1	4	1.0

In this case, the model was correct in all five cases, yielding the coincidence matrix in Table 6.14.

Application to the new cases initially given in Table 4.12 is shown in Table 6.15.

A linear discriminant function can also be obtained through regression over the training set. The regression over the data in Table 6.12 is shown in Table 6.16.

The discriminant function is 0.430 − 0.421 Age + 0.333 Gender − 0.648 Claim + 0.584 Tickets − 1.091 Prior Claims + 0.573 Attorney. The R Square of 0.64 looks fairly good, but the adjusted R Square is negative, indicating that too many variables were added to the model. Looking at the P-values based on t statistics indicates none of the variables are significant, another indication that too many variables were included (also indicated by the 95-percent confidence intervals for each beta coefficient spanning 0). However, this model was also based on very few observations, and our purpose is to demonstrate the method. To use the model, we need a cutoff. The discriminant function value for each of the 10 training cases is shown in Table 6.17.

The average functional value for the seven cases with 0 outcome was 0.106, while the average for the three cases with an outcome of 1 was 0.753. The cutoff can be the average of these two, or 0.429. If this discriminant function were applied to a new observation, and the functional value was below 0.429, the prediction would be an outcome of 0. Conversely, if the functional value for the new observation were above 0.429, the prediction would be an outcome of 1. Applying this discriminant function to the standardized test data in Table 5.6 resulted in the results shown in Table 6.18.

Table 6.19 shows the coincidence matrix for this model.

The model was correct in 0.6 of the cases.

Job Applicant Data

A nice feature of discriminant analysis is that it can be applied to any number of known outcomes. Table 6.20 gives a small database of normalized scores for personnel recruitment from Table 6.12 (based on coding from Table 5.1). The only

TABLE 6.15
Squared Distance to
the Centroid Model
Applied to
Insurance Fraud
New Cases

Case	Age	Gender	Claim	Tickets	Prior	Atty	Dist(0)	Dist(1)	Model
1	0.15	1	0.64	0.6	0.5	0	1.268	0.815	1
2	0.60	0	0.58	1	1	0	1.609	1.129	1
3	0	0	0.68	1	1	0	1.592	1.189	1
4	0	0	0.34	0	1	0	1.886	0.508	1
5	1	1	0.20	1	1	1	1.313	1.620	0
6	1	1	0.48	0.6	0.5	0	1.318	0.743	1
7	0.90	0	0.38	1	1	0	1.703	1.071	1
8	0.05	1	0.50	0.6	1	0	1.345	0.499	1
9	0	0	0.10	0.6	0	1	1.790	2.326	0
10	0.20	1	0.48	0.6	0.5	0	1.318	0.743	1

TABLE 6.16
Fraud Data
Discriminant
Function from
Regression

SUMMARY OUTPUT

Regression Statistics

Multiple R	0.804
R Square	0.647
Adj R Square	−0.059
Standard Error	0.497
Observations	10

ANOVA

	df	SS	MS	F	Significance F
Regression	6	1.358629	0.226438	0.916	0.578
Residual	3	0.741371	0.247124		
Total	9	2.1			

	Coefficients	Std Error	t Stat	P-value	Low 95%	Up 95%
Intercept	0.430	0.914	0.471	0.6701	−2.480	3.341
Age	−0.421	0.899	−0.468	0.6716	−3.283	2.441
Gender	0.333	0.891	0.374	0.7334	−2.504	3.170
Claim	−0.648	0.784	−0.827	0.4690	−3.144	1.848
Tickets	0.584	0.908	0.643	0.5660	−2.306	3.473
Prior Claims	−1.091	1.112	−0.982	0.3986	−4.629	2.446
Attorney	0.573	0.99987	0.573	0.6072	−2.610	3.755

TABLE 6.17
Discriminant
Function Scores for
Fraud Training Data

Case	1	2	3	4	5	6	7	8	9	10
Function	−0.008	0.035	0.993	0.549	0.193	0.823	0.151	0.443	0.015	−0.193
Outcome	0	0	1	0	0	1	0	1	0	0

TABLE 6.18
Discriminant
Function Results for
Fraud Test Data

Case	1	2	3	4	5
Function	0.480	−0.203	0.491	1.089	−0.606
Prediction	1	0	1	1	0
Outcome	0	0	1	0	0

TABLE 6.19
The Coincidence
Matrix for Insurance
Fraud Test Cases—
Discriminant
Function

Actual	Fraudulent	OK	Total
Fraudulent	1	0	1
OK	2	2	4
Total	3	2	0.6

TABLE 6.20
Personnel Applicant
Database—
Coded

Record	Age	State	Degree	Major	Experience	Outcome
1	0.233	1	0	0.9	0.4	Excellent
6	0.200	1	1	0.7	0.0	Excellent
2	0.433	0	1	0.7	1.0	Adequate
3	0.333	1	1	0.9	0.0	Adequate
7	0.167	1	0	0.9	0.6	Adequate
8	0.267	0	1	0.9	0.4	Adequate
10	0.133	1	0	1.0	0.2	Adequate
5	0.267	1	0	1.0	0.4	Minimal
9	0.167	1	0	1.0	0.4	Minimal
4	0.067	1	0	1.0	0.0	Unacceptable

TABLE 6.21
Centroid Averages for Job Application Data

	Age	State	Degree	Major	Experience
Excellent	0.217	1	0.5	0.8	0.20
Adequate	0.267	0.6	0.6	0.88	0.44
Minimal	0.217	1	0	1	0.40
Unacceptable	0.067	1	0	1	0

TABLE 6.22
Distance Calculations for Test Record 11 to Training Means for Excellent Group

Variable	Record 11	Record 11 Coded	Excellent Coded	Squared Distance
Age	36	0.533	0.217	0.100
State	CA	1	1	0
Degree	MS	1	0.5	0.25
Major	Information S	1.0	0.8	0.04
Experience	0	0	0.2	0.04
			Sum	0.43

TABLE 6.23
Centroid Distance Calculations for First Job Applicant Test Set Member

Variable	Case 11	Unacceptable	Minimal	Adequate	Excellent
Age	0.533	0.100	0.071	0.100	0.217
State	1.000	0	0.160	0	0
Degree	1.000	0.250	0.160	1	1
Major	1.000	0.040	0.014	0	0
Experience	0.000	0.040	0.194	0.160	0
Total		**0.430**	**0.599**	**1.260**	**1.217**

TABLE 6.24
The Coincidence Matrix for the Centroid Discriminant Model of Job Applicants

Actual	Unacceptable	Minimal	Adequate	Excellent	Total
Unacceptable			1		1
Minimal		1		1	2
Adequate		1			1
Excellent			1		1
Total	**0**	**2**	**2**	**1**	**5**

TABLE 6.25
Distance Calculations for Applicant 1

	Age	State	Degree	Major	Exp	Calculation	Distance
Applicant 1	0.267	1.0	1.0	0.9	0		
Excellent	0.217	1.0	0.5	0.80	0.2	0.0025 + 0 + 0.25 + 0.01 + 0.04	= 0.3025
Adequate	0.267	0.6	0.6	0.88	0.44	0 + 0.16 + 0.16 + 0.0004 + 0.194	= 0.5144
Minimal	0.217	1.0	0.0	1.00	0.40	0.0025 + 0 + 1 + 0.01 + 0.16	= 1.1725
Unacceptable	0.067	1.0	0.0	1.00	0.00	0.04 + 0 + 1 + 0.01 + 0	= 1.0500

TABLE 6.26 Squared Distance Calculations for Applicant 2

	Age	State	Degree	Major	Exp	Calculation	Distance
Applicant 2	0.2	0	0	0.90	0.6		
Excellent	0.217	1.0	0.5	0.80	0.2	0.0003 + 1 + 0.25 + 0.01 + 0.16	= 1.4203
Adequate	0.600	0.6	0.6	0.88	0.44	0.0045 + 0.36 + 0.36 + 0.0004 + 0.0256	= 0.7505
Minimal	0.217	1.0	0.0	1.00	0.40	0.0003 + 1 + 0 + 0.01 + 0.04	= 1.0503
Unacceptable	0.067	1.0	0.0	1.00	0.00	0.0177 + 1 + 0 + 0.01 + 0.36	= 1.3877

difference would be to measure the distance to the mean of variable values for each group rather than measuring the distance to each observation.

A simple clustering could be Adequate or better, versus Minimal or worse. In this case, as shown in Table 6.21, the first cluster would consist of the top seven records, and the second cluster would be the last three (original records 4, 5, and 9).

We can apply this model to the test set of applicants from Chapter 4. Record 11 was 36, from California, with a master's degree in information systems. This codes to an age value of 0.533. The squared distance to the Excellent group average is thus $(0.533 - 0.217)^2 = 0.100$. The ordinary least squares distances for Case 11 over each variable to the Excellent group are shown in Table 6.22.

The results for each of the test set members are shown in Table 6.23.

The minimum sum of squared distances in this case is to the Excellent group. Thus, the model predicts that this case will have an Excellent outcome (the actual outcome for Case 11 was Minimal). The coincidence matrix for the five test cases is given in Table 6.24.

In this case, the model got only one of the five records classified correctly. Thus, this model is not expected to do very well, although we will test it more thoroughly near the end of the chapter when we deal with the larger data set.

We can also apply the model to new applicants. Squared distance measures for two new applicants (the first two rows from Table 4.9) are given in Tables 6.25 and 6.26, respectively.

The first applicant is closest to the Excellent cluster, followed by the Adequate cluster. Thus, this would seem like a good prospect (keeping in mind the relatively poor fit of the model).

The second applicant is closest to the Adequate cluster, followed by the Minimal cluster.

Real Applications of Regression in Data Mining

The number of applications of these methods to business problems is manifold. Note that since most major data mining software products include both regression (linear and logistic) and neural networks (often with choices of different variants) as basic tools to select from, usually all available model forms are applied to a given set of data, and that form that seems to fit best is applied. We present only a few of many applications.

Stepwise Regression in Bankruptcy Prediction Models

One of the most important business applications of data mining is the prediction of bankruptcy by lenders. There are large datasets gathered on credit card operations, with many variables typically available. Stepwise regression is a procedure that uses the computer to select independent variables to include in a regression model. This is attractive when dealing with large numbers of variables. While it is ideally better to base variable selection on substantive expertise, there are limits to what humans can do, and having the computer build models more automatically is useful.

Stepwise regression begins with a forward selection of variables based on simple regressions, and selecting variables based on partial F statistics.[2] Variable significance is evaluated, and if significance is identified, the variable is added to the model, and the partial F statistics recalculated for the next iteration. Partial F statistics change as variables are added and deleted from the model. After adding a new variable, coefficients of previously added variables are rechecked, and if the significance of a variable is not present in the new model, that variable is eliminated. Once no variables outside of the model test are significant, the method stops.

Foster and Stine[3] studied the use of stepwise regression on a dataset of 244,000 credit card accounts over a twelve-month period. The dataset included a pool of 255 predictor variables, including lagged variables. The outcome was the binary result of 1 for bankruptcy and 0 otherwise. Interactions among variables are important in stepwise regression, and there were 66,430 interactions that were treated as independent variables, creating a very large number of candidate predictor variables. The dataset included a small proportion (about 1 percent) of defaults. Furthermore, the cost of error of granting a loan that turned out bad was roughly 100 times the cost of denying a loan that ultimately would be good.

Foster and Stine conducted a series of experiments to deal with their large dataset of credit card accounts. The data set was variables that were randomly divided into five groups, using 20 percent of the data set for training and retaining 80 percent for testing. They compared their stepwise regression model with decision tree models. They found that regression performed well on the basis of minimizing costs even though cost was not considered in building the model (while it would be in decision tree models). They also found that smaller sample sizes resulted in less accurate models, primarily due to the very small number of bankruptcies.

Application of Models to Larger Data Sets

For ordinary least squares regression, both SAS and Excel were used. Both obviously provide identical models. The only limitation we perceive to using Excel is that Excel regression is limited to 16 independent variables. Basic SAS has the ability to do ordinary least squares regression (so does Excel) and logistic regression.

Insurance Fraud Data

The first 4,000 observations of the data set were used for training. Standardized scores (between 0 and 1, as in Table 5.1) were used, although continuous data, or even categorical data, could have been used. Standardizing the data transforms it so that scale doesn't matter. There are reasons to do that, if different variables have radically different scales. Regression results should be identical between standardized and original data (standardized data is continuous, just like the original—it's just transformed). As a check, you could run against the original data and see if you get the same R Square and t statistics. The coefficients will be different and categorical data is transformed into a form where details are lost. You'll get different results between regressions over original continuous data and categorical data.

The Regression Discriminant Model

For the regression model over standardized data, the result is shown in Table 6.27.

Of course, the same model was obtained with SAS. Only the presence of an attorney (highly significant) and number of tickets on record (marginally significant) had any significance. The beta coefficients give the discriminant function. A cutoff value for this function is needed. We applied the model to the training set and then sorted the results. There were 60 fraudulent cases in the training set of

TABLE 6.27 OLS Regression Output—Insurance Fraud Data

SUMMARY OUTPUT					
Regression Statistics					
Multiple R	0.203298				
R Square	0.04133				
Adjusted R Square	0.03989				
Standard Error	0.119118				
Observations	4000				

ANOVA					
	df	SS	MS	F	Significance F
Regression	6	2.442607	0.407101	28.69096	8.81E-34
Residual	3993	56.65739	0.014189		
Total	3999	59.1			

	Coefficients	Standard Error	t Stat	P-value	Lower 95%	Upper 95%
Intercept	**0.0081**	0.012594	0.643158	0.520158	−0.01659	0.032792
Age	**0.001804**	0.005147	0.350421	0.726041	−0.00829	0.011894
Gender	**−0.00207**	0.003772	−0.54928	0.582843	−0.00947	0.005323
Claim	**0.007607**	0.0191	0.398289	0.690438	−0.02984	0.045054
Tickets	**−0.0076**	0.004451	−1.70738	**0.08783**	−0.01633	0.001127
Prior	**0.000148**	0.004174	0.035408	0.971756	−0.00804	0.008332
Atty	**0.201174**	0.018329	10.97554	**1.24E-27**	0.165238	0.237109

4,000 observations. Therefore, a logical cutoff would be the 60th-largest functional value in this training set. The 60th-largest model value was 0.196197. The cutoff for prediction of 0.19615 was used. This yielded the coincidence matrix shown in Table 6.28.

This model had a correct classification rate of 0.966, which is very good. The model applied to the test data predicted 22 fraudulent cases, and 978 not fraudulent. Of the 22 test cases that the model predicted to be fraudulent, five actually were. Therefore, the model would have triggered an investigation of 17 cases in the test set that were not actually fraudulent. Of the 978 test cases that the model predicted to be OK, 17 were actually fraudulent, and would not have been investigated. If the cost of an investigation were $500, and the cost of loss were $2,500, this would have an expected cost of $500 × 17 + $2,500 × 17, or $51,000.

The Centroid Discriminant Model

We can compare the preceding model with a centroid discriminant model. The training set is used to identify the mean variable values for the two outcomes (Fraud and OK) shown in Table 6.29.

The squared distance to each of these clusters was applied on the 1,000 test observations, yielding the coincidence matrix shown in Table 6.30.

TABLE 6.28
Coincidence
Matrix—OLS
Regression of
Insurance Fraud
Test Data

Actual	Model Fraud	Model OK	Total
Fraud	5	17	22
OK	17	961	978
Totals	22	978	1000

TABLE 6.29
Centroid Discriminant Function Means

Cluster	Age	Gender	Claim	Tickets	Prior	Attorney
OK	0.671	0.497	0.606	0.068	0.090	0.012
Fraud	0.654	0.467	0.540	0.025	0.275	0.217

TABLE 6.30
Coincidence Matrix—Centroid Discriminant Model of Insurance Fraud Test Data

Actual	Model Fraud	Model OK	Total
Fraud	7	15	22
OK	133	845	978
Totals	140	860	1000

TABLE 6.31
The Logistic Regression Model—Insurance Fraud Data

Parameter	DF	Estimate	Std. Error	Chi-Square	Pr > ChiSq
Intercept	1	−2.9821	0.7155	17.3702	<0.0001
Age	1	0.1081	0.3597	0.0903	0.7637
Claim	1	0.3219	1.2468	0.0667	0.7962
Tickets	1	−0.8535	0.5291	2.6028	0.1067
Prior	1	0.0033	0.3290	0.0001	0.9920
Gender 0	1	0.0764	0.1338	0.3260	0.5680
Atty 0	1	−1.6429	0.4107	15.9989	<0.0001

TABLE 6.32
Coincidence Matrix—Logistic Regression of Insurance Fraud Data

Actual	Model Fraud	Model OK	Total
Fraud	5	17	22
OK	16	962	978
Totals	21	979	1000

TABLE 6.33
Average Transformed Variable Values for Job Applicant Data

	Age	State	Degree	Major	Experience
Unacceptable	0.156322	0.137931	0.241379	0.186207	0.475862
Minimal	0.232068	0.303797	0.594937	0.517722	0.772152
Adequate	0.292346	0.237037	0.707407	0.833333	0.903704
Excellent	0.338095	0.285714	0.571429	0.985714	0.942857

TABLE 6.34 Calculation of Squared Distances

Average	Age	State	Degree	Major	Experience	Total
Unaccept	$(0.267 - 0.156)^2$	$(0 - 0.138)^2$	$(0 - 0.241)^2$	$(0 - 0.186)^2$	$(1 - 0.476)^2$	
	0.012176	0.019025	0.058264	0.034673	0.274721	0.398859
Minimal	$(0.267 - 0.232)^2$	$(0 - 0.304)^2$	$(0 - 0.594)^2$	$(0 - 0.518)^2$	$(1 - 0.772)^2$	
	0.001197	0.092293	0.35395	0.268036	0.051915	0.76739
Adequate	$(0.267 - 0.292)^2$	$(0 - 0.237)^2$	$(0 - 0.707)^2$	$(0 - 0.833)^2$	$(1 - 0.904)^2$	
	0.000659	0.056187	0.500425	0.694444	0.009273	1.260989
Excellent	$(0.267 - 0.338)^2$	$(0 - 0.286)^2$	$(0 - 0.571)^2$	$(0 - 0.986)^2$	$(1 - 0.943)^2$	
	0.005102	0.081633	0.326531	0.971633	0.003265	1.388163

Here, the correct classification rate was 0.852—quite a bit lower than with the regression model. The model had many errors where applicants who turned out to be OK were denied loans. There were also two fewer cases where applicants who turned out bad were approved for loans. The cost of error here is $500 \times 133 + \$2,500 \times 15$, or $104,000.

The Logistic Regression Model

A logistic regression model was run on SAS. The variables gender and attorney were 0–1 variables, and thus categorical. The model, based on maximum likelihood estimates, is shown in Table 6.31.

The output obtained was all between 0 and 1, but the maximum was 0.060848. The division between the 60th- and 61st-largest training values was 0.028. Using this cutoff, the coincidence matrix shown in Table 6.32 was obtained.

The correct classification rate is up very slightly, to 0.967. The cost of error here is $500 \times 16 + \$2,500 \times 17$, or $50,500.

Job Applicant Data

The Job Applicant Data set involves 500 cases. Since there are four distinct outcomes, discriminant analysis is appropriate. (Cluster analysis might have been appropriate to identify these four outcomes in the first place.) We will use 250 for training, and test on the remaining 250. Excel turns out to be very easy to use for distance calculation. The first–step is to convert data to a zero-one scale.

Age	< 20	0
	20–50	(Age–20)/30
	> 50	1.0
State	CA	1.0
	Rest	0
Degree	Cert	0
	UG	0.5
	Rest	1.0
Major	IS	1.0
	Csci, Engr, Sci	0.9
	BusAd	0.7
	Other	0.5
	None	0
Experience	Max	Years/5

In Excel, we place the outcome variable to the left of the four columns with the converted data so that we can sort the 250 training observations on outcome. This simplifies the calculation of averages for each of the four variables by each of the four outcomes. Table 6.33 provides that information.

The distance of each of the 250 test observations was measured to these averages using the squared distance metric. Observation 251 was a 28-year-old applicant from Utah with a professional certification (no major) and six years of experience (outcome minimal). First, the data needs to be transformed. Age 28 is eight years above the minimum, yielding a transformed value of 0.267. The transformed State value is 0, the transformed Degree value is 0, and the transformed Major is 0. Experience of six years transforms to a value of 1.0. The distance calculation is shown in Table 6.34.

The minimum sum of squared distances was to the unacceptable group. Here, the minimum distance is to the unacceptable average. Table 6.35 shows the coincidence matrix for all 250 test cases.

TABLE 6.35
The Coincidence Matrix for the Job Applicant Matching Model Using Squared Error Distance

Actual	Unacceptable	Minimal	Adequate	Excellent	Total
Unacceptable	19	5	6	0	30
Minimal	28	14	33	1	76
Adequate	2	16	73	37	128
Excellent	0	0	3	13	16
Total	49	35	115	51	250

TABLE 6.36
The Coincidence Matrix for the Regression Model of Loan Application Data

	Model Fraud	Model OT	Total
Actual Late	8	12	20
Actual OT	18	212	230
Totals	26	224	250

TABLE 6.37
The Logistic Regression Model for Loan Applicant Data

Parameter	Category	Estimate	Chi-Square	Pr>ChiSq
Intercept		2.0909	13.1026	0.0003
Age	Middle	0.6186	1.5904	0.2073
Age	Old	−0.8939	1.0538	0.3046
Income	Average	−0.2897	0.6358	0.4252
Income	High	1.1789	4.4098	0.0357
Risk	Average	0.4902	0.3986	0.5278
Risk	High	−1.0750	4.5589	0.0327
Credit	Amber	−0.5198	2.7202	0.0991
Credit	Green	1.4185	16.7962	<0.0001

TABLE 6.38
Coincidence Matrix—Loan Applicant Training Data, Logistic Regression

Actual	Model Fraud	Model OK	Total
Fraud	9	0	9
OK	25	216	241
Totals	34	216	250

This metric correctly classified 119 out of 250 chances, for a correct classification rate of 0.476. It was quite good at predicting the extreme cases.

Loan Applicant Data

Clementine was used to build a continuous regression model over the training set of the first 400 observations. This yielded the following model:

Pred = 0.5527 + 0.1138 Age + 0.2073 Credit + .08547 Income + 0.1355 Risk

The credit variable was highly significant, although the probability measure of significance for Risk was only 0.065, for Income 0.247, and for Age 0.263. Overall, model r-squared was 0.125. Of the 400 training observations, 45 were 0 (not on-time) and 355 were 1 (on-time repayment). The model was applied in Excel to the training data, and the model results sorted. The 45th-smallest observations were all below 0.251, which was used as a cutoff. The model was then applied (in Excel) to the 250 training cases, using the cutoff to predict. The results are shown in Table 6.36.

The model had a correct classification rate of 0.88—fairly good. The model was not very good at predicting late payment cases, however (it was correct only 40 percent of the time).

A logistic regression model was obtained through SAS using a training set of 250 observations of categorical data. Each of the four variables had the three categories described earlier. The SAS model for this data is shown in Table 6.37.

The output indicates that green credit rating is an extremely effective predictor, while high income and high risk (negatively) also are very significant. Amber credit rating is slightly significant in a negative way.

In order to use this model, we need to know a cutoff for observation scores. The training data was sorted by model score, with 29 negative observations in this training set. The 29th-smallest model score was 0.7262 (shared by 12 observations, because the categorical data consists of only 81 discrete combinations of variable values). Applying this model to the 250 remaining observations, we obtained the coincidence matrix shown in Table 6.38.

Thus, this model had a correct classification rate of 0.90. There was a heavy skew toward calling all cases OK, but all 9 of the 25 cases that were actually fraudulent were correctly classified.

Summary

Regression models have been widely used in classical modeling. They continue to be very useful in data mining environments, which differ primarily in the scale of observations and number of variables used. Classical regression (usually ordinary least squares) can be applied to continuous data. If the output variable (or input variables) are categorical, logistic regression can be applied. Regression can also be applied to identify a discriminant function, separating observations into groups. If this is done, cutoff limits to separate observations based upon discriminant function scores need to be identified. While discriminant analysis can be applied to multiple groups, it is much more complicated if there are more than two groups. Thus, other discriminant methods, such as the centroid method demonstrated in this chapter, are often used.

Regression can be applied by conventional software such as SAS, SPSS, or Excel. Additionally, there are many refinements to regression that can be accessed, such as stepwise linear regression, which is the algorithm used in PolyAnalyst. Stepwise regression uses partial correlations to select entering independent variables iteratively, providing some degree of automatic machine development of a regression model, but it has its proponents and opponents.

Glossary

analysis of variance (ANOVA) Analysis of model error (specifically, differences among group means).

discriminant analysis Identifies which category an observation most likely belongs to.

linear discriminant analysis Discriminant analysis based on a discriminant function identified through linear regression.

logistic regression Regression based on probability of membership in one of two or more groups.

neural network Artificial intelligence model based on fitting data with a network of arcs using weights adjusted to optimize the fit.

regression Mathematical model to fit data based on the minimization of one of many possible error metrics.

sum of squared errors (SSE) Model error squared and added.

time series Data set of a variable measured over time.

Exercises

1. Apply the regression algorithm to the Job Applicant data file. Use the first 400 observations as the training set, and apply it to the last 100 observations. Employ the scoring scheme described for Table 6.14. If data mining software is available, compare regression, logistic regression, and neural network output. Use data mining software if available, or Excel if not. Develop the coincidence matrix for this data.

2. If data mining software is available, compare regression and logistic regression (coding the output variable into the four given categories) models to the Job Applicant data file. Use the first 400 observations as the training set, and the last 100 observations for testing. Compare the coincidence matrices for this data.

3. Apply the ordinary regression algorithm to the Loan Application data set. Use the first 500 observations as the training set, and apply it to the last 100 observations. Employ data mining software if available, or Excel if not. Develop the coincidence matrix.

4. If data mining software is available, compare ordinary regression and logistic regression (using binary codes for results) models to the Loan Application data file. Employ the first 500 observations as the training set, and apply it to the last 100 observations. Use data mining software if available, or Excel if not. Develop the coincidence matrix. Compare the coincidence matrices for this data with the results from problem 3.

5. Apply the linear regression algorithm to the Insurance Fraud data set. Transform age by making 20 (or younger) = 0, 50 (or older) 1.0, and every age between = age/30. Leave gender as is (0 or 1). Transform claim by dividing claim by 5,000. Transform tickets and prior claims by making 0 = 0, 1 = 0.5, and 2 or more = 1.0. Transform attorney by making "none" = 0 and all others = 1. Use the first 1,000 observations as the training set, and apply it to test the last 1,000 observations. Use data mining software if available, or Excel if not. Develop the coincidence matrix.

6. If data mining software is available, compare regression and logistic regression (coding output to 0 and 1) models to the Insurance Fraud data file. Use the first 1,000 observations as the training set, and apply it to test the last 1,000 observations. Use data mining software if available, or Excel if not. Develop the coincidence matrix. Compare the coincidence matrices for this data with the results from problem 5.

7. Apply the logistic regression algorithm to the Customer Expenditure data set with the intent of identifying the type of people who spend the following portion of their income on restaurants: less than 1 percent, between 1 and 5 percent, 5 to 10 percent, and over 10 percent. Use the first 12 variables (age through churn) in standardized form. Employ 5,000 observations as the training set, and apply it to 1,000 test observations. Use data mining software if available. Develop the coincidence matrix.

8. Using the Expenditure Data file, apply a logistic regression model identifying the type of people who spend the following portion of their income on groceries: less than 1 percent, between 1 and 5 percent, 5 to 10 percent, and over 10 percent. Use standardized data for the first 12 variables (age through churn) as independent variables. Employ 5,000 observations as the training set, and apply it to 1,000 test observations. Use data mining software if available. Develop the coincidence matrix.

9. Using the Expenditure Data file, apply a logistic regression model identifying the type of people who spend the following portion of their income on housing: less than 10 percent, between 10 and 30 percent, 30 to 50 percent, and over 50 percent. Use standardized data for the first 12 variables (age through churn) as independent variables. Employ 5,000 observations as the training set, and apply it to 1,000 test observations. Use data mining software if available. Develop the coincidence matrix.

10. Using the Expenditure Data file, apply a logistic regression model identifying the type of people who spend the following portion of their income on utilities: less than 1 percent, between 1 and 5 percent, 5 to 10 percent, and over 10 percent. Use standardized data for the first 12 variables (age through churn) as independent variables. Employ 5,000 observations as the training set, and apply it to 1,000 test observations. Use data mining software if available. Develop the coincidence matrix.

11. Using the Expenditure Data file, apply a logistic regression model identifying the type of people who spend the following portion of their income on owning and operating automobiles: less than 1 percent, between 1 and 5 percent, 5 to 10 percent, and over 10 percent. Use standardized data for the first 12 variables (age through churn) as independent variables. Employ 5,000 observations as the training set, and apply it to 1,000 test observations. Use data mining software if available. Develop the coincidence matrix.

12. Using the Expenditure Data file, apply a logistic regression model identifying the type of people who spend the following portion of their income on clothing: less than 5 percent, between 5 and 10 percent, 10 to 20 percent, and over 20 percent. Use standardized data for the first 12 variables (age through churn) as independent variables. Employ 5,000 observations as the training set, and apply it to 1,000 test observations. Use data mining software if available. Develop the coincidence matrix.

13. Using the Expenditure Data file, apply a logistic regression model identifying the type of people who spend the following portion of their income on entertainment: less than 1 percent, between 1 and 5 percent, 5 to 10 percent, and over 10 percent. Use standardized data for the first 12 variables (age through churn) as independent variables. Use 5,000 observations as the training set, and apply it to 1,000 test observations. Use data mining software if available. Develop the coincidence matrix.

Endnotes

1. T. Dielman, *Applied Regression Analysis for Business and Economics*, 3rd ed., Duxbury, 2001, pp. 563–570.

2. Ibid.

3. D. P. Foster and R. A. Stine, "Variable Selection in Data Mining: Building a Predictive Model for Bankruptcy," *Journal of the American Statistical Association*, volume 99, number 466, 2004, pp. 303–313.

CHAPTER SEVEN

Neural Networks in Data Mining

This chapter:

Describes neural networks as used in data mining

Reviews real applications of each model

Shows the application of models to larger data sets

Commercial banks provide funds to businesses. This loan market involves some risk, probably more risk than is found in personal banking, because by no means do all business ventures turn out to be profitable.

As with many similar business data mining applications, the ability to predict customer success would make decision making a lot easier. While perfect prediction models cannot be expected, there are a number of data mining techniques that can improve predictive ability. Neural network models are applied to data that can be analyzed by alternative models. The normal data mining process is to try all alternative models and see which works best for a specific type of data over time. But there are some types of data where neural network models usually outperform alternatives, such as regression or decision trees. Neural networks tend to work better when there are complicated relationships in the data, such as high degrees of nonlinearity. Thus, they tend to be viable models in problem domains where there are high levels of unpredictability. Commercial banking is one such area.

Neural networks can be applied to a variety of data types. One of the early applications of neural networks was in deciphering letters of the alphabet in character recognition. This involved 26 different letters and a finite number of outcomes (but much more than two). Many business prediction problems involve more than two outcomes, such as categories of employee performance. Often, however, two outcome categories will do nicely, such as on-time repayments or late payments. Neural networks can deal with either continuous data input or categorical data input, making them flexible models that are applicable to a number of data mining applications. The same is true of regression models and decision trees, all three of which support the data mining process of modeling.

Neural networks are the most widely used method in data mining. They are computer programs that take previously observed cases and use them to build a system of relationships within a network of nodes connected by arcs. Figure 7.1 shows a simple sketch of a neural network.

The idea of neural networks was derived from how neurons operate in the brain. Real neurons are connected to each other, and accept electrical charges across synapses (small gaps between neurons). They in turn pass on an electrical charge to other neighboring neurons. The relationship between real neural systems and artificial neural networks probably ends at that point. Human brains

FIGURE 7.1
Simple Neural Network

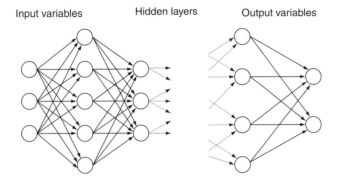

Input variables   Hidden layers   Output variables

contain billions of synaptic connections, each of which contributes only a tiny bit to the overall transformation of electrical synapses that encode knowledge.[1] This provides a tremendous amount of storage capacity, and makes the loss of a few thousand synaptic connections (due to minor damage or cell death) immaterial. Artificial **neural networks** are usually arranged in at least three layers, and have a defined and constant structure that is capable of reflecting complex nonlinear relationships, although they do not have anything near the capacity of the human brain. Each variable of input data (akin to independent variables in regression analysis) have a node in the first layer. The last layer represents output. For classification neural network models, this output layer has one node for each classification category (in the simplest case, output such as the prediction of system success is either true or false). Neural networks almost always have at least one middle (hidden) layer of nodes that add complexity to the model. (Two layer neural networks have not proven to be very successful.)

Each node is connected by an arc to nodes in the next layer. These arcs have weights, which are multiplied by the value of incoming nodes and summed. The input node values are determined by variable values in the data set. Middle layer node values are the sum of incoming node values multiplied by the arc weights. These middle node values in turn are multiplied by the outgoing arc weights to successor nodes. Neural networks "learn" through feedback loops. For a given input, the output for starting weights is calculated. Output is compared to target values, and the difference between attained and target output is fed back to the system to adjust the weights on arcs.

This process is repeated until the network correctly classifies the proportion of learning data specified by the user (tolerance level). Ultimately, a set of weights might be encountered that explain the learning (training) data set very well. The better the fit that is specified, the longer the neural network will take to train, although there is really no way to accurately predict how long a specific model will take to learn. The resulting set of weights from a model that satisfies the set tolerance level is retained within the system for application to future data.

Neural Networks

These programs can be used to apply learned experience to new cases, for decisions, classifications, and forecasts. Because they can take data sets with many inputs and relate them to a set of categorical outputs, they require little modeling. This is not to say that they are simply a black box into which the data miner can throw data and expect good output. Sarle (1994) stated that multilayer perceptrons, the most commonly used artificial neural networks, are nothing more than nonlinear regression and discriminant models.[2] Smith and Gupta (2000) call neural networks function approximation tools which learn the relationship between independent and dependent variables, similar to regression in that respect.[3] However, neural networks have relative advantages in that they make no assumptions about data properties or statistical distributions. They also tend to be more accurate when dealing with complex data patterns, such as nonlinear relationships.

There is modeling required when using neural networks in the sense of input variable selection, to include manipulation of input data, as well as the selection of neural network parameters, such as the number of hidden layers used. But computer software can perform complex calculations, applying nonlinear regression to relate inputs to output.

There are many neural network models. About 95 percent of business applications were reported to use **multilayered feedforward neural networks** with the **backpropogation** learning rule.[4] This model supports prediction and classification when fed inputs and known outputs. Backpropogation is a supervised learning technique in that it uses a training set to fit relationships (or learn). This model uses one or more hidden layers of neurons between inputs and outputs. Each element in each layer is connected to all elements of the next layer, and each connecting arc has a weight which is adjusted until the rate of explanation is at, or above, a prescribed level of accuracy. The hidden layers provide a means to reflect nonlinearities quite well relative to regression models. The neural network model is computationally intensive.

Many business applications do not have as much data as would be ideal. In such situations, neural network software products take over at this point. Backpropogation is a means to explore the vector space of its hidden nodes and to find effective linear or nonlinear transformations.[5] Philosophers in artificial intelligence view this feature as a potential means for artificial neural network models to learn, by recognizing a complex set of weights that we never could have identified *a priori*.

While multilayered feedforward neural networks are analogous to regression and discriminant analysis in dealing with cases where training data is available, **self-organizing neural networks** are analogous to clustering techniques used when there is no training data. The intent is to classify data to maximize the similarity of patterns within clusters while minimizing the similarity to patterns of different clusters. Kohonen self-organizing feature maps were developed to detect strong features of large data sets.[6]

An Example Neural Network Application

Assume a savings and loan institution has a lot of credit applications to process for approval. This decision is repetitive and time consuming, and every attempt should be made to make the decision in a manner that is fair to the applicant, while reducing the risk of default to the lender. The overall process of applying a neural network was given by Klimasauskas (1991).[7] We will use that outline of the process with this example.

1. *Collect data:* All data pertinent to the decision that is available is collected. This includes sex, marital status, number of dependent children, occupation, monthly income, monthly expenses, home ownership, checking account, savings account, credit cards held, and the history of payments on all loans over the last 12 months. Data categories need to be screened so that only legitimate variables are considered.

2. *Separate data into training and test sets:* The data set needs to be split into two important parts. A portion of the data is used for the neural network to "learn" on. This is the data for which arc weights on input arcs and weights on arcs from middle layer nodes to output nodes are adjusted until they match output variable values with sufficient accuracy. The learning set should ideally have at least 100 observations, although this quantity of data may not always be available.

Another portion of the data needs to be saved as a test set. This test set should be large enough to give valid inferences about how well the neural network learned. A test set size of at least 100 would be appropriate, although statistical sampling is often based on 50, or even 30, observations.

3. *Transform the data into network appropriate inputs:* Neural networks require numeric data. If the data is qualitative originally, such as marital status or occupation, it needs to be converted to some code (assigning a number to each group, with the number not necessarily implying any order). The downside to this is that results can be very sensitive to coding. Fortunately, data mining software does this internally, so that the user does not have to get involved with transformation. For the purpose of orientation, we demonstrate how coding could be done.

For categorical input data, such as marital status, each category can be assigned a particular value, such as single = 1, married = 2, widowed = 3, and divorced = 4. Each of these categories is assigned an input variable, with possible values of 0 or 1 (1 if that variable matches the group, 0 if not). Only one of the four input variables would have a value of 1 for a particular observation.

For variables such as occupation, the same approach is used, although occupations need to be grouped into a reasonably small number of categories. For variables with yes/no answers, observations with yes can be assigned values of 1, and no can be assigned values of 0.

Numerical data should be scaled to a 0–1 range. Things like monthly income and expenses can be divided by some maximum amount, or could be converted into ranges, each with an assigned score.

4. *Select, train, and test the network:* A number of optional network configurations can be used, depending upon neural network software. Options include the number of middle layer nodes (and possibly even the number of middle layers), transfer functions, and learning algorithms. Too many middle layer nodes result in the neural network memorizing the input data, without learning a generalizable pattern for the accurate analysis of new data. Too few middle layer nodes require more training time, and result in less accurate models. Usually the best place to start is the documentation for the neural network software you use, which should explain the options available to you. Most will default to a reasonable selection.

There are also a number of parameters to set for each problem. The number of inputs is a function of the data, akin to independent variables in a regression model, expanded some by the use of 0–1 variables to depict categorical input as described earlier. The number of output variables equals the possible dependent variable categories. The tolerance for learning can often be set. A very high rate of the learning set that is to be correctly classified may cause the network to take a very long time to learn. On the other hand, a relatively low tolerance level will learn quickly, but not be very useful. One approach is to start with a very high value, and if it takes longer than you have to wait, lower it a bit and start over. If you are in a hurry, it's best to set a slightly lower tolerance level.

Once the neural network has correctly classified the learning set to at least the prescribed tolerance, it can be tested on the part of the data set withheld for this purpose. If the model performs less accurately than desired, new data can be added in the form of extra variables and/or extra observations. Some variables that are thought to be marginally important could be deleted, although deleting variables will not generally improve the fit.

Steps 1 through 4 are repeated as needed, until the prescribed tolerance level has been attained.

5. *Apply the neural network model:* Once a model successfully classifies the desired portion of the test data set, it can be used on the real problem. It would be wise to monitor the success rate of the model on real data, and if this performance is less than desired, a new model might be called for.

Neural Networks in Data Mining

Artificial neural networks are the most common form of data mining model. They are extremely attractive because they can be fed data without a starting model estimation. This does not mean that they are best applied by automatically letting them operate on the data without model design. However, they are capable of going a long way toward the idea of the computer generating its own predictive model.

Neural network applications span most data mining activity, except for rule-based systems that are applied when an explanation of model results is emphasized, and the more exploratory data mining operations of market-basket analysis. One of the many neural network applications is fraud control. In health care,[8] the automobile insurance,[9] and other places, people continually try to outwit the insurance system. Neural network analysis to credit card use is a classical data mining application (including bank loans, home loans, automobile loans, and many other variants).[10] Neural networks have also been applied to stock market trading, electricity trading, and many other transactional environments. A common theme is to classify a new case for which multiple measures are available into a finite set of classes, such as on-time repayment, late repayment, or default.

Artificial neural networks operate much like regression models except that they try many different coefficient values to fit the training set of data until they obtain a fit as good as the modeler specifies. Artificial neural network models have the added benefit of considering variable interactions, giving it the ability to estimate training data contingent upon other independent variable values. (This could also be done with regression, but would lead to a tremendous amount of computational effort.)

Business Applications of Neural Networks

Neural networks are a fundamental modeling tool for prediction in data mining. Therefore, they are widely used, but usually in conjunction with other prediction models, especially various forms of regression described in Chapter 6. Here we present two specific applications of neural networks in data mining that involve classical business applications of data mining.

Neural Network Models for Bankruptcy Prediction

Analysis of company financial stability has long been a key issue in accounting. Monitoring the financial performance of the firm is very useful in identifying internal problems, investment evaluation, and auditing. A common approach is to try to predict firm bankruptcies employing multivariate discriminant analysis that uses a number of financial ratios. Discriminant analysis classifies objects into distinct groups on the basis of a linear function. This approach assumes that discriminating variables are jointly multivariate normal in distribution, an assumption not always accurate in practice.

Neural network models have been successfully applied to a number of business decisions, including evaluation of loan applications, mortgage applicant solvency, credit card fraud prevention, and the validation of bank signatures. Wilson and Sharda developed a neural network model to predict bankruptcy and compare its performance with discriminant analysis.[11]

The neural network model was fed the same data as a published multivariate discriminant analysis study that used five financial ratios. These ratios were working capital/total assets, retained earnings/total assets, earnings before interest and taxes/total assets, market value of equity/total debt, and sales/total assets. Data was gathered for these ratios on firms in operation or bankrupt over the period 1975 through 1982, taken from *Moody's Industrial Manuals*. There were 129 firms in this data set, including 65 that went bankrupt during the period. The prediction of bankruptcy was to be made about one year in advance of the event.

In order to test the accuracy of the discriminant analysis model and the neural network, the data set was divided into two parts. The first part of the data was used for developing the models, and the second part was used to test the models. This operation was repeated, using sampling methods to assign the 129 observations into either the first or second set. The proportion of bankrupt to nonbankrupt cases was controlled for both sets. A total of 180 distinct training and testing data set pairs were generated from the original data. Firms were not allowed to be included in both sets for the same test.

For each of the 180 data set pairs, the training set was used to develop the models. SYSTAT was used for discriminant analysis. BRAINMAKER was used for the neural network model. For each network trained in the study, five input neurons (one for each variable), 10 middle layer neurons, and two output neurons (one for each output classification) were used. A heuristic backpropogation algorithm was used to ensure convergence. All firms in each of the 180 training sets were classified correctly.

The holdout part of each data set was used to test the accuracy of the discriminant analysis and neural network models. Three treatments were applied, reflecting different ratios of bankrupt to nonbankrupt data for each of the two data set parts. In each of the nine combinations of these ratios, the neural network model had a superior correct classification rate to the discriminant analysis model. These differences were significant at the 0.05 error level in seven of the nine combinations.

Data Mining to Target Customers

Customer relationship management (CRM) is a major focal point of modern marketing. The aim of CRM is to develop and retain profitable customers. Data mining is a valuable tool in support of CRM, identifying which customers to target based upon the anticipated future value to the firm.

Drew et al. (2001) analyzed alternative methods to estimate a customer's hazard function (their likelihood to leave the company, or churn).[12] These methods provided management with measures of Gain in Lifetime Value (GLTV), an extension of traditional lifetime value. Traditional lifetime value weights monthly revenues by the probability that a customer will not leave, subtracting company costs. GLTV quantified the potential financial effects of company actions to retain customers for future business. Data mining provided a clearer understanding of customer relationships and allowed the segmentation of customer populations.

A neural network model was applied to estimate hazard functions for individual customers. The standard technique for this purpose has been classical proportional hazards regression, but that method was difficult to apply in this case. Neural network models provided a means to produce better estimates of hazards and customer retention. Retention was modeled with numeric customer tenure data and a binary service termination variable.

Neural network models involve high levels of instability. If new conditions were imposed, such as promotions, neural network models would change substantially. There was a need for traditional statistical models to baseline hazards and obtain models for longitudinal analysis.

Data was obtained from the cellular telephone division of a major U.S. telecommunications corporation. Their data warehouse contained billing, usage, and demographic information on customers. The warehouse was updated monthly with summary information, including the identities of canceling customers. Five types of data were extracted:

1. Billing data, including previous balance, access charges, minutes used, toll charges, roaming charges, and optional features.
2. Usage data, including the number of calls, and minutes used pertaining to local, toll, peak, and off-peak categories.
3. Subscription data, including the number of months in service, the rate plan, contract type, date, and duration.
4. Churn data, a flag indicating if the customer had canceled service.
5. Other data, including age, current and historical profitability to the firm, and optional features.

A sample of about 21,500 subscribers for April 1998 was used to model tenure for 1 to 36 months. The model were developed using 15,000 of these samples. The remainder of the samples was used as a holdout sample. Neural network models were found to provide superior modeling of customer tenure to classical statistical models.

Early applications of neural networks to business focused on classification, with categorical output (usually binary). This example provides a method extending the use of neural networks to support an important class of business problem, providing rank ordering of alternatives.

Application of Neural Networks to Larger Data Sets

For ordinary least squares regression, both SAS and Excel were used. Both obviously provide identical models. The only limitation we perceive to using Excel is that Excel regression is limited to 16 independent variables. Basic SAS has the ability to do ordinary least squares regression (so does Excel) and logistic regression.

Insurance Fraud Data

Standardized scores (between 0 and 1) were used, although continuous data, or even categorical data, could have been used. Standardizing the data transforms it so that scale doesn't matter. There are reasons to do that, if different variables have radically different scales. Regression results should be identical between standardized and

TABLE 7.1
Coincidence
Matrix—Test Data,
Neural Network,
5,000 Epochs

Actual	Model Fraud	Model OK	Total
Fraud	13	9	22
OK	1546	3311	4857
Totals	1559	3320	4879

original data (standardized data is continuous, just like the original—it is just transformed). As a check, you could run it against the original data, and see if you get the same R Square and t statistics. The coefficients will be different, and categorical data will be changed into a form where details are lost. You will thus get different results between regressions over original continuous data and categorical data.

This data was also solved with the Matlab Neural Network Toolkit, using a backpropogation algorithm. Two runs were made: one with 5,000 epochs, the second with 20,000 epochs. In an effort to obtain a better fit, 60 cases of no fraud and 60 cases of fraud were used for training. The training data had a fairly good fit, with balanced errors, and a correct classification rate of $109/120 = 0.91$. Test data results are shown in Table 7.1. This model correctly classified 59 percent of the fraudulent cases, and 68 percent of the OK cases, for an overall correct classification rate of 68 percent (the overwhelming number of cases were OK).

When the number of neural network epochs was increased to 20,000, the training model fit better, with a correct classification rate of $113/120 = 94$ percent. However, the fit on the test data was worse, as shown in Table 7.2.

Here, the majority of actually fraudulent cases were misclassified, while 44 percent of the OK cases were identified as fraudulent. Increasing the number of epochs did not improve the model.

The Clementine neural network model, using 4,000 training observations on continuous age, claim amount, gender, tickets, and prior claims, with categorical data for attorney and binary outcomes, took the easy way out and classified all cases as fraudulent. Thus, it was 0.978 accurate, although it missed all the actual fraudulent cases. This demonstrates the value of balancing data (which can be done in Clementine as well).

Job Applicant Data

The job application data can be coded as in Table 5.1, providing continuous variable values from 0 to 1 for the five independent variables. There are four output values, which do not have a continuous value function available. We used the first 400 observations for training, and tested the model on the last 100 observations.

The Matlab backpropogation neural network tool was also applied to this data. The training set included 90 percent of the observations. The neural network algorithm was run for 20,000 epochs. The correct classification rate of the training model was 77 percent. Test results are shown in Table 7.3.

Here, the model correctly classified 12 of the 40 test cases for a correct classification rate of 0.30. However, this is with four possible outcomes, and thus is not as bad as 30 percent would be when there were only two outcomes.

TABLE 7.2
Coincidence
Matrix—Test Data,
Neural Network,
20,000 Epochs

Actual	Model Fraud	Model OK	Total
Fraud	10	12	22
OK	2145	2712	4857
Totals	2155	2724	4879

TABLE 7.3
Coincidence Matrix
for Matlab Neural
Net Applied to Job
Applicant Data

	Unacceptable	Minimal	Adequate	Excellent	Totals
Actual unacceptable	3	7	3	0	13
Actual minimal	4	3	9	1	17
Actual adequate	1	1	6	0	8
Actual excellent	2	0	0	0	2
Totals	10	11	18	1	50

TABLE 7.4
Coincidence Matrix
for Clementine
Neural Net Applied
to Job Applicant
Data

	Unacceptable	Minimal	Adequate	Excellent	Totals
Actual unacceptable	10	9	6	0	25
Actual minimal	11	20	28	0	59
Actual adequate	0	18	83	0	101
Actual excellent	0	0	15	0	15
Totals	21	47	132	0	200

TABLE 7.5
Coincidence
Matrix—Loan Test
Data, Neural
Network, 2,000
Epochs

Actual	Model Fraud	Model OK	Total
Fraud	6	9	15
OK	74	311	385
Totals	80	320	400

Running the training data set of 450 cases on Clementine and testing it on the last 200 yielded the coincidence matrix shown in Table 7.4.

In this case, the correct classification rate was much higher, at 0.565. This model was never wrong by more than one classification level. However, it was very conservative in that it never classified any outcomes as excellent.

Loan Applicant Data

The Matlab backpropogation neural network algorithm was applied to the first 250 observations for training. This was a different 250 cases than used in the logistic regression, providing the neural network model with more balance among fraudulent and OK cases. Three different durations of modeling were used. The first model used 2,000 epochs, and correctly classified 246 of the 250 cases (98 percent). Using 5,000 epochs, the model correctly classified 247 cases, while using 10,000 epochs 248 training cases were correctly classified. All three runs correctly classified all of the training cases with OK outcomes. However, the test results (on the remaining 400 observations) were inversely related to the training results. The best classification rate among these three models was the model with 2,000 epochs, shown in Table 7.5.

This model had a correct classification rate of 317/400, or 79 percent. The correct classification rate for actually fraudulent cases was 40 percent.

Neural Network Products

Many data mining software products include neural network technology. This is a black box in that much of the control is internal to the software, although some allow parameters such as the number of layers to be controlled by the user. There also are many neural network products listed on the Web. The site www.kdnuggets.com has a section on software, including a portion on neural products. This dynamic market includes products that are free for download.

Neural network products fall into at least three categories for our purposes. Some software provides neural network modeling capability in general. There are also a number of products built around a specific problem. Finally, neural networks have been included in more general software, such as other techniques like statistical software and expert system software.

General neural network software products can be used to build neural networks for whatever data set is provided (once the data is properly transformed). Some products allow the user to enter any data, with the software transforming the data in the form required. Other products provide very useful visual supplements to help the modeler build the model, and help the user see the output in a clearer form. Prices vary over a wide range, with a number of products below $100, and a few products in the $2,000 range. Many systems allow the user to access a number of architectures, such as backpropagation or Kohonen learning networks. Back propagation is a general learning rule applied to networks with middle layers. Initial input weights are set at some value (like +1), and other weights are randomized. For each input pattern, weights are adjusted considering the degree of error. Kohonen networks (used in cluster analysis) consist of two layers, but there are interconnections within layers. Initial random weights must be normalized. The network then uses the best fit in selecting modifications to weights. Other architectures are also available.

Neural network software is found in a number of more general packages, such as the Network Cybernetics' product Owl, which is a neural network library that allows the user to encode his or her own neural network.

Neural networks have proven very attractive in trading venues, where a very complex system with high time pressures exists. Neural networks have also been applied to construction bidding, allowing the user to enter data on past bid experience. The software then produces a suggested bid markup seeking improved profit margins.

Summary

Neural networks have the very important strength that they can be applied to most data mining applications, and require minimal model building. They provide good results in complicated applications, especially when there are complex interactions among variables in the data. Neural networks can deal with categorical and continuous data. Many packages are available.

The method has some weaknesses, however. For instance, data needs to be massaged a bit, but that's not a major defect. The primary problem is that neural network output tends to have a black-box effect, in that explanations in the form of a model are not available. Neural networks also have the technical defect of potentially converging to an inferior solution. However, this technical defect is detectable when applied to the test set of data.

Neural networks are therefore very attractive for problems where an explanation of conclusions aren't needed. This is often the case in classification and prediction problems. Neural networks should not be applied with excessive numbers of variables. Decision tree methods can be used to prune variables in that case. Genetic algorithms can also be applied to improve neural network performance.

Glossary

backpropogation Commonly used learning rule in neural networks, where results of prior iterations are used to guide model adjustments in future iterations.

multilayered feedforward neural networks Common structure of a neural network model, with multiple hidden layers connecting arcs with data inputs leading through the hidden layers to output.

neural network Artificial intelligence model based upon fitting data with a network of arcs that has weights adjusted to optimize fit.

self-organizing neural networks Neural networks capable of adjusting the number of clusters.

Exercises

1. Apply a neural network algorithm to the Job Applicant data file. Use the first 250 observations as the training set, and apply it to the last 250 observations. Use standardized data, as in the scoring scheme described before Table 6.33. If data mining software is available, compare regression, logistic regression, and neural network output. Develop the coincidence matrix for this data.

2. Apply a neural network algorithm to the Job Applicant data file. Use the first 250 observations as the training set, and apply it to the last 250 observations. Use categorical data. If data mining software is available, compare regression, logistic regression, and neural network output. Develop the coincidence matrix for this data.

3. If data mining software is available, apply a neural network algorithm to the standardized Loan Application data set. Use the first 500 observations as the training set, and apply it to the last 100 observations. Use data mining software if available, or Excel if not. Develop the coincidence matrix.

4. If data mining software is available, apply a neural network model to categorical data (using binary codes for results) in the Loan Application data file. Use the first 500 observations as the training set, and apply it to the last 100 observations. Use data mining software if available, or Excel if not. Develop the coincidence matrix. Compare the coincidence matrices for this data with the results from problem 3.

5. If data mining software is available, apply the neural network algorithm to the Insurance Fraud data set. Transform age by making 20 (or younger) = 0, 50 (or older) = 1.0, and every age between = age/30. Leave gender as is (0 or 1). Transform claim by dividing it by 5,000. Transform tickets and prior claims by making 0 = 0, 1 = 0.5, and 2 or more = 1.0. Transform attorney by making "none" = 0 and all others = 1. Use the first 1,000 observations as the training set, and apply it to test the last 1,000 observations. Use data mining software. Develop the coincidence matrix.

6. If data mining software is available, compare neural network models on standardized and categorical data (coding output to 0 and 1) models to the Insurance Fraud data file. Use the first 1,000 observations as the training set, and apply it to test the last 1,000 observations. Use data mining software if available, or Excel if not. Develop the coincidence matrix. Compare the coincidence matrices for this data with the results from problem 5.

7. Apply the neural network algorithm to the Customer Expenditure data set with the intent of identifying the type of people who spend the following portion of their income on restaurants: less than 1 percent, between 1 and 5 percent, 5 to 10 percent, and over 10 percent. Use the first 12 variables (age through churn)

in standardized form. Use 5,000 observations as the training set, and apply it to 1,000 test observations. Use data mining software if available. Develop the coincidence matrix.

8. Using the Expenditure Data file, apply a neural network model identifying the type of people who spend the following portion of their income on groceries: less than 1 percent, between 1 and 5 percent, 5 to 10 percent, and over 10 percent. Use standardized data for the first 12 variables (age through churn) as independent variables. Use 5,000 observations as the training set, and apply it to 1,000 test observations. Use data mining software if available. Develop the coincidence matrix.

9. Using the Expenditure Data file, apply a neural network model identifying the type of people who spend the following portion of their income on housing: less than 10 percent, between 10 and 30 percent, 30 to 50 percent, and over 50 percent. Use standardized data for the first 12 variables (age through churn) as independent variables. Use 5,000 observations as the training set, and apply it to 1,000 test observations. Use data mining software if available. Develop the coincidence matrix.

10. Using the Expenditure Data file, apply a neural network model identifying the type of people who spend the following portion of their income on utilities: less than 1 percent, between 1 and 5 percent, 5 to 10 percent, and over 10 percent. Use standardized data for the first 12 variables (age through churn) as independent variables. Use 5,000 observations as the training set, and apply it to 1,000 test observations. Use data mining software if available. Develop the coincidence matrix.

11. Using the Expenditure Data file, apply a neural network model identifying the type of people who spend the following portion of their income on owning and operating automobiles: less than 1 percent, between 1 and 5 percent, 5 to 10 percent, and over 10 percent. Use standardized data for the first 12 variables (age through churn) as independent variables. Use 5,000 observations as the training set, and apply it to 1,000 test observations. Use data mining software if available. Develop the coincidence matrix.

12. Using the Expenditure Data file, apply a neural network model identifying the type of people who spend the following portion of their income on clothing: less than 5 percent, between 5 and 10 percent, 10 to 20 percent, and over 20 percent. Use standardized data for the first 12 variables (age through churn) as independent variables. Use 5,000 observations as the training set, and apply it to 1,000 test observations. Use data mining software if available. Develop the coincidence matrix.

13. Using the Expenditure Data file, apply a neural network model identifying the type of people who spend the following portion of their income on entertainment: less than 1 percent, between 1 and 5 percent, 5 to 10 percent, and over 10 percent. Use standardized data for the first 12 variables (age through churn) as independent variables. Use 5,000 observations as the training set, and apply it to 1,000 test observations. Use data mining software if available. Develop the coincidence matrix.

Endnotes

1. P. Churchland, *Matter and Consciousness*, 8th printing, Cambridge, MA: Bradford Books/The MIT Press, 1997, p. 154.
2. W. S. Sarle, "Neural Networks and Statistical Models," *Proceedings of the Nineteenth Annual SAS Users Group International Conference*, April 1994, pp. 1–13.

3. K. A. Smith and J. N. D. Gupta, "Neural Networks in Business: Techniques and Applications for the Operations Researcher," *Computers & Operations Research*, volume 27, numbers 11–12, 2000, pp. 1023–1044.
4. B. K. Wong, T. A. Bodnovich, and Y. Selvi, "Neural Network Applications in Business: A Review and Analysis of the Literature (1988–1995)," *Decision Support Systems*, volume 19, 1997, pp. 301–320, cited in Smith and Gupta, op. cit.
5. Wong, Bodnovich, and Selvi, op. cit.
6. T. Kohonen, *Self-Organization and Associative Memory* (New York: Springer, 1988).
7. C. C. Klimasauskas, "Applying Neural Networks: Part I: An Overview of the Series," *PC AI*, January/February 1991, pp. 30–33.
8. D. Pearson, "Instant Inspections," *CIO*, volume 11, number 18, section 1, July 1, 1998, pp. 34–35.
9. T. Goveia, "Short Circuiting Crime," *Canadian Insurance*, volume 104, number 5, May 1999, pp. 16–17+.
10. J. M. Donato, J. C. Schryver, G. C. Hinkel, R. L. Schmoyer, Jr., M. R. Leuze, and N. W. Grandy, "Mining Multi-Dimensional Data for Decision Support," *Future Generation Computer Systems*, volume 15, 1999, pp. 433–441.
11. R. L. Wilson and R. Sharda, "Bankruptcy Prediction Using Neural Networks," *Decision Support Systems*, volume 11, 1994, pp. 545–557.
12. J. H. Drew, D. R. Mani, A. L. Betz, and P. Datta, "Targeting Customers with Statistical and Data-Mining Techniques," *Journal of Service Research*, volume 3, number 3, 2001, pp. 205–219.

CHAPTER EIGHT

Decision Tree Algorithms

This chapter:

Presents the concept of decision tree models

Discusses the concept of rule interestingness

Demonstrates decision tree rules on a case

Reviews real applications of decision tree models

Shows the application of decision tree models to larger data sets

Demonstrates See5 decision tree analysis in the appendix

Contemporary grocery stores handle literally hundreds of thousands of items (given various product flavors, sizes, and so on). This presents a massive data problem in inventory control, dealt with to a high degree by bar-coding technology. Technology of this kind enables the checkout recording of withdrawals of products, which provides a massive database of transactions that can be mined to monitor customer demand. Grocery stores generate very large quantities of data about purchases (even more than Wal-Mart stores do). This creates a massive amount of data that can be mined for a variety of purposes related to inventory management.

The vast number of products makes automatic generation of specific prediction models useful. Decision trees provide a means to obtain product-specific forecasting models in the form of rules that are easy to implement. These rules have an IF-THEN form, which is easy for grocery employees to implement. This data mining approach can be used by grocery stores in a number of policy decisions, including ordering inventory replenishment and evaluating alternative promotion campaigns.

As was the case with regression models and neural networks, decision tree models support the data mining process of modeling.

Decision trees in the context of data mining refer to the tree structure of rules (often called association rules). The data mining decision tree process involves collecting those variables that the analyst thinks might bear on the decision at issue, and analyzing these variables for their ability to predict the outcome. Decision trees are useful for gaining further insight into customer behavior, and for finding ways to profitably act on the results.[1] The algorithm automatically determines which variables are most important, based on their ability to sort the data into the correct output category. The method has a relative advantage over neural network and genetic algorithms in that a reusable set of rules are provided, thus explaining model conclusions.[2] There are many examples where decision trees have been applied to business data mining, including classifying loan applicants, screening potential consumers, and rating job applicants.

Decision trees provide a way to implement rule-based system approaches. The ID3 system selects an attribute as a root, with **branches** for different values of the attribute.[3] All objects in the training set are classified into these branches. If all objects in a branch belong to the same output class, the **node** is labeled and this branch is terminated. If there are multiple classes on a branch, another attribute is selected as a node, with all possible attribute values branched. An entropy **heuristic** is used to select the attributes with the highest information. In other data mining tools, the ways of selecting branches vary.

Decision Tree Operation

A bank may have a database of past loan applicants for short-term loans. This data base (a simplification of Table 4.4) consists of the age of the applicant, the applicant's income, her or his risk rating, and whether the outcome of the loan was paid on-time or not). The bank's policy treats applicants differently by age group, income level, and risk. Age groups are less than or equal to 30, over 30 but less than or equal to 60, and over 60 years of age, respectively. Income levels are less than or equal to $30,000 per year, over $30,000 but less than or equal to $80,000 per year, and over $80,000 per year. High risk is defined as applicants with greater debt than assets. If an applicant's assets minus the requested loan amount exceeds debt, the applicant is classified as low risk. Applicants with asset-debt relationships between these values are classified as medium risk. A tree sorts the possible combination of these variables. An exhaustive tree enumerates all combinations of variable values in Table 8.1. The tree for this set of rules is partially shown in Figure 8.1.

A **rule-based system** model would require that bank loan officers who had respected judgment be interviewed to classify (and justify) the decision for each

FIGURE 8.1

Partial Tree for Loan Application Data

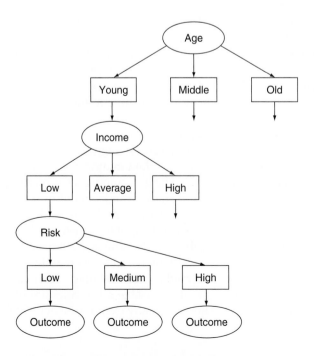

TABLE 8.1
Enumeration of
Appliance Loan
Variable
Combinations

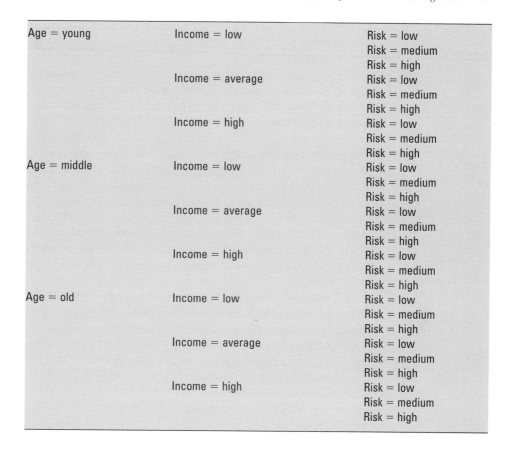

Age = young	Income = low	Risk = low
		Risk = medium
		Risk = high
	Income = average	Risk = low
		Risk = medium
		Risk = high
	Income = high	Risk = low
		Risk = medium
		Risk = high
Age = middle	Income = low	Risk = low
		Risk = medium
		Risk = high
	Income = average	Risk = low
		Risk = medium
		Risk = high
	Income = high	Risk = low
		Risk = medium
		Risk = high
Age = old	Income = low	Risk = low
		Risk = medium
		Risk = high
	Income = average	Risk = low
		Risk = medium
		Risk = high
	Income = high	Risk = low
		Risk = medium
		Risk = high

of these combinations of variables. Some trees may be simplified. For instance, if income is high, the loan might be automatically granted by some loan officers. This would reduce the tree, as age and risk would not matter in that case. Further, for those without low income, if risk were high, the loan might not be granted. The first rule would be as shown in Table 8.2.

This structure uses classification data because there are a clear, finite number of outcomes (don't grant the loan, grant the loan, and possibly authorize part of the loan). This form of tree is referred to as a classification tree. Trees can also be used on data with continuous outcomes, in an estimating or predicting mode. In these cases, the terminology is a **regression tree.**

Rule Interestingness

Data, even categorical data, can potentially involve many rules. For instance, in the loan application data just presented, there were four variables, each of which could take on three values. There were 3 _ 3 _ 3 = 27 combinations, each given in Table 8.1. If there were 10 variables, each with four possible values, the number of combinations would be over a million (1,048,576). Clearly, the brute-force generation of rule

TABLE 8.2
Initial Rule

Age	Income	Risk	Rule
	High		Grant loan
	Not High		Deny loan

outcomes is unreasonable. Fortunately, decision tree methods identify the most useful rules in terms of predicting outcomes. Rule effectiveness is measured in terms of confidence and support. Confidence is the degree of accuracy of a rule, while support is the degree to which the antecedent conditions occur in the data. For instance, a book retailer may find that of all the cases where Zane Grey's baseball book *The Short Stop* was purchased, his other book, *The Young Pitcher*, was also purchased. This may have happened 8 of 10 times, giving a confidence of 0.8 for the rule: If purchased *The Short Stop*, then will purchase *The Young Pitcher*. In fact, let us suppose that these were the only eight purchases of *The Young Pitcher*. However, this rule may not be very useful, as both purchases were rare. **Support** for an association rule indicates the proportion of records covered by the set of attributes in the association rule. If there were 10 million book purchases, support for the given rule would be 10/10,000,000, a very small support measure of 0.000001. These concepts are often used in the form of threshold levels in machine learning systems. Minimum **confidence levels** and support levels can be specified to retain rules identified by decision tree (or other association rule) methods.

For rules to be interesting, they must identify something useful (have a high confidence level and sufficiently high support) and novel. For instance, a grocer applying data mining finding that eggs and bacon are purchased together at a confidence level of 0.9 and a support level of 0.2 might not be impressed. The grocer knew that prior to data mining. **Interestingness** is the idea that the data mining analysis found out something that was unexpected (knowledge discovery). It is still useful to confirm the hypothesis that eggs and bacon sell together. But it is more useful to discover the knowledge that blackberry jam and eggs go together at a similar rate. (Please note that we do not know of such a real relationship.) Such information could lead to the rearrangement of store displays and/or promotions.

Machine Learning

Rule-induction algorithms have been developed to automatically process categorical data (it also can work on continuous data). For this approach to work, a clear outcome is needed.[4] Thankfully, in this case a clear outcome exists: two categories of payoff results. Rule induction works by searching through data for patterns and relationships. Records can be clustered into specific categories. **Machine learning** starts with no assumptions, looking only at input data and results. The judgment developed by human experts is not considered, which might sound inefficient, but it means that human biases can be eliminated. Recursive partitioning algorithms split data (original data, not grouped as shown earlier) into finer and finer subsets leading to a decision tree.[5]

For instance, let's consider the 20 past loan application cases displayed in Table 8.3, with known outcomes.

There are three variables here, each with three possible levels. In practice, we would expect thousands of observations, making it unlikely that any combinations would be empty. We use 20 observations to demonstrate the principles of the calculations, and of the 27 combinations, many here are empty. The combinations with representative observations are given in Table 8.4.

Automatic machine learning begins with identifying those variables that offer the greatest likelihood of distinguishing between the possible outcomes. For each of the three variables, we can identify the outcome probabilities in Table 8.5.

TABLE 8.3
Twenty Past Loan
Application Cases

Age	Income	Assets	Debts	Want	Risk	Result
20 (young)	17,152 (low)	11,090	20,455	400	high	On-time
23 (young)	25,862 (low)	24,756	30,083	2,300	high	On-time
28 (young)	26,169 (low)	47,355	49,341	3,100	high	Late
23 (young)	21,117 (low)	21,242	30,278	300	high	Default
22 (young)	7,127 (low)	23,903	17,231	900	low	On-time
26 (young)	42,083 (average)	35,726	41,421	300	high	Late
24 (young)	55,557 (average)	27,040	48,191	1,500	high	On-time
27 (young)	34,843 (average)	0	21,031	2,100	high	On-time
29 (young)	74,295 (average)	88,827	100,599	100	high	On-time
23 (young)	38,887 (average)	6,260	33,635	9,400	low	On-time
28 (young)	31,758 (average)	58,492	49,268	1,000	low	On-time
25 (young)	80,180 (high)	31,696	69,529	1,000	high	Late
33 (middle)	40,921 (average)	91,111	90,076	2,900	average	Late
36 (middle)	63,124 (average)	164,631	144,697	300	low	On-time
39 (middle)	59,006 (average)	195,759	161,750	600	low	On-time
39 (middle)	125,713 (high)	382,180	315,396	5,200	low	On-time
55 (middle)	80,149 (high)	511,937	21,923	1,000	low	On-time
62 (old)	101,291 (high)	783,164	23,052	1,800	low	On-time
71 (old)	81,723 (high)	776,344	20,277	900	low	On-time
63 (old)	99,522 (high)	783,491	24,643	200	low	On-time

Most data mining packages use an **entropy** measure to gauge the discriminating power of each variable, selecting that variable with the greatest discriminating power as the first to split data with. (Chi-square measures can also be used to select variables.) Three of the nine categories are shown here, with all observations in one outcome category or the other (age = old and risk = low both have all cases in the on-time category; risk = average has only one observation, and it is in the late category; this is suspicious logically and is based on the minimum possible sample size, but remember we're trying to demonstrate the procedure with a small data set).

One formula for entropy (Koonce, et al., 1997) where p is the number of positive examples and n is the number of negative examples in the training set for each value of the attribute:[6]

$$\text{Inform} = -\frac{p}{p+n}\log_2\frac{p}{p+n} - \frac{n}{p+n}\log_2\frac{n}{p+n}$$

TABLE 8.4
Grouped Data

Age	Income	Risk	Total	On-time	Not on-time	Probability
Young	Low	High	4	2	2	0.50
Young	Low	Low	1	1	0	1.00
Young	Average	High	4	3	1	0.75
Young	Average	Low	2	2	0	1.00
Young	High	High	1	0	1	0.00
Middle	Average	Average	1	0	1	0.00
Middle	Average	Low	2	2	0	1.00
Middle	High	Low	2	2	0	1.00
Old	High	Low	3	3	0	1.00

TABLE 8.5
Combination
Outcomes

Variable	Value	Cases	On-Time	Late	Prob {On-Time}
Age	Young	12	8	4	0.67
	Middle	5	4	1	0.80
	Old	3	3	0	1.00
Income	Low	5	3	2	0.60
	Average	9	7	2	0.78
	High	6	5	1	0.83
Risk	High	9	5	4	0.55
	Average	1	0	1	0.00
	Low	10	10	0	1.00

This formula has a problem if either p or n are 0 (which would happen if there were unanimous outcomes for a category), then the log to base 2 is undefined, and the formula does not work. However, for values just above 0, the Inform formula will converge to 0. For the variable Age, there are three outcomes. Entropy for each Age category generated by this formula is shown in Table 8.6.

For category Young, the calculation is $[-(8/12) \times (-0.585) - (4/12) \times (-1.585)] \times (12/20) = 0.551$. The lower this entropy measure, the greater the information content (the greater the agreement probability). The entropy measures for the three variables are

Age	0.731
Income	0.782
Risk	0.446

By this measure, Risk has the greatest information content. If Risk is low, the data indicates a 1.0 probability (10 of 10 cases) that the applicant will pay the loan back on time. If Risk is not low, this data indicates a 0.5 probability that the applicant will pay the loan back on time. This would be the first rule selected by the machine learning algorithm.

IF (Risk = Low)	THEN Predict On-time payment
ELSE	Predict Late

This rule is subject to two types of error. First, those applicants rated as low risk may actually not pay on time. (From the data, the probability of this happening is 0.0.) Second, those applicants rated as high or average risk may actually have paid if given a loan. (From the data, the probability of this happening is 0.5.) The expectation of this is the probability of an applicant being rated as high or average in risk (10/20, or 0.5) times the probability of being wrong (0.5),

TABLE 8.6
Entropy Calculation
for Age

	p/(p + n)	Log(base 2)	n/(p + n)	Log(base 2)	Sum of Products	Probability {Young}	Product
Young	8/12	−0.585	4/12	−1.585	0.918	12/20	0.551
Middle	4/5	−0.322	1/5	−2.322	0.722	5/20	0.180
Old	3/3	0*	0/3	0*	0*	3/20	0*
SUM							**0.731**

*Formula is strictly undefined, but converges to zero.

TABLE 8.7
Probabilities
by Case

Risk	Age	Count	Probability {On-Time}
Low		10/20	1.0
NOT low	Middle	1/20	0.0
NOT low	Young	9/20	0.56

yielding an expected error of 0.25. To test this rule, it is best to apply it to a second set of data, different from the data set used to develop the rule.

The set of rules may be examined further to see if greater accuracy can be obtained. The entropy formula for Age, given that risk was not low, is 0.991, while the same calculation for income is 1.971. This indicates that Age has greater discriminating power. With this data, if Age is middle, the one case did not pay on time. There were no old cases in this group. Therefore, the second rule is the following:

IF (Risk is NOT low)	AND (Age = Middle)	THEN Predict Late
ELSE		Predict On-time

In this case, the data would indicate probabilities, as shown in Table 8.7.

All 10 of this subset of the data with Low risk rating paid on time. Of the other 10 cases that were not low, the one that was Middle aged did not pay on time (as stated earlier), while five of the nine Young cases paid on time. The expected error here is the 4/9 probability for the nine cases out of 20 total, or 0.2. This is an improvement over the prior case where the expected error was 0.25.

For the last variable, Income, given that Risk was not low, and Age was not Middle, there are nine cases left, shown in Table 8.8.

Four of these nine cases were Low income, with two paying on time and two not. Four were Average income, three of which paid on time and one that did not. The last case was High income, which was not paid on time.

A third rule, taking advantage of the case with unanimous outcome, is

IF (Risk NOT low)	AND (Age NOT middle)	AND (Income high)	THEN predict Late
ELSE			Predict On-time

The expected accuracy of the three rules together is shown in Table 8.9. The expected error here is 8/20 times 0.375 = 0.15.

An additional rule could be generated. For the case of Risk NOT low, Age = Young, and Income NOT high, there are four cases with low income (probability of on-time = 0.5) and four cases with average income (probability of on-time = 0.75). The greater discrimination is provided by average income, resulting in the following rule:

IF (Risk NOT low)	AND (Age NOT middle)	AND (Income average)	THEN predict On-time
ELSE			Predict Either

There is no added accuracy obtained with this rule, shown in Table 8.10.

TABLE 8.8
Probabilities
Recalculated

Income	On-Time	Late	Probability {On-time}
Low	2	2	0.50
Average	3	1	0.75
High	0	1	0.00

TABLE 8.9
Expected Accuracy
of Three Rules

Risk	Age	Income	Count	Probability {On-time}
Low			10/20	1.0
NOT low	Middle		1/20	0.0
NOT low	Young	High	1/20	0.0
NOT low	Young	NOT high	8/20	0.625

TABLE 8.10
Accuracy of the
Fourth Rule

Risk	Age	Income	Count	Probability {On-time}
Low			10/20	1.0
NOT low	Middle		1/20	0.0
NOT low	Young	High	1/20	0.0
NOT low	Young	Average	4/20	0.75
NOT low	Young	Low	4/20	0.50

TABLE 8.11
Rules Applied to
Test Cases

Record	Actual	Rule Prediction	By Rule	Result
1	On-Time	On-Time	1	match
2	On-Time	On-Time	1	match
3	On-Time	On-Time	1	match
4	On-Time	On-Time	Else	match
5	On-Time	On-Time	1	match
6	On-Time	On-Time	Else	match
7	Late	On-Time	Else	miss
8	On-Time	On-Time	1	match
9	On-Time	Late	3	miss
10	On-Time	On-Time	1	match

FIGURE 8.2
Decision Tree
for Rules

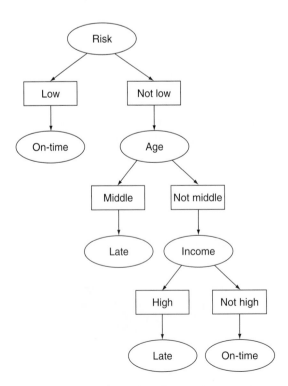

TABLE 8.12
Coincidence Matrix
for Rule Set

Actual	Late	On-Time	Total
Late	0	1	1
On-Time	1	8	9
Total	1	9	10

The expected error is 4/20 times 0.25 + 4/20 times 0.5, equals 0.15, the same as without the rule. When machine learning methods encounter no improvement, they generally stop. (Here, we've exhausted all combinations anyway.) Therefore, the last rule would NOT be added to the first three. The machine learning algorithm would stop at:

IF (Risk low)			THEN predict On-time
ELSE			
IF (Risk NOT low)	AND (Age middle)		THEN predict Late
ELSE			
IF (Risk NOT low)	AND (Age NOT middle)	AND (Income high)	THEN predict Late
ELSE			Predict On-time

This model can be tested with the data given in Table 4.5. Table 8.11 shows the results.

Figure 8.2 displays the decision tree for this set of rules.

In this case, the coincidence matrix is shown in Table 8.12.

In this case, the accuracy of the model is 8/10, or 80 percent. There were errors of both types (denying a good loan application, accepting one bad application).

Decision Tree Applications

In this section, we present brief summaries of decision tree applications. The first involves inventory forecasting, the second medical data mining, and the third software engineering. We then present a description of decision tree development applied to software development quality.

Inventory Prediction

Grocery stores carry many items, with a multitude of product variations and sizes. Stock keeping units are specific items, each of which is associated with a price that enables expeditious bar-code checkout. Large grocery stores may carry over 100,000 stock keeping units. Bar-code checkout provides fast service to customers, but also provides a flood of data needed by grocers to manage their inventories. While many items are quite predictable within a small variation, events such as sales promotions introduce an irregular pattern of variation. A large number of interactions between manufacturers, merchandise divisions, and individual store effects challenge traditional forecasting techniques.

A data mining tool was designed and implemented to discover patterns in forecasting model residuals reflecting local knowledge.[7] A random sample of over 1.6 million records over a 30-month period (from a population of over 19 million records) was used to reflect retail grocery promotions from 95 grocery outlets of a major retailer in a large urban area. The model was validated on a hold-out sample of over 400,000 records collected after calibration of the model.

A forecasting model, including manufacturer and subcommodity, would have involved over 2,000 dummy variables. Thus, they would have been unattractive to include in the traditional forecasting model for this application. Data mining was used to develop a rule-induction model to discover when information in the two excluded variables would be important. When the rule-induction model identified that these variables were important, the traditional forecast was adjusted to yield more accurate forecasts.

The data mining analysis yielded over 28,000 rules. In about half of the forecasting cases involving promotions, no adjustment to the traditional forecast was needed. The rule-based adjusted forecast was very accurate, within one case of product in over 80 percent of the cases, and within two cases of product in 90 percent of the cases. Improvement over the traditional model ranged from 0 for shampoo subcommodities to over 27 percent for yogurts.

The Mining of Clinical Databases

Medical experts use both positive reasoning and negative reasoning when diagnosing cases. There are over 60 possible tests that might involve various causes of headache. Exclusive reasoning (represented by negative rules) excludes particular diseases when a related symptom is absent. Inclusive reasoning (represented by positive rules) suspects a particular disease when a related symptom is present.

A probabilistic rule-based induction system was developed based on a rough set theory for medical domains of headache, cerebulovasular diseases (CVD), and meningitis.[8] Training samples were over 50,000 for the headache domain, which involved 45 classes and 147 attributes. There were over 7,500 samples for training of the CVD model, which had 285 attributes available to classify cases into 22 categories. The meningitis model had over 1,200 samples to train on 41 attributes into four classes of output variable.

Comparison of model performance was conducted. Samples were randomly divided into new training samples and new test samples. Conventional rule induction methods AQ15 and C4.5 were used on the new training samples. Rules were also manually obtained from experts. These induced rules and expert rules were tested on the new test samples. This process was repeated 100 times, thus applying a two-fold cross-validation. Rules based on expert input had over 92-percent accuracy in all three disease domains. The AQ15 model and C4.5 model averaged about 82-percent accuracy, with AQ15 having a slightly higher average, and C4.5 a slightly higher minimum performance. The rough set rule system based only on positive rules had more errors, averaging around 70-percent accuracy. However, the model based on both positive and negative rules from rough sets averaged over 90-percent accuracy, nearly matching the models based on expert opinion.

An additional value of the rule system model developed was insight into new relationships that experts had not realized. This is a case of automated knowledge acquisition.

Software Development Quality

Software engineering includes the development of modules of software that include probabilities of faults. Faults were defined in this context as a program defect causing incorrect execution of the software. The goal of this knowledge discovery application was to find patterns in data of past module development that would enable better prediction of software modules likely to contain faults discovered by customers. The intent was to identify faults as early in the software development process as possible, so that reliability enhancement (such as more stringent specification, testing, and inspection) could be applied to reduce the risk of customer-identified faults.[9]

The study was conducted for a large telecommunications company. The fault rate for modules that were not updated was quite low (about 99 percent of the modules did not have faults). Thus, the study focused on modules that were updated after release. Typical modules contained several million lines of code in a few thousand modules. Of these updated modules, the probability of fault was 0.074. The data was divided approximately in half, with one half used for training and the other half for testing.

Preprocessing involved development of a clean set of module identifiers, and measurements of source code features. There were two call graph metrics (such as the number of calls from one module to another), 13 control flow graph metrics (such as the number of entry nodes, or the number of exit nodes), and nine statement metrics (including the number of lines of code). Those modules with missing data were excluded.

Data was reduced by extracting customer-discovered fault data and software process variables from the company's database. Usage was forecast from deployment records and installation plans.

A module is a set of source files, where a transaction occurs with each change to a source file. Data reduction was used to extract seven module-level variables. These included code churn, or the amount of code changed in the module, as well as programmer experience in terms of the number of updates previously performed.

There also was deployment data, identifying the four variable values of customer site identifier, module identifier, version installed, and date installed. These records were used to calculate the variable USAGE. Problem reporting data was based on nine variables relating to a problem reporting system. This information was used to generate eight variables for the data mining study.

Classification trees were used for this knowledge discovery analysis using the Classification and Regression Trees algorithm CART. CART allowed specification of prior probabilities and the use of costs of misclassification. Here both types of error were considered equally important, so the ratio of costs of misclassification rates was set at 1.0. CART worked by starting with all 40 variables and then pruning until the ratio of errors was within a specified limit.

The first model identified by the CART algorithm used the variables FILINCUQ (number of distinct include-files, a statement metric), SRC_MOD (net new and changed lines of code), CTRNSTMX (maximum control structure nesting), UPD_CAR (number of updates designers had done in their company career), STMCTL (number of control statements), and USAGE (fraction of customer sites with a module assigned for the release of interest). The model consisted of the following rules:

Rule	Condition	Outcome
1	If FILINCUQ $\leq$ 27	Not Fault-prone
2	If FILINCUQ $>$ 27 & SRC_MOD $\leq$ 30 & CTRNSTMX $\leq$ 6	Not Fault-prone
3	If FILINCUQ $>$ 27 & SRC_MOD $\leq$ 30 & CTRNSTMX $>$ 6 & UPD_CAR $\leq$ 10	Not Fault-prone
4	If 27 $<$ FILINCUQ $\leq$ 29 & SRC_MOD $\leq$ 30 & CTRNSTMX $>$ 6 & UPD_CAR $>$ 10 & STMCTL $<$ 630	Fault-prone
5	If 29 $<$ FILINCUQ $\leq$ 34 & SRC_MOD $\leq$ 30 & CTRNSTMX $>$ 6 & UPD_CAR $>$ 10 & STMCTL $<$ 630	Not Fault-prone
6	If FILINCUQ $>$ 34 & SRC_MOD $\leq$ 30 & CTRNSTMX $>$ 6 & UPD_CAR $>$ 10 & STMCTL $<$ 630	Fault-prone
7	If FILINCUQ $>$ 27 & SRC_MOD $\leq$ 30 & CTRNSTMX $>$ 6 & UPD_CAR $>$ 10 & STMCTL $\geq$ 630	Not Fault-prone
8	If FILINCUQ $>$ 27 & SRC_MOD $>$ 30 & USAGE $\leq$ 0.005	Not Fault-prone
9	If FILINCUQ $>$ 27 & SRC_MOD $>$ 30 & USAGE $>$ 0.005	Fault-prone

TABLE 8.13
Coincidence Matrix
Software Quality
Test Data

	Not Fault-prone	Fault-prone
Actual Not Fault-prone	73.8%	26.2%
Actual Fault-prone	28.9%	71.1%

The second simple model identified by CART considered the six variables scored as most important in the first model. The final model generated an even simpler set of rules using variables FILINCUQ and VARSPNSM (total span of variables; another statement metric):

Rule	Condition	Outcome
1	If FILINCUQ $\leq$ 27	Not Fault-prone
2	If 27 < FILINCUQ $\leq$ 49 & VARSPNSM $\leq$ 15657	Not Fault-prone
3	If 27 < FILINCUQ $\leq$ 49 & VARSPNSM > 15657	Fault-prone
4	If FILINCUQ > 49	Fault-prone

Evaluation

The first model yielded the following coincidence matrix over the test data, expressed in percentages in Table 8.13.

The simpler second model had the error rates shown in Table 8.14.

The two models were very close in accuracy. The first model was better at cross-validation accuracy, but its variables were available just prior to release. The second model had the advantage of being based on data available at an earlier state, and also required less extensive data reduction.

There are many other applications of decision tree models in data mining. The paper industry is an example of a continuous manufacturing process. A decision tree model was used by a paper-producing company.[10] The manufacturing goal in this application was to reduce the level of salvage in the production of paper. Manufacturing quality data was saved at various stations in the mill, to include paper measurements such as weight, moisture content, and thickness. Data from each reel of paper was compared with past data by paper grade produced. Several months were spent identifying good and bad profiles for production output. Induction was selected as a data mining tool, because of the desire for an explanation of model conclusions. The system produced very good results, correctly predicting 96 percent of good reels, and 88 percent of faulty reels. Some aspects of the predictive model were counter-intuitive, leading to study that improved understanding of the paper production process.

Other applications of decision tree algorithms include a probabilistic, inductive learning decision tree algorithm applied to improve the decision-making process for the New York State Workers' Compensation Board.[11] Reduction in administrative costs was sought from applying more efficient processing for low-dollar claims. The system generated rules that could be used to assign cases to different processing routes. In this case, the system automatically generated the rules, which were then applied as in production rule **expert systems**.

TABLE 8.14
Coincidence Matrix
Software Quality
Test Data

	Not Fault-prone	Fault-prone
Actual Not Fault-prone	73.0%	27.0%
Actual Fault-prone	27.4%	72.6%

TABLE 8.15
Grouped Data—
Young

Age	Income	Risk	Credit Rating	On-Time	Not On-Time	Probability
Young	Low	High	Red	3	1	0.750
			Amber	7	1	0.875
			Green	17	1	0.944
		Average	Red	1	1	0.500
			Green	1	0	1.000
		Low	Green	7	0	1.000
	Average	High	Red	9	9	0.500
			Amber	24	10	0.706
			Green	42	6	0.875
		Average	Amber	1	0	1.000
			Green	4	0	1.000
		Low	Red	2	0	1.000
	High	High	Red	1	1	0.500
			Amber	5	3	0.625
			Green	12	0	1.000

Application of Methods to Larger Data Sets

We use the Loan Application Data set to demonstrate decision tree operation.

Loan Application Data

The full Loan Application Data set had 650 observations over four variables. We can use the first 400 observations for training, reserving the last 250 observations for testing. The 400 training observations fall into the categories shown in Tables 8.15 through 8.17.

Table 8.16 gives the categorical counts for middle-aged loan applicants.

Finally, we have the Old applicants in Table 8.17.

Most of the possible old categories were vacant. Furthermore, all of the old applicant categories had unanimity in their outcome. Automatic machine learning

TABLE 8.16
Grouped Data—
Middle-Aged

Age	Income	Risk	Credit Rating	On-Time	Not On-Time	Probability
Middle	Low	Average	Green	3	0	1.000
		Low	Red	0	1	0
			Amber	1	0	1.000
			Green	2	0	1.000
	Average	High	Red	1	1	0.500
			Amber	4	2	0.667
			Green	17	1	0.944
		Average	Amber	4	0	1.000
			Green	4	0	1.000
		Low	Red	13	1	0.929
			Amber	37	4	0.902
			Green	64	1	0.985
	High	High	Amber	1	0	1.000
			Green	7	0	1.000
		Low	Red	8	0	1.000
			Amber	14	0	1.000
			Green	30	0	1.000

TABLE 8.17
Grouped Data—
Age Equals Old

Age	Income	Risk	Credit Rating	On-Time	Not On-Time	Probability
Old	Average	Low	Red	0	1	0
			Amber	1	0	1.000
			Green	2	0	1.000
	High	Low	Red	2	0	1.000
			Amber	1	0	1.000
			Green	3	0	1.000

begins with identifying those variables that offer the greatest likelihood of distinguishing between the possible outcomes. For each of the four variables, we can identify the outcome probabilities in Table 8.18.

For the variable Age, there are three outcomes. Entropy for Age by this formula would be as shown in Table 8.19.

Under the Sum heading is the following calculation. For Young, the first term of the Inform equation multiplies the ratio 136/169 times –0.313, and by –1. The second term multiplies the ratio 33/169 times –4.328, and by –1. The sum of these terms is 0.712. This represents 169 of the 400 training cases. The Product heading is the product of sum by probability. For Young, this is 0.712 times 169/400, yielding 0.301. The sum of the three products yields the entropy measure. The lower this entropy measure, the greater the information content (the greater the agreement probability). The entropy measures for the four variables are

Age	0.473
Income	0.500
Risk	0.470
Credit Rating	**0.461**

By this measure, Credit Rating has the greatest information content. Among the Credit Rating categories, we want to select the one with the greatest ability to accurately categorize data (the closest probability to 1.0 for Loan, or 0.0 for Deny Loan). We can consider the relative cost of error. An error of granting a loan to a case where it is not paid on-time may cost nine times ($900) as much as one that does pay on time (but was denied, $100). We can therefore use a cutoff limit of 0.90 probability. If the category being considered has a probability greater than or

TABLE 8.18
Combination
Outcomes

Variable	Value	Cases	On-Time	Late	Prob {On-Time}
Age	Young	169	136	33	0.805
	Middle	221	210	11	0.950
	Old	10	9	1	0.900
Income	Low	47	42	5	0.894
	Average	265	229	36	0.864
	High	88	84	4	0.955
Risk	High	186	150	36	0.806
	Average	19	18	1	0.947
	Low	195	187	8	0.959
Credit Rating	Red	56	40	16	0.714
	Amber	120	100	20	0.833
	Green	224	215	9	0.960

TABLE 8.19
Entropy Calculation for Age

	p/(p+n)	Log(base 2)	n/(p+n)	Log(base 2)	Sum	Probability	Product
Young	136/169	−0.313	33/169	−2.356	0.712	169/400	0.301
Middle	210/221	−0.074	11/221	−4.328	0.285	221/400	0.158
Old	9/10	−0.152	1/10	−3.322	0.469	10/400	0.012
SUM							**0.470**

equal to 0.9, we will create a rule granting the loan. If the category being considered has a probability less than 0.9, we will deny the loan. If Credit Rating is green, the data indicates a 0.953 probability (244 of 256 cases) that the applicant will pay the loan back on time. If Credit Rating is not green, this data indicates a 0.815 probability that the applicant will pay the loan back on time. This would be the first rule selected by the machine learning algorithm.

IF (Credit=Green)	THEN Predict On-Time Payment
ELSE	Predict Late

This rule is subject to two types of error. First, those applicants rated as green may actually not pay on time. (From the data, the probability of this happening is 0.040.) Second, those applicants rated as amber or red may actually have paid if given a loan. (From the data, the probability of this happening is 0.815.) The expectation of this is the probability of an applicant being rated as green (224/400, or 0.550) times the probability of being wrong (0.040), plus the probability of not being green (176/400, or 0.440) times the probability of being wrong (0.795), yielding an expected error of 0.022 + 0.350 = 0.372. We can also calculate the error cost function. This would be $900 times 0.022 + $100 times 0.350, or $55.14. To test this rule, it is best to apply it to a second set of data, different from the data set used to develop the rule. Using the last 250 observations as the test set, Table 8.20 shows the coincidence matrix.

The correct classification rate was 0.620. The cost function for this result would be $900 times 7 plus $100 times 88, or $15,100. Since we had 250 cases, the average error cost would have been $60.40 per case.

The set of rules can be examined further to see if greater accuracy can be obtained. The entropy formula for Age, given that Credit Rating was not green, is 0.672, for Income 0.720, for Risk 0.657, and for the difference between red and amber Credit Rating is 0.718. This indicates that Risk has the greater discriminating power at this point. With this data, if Risk is low, 79 of the 86 cases paid on time (0.919). The other two states had 61 of 90 pay on time (0.678). Therefore, the second rule is

IF (Credit Rating is NOT green)	AND (Risk = Low)	THEN Predict On-Time
ELSE		Predict Late

In this case, the data would indicate probabilities shown in Table 8.21.

The expected error here is the 224/400 times (1 − 0.960) + 86/400 times (1 − 0.919) + 90/400 times (1 − 0.678), or 0.112. The cost function is $900 times 224/400 times 0.040 ($20.16) plus $900 times 86/400 times 0.081 ($15.67) plus $100 times 90/400 times 0.678 ($15.26), or $51.09 per case. This is an improvement over the prior case where the expected error was 0.380 with an expected cost per case of $60.40. The coincidence matrix is as shown in Table 8.22.

TABLE 8.20
Coincidence Matrix
for First Rule

Actual	Late	On-Time	Total
Late	**13**	7	20
On-Time	88	**142**	230
Total	101	149	250

TABLE 8.21
Probabilities
by Case

Credit Rating	Risk	Count	Probability {On-Time}
Green		224/400	0.960
NOT green	Low	86/400	0.919
NOT green	NOT Low	90/400	0.678

TABLE 8.22
Coincidence Matrix
for First Two Rules

Actual	Late	On-Time	Total
Late	**11**	9	20
On-Time	43	**187**	230
Total	54	196	250

TABLE 8.23
Probabilities
Recalculated

Credit Rating	On-Time	Late	Probability {On-Time}
Red	15	13	0.536
Amber	46	16	0.742

TABLE 8.24
Expected Accuracy
of Three Rules

Credit Rating	Risk	Credit Rating	Count	Probability {On-Time}
Green			224/400	0.960
NOT green	High		86/400	0.919
NOT green	NOT high	Amber	62/400	0.742
NOT green	NOT high	NOT high	28/400	0.536

TABLE 8.25
Coincidence Matrix
for Three Rules

Actual	Late	On-Time	Total
Late	**3**	17	20
On-Time	11	**219**	230
Total	14	236	250

TABLE 8.26
Results from
Balancing the
Data Set

Train Set	Late	On-Time	Proportion	Predict 0 = 1	Predict 1 = 0	Correct Rate	Cost
400	45	355	0.1125	20	0	0.920	$18,000
325	45	280	0.1385	20	0	0.920	$18,000
225	45	180	0.2000	9	39	0.808	$12,000
180	45	135	0.2500	9	39	0.808	$12,000
150	45	105	0.3000	9	32	0.956	$11,300

The correct classification rate was 0.792, much better than in Table 8.20. The cost function here would be $900 times 9 plus $100 times 43, or $12,400, or $49.60 per case.

We recalculate entropy, eliminating Credit Rating green and Risk rating Low. The values obtained were 0.902 for Age, 0.893 for Income, 0.897 for Risk, and 0.877 for Credit Rating. The lowest of these values was for Credit. Given that Credit Rating was not green, and Risk was not high. That leaves 90 training cases, as shown in Table 8.23.

While below the specified cutoff limit of 0.9, those with Amber credit ratings clearly had a higher probability of on-time payment than did those with credit ratings of red. A third rule is

IF (Credit Rating NOT green)	AND (Risk NOT high)	AND (Credit Rating amber)	THEN predict On-Time
ELSE			Predict Late

The expected accuracy of the three rules together is shown in Table 8.24.

The expected error here is 0.117, with an expected cost function per case of $75.57 (due to the high error rate for the third rule). The expected classification error went down, although the expected cost function went up. Table 8.25 gives the coincidence matrix for this set of rules using the test data.

Here the correct classification rate increased to 0.888 (it was 0.792 after two rules), while the average cost per case increased to $65.60 from $49.60. When machine learning methods encounter no improvement, they generally stop. Therefore, the last rule would NOT be added to the first two. The machine learning algorithm would stop at:

IF (Credit Rating is green)		THEN Predict On-Time
IF (Credit Rating is NOT green)	AND (Risk = Low)	THEN Predict On-Time
ELSE		Predict Late

Note that this approach does not guarantee optimality. In that sense, it is heuristic, which means it tends to give good models, but there might be better ones.

The model was also run using See5 (see the demonstration of See5 decision tree analysis in the appendix to this chapter). The initial model, using 400 training observations of categorical, degenerated to classifying all cases as On-Time. Due to the highly skewed data set (where 45 cases were Late and 355 were On-Time), this had a fairly high correct classification rate of 0.920. However, it was very bad at predicting applications that would end up late. Balancing the data can improve results. We pruned observations from the training set to control the proportion of late cases, as shown in Table 8.26. Using 325 observations again yielded all forecasts to be On-Time. The model, based on 225 observations (as well as the model based on 180 observations), was to classify all cases as On-Time unless risk was High, and credit was either red or amber. The model using 150 training cases was to classify all cases as On-Time unless the applicant was Young and credit was either red or amber. Models obtained were tested on the same test set of 250 observations.

This data shows a clear trend toward more useful model results by balancing data.

Insurance Fraud Data

A training set of 4,000 observations was used with continuous data (with age and claims standardized to between 0 and 1) using See5. This dataset had only 60 cases of fraud, and thus was highly skewed. See5 responded with a model assigning all cases as not fraudulent. This demonstrates the need to balance data. A new training set was generated, retaining all 60 fraudulent cases, and randomly pruning the not-fraudulent cases down to 600, 10 times the number of fraudulent cases. This yielded the following model:

			Cases	Errors
IF(claim > 0.38)		THEN(not fraud)	634	48
IF(claim ≤ 0.38)	IF(prior ≤ 1)	THEN(not fraud)	8	0
"	IF(prior > 1)	THEN(fraud)	18	6

This model thus had 54 errors out of 660 opportunities, for a correct classification rate of 0.918. (The model missed 48 of 60 actual fraudulent cases, or an 80-percent error in the important category.) The results applied to 1,000 test cases, as shown in Table 8.27.

The model had a correct classification rate of 0.968, which is quite good. However, of the 22 fraudulent test cases, it missed 86 percent. The primary point, however, is that balancing the data may be necessary in order to get a useful model. Data mining software usually has that capability.

Job Application Data

Job application data is highly skewed, with very few cases rated "excellent." However, we can apply See5 on the data, either in categorical form or in standardized numeric form. Using the first 300 observations for training over the categorical data, we obtain the following rules:

				Cases	Errors
IF (major = none)			THEN (minimal)	53	27
IF (major = other)			THEN (minimal)	21	7
IF (major = Csci)			THEN (adequate)	34	6
IF (major = Engr)			THEN (adequate)	38	1
IF (major = Sci)			THEN (adequate)	18	2
IF (major = IS)			THEN (adequate)	34	8
IF (major = BusAd)	AND (experience = none)		THEN (unacceptable)	1	0
"	AND (experience < 3)		THEN (minimal)	11	3
"	AND (experience > 2)	AND (age < 25)	THEN (adequate)	0	0
"	"	AND (age 25 − 30)	THEN (minimal)	71	37
"	"	AND (age > 30)	THEN (adequate)	19	5

This model was correct 68 percent of the time on the training data, which is not bad for four outcomes. Application of the test data yielded the coincidence matrix given in Table 8.28.

This model was correct 116 of 200 times, or 58 percent of the time. Note that the model never predicted an excellent outcome, and only five unacceptable outcomes (and was wrong in four of those cases). The lack of excellent outcomes is due to the sparsity of cases in the training set. Of 300 training cases, 34 were unacceptable, 96 minimal, 162 adequate, and only eight excellent.

TABLE 8.27
Coincidence Matrix for the See5 Fraud Model

Actual	Not Fraud	Fraud	Total
Not fraud	965	13	978
Fraud	19	3	22
Total	984	16	1000

TABLE 8.28
Coincidence Matrix
for the Job
Application
Categorical Model
on Test Data

Actual	Unacceptable	Minimal	Adequate	Excellent	Totals
Unacceptable	**1**	24			25
Minimal	4	**48**	7		59
Adequate		34	**67**		101
Excellent			15		15
Totals	5	106	89	0	200

The continuous standardized data set was also analyzed with a decision tree model from See5. The resulting decision tree was as follows:

				Cases	Errors
IF(degree = 0)	IF(state>0)		THEN(minimal)	11	3
"	"	IF(experience≤0.8)	THEN(unacceptable)	34	14
"	"	IF(experience>0.8)	THEN(minimal)	8	2
IF(degree > 0)	IF(major>0.7)		THEN(adequate)	124	17
"	IF(major≤0.7)	IF(age≤0.333)	THEN(minimal)	101	46
"	"	IF(age>0.333)	THEN(adequate)	22	6

Again, this decision tree did not identify any cases as excellent (still due to the sparsity of such cases in the training data set). Over the training set, this model was correct 212 of 300 times for a correct classification rate of 0.71. The coincidence matrix for this model over the test set is given in Table 8.29.

Over the test data, this model had a correct classification rate of 119/200, or 0.595. This is practically the same as the model based upon categorical data.

Decision Tree Software Products

Algorithms are marketed, such as CART (classification and regression trees), CHAID (chi-squared automatic interaction detection), ID3, and ID4.5. Nock and Jappy (1999) classified algorithms that learn decision lists.[12] Greedy, iterative algorithms such as CN2 add rules one at a time until the dataset is exhausted. Algorithms that search the rule space before adding to the decision list use branch and bound, such as BruteDL. The last class of algorithms used stochastic search, such as SDL does with simulated annealing.

Many data mining software systems include rule-induction/decision tree algorithms, such as C4.5 (and See5), successors to ID3.[13] DBMine includes ID3 decision tree methodology.[14] Other systems, such as BusinessObjects Version 4.0 are based on intuitive decision tree technology. CART (Classification and Regression Trees) provides reliable classification and prediction models for profiling the best customers, targets for direct mailings, fraud detection, and credit risk analysis.[15] Cognos' Scenario software provides a range of decision tree products.[16]

TABLE 8.29
Coincidence
Matrix for the
Job Application
Categorical
Model on
Test Data

Actual	Unacceptable	Minimal	Adequate	Excellent	Totals
Unacceptable	**9**	15	1		25
Minimal	7	**37**	15		59
Adequate		28	**73**		101
Excellent			15		15
Totals	16	80	104	0	200

Appendix

Demonstration of See5 Decision Tree Analysis

We demonstrate the use of See5 data mining software on the expenditure data file, analyzing the amount spent on various categories such as owning and operating automobiles, clothing, entertainment, groceries, housing, and restaurants.

DATA CLEANING

The data file has 19 variables and 1,000 records. There are two types of variables: demographic and expenditure (showing proportion of income spent on a number of categories), as shown in Table 8A.1.

The target of the data mining task is to find the characteristics of potential customers for each expenditure category. A simple case is to categorize clothing expenditures (or other expenditures in the data set) per year as a 2-class classification problem. Based on the existing source data, some derived variables are added to make more details for the 2-class classification problem. This process could be the following:

1. Create new variables by multiplying the "income" and each ratio, respectively. For example: the new variable "Cloth" is the value of "income" multiplied by "ProCloth." In the same way, other variables such as Rest, Hous, Util, Auto, Groc, and Ent are added in.
2. Count the average value of each new variable. Then create a binary variable for each target variable (Groc, Rest, Hous, Util, Auto, Cloth, and Ent). These binary variables have values of 1 or 0. For each new variable, when its value is bigger than the average value, it's assigned a value of 1. Otherwise, it's assigned a value of 0. These new binary variables are called GrocClass, RestClass, HousClass, UtilClass, AutoClass, ClothClass, and EntClass.
3. Data for mining. Take "Cloth" as an example to illustrate this point. Before deciding whether the customer is interested in this field, it is necessary to figure out "which variables are needed." The new variable "Cloth" itself cannot be

TABLE 8A.1
Variables in the Expenditure Data File

Demographic Variables	Description	Consumer Variables	Proportion of Income Spent
Age	Integer, 16 and up	ProGroc	At groceries
Gender	0-female, 1-male	ProRest	At restaurants
Marital status	0-single, 0.5-divorced, 1-married	ProHous	On housing
Dependents	Integer	ProUtil	On utilities
Income	$ annual	ProAuto	Owning & operating autos
Job years	Integer, current job	ProCloth	On clothing
Town years	Integer, this town	ProEnt	On entertainment
Years education	Integer, completed		
Drivers License	0-no, 1-yes		
Own Home	0-no, 1-yes		
Credit Cards	Integer, number		
Churn	Integer, canceled last year		

TABLE 8A.2
First Five
Observations in
Cloth2.data

Variable	Obs. 1	Obs. 2	Obs. 3	Obs. 4	Obs. 5
Age	87	64	23	48	56
Gender	0	0	0	0	1
Marital	0.5	1	0	1	1
Dependents	0	0	0	1	0
Income	80.054	51.253	41.426	59.073	57.397
Job Yrs	5	4	7	13	21
Town Yrs	0	0	23	0	18
Yrs Ed	13	11	11	13	13
Dri. Lic.	0	1	1	1	1
Own Home	0	0	0	1	1
# Cred Card	1	13	1	4	9
Churn	0	1	0	0	1
ProGroc	0.031	0.044	0.000	0.073	0.037
ProRest	0.009	0.032	0.080	0.002	0.019
ProHous	0.132	0.210	0.247	0.248	0.237
ProUtil	0.031	0.042	0.081	0.098	0.079
ProAuto	0.000	0.069	0.081	0.059	0.067
ProCloth	0.066	0.119	0.146	0.106	0.116
ProEnt	0.049	0.062	0.091	0.035	0.050
Groceries	2.458	2.271	0	4.319	2.140
Restaurant	0.759	1.633	3.331	0.133	1.098
Housing	10.596	10.779	10.219	14.663	13.578
Utilities	2.458	2.133	3.341	5.805	4.553
Auto	0	3.539	3.354	3.512	3.872
Clothing	5.308	6.118	6.038	6.259	6.643
Entertain	3.936	3.174	3.751	2.059	2.850
ClothClass	0	0	0	0	0

used for mining because in reality this value is unknown before the prediction. There are 25 variables for mining "Cloth" (the first record in the database). The first five observations are shown in Table 8A.2.

DATA MINING PROCESS

In this section, we'll still be mining "Cloth" as our example. First, the data must be transformed into the See5 required format. The first record of the data for mining "Cloth" is

87.00,0.00,0.50,0.00,80.05,5.00,0.00,13.00,0.00,0.00,1.00,0.00,0.03,9.47623172478198e −03,0.13,0.03,0.00,0.06,0.04,0.75,10.59,2.45,0.00,5.30,3.93,0.00

After the last comma, the variable ClothClass is the class to which the case is assigned. The data file is named "Cloth2.data." There is another file called "Cloth2.names," which summarizes the data. It is organized as follows:

```
       0.00,1.00. | classes
A1:              continuous.
A2:              continuous.
. . .
A25:             continuous.
```

"0.00,1.00.|classes" means that the file contains two classes which are represented by 1 and 0.A1–A25 are the variables in the data set. Figure 8A.1 gives a screenshot of the See5 analysis for the data set Cloth.data.

FIGURE 8A.1
Locate Data for
Loading

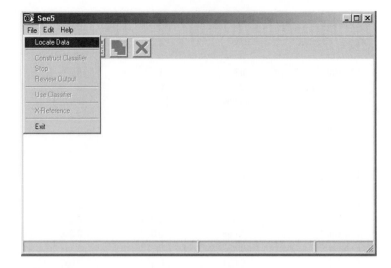

FIGURE 8A.2
Data Is Now
Loaded

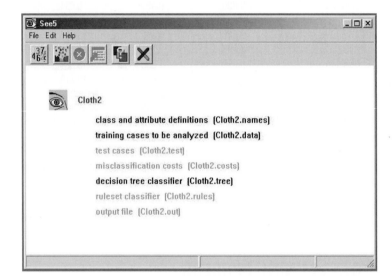

FIGURE 8A.3
Choose the
Construct Classifier

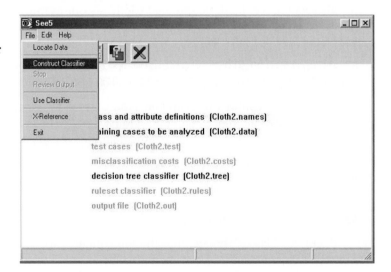

FIGURE 8A.4
Construct
Configuration

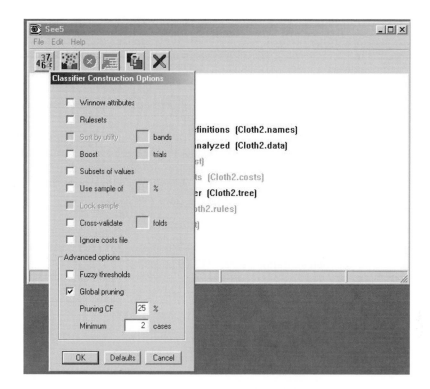

Figure 8A.2 shows the screen after data is loaded.

Figure 8A.3 shows the command to choose the classification construct.

Figure 8A.4 offers options to include the pruning confidence factor, and a minimum setting for cases required in a class (in this instance, 2 is entered).

Figure 8A.5 shows the resulting decision tree after the training set is analyzed. In this case, 50 percent of the 10,000 observations were used for training. Note

FIGURE 8A.5
Decision Tree
Created after
Training

that data mining software randomly selects observations at this rate, while our examples using Excel are controlled for the specific observations used for training and testing. Randomness is a favorable feature. However, it also guarantees that a particular study cannot be replicated (unless some random number seed is applied).

Figure 8A.6 shows the See5 screen applied to use the classifier (apply the decision tree model to the test cases).

Figure 8A.7 shows the inputting of a particular sample set of data.

Figure 8A.8 shows the result for the decision tree model from the given input.

Results from the decision tree model are reported in coincidence matrices. First, a report is given treating all observations as training data. This provides a global picture of the model's fit to the data.

1.2 Cloth
(a) All data for training
Evaluation on training data   (10000 cases):

Decision Tree

Size	Errors	
91	227(2.3%)	<<

(a)	(b)	<-classified as
6670	124	(a) : class 0.00
103	3103	(b) : class 1.00

In this case, there was a very good fit, with only a 2.3-percent error (fairly evenly distributed over the two output classes). Next, results are reported by training (the 5,000 cases used to build the model) and test data (the 5,000 cases that the software held out).

FIGURE 8A.6
Choose Use
Classifier

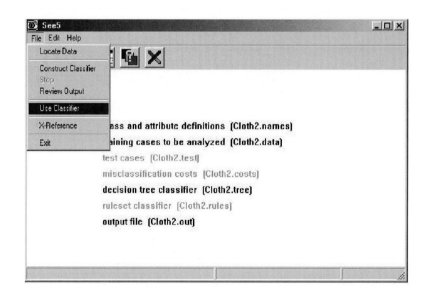

FIGURE 8A.7
Input Sample Data

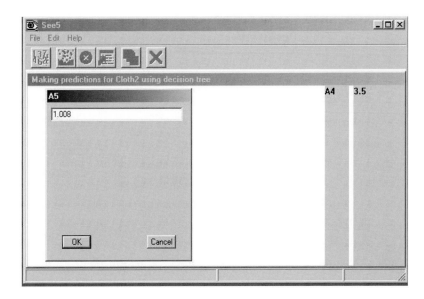

(b)   **50% for training and 50% testing**
Evaluation on training data   (5000 cases):
           Decision Tree

Size	Errors	
68	107(2.1%)	<<

(a)	(b)	<-classified as
3310	46	(a): class 0.00
61	1583	(b): class 1.00

FIGURE 8A.8
Prediction Result

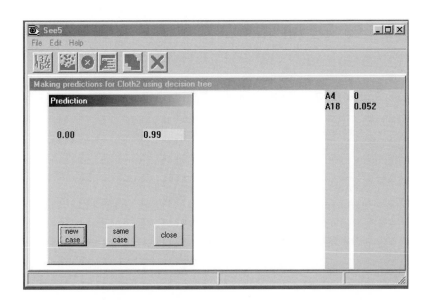

Evaluation on test data (5000 cases):
Decision Tree

Size	Errors	
68	221(4.4%)	<<

(a)	(b)	<-classified as
3359	79	(a): class 0.00
142	1420	(b): class 1.00

The model had a classification error rate of 4.4 percent over the test data.

Summary

Decision trees are very effective and useful data mining models. They are automatic, an application of machine learning, which in itself makes them attractive. They are relatively robust, in that they are not adversely affected by noisy or missing data. They can handle very large data sets, and can deal with data in categorical or numeric form. They are also very strong in their ability to explain their conclusions (rules can be expressed in natural language, and communication to managers is excellent). As shown in the preceding section, there are many software products available to support decision tree modeling.

Glossary

branches The subcategories on a decision tree.

confidence level The number of events where items were associated divided by the total number of events for the base item.

decision trees Logical branching on variables; enumerating cases with outputs.

entropy The measure of information, or more specifically, the degree of randomness in data. Lower scores indicate a greater ability to discriminate outcome categories.

expert system Artificial intelligence system to replicate the behavior of an expert. Usually implemented through a series of production rules (IF–THEN).

goal driven Method of generating rules through induction based on improved successful performance.

heuristic Method of reaching conclusions that works fairly successfully, but does not guarantee optimality.

interestingness Characteristic of rules identified that are important and unexpected.

machine learning A system to develop rules automatically.

node A decision tree element where branching takes place.

regression tree Decision tree based on continuous outcomes.

rule induction Algorithms capable of generating sets of rules based upon the analysis of data.

rule-based system Algorithm that classifies cases based upon a set of association rules developed from a training set.

support The proportion of records covered by the set of attributes.

Exercises

1. Apply the decision tree algorithm to the Job Applicant data file. Use the categorical data. Employ all 500 observations, with 50 percent for training and 50 percent for testing. Use data mining software if available, or Excel if not. Develop the coincidence matrix for this data.

2. Apply the decision tree algorithm to the Job Applicant data file. Use standardized continuous data. Employ all 500 observations, with 50 percent for training and 50 percent for testing. Use data mining software if available, or Excel if not. Develop the coincidence matrix for this data.

3. Apply the decision tree algorithm to the Loan Application data set. Use the categorical variables: age, income, risk, and credit rating. Employ all 650 observations, selecting 50 percent for training. Develop the coincidence matrix. Comment on the results.

4. Apply the decision tree algorithm to the Loan Application data set. Use continuous data for variables age, income, risk, and credit rating. Employ all 650 observations, selecting 50 percent for training. Develop the coincidence matrix. Comment on the results.

5. Apply the decision tree algorithm to all 5,000 observations of the Insurance Fraud data set. Transform age by making 20 (or younger) =0, 50 (or older) 1.0, and every age between =age/30. Leave gender as is (0 or 1). Transform claim by dividing claim by 5000. Transform tickets and prior claims by making 0 = 0, 1 = 0.5, and 2 or more = 1.0. Transform attorney by making "none" = 0 and all others = 1. Use 60 percent of the data for training. Employ data mining software if available, or Excel if not. Develop the coincidence matrix and comment on the results.

6. Apply the decision tree algorithm to all 5,000 observations of the Insurance Fraud data set. Use categorical dataUse 60 percent of the data for training. Use data mining software if available, or Excel if not. Develop the coincidence matrix and then comment on the results.

7. Apply the decision tree algorithm to the Customer Expenditure data set with the intent of identifying the type of people who spend the following proportion of their income on groceries: less than 1 percent, between 1 and 5 percent, 5 to 10 percent, and over 10 percent. Use standardized data for the input variables. Employ 8,000 observations as the training set, and apply it to 2,000 test observations. Use data mining software if available, or Excel if not. Develop the coincidence matrix and then count the number of rules obtained.

8. Apply the decision tree algorithm to the Customer Expenditure data set with the intent of identifying the type of people who spend the following proportion of their income on restaurants: less than 1 percent, between 1 and 5 percent, 5 to 10 percent, and over 10 percent. Use standardized data for the input variables. Employ 8,000 observations as the training set, and apply it to 2,000 test observations. Use data mining software if available, or Excel if not. Develop the coincidence matrix and then count the number of rules obtained.

9. Apply the decision tree algorithm to the Customer Expenditure data set with the intent of identifying the type of people who spend the following proportion of their income on housing: less than 1 percent, between 1 and 5 percent, 5 to 10 percent, and over 10 percent. Use standardized data for the input variables. Use 8,000 observations as the training set, and apply it to 2,000 test observations. Use data mining software if available, or Excel if not. Develop the coincidence matrix and then count the number of rules obtained.

10. Apply the decision tree algorithm to the Customer Expenditure data set with the intent of identifying the type of people who spend the following portion of their income on utilities: less than 1 percent, between 1 and 5 percent, 5 to 10 percent, and over 10 percent. Use standardized data for the input variables. Employ 8,000 observations as the training set, and then apply it to 2,000 test observations. Use data mining software if available, or Excel if not. Develop the coincidence matrix and then count the number of rules obtained.

11. Apply the decision tree algorithm to the Customer Expenditure data set with the intent of identifying the type of people who spend the following portion of their income on operating and owning automobiles: less than 1 percent, between 1 and 5 percent, 5 to 10 percent, and over 10 percent. Use standardized data for the input variables. Employ 8,000 observations as the training set, and apply it to 2,000 test observations. Use data mining software if available, or Excel if not. Develop the coincidence matrix and then count the number of rules obtained.

12. Apply the decision tree algorithm to the Customer Expenditure data set with the intent of identifying the type of people who spend the following proportion of their income on clothing: less than 1 percent, between 1 and 5 percent, 5 to 10 percent, and over 10 percent. Use standardized data for the input variables. Employ 8000 observations as the training set, and apply it to 2,000 test observations. Use data mining software if available, or Excel if not. Develop the coincidence matrix and count the number of rules obtained.

13. Apply the decision tree algorithm to the Customer Expenditure data set with the intent of identifying the type of people who spend the following proportion of their income on entertainment: less than 1 percent, between 1 and 5 percent, 5 to 10 percent, and over 10 percent. Use standardized data for the input variables. Employ 8,000 observations as the training set, and apply it to 2,000 test observations. Use data mining software if available, or Excel if not. Develop the coincidence matrix and then count the number of rules obtained.

Endnotes

1. G. Linoff, "Which Way to the Mine?" *As/400 Systems Management*, volume 26, number 1 (January 1998), pp. 42–44.
2. D. Michie, "Learning Concepts from Data," *Expert Systems with Applications*, volume 15, number 34 (1998), pp. 193–204.
3. D. A. Koonce, C.-H. Fang, and S.-C. Tsai, "A Data Mining Tool for Learning from Manufacturing Systems," *Computers & Industrial Engineering*, volume 33, numbers 1–2 (1997), pp. 27–30.
4. V. Dhar and R. Stein, *Intelligent Decision Support Methods: The Science of Knowledge Work*, (Upper Saddle River, NJ: Prentice Hall, 1997).
5. V. Dhar and R. Stein, *Intelligent Decision Support Methods: The Science of Knowledge Work*. (Upper Saddle River, NJ: Prentice Hall, 1997).
6. D. A. Koonce, C.-H. Fang, and S.-C. Tsai, "A Data Mining Tool for Learning from Manufacturing Systems," *Computers & Industrial Engineering*, volume 33, numbers 1–2 (1997), pp. 27–30.
7. L. G. Cooper and G. Guiffrida, "Turning Datamining into a Management Science Tool: New Algorithms and Empirical Results," *Management Science*, volume 46, number 2 (2000), pp. 249–264.
8. S. Tsumoto, "Automated Knowledge Discovery in Clinical Databases Based on Rough Set Model," *INFOR*, volume 38, number 3 (2000), pp. 196–207.

9. T. M. Khoshgoftaar, E. B. Allen, W. D. Jones, and J. P. Hudepohl, "Data Mining for Predictors of Software Quality," *International Journal of Software Engineering and Knowledge Engineering*, volume 9, number 5 (1999), pp. 547–563.

10. R. Milne, M. Drummond, and P. Renoux, "Predicting Paper Making Defects On-line Using Data Mining," *Knowledge-Based Systems*, volume 11 (1998), pp. 331–338.

11. R. G. Arunasalam, J. T. Richie, W. Egan, O. Gur-Ali, and W. A. Wallace, "Reengineering Claims Processing Using Probabilistic Inductive Learning," *IEEE Transactions on Engineering Management*, volume 46, number 3 (August 1999), pp. 335–345.

12. R. Nock and P. Jappy, "Decision Tree Based Induction of Decision Lists," *Intelligent Data Analysis*, volume 3 (1999), pp. 227–240.

13. S. Lavington, N. Dewhurst, E. Wilkins, and A. Freitas, "Interfacing Knowledge Discovery Algorithms to Large Database Management Systems," *Information & Software Technology*, volume 41, number 9 (June 1999), pp. 605–617.

14. Koonce et al. (1997), op. cit.

15. R. McLaughlin, "Answering the Age-Old Question of 'When?'" *Zip/Target Marketing*, volume 21, number 8, (August 1998), p. 24.

16. B. De Ville, "Data Mining for the Desktop," *Marketing Research: A Magazine of Management & Applications*, volume 9, number 4 (Winter 1997), pp. 57–59.

CHAPTER NINE

Linear Programming–Based Methods

This chapter:

Describes linear discriminant analysis

Describes multiple criteria linear programming classifications

Describes fuzzy linear programming classifications

Demonstrates credit card portfolio management

Reviews the linear programming–based software support available

One of the features of modern business is the existence of large pooled data sets by industry. For instance, corporations exist to gather data on entire industries. This can include the grocery industry for a specific metropolitan area, where detailed sales data is collected on a daily basis from each store, which is then combined and aggregated to identify what sales activity was occurring according to specific products in the metropolitan region. This traffic in data has led to entire industries providing highly useful information to members of those industries.

In addition to grocery sales, a similar market exists for the bank credit card arena. This chapter includes a real application where credit card data is gathered nationally, and then mined in order to identify industrywide data about the credit card business. Within that application, linear programming models were developed as an alternative type of predictive model. This is a form of discriminant analysis, covered earlier in Chapter 6 as a form of regression. Linear programming is an optimization technique, capable of identifying the combination of variable values in a system of equations that is the least (or most) of some function. In this case, the model purpose is to minimize error in a data set (just as regression models minimized error). Linear programming provides more flexibility than ordinary least squares regression in terms of constraints on the model. The credit card data firm in the real application experimented with linear programming–based prediction models, and found them to have relatively attractive features to regression models.

Linear programming models, like regression, neural network, and decision tree models, support the modeling phase of the data mining process. Each of these systems tends to be better for particular data sets. The general practice in data mining is to try all available models, and see which works best in terms of coincidence matrices, or cost function. Linear programming models expand the toolbox, although thus far it usually is not found in commercial data mining software. It is a developing topic in data mining, but one with useful potential.

Data mining developments include consideration of alternative algorithms. Linear programming supports a number of data mining alternative techniques. It is an optimization technique that identifies the combination of variable values in a linear system of relationships that is best measured by some linear function. Linear programming (LP) models are formulated with an **objective function** and a number of **constraints** with a fixed resource availability level (right-hand side). Both objective function and constraints are linear combinations of decision variables.[1] Linear programming–based data mining techniques include linear discriminant analysis, multiple criteria programming classification, and fuzzy linear programming classification. In the U.S., roughly about 85 percent of the Fortune 500 companies have used linear programming in business decision making. Application areas of linear programming include transportation, agriculture, economic analysis, finance, energy industries, military, production, and public policy.

A key idea in linear programming–based data mining is that the misclassification of data can be reduced by using two objectives in a linear system. One is to **maximize the minimum distances (MMD)** of data records from a critical value. Another separates the data records by **minimizing the sum of the deviations (MSD)** of the data from the critical value.[2] Compared with traditional mathematical tools of classification, such as decision trees, statistics, and neural networks, this approach is simple and direct, free of statistical assumptions, and allows decision makers to play an active part in the analysis. However, managing this tool requires certain skills of formulating LP problems, and effective and flexible use of existing commercial software packages. Unlike some of the other methods we've discussed in this book, the format of data for linear programming–based data mining has to be quantitative. If the available data is qualitative, it needs to be transformed before analysis.

Linear Discriminant Analysis

The fundamental framework of linear discriminant analysis can be described as follows:

Suppose each evaluated target $a = (a_1, \ldots, a_r)$ is described by r attributes (or variables). Consider n targets where data observation of the ith target is $A_{i1} = (A_{i1}, \ldots, A_{ir})$ for $i = 1, \ldots, n$. In linear discriminant analysis, we want to determine the **optimal coefficients** (or weights) for the attributes, denoted by $X = (x_1, \ldots, x_r)$, and a boundary value (scalar) b to separate two predetermined classes: G (Good) and B (Bad); that is

$$A_{i1} x_1 + \cdots + A_{ir} x_r \leq b, A_i \in B \text{ (Bad)} \text{ and } A_{i1} x_1 + \cdots + A_{ir} x_r \geq b, A_i \in G \text{ (Good)}$$

To measure the separation of Good and Bad, we define α_i to be the overlapping of the two-class boundary for case A_i (external measurement). Then, α is denoted as the max overlapping of the two-class boundary for all cases A_i ($\alpha_i < \alpha$). We also define β_i to be the distance of case A_i from its adjusted boundary (internal measurement), while β is the minimum distance of all cases A_i to the adjusted boundary ($\beta_i > \beta$).

Linear programs for data separation can be formulated in several ways. We present two basic formulations.[3]

(1) MSD:

Minimize $\alpha_1 + \cdots + \alpha_r$
Subject to:

$$A_{11} x_1 + \cdots + A_{1r} x_r \leq b + \alpha_1, \quad \text{for } \mathbf{A}_1, \in B,$$

$$\cdots\cdots\cdots$$

$$A_{n1} x_1 + \cdots + A_{nr} x_r \geq b - \alpha_r, \quad \text{for } \mathbf{A}_n, \in G,$$

$$\alpha_1, \ldots, \alpha_r \geq 0,$$

(2) MMD:

Maximize $\beta_1 + \cdots + \beta_r$
Subject to:

$$A_{11} x_1 + \cdots + A_{1r} x_r \geq b - \beta_1, \quad \text{for } \mathbf{A}_1, \in B,$$

$$\cdots\cdots\cdots$$

$$A_{n1} x_1 + \cdots + A_{nr} x_r \leq b + \beta_r, \quad \text{for } \mathbf{A}_n, \in G,$$

$$\beta_1, \ldots, \beta_r \geq 0.$$

Let's use a simple example to show how linear discriminant analysis works. Assume that a credit-rating problem has two variables (attributes) involving two people. Let the variables a_1 = age and a_2 = salary with the same quantitative measurement. The observations of A_1 and A_2 are given from a database (see Table 9.1). Our goal is to identify a boundary value b and the optimal solution of LP $(x_1{}^*, x_2{}^*)$ so that the two people can be separated into categories of Bad and Good. This LP problem can be modeled as:

Minimize $\alpha_1 + \alpha_2$
Subject to:

$$6\, x_1 + 8\, x_2 \leq b + \alpha_1, \quad \text{for } A_1 \in B,$$

$$15\, x_1 + 31\, x_2 \geq b - \alpha_2, \quad \text{for } A_2 \in G,$$

$$\alpha_1, \alpha_2 \geq 0.$$

To further simply the problem, suppose we use $b = 9$. If the commercial software, such as LINDO, is employed to solve the problem, its optimal solution is found as $x_1{}^* = 0$ and $x_2{}^* = 0.290323$. Then we have the following:

For A_1: because its LP score is $6\,(0) + 8\,(0.290323) = 2.345840 < 9$, it is Bad, and
For A_2: because its LP score is $15\,(0) + 31\,(0.290323) = 9.000013 > 9$, it is Good.

The separation of the preceding example is perfect with no overlapping (see Figure 9.1). In most cases, overlapping data exists, as shown in Figure 9.2.

TABLE 9.1
A Simple Separation

Cases	a_1	a_2	Boundary b	The Best Coefficients $x_1{}^*$	$x_2{}^*$	LP Score
A_1	6	8	9	0	.290323	2.345840
A_2	15	31	9	0	.290323	9.000013

FIGURE 9.1
A Perfect Separation

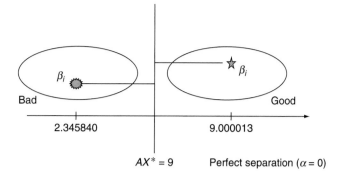

FIGURE 9.2
Overlapping Data in Linear Discriminant Analysis

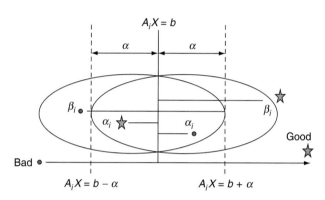

FIGURE 9.3
Three-Class Linear Discriminant Analysis

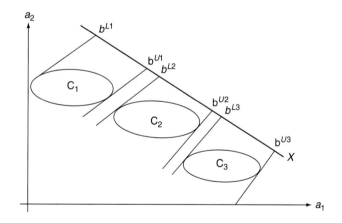

Because its separation power is demonstrated by using the boundary of the constraints, the linear discriminant analysis can be flexibly extended from a two-class separation into a multiclass separation (see the appendix at the end of this chapter). A graphical representation of three-class separation without overlapping can be viewed in Figure 9.3.

As illustrated, we should consider a three-class linear discriminant analysis for assigning credit applicants to different risk classes. An applicant is to be classified as a "poor" (C_1), "fair" (C_2), or "good" (C_3) credit risk based on his/her responses to two questions appearing on a standard credit application. Columns 1 through 3 of Table 9.2 show previous experience with 12 customers.

To build a linear program, we can define θ_1 as the overlapping between the C_1 and C_2, while θ_2 is the overlapping between the C_2 and C_3. Assume p_i to be the penalties

TABLE 9.2
A Small Example of Credit Applicants Risk Classification

Customer	# of Credit	Responses		LP Scores at the Coefficients	
		Quest 1	Quest 2	$x_1^* = 1$	$x_2^* = -4$
Class 1	1	1	3	-11	$b^{L1} = -20$
(Poor risk)	2	2	5	-18	
	3	3	4	-13	
	4	4	6	-20	$b^{U1} = -11$
Class 2	5	5	7	-23	$b^{L2} = -21$
(Fair risk)	6	6	9	-30	
	7	7	8	-25	
	8	7	7	-21	
	9	9	9	-27	$b^{U2} = -30$
Class 3	10	6	2	-2	$b^{L3} = -10$
(Good risk)	11	6	4	-10	
	12	8	3	-4	$b^{U3} = -2$

for θ_i (a "cost" of misclassification), $i = 1, 2$. If version 1 of the three-class formulation in the later appendix is used, then the classification problem is expressed as:

Minimize $p_1\theta_1 + p_2\theta_2$
Subject to:

$$x_1 + 3x_2 \geq b^{L1}, \quad x_1 + 3x_2 \leq b^{U1}$$
$$2x_1 + 5x_2 \geq b^{L1}, \quad 2x_1 + 5x_2 \leq b^{U1}$$
$$3x_1 + 4x_2 \geq b^{L1}, \quad 3x_1 + 4x_2 \leq b^{U1}$$
$$4x_1 + 6x_2 \geq b^{L1}, \quad 4x_1 + 6x_2 \leq b^{U1}$$
$$5x_1 + 7x_2 \geq b^{L2}, \quad 5x_1 + 7x_2 \leq b^{U2}$$
$$6x_1 + 9x_2 \geq b^{L2}, \quad 6x_1 + 9x_2 \leq b^{U2}$$
$$7x_1 + 8x2 \geq b^{L2}, \quad 7x_1 + 8x2 \leq b^{U2}$$
$$7x_1 + 7x_2 \geq b^{L2}, \quad 7x_1 + 7x_2 \leq b^{U2}$$
$$9x_1 + 9x_2 \geq b^{L2}, \quad 9x_1 + 9x_2 \leq b^{U2}$$
$$6x_1 + 2x_2 \geq b^{L3}, \quad 6x_1 + 2x_2 \leq b^{U3}$$
$$6x_1 + 4x_2 \geq b^{L3}, \quad 6x_1 + 4x_2 \leq b^{U3}$$
$$8x_1 + 3x_2 \geq b^{L3}, \quad 8x_1 + 3x_2 \leq b^{U3}$$
$$b^{U1} + 1 < b^{L2} + \theta_1, \quad b^{U2} + 1 < b^{L3} + \theta_2$$

where b^{U1}, b^{U2}, and b^{U3} are the upper bounds, and b^{L1}, b^{L2}, b^{L3} are lower bounds.

Using LINDO to solve this problem with the assumption that $x_1 \geq 1$, the solution of data separation is found as $x_1^* = 1$, $x_2^* = -4$ and $b^{L1} = -20$, $b^{L2} = -21$, $b^{L3} = -10$, $b^{U1} = -11$, $b^{U2} = -30$, and $b^{U3} = -2$ (the fourth column of Table 9.2).

Multiple Criteria Linear Programming Classification

Computational experience on MMD and MSD showed that, generally, the classification results of MMD often are opposite to those of MSD because of the extreme cases of MMD and MSD in terms of optimization. The formulation of linear discriminant analysis could be improved for a certain combination of MMD and MSD for a better data separation. Instead of maximizing the minimum distances

(MMD) of data records from a boundary b or minimizing the sum of the deviations (MSD) of the data from b, **multiple criteria linear programming** (MCLP) classification considers all of the scenarios of **trade-offs** between MMD and MSD and finds a **compromise solution.** To find the compromise solution of MMD and MSD for data separation, we want to minimize the sum of α_i and maximize the sum of β_i simultaneously, as follows.

(3) *Two-Class MCLP:*

Minimize $\alpha_1 + \cdots + \alpha_r$ and *Maximize* $\beta_1 + \cdots + \beta_r$
Subject to:

$$A_{11} x_1 + \cdots + A_{1r} x_r = b + \alpha_1 - \beta_1, \quad \text{for } \mathbf{A}_1 \in B,$$

$$\ldots\ldots\ldots$$

$$A_{n1} x_1 + \cdots + A_{nr} x_r = b - \alpha_r + \beta_r, \quad \text{for } \mathbf{A}_n \in G,$$

$$\alpha_1, \ldots, \alpha_r \geq 0, \quad \beta_1, \ldots, \beta_r \geq 0.$$

Even though the preceding problem can be solved by conventional multiple criteria linear programming algorithms, commercial software for linear programming can be readily utilized to solve this problem after it has been modified as the revised MCLP in the appendix.[4] The idea is illustrated by Figure 9.4. Instead of seeking MMD (*Maximize* $\beta_1 + \cdots + \beta_r$) or MSD (*Minimize* $\alpha_1 + \cdots + \alpha_r$) separately, we set up the ideal point of both as (α^*, β^*). Then, the shortest "distance" (through *Minimize* $d_\alpha^- + d_\alpha^+ + d_\beta^- + d_\beta^+$) to the frontier of MMD and MSD will be used to determine the data separation.

We continue using the simple problem presented by Table 9.1 to show how to use the revised version of the MCLP classification method via linear programming software. According to the formulation of the appendix, we have the following:

Minimize $d_\alpha^- + d_\alpha^+ + d_\beta^- + d_\beta^+$
Subject to:

$$\alpha^* + \alpha_1 + \alpha_2 = d_\alpha^- - d_\alpha^+,$$
$$\beta^* - \beta_1 + \beta_2 = d_\beta^- - d_\beta^+,$$
$$6 x_1 + 8 x_2 = b + \alpha_1 - \beta_1, \text{ for } \mathbf{A}_1 \in B,$$
$$15 x_1 + 31 x_2 = b - \alpha_2 + \beta_2, \text{ for } \mathbf{A}_2 \in G,$$
$$\alpha_1, \alpha_2, \beta_1, \beta_2, d_\alpha^-, d_\alpha^+, d_\beta^-, d_\beta^+ \geq 0$$

FIGURE 9.4
An MCLP
Formulation

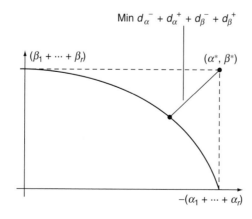

Suppose that we assign $b = 9$, $\alpha^* = 0.001$, and $\beta^* = 1000$, then the separation solution by using LINDO would be $x_1^* = 0$ and $x_2^* = 32.548390$, $\alpha_1 = 251.387100$, $\beta_1 = 0$, $\alpha_2 = 0$, and $\beta_2 = 1000.000000$. The calculation of MCLP score with the adjusted boundary is

For A_1: $6(0) + 8 (32.548390) = 260.3864$, which is Bad, and
For A_2: $15(0) + 31 (32.548390) = 1009.0001$, which is Good.

Similar to the two-class situation, a three-class MCLP model can be written as in the appendix of this chapter.[5] The small three-class problem in Table 9.2 can be formulated by this MCLP method as:

Minimize $d_1 + d_2 + d_3 + d_4 + d_5 + d_6 + d_7 + d_8$
Subject to:

$$d_1 - d_2 - \alpha_1 - \alpha_2 - \alpha_3 - \alpha_4 - \alpha_5 - \alpha_6 - \alpha_7 - \alpha_8 - \alpha_9 - \alpha_{10} - \alpha_{11} - \alpha_{12} = 0.1$$
$$d_3 - d_4 + \beta_1 + \beta_2 + \beta_3 + \beta_4 + \beta_5 + \beta_6 + \beta_7 + \beta_8 + \beta_9 + \beta_{10} + \beta_{11} + \beta_{12} = 10$$
$$d_5 - d_6 - s_1 - s_2 - s_3 - s_4 - s_5 - s_6 - s_7 - s_8 - s_9 - s_{10} - s_{11} - s_{12} = 0.2$$
$$d_7 - d_8 + t_1 + t_2 + t_3 + t_4 + t_5 + t_6 + t_7 + t_8 + t_9 + t_{10} + t_{11} + t_{12} = 9$$
$$\alpha_1 + s_1 + b_1 - b_2 < 0$$
$$\alpha_2 + s_2 + b_1 - b_2 < 0$$
$$\alpha_3 + s_3 + b_1 - b_2 < 0$$
$$\alpha_4 + s_4 + b_1 - b_2 < 0$$
$$\alpha_5 + s_5 + b_1 - b_2 < 0$$
$$\alpha_6 + s_6 + b_1 - b_2 < 0$$
$$\alpha_7 + s_7 + b_1 - b_2 < 0$$
$$\alpha_8 + s_8 + b_1 - b_2 < 0$$
$$\alpha_9 + s_9 + b_1 - b_2 < 0$$
$$\alpha_{10} + s_{10} + b_1 - b_2 < 0$$
$$\alpha_{11} + s_{11} + b_1 - b_2 < 0$$
$$\alpha_{12} + s_{12} + b_1 - b_2 < 0$$
$$x_1 + 3x_2 + \alpha_1 - \beta_1 - b_1 = 0$$
$$2x_1 + 5x_2 + \alpha_2 - \beta_2 - b_1 = 0$$
$$3x_1 + 4x_2 + \alpha_3 - \beta_3 - b_1 = 0$$
$$4x_1 + 6x_2 + \alpha_4 - \beta_4 - b_1 = 0$$
$$5x_1 + 7x_2 - \alpha_5 + \beta_5 + b_1 = 0, \quad 5x_1 + 7x_2 + s_5 - t_5 - b_2 = 0$$
$$6x_1 + 9x_2 - \alpha_6 + \beta_6 + b_1 = 0, \quad 6x_1 + 9x_2 + s_6 - t_6 - b_2 = 0$$
$$7x_1 + 8x_2 - \alpha_7 + \beta_7 + b_1 = 0, \quad 7x_1 + 8x_2 + s_7 - t_7 - b_2 = 0$$
$$7x_1 + 7x_2 - \alpha_8 + \beta_8 + b_1 = 0, \quad 7x_1 + 7x_2 + s_8 - t_8 - b_2 = 0$$
$$9x_1 + 9x_2 - \alpha_9 + \beta_9 + b_1 = 0, \quad 9x_1 + 9x_2 + s_9 - t_9 - b_2 = 0$$

TABLE 9.3
MCLP
Classification on
Credit Applicants
Risks

		Responses		LP Scores at the Coefficients
	# of Credit Customer	Quest 1	Quest 2	$x_1^* = 11$ $x_2^* = -5$
Class 1 (Poor risk)	1	1	3	−5
	2	2	5	−4
	3	3	4	15
	4	4	6	16
Class 2 (Fair risk)	5	5	7	23
	6	6	9	24
	7	7	8	43
	8	7	7	49
	9	9	9	63
Class 3 (Good risk)	10	6	2	66
	11	6	4	54
	12	8	3	86

$$6x_1 + 2x_2 - s_{10} + t_{10} + b_2 = 0$$
$$6x_1 + 4x_2 - s_{11} + t_{11} + b_2 = 0$$
$$8x_1 + 3x_2 - s_{12} + t_{12} + b_2 = 0$$

where $d_1, d_2, d_3, d_4, d_5, d_6, d_7$, and d_8 represent $d_{\alpha_1}^-, d_{\alpha_1}^+, d_{\beta_1}^-, d_{\beta_1}^+, d_{\alpha_2}^-, d_{\alpha_2}^+, d_{\beta_2}^-$, and $d_{\beta_2}^+$, respectively; $a_1, a_2, \ldots, a_{12}$ represent α_i^1 ($i = 1, 2, \ldots 12$), respectively; $s_1, s_2, \ldots, s_{12}$ represent α_i^2 ($i = 1, 2, \ldots, 12$), respectively; $b_1, b_2, \ldots, b_{12}$ represent β_i^1 ($i = 1, 2, \ldots, 12$) respectively; $t_1, t_2, \ldots, t_{12}$ represent β_i^2 ($i = 1, 2, \ldots, 12$), respectively. The ideal values are set as $\alpha_*^1 = 0.1$, $\beta_*^1 = 10$, $\alpha_*^2 = 0.2$, and $\beta_*^2 = 9$.

Solving this problem with no restrictions on x_1 and x_2, we found the coefficients are $x_1^* = 11$ and $x_2^* = -5$. The MCLP scores are calculated for each applicant using the resulting coefficients as shown in Table 9.3. From Figure 9.5, one can see that except for one case of overlapping between Class 2 and Class 3 (the ninth applicant's score = 63), all of the other 11 applicants are appropriately classified.

FIGURE 9.5
MCLP Classification
on the Small
Example

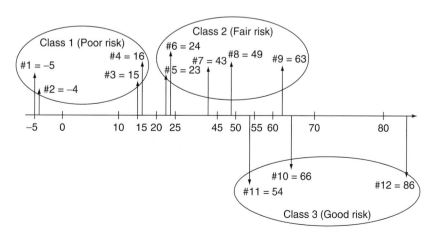

Fuzzy Linear Programming Classification

It has been recognized that in many decision making problems, instead of finding the existing "**optimal solution**" (a goal value), decision makers often approach a "satisfying solution" between upper and lower aspiration levels that can be represented by the upper and lower bounds of acceptability for objective payoffs, respectively. This idea, which has an important and pervasive impact on human decision making, is called the decision makers' goal-seeking concept. Zimmermann[6] employed it as the basis of his pioneering work on fuzzy linear programming (FLP). When FLP is adopted to classify two-class data separation problems (Good and Bad accounts, for instance), a fuzzy (satisfying) solution is used to meet a threshold for the accuracy rate of classifications although the fuzzy solution is a **near optimal solution.**

Given a two-class problem described in this chapter, suppose that a threshold τ is set up as *priori*. The FLP approach on classifications is to first train (for example, solve repeatedly) model (1) for MSD and model (2) for MMD, respectively. If the accuracy rate of either model (1) and/or (2) exceeds **threshold τ**, the approach terminates. Generally, if both model (1) and model (2) cannot offer the results to meet threshold τ, then the following fuzzy approach is applied.

The concept of fuzzy linear programming (FLP) classification is to seek a satisfying solution among the objective space formed by MSD and MMD as data separation. Theoretically speaking, if the objective value of MSD, say y_{1L}, and that of MMD, say y_{2U}, are found, then we can assume that the objective value of *Maximize* $\Sigma_i \alpha_i$ to be y_{1U} (*Max* in Figure 9.6) and that of *Minimize* $\Sigma_i \beta_i$ to be y_{2L} (*Min* in Figure 9.6). With such information, we define the membership functions $\mu_{F_1}(x)$ and $\mu_{F_2}(x)$ for $\Sigma_i \alpha_i$ and $\Sigma_i \beta_i$, respectively. Thus, the satisfying solution can be determined by a fuzzy linear program with *Maximize* ξ, $0 < \xi < 1$ subject to the membership expressions and constraints of MCLP classification (3) (see the appendix section later in this chapter).

In two-class data separation, finding *Maximum* ξ in the FLP approach becomes the standard of determining the classifications between Good and Bad accounts in the database. A graphical illustration of this approach can be seen in Figure 9.6, where any point of hyperplane $0 < \xi < 1$ over the shadow area represents the possible determination of classifications by the FLP method. Whenever the FLP model has been trained to meet the given threshold τ, it is said that the better classifier has been identified.

A procedure of using the FLP method for data classification is shown by the flowchart in Figure 9.7. Note that although the boundary of two classes b is unrestricted

FIGURE 9.6
**A Fuzzy
Classification
Formulation**

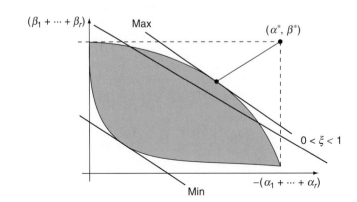

FIGURE 9.7
A Flowchart of an
FLP Classification
Method

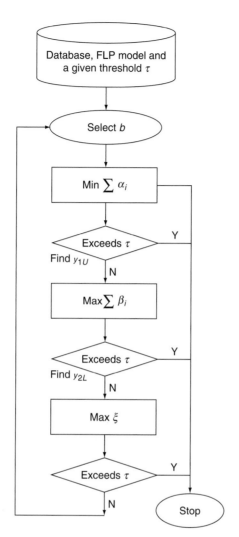

in the FLP model, it can be presumed by the analyst according to the structure of a particular database. Choosing a proper value of b can speed up the process of solving the FLP. For this reason, the procedure in Figure 9.7 uses b as an important control parameter in the FLP classification method.

Consider the simple credit rating problem presented by Table 9.1 again. According to Figure 9.7, we choose $b = 9$, and the threshold $\tau = 99$ percent for either Good and Bad (since there are only two data figures involved). By using LINDO, we solved model (1) MSD and model (2) MMD, respectively, as:

a. At MSD, $y_{1L} = 0$, $x_1{}^* = 0$, $x_2{}^* = 0.290323$, $\alpha_1 = \alpha_2 = 0$. The data are separated (see Table 9.1).

b. At MMD, $y_{2U} = 99999900$, $x_1{}^* = 0$, $x_2{}^* = 99999900$, $\beta_1 = 0$, $\beta_2 = 99999900$. The data are *not* separated.

c. At the *Maximize* $\Sigma_i \alpha_i$, $y_{1U} = 99999900$, $x_1{}^* = 0$, $x_2{}^* = 0$, $\alpha_1 = 0$, $\alpha_2 = 99999900$. The data are separated.

d. At the *Minimize* $\Sigma_i \beta_i$, $y_{2L} = 5.4$, $x_1{}^* = .6$, $x_2{}^* = 0$, $\beta_1 = 5.4$, and $\beta_2 = 0$. The data are separated.

From this information, the FLP problem is constructed as:

Maximize ξ
Subject to:

$$\xi \leq \frac{\alpha_1 + \alpha_2 - 0}{99999900 - 0}$$

$$\xi \leq \frac{\beta_1 + \beta_2 - 5.4}{99999900 - 5.4}$$

$$6x_1 + 8x_2 = b + \alpha_1 - \beta_1, \quad \text{for } A_1 \in B,$$

$$15x_1 + 31x_2 = b - \alpha_2 + \beta_2, \quad \text{for } A_2 \in G,$$

$$\alpha_1, \alpha_2, \beta_1, \beta_2, \xi \geq 0.$$

Before solving this problem using LINDO, we set up $\xi > .7 \geq 0$. The fuzzy satisfying solution then is found as $\xi = 1$, $x_1^* = .6$, $x_2^* = 0$, $\alpha_1 = 99999900$, $\alpha_2 = 0$, $\beta_1 = 99999910$, $\beta_2 = 0$. The data are separated in terms of $b = 9$. By Figure 9.7, we see that both the MSD model (1) and the FLP model are satisfied with the threshold $\tau = 99$ percent. Therefore, the FLP heuristic classification method should suggest using either MSD or FLP as the classifier for data interpretation and prediction.

As another example for the FLP method, if the employees of a company are evaluated based on two criteria: their performance (a 1–10 scale with 1 as worst and 10 as best) and communication skill (a 1–5 scale with 1 as worst and 5 as best), all of them are divided into two classes: "successful group" and "unsuccessful group."[7] Suppose there are 10 employees whose criteria evaluations and predetermined classes are given in the first three columns of Table 9.4, we can use the FLP classification method to separate the given data as follows.

Choosing $b = 10$, we have
For MSD (y_{1L}),

Minimize $\alpha_1 + \alpha_2$
Subject to:

$$x_1 + x_2 \leq 10 + \alpha_1,$$

$$3x_1 + x_2 \leq 10 + \alpha_1,$$

$$2x_1 + 2x_2 \leq 10 + \alpha_1,$$

$$6x_1 + 3x_2 \leq 10 + \alpha_1,$$

$$3x_1 + 3x_2 \leq 10 + \alpha_1,$$

$$4x_1 + x_2 \geq 10 - \alpha_2,$$

$$5x_1 + 2x_2 \geq 10 - \alpha_2,$$

$$7x_1 + 2x_2 \geq 10 - \alpha_2,$$

$$9x_1 + x_2 \geq 10 - \alpha_2,$$

$$8x_1 + 4x_2 \geq 10 - \alpha_2,$$

$$\alpha_1, \alpha_2 \geq 0.$$

By using LINDO, the solution is $y_{1L} = 3.3$, $x_1^* = 1.67$, $x_2^* = 0$, $\alpha_1 = 0$, $\alpha_2 = 3.3$. The MSD score is given in Table 9.4 where the fourth and sixth employees are misidentified.

TABLE 9.4
Employee
Evaluations by the
FLP Classification
Method

| Employee # | Unsuccessful Group | | FLP Classification Scores Against $b = 10$ | | | | |
	Performance	Communication Skill	MSD y_{1L}	y_{1U}	MMD y_{2U}	y_{2L}	FLP
1	1	1	1.67	X	X	10	−7.5
2	3	1	5.01	X	X	11	9.5
3	2	2	3.34	X	X	12	7
4	6	3	10.02	X	X	15.5	9.5
5	3	3	5.01	X	X	15	6.5
	Successful Group		**FLP Classification Scores**				
6	4	1	9.98	X	X	3.5	10.8
7	5	2	11.65	X	X	5.5	10
8	7	2	14.99	X	X	6.5	12
9	9	1	18.33	X	X	6	15.5
10	8	4	16.66	X	X	10	10

Both of the problems for y_{1U} and MMD (y_{2U}) resulted in an **unbounded solution.** Therefore, we set up $y_{1U} = y_{2U}$ for the FLP formulation as shown next.

For y_{2L},

Minimize $\beta_1 + \beta_2$
Subject to:

$$x_1 + x_2 \geq 10 - \beta_1,$$
$$3x_1 + x_2 \geq 10 - \beta_1,$$
$$2x_1 + 2x_2 \geq 10 - \beta_1,$$
$$6x_1 + 3x_2 \geq 10 - \beta_1,$$
$$3x_1 + 3x_2 \geq 10 - \beta_1,$$
$$4x_1 + x_2 \leq 10 + \beta_2,$$
$$5x_1 + 2x_2 \leq 10 + \beta_2,$$
$$7x_1 + 2x_2 \leq 10 + \beta_2,$$
$$9x_1 + x_2 \leq 10 + \beta_2,$$
$$8x_1 + 4x_2 \leq 10 + \beta_2,$$
$$\beta_1, \beta_2 \geq 0.$$

This solution is $y_{2L} = 8$, $x_1^* = 0.5$, $x_2^* = 1.5$, $\beta_1 = 8$, $\beta_2 = 0$. The score of data separation is calculated in Table 9.2 where the first and the tenth employees are on the boundary of successful and unsuccessful.

The FLP formulation is built as:

Maximize ξ
Subject to:

$$\xi \leq \frac{\alpha_1 + \alpha_2 - 3.3}{10 - 3.3}$$

$$\xi \leq \frac{\beta_1 + \beta_2 - 8}{10 - 8}$$

$$x_1 + x_2 < 10 + \alpha_1 - \beta_1,$$
$$3x_1 + x_2 < 10 + \alpha_1 - \beta_1,$$
$$2x_1 + 2x_2 < 10 + \alpha_1 - \beta_1,$$
$$6x_1 + 3x_2 < 10 + \alpha_1 - \beta_1,$$
$$3x_1 + 3x_2 < 10 + \alpha_1 - \beta_1,$$
$$4x_1 + x_2 \geq 10 - \alpha_2 + \beta_2,$$
$$5x_1 + 2x_2 \geq 10 - \alpha_2 + \beta_2,$$
$$7x_1 + 2x_2 \geq 10 - \alpha_2 + \beta_2,$$
$$9x_1 + x_2 \geq 10 - \alpha_2 + \beta_2,$$
$$8x_1 + 4x_2 \geq 10 - \alpha_2 + \beta_2,$$
$$\alpha_1, \alpha_2, \beta_1, \beta_2 \geq 0.$$

To avoid an **infeasible solution,** we use a constraint sign "<" for the unsuccessful group and "≥" for the successful group, as well as conditions $\xi > .7$, $\alpha_2 \leq 9$, and $\beta_2 \leq 9$. The solution is found as $x_1^* = 1$, $x_2^* = -1.5$, $\alpha_1 = 1$, $\alpha_2 = 9$, $\beta_1 = 9$, and $\beta_2 = 1$. The FLP scores are shown in Table 9.4. Under our conditions, the data has been completely separated.

Credit Card Portfolio Management: A Real-Life Application

Credit card portfolio management problems can be data mined using large real-life data sets. A typical credit card portfolio management problem is to predict cardholders' behavior (for instance, either "Bad" for bankruptcy or "Good" for otherwise). In the financial business, practitioners have applied a number of data mining techniques to support credit card portfolio management. These techniques include (1) the Behavior Score developed by Fair Isaac Corporation (FICO); (2) Credit Bureau Scores, most of which are also developed by FICO;[8] (3) First Data Resource (FDR)'s Proprietary Bankruptcy Score;[9] and (4) Set Enumeration (SE) decision tree.[10]

As an alternative, linear system–based methods introduced in this chapter have been tested and used in FDR, the largest credit card processing company in the world, to classify the different cardholder behaviors in terms of their payment to the credit card issuing companies (such as banks and mortgage loan firms). While all credit card companies use some of the same variables, some credit card companies find different variables important in describing cardholders' behavior. Common variables are balance, purchase, payment, and cash advance. Some credit card companies may consider state of residence and job security as important variables. Based on 38 original variables from common variables used over the past seven months, FDR built a set of 65 derived variables internally generated from the 38 variables to perform its data mining tasks. The best separation can be interpreted in terms of many different criteria. For instance, information value, which is the quotient of the difference between means and standard deviation, is used to measure the separation in terms of the pair of the center and the dispersion. The concordance measures the separation in terms of matching pairs of Good and Bad outcomes. Kolmogorov–Smirnov (KS) value can measure the largest separation of two cumulative distributions of Good and Bad.[11] Comparing these available measurements of separation, the KS measurement has empirically

FIGURE 9.8
KS Value (MCLP) =
56.43 on 6,000
Records

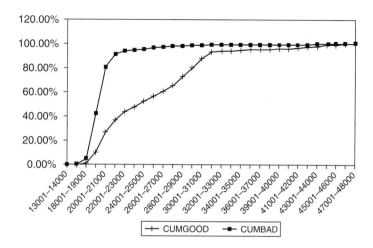

demonstrated to be good at identifying Bads. Thus, it has been widely accepted in the credit risk management area. Furthermore, it also makes sense in the credit risk area that the bigger the value of KS, the better the separation. For the problem of the two-class classification in this paper, the KS separation is given as:

KS = *max* | Cum. distribution of Good - Cum. distribution of Bad |.

A sample set of 6,000 credit card records taken from the database of a major U.S. bank was used to identify a classification model from the two-class formulation at the FDC's SAS platform. The total of more than 50 LP and MCLP score solutions has been computed within a set of 65 attributes in FDC on samples of 1,000, 2,000, and 6,000 records. Figure 9.8 is the chart of the KS score on 6,000 records. The control parameters, such as α^*, β^*, and b, varied many times on different values. Table 9.5 summarizes the comparison study between the LP score, MCLP score, and the known score models: Behavior Score, Credit Bureau Score, FDC Bankruptcy Score, and SE Decision Tree Score. These findings have shown that the MCLP model provides both robustness and stability. The training result, in fact, was consequently applied to find the business solutions for some commercial banks. The MCLP prediction of bankruptcy (the Bad group) of real-life data was more accurate than the previously used business scores. Therefore, the MCLP model has proved to be an attractive technology for two-class behaviors in credit card portfolio management.

In a comparison study, decision tree, neural network, MCLP, and FLP were trained using a balanced data set of 280 records, and tested on 5,000 credit card holder records (both are drawn from the set of 6,000 records). The decision tree software used was the commercial version C5.0 (the newly updated version of C4.5)[12] while software for both neural network and MCLP were developed at the Data Mining Lab, University of Nebraska at Omaha. In the results of both Table 9.6

TABLE 9.5
Summary of Real-Life Learning on a Two-Class Model

Methods	KS Value of 1,000 records	KS Value of 3,000 records	KS Value of 6,000 records
Behavior Score	55.26	54.26	53.21
Credit Bureau Score	45.55	45.01	44.43
FDC Score	59.16	57.21	54.46
SE Score	60.22	56.21	53.23
LP Score	49.88	55.00	47.55
MCLP Score	61.49	60.43	56.43

TABLE 9.6
Learning
Comparisons on 280
Records

Decision Tree	T_g	T_b	Total
Good	138	2	140
Bad	13	127	140
Total	151	129	280
Neural Network			
Good	116	24	140
Bad	14	126	140
Total	130	150	280
MCLP			
Good	134	6	140
Bad	7	*133*	140
Total	141	139	280
FLP			
Good	127	13	140
Bad	13	127	140
Total	140	140	280

and Table 9.7, columns T_g and T_b, respectively, represent the number of Good and Bad accounts identified by a method, while the rows of Good and Bad represent the actual number of the accounts.

In Table 9.6, the process of selecting the final training result using decision trees was controlled by C.5.0. The configuration used for training the neural network result includes a backpropagation algorithm, one hidden layer with 16 hidden nodes, random initial weight, sigmoid function, and 8,000 training periods. The boundary value of *b* in both the MCLP and FLP methods were –1.10. As you can see, the best training comparison on Good (non-bankruptcy) accounts is the decision tree with 138 out of 140 (98.57 percent) while the best for Bad (bankruptcy) accounts is the MCLP method with 133 out of 140 (95 percent). However, the FLP method has equally identified 127 out of 140 (90.71 percent) for Good and Bad. The neural network method underperformed others in this case.

Table 9.7 shows prediction (or test) results on 5,000 records by using the classifiers based on the results of 280 balanced data sets. The MCLP method outper-

TABLE 9.7
Comparisons on the
Prediction of 5,000
Records

Decision Tree	T_g	T_b	Total
Good	2180	2005	4185
Bad	141	674	815
Total	2321	2679	5000
Neural Network			
Good	2814	1371	4185
Bad	176	639	815
Total	2990	2010	5000
MCLP			
Good	3160	1025	4185
Bad	484	331	815
Total	3644	1356	5000
FLP			
Good	2498	1687	4185
Bad	113	702	815
Total	2611	2389	5000

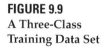

FIGURE 9.9
A Three-Class
Training Data Set

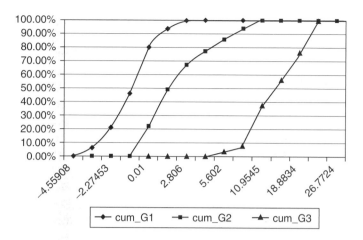

formed others in terms of predicting Good accounts with 3,160 out of 4,185 (75.51 percent), but the FLP method proposed in this paper is the best for predicting Bad accounts with 702 out of 815 (86.14 percent). If the business strategy of black listing Bad accounts is chosen, then the FLP method should be used to conduct the data mining project. Therefore, the proposed FLP method has some validity as an alternative tool to the other well-known data mining techniques in classification.

Even though the LP, MCLP, and FLP classification models that we discussed in this chapter are for two-class data separation, in reality, a multiclass model may be needed. We'll now demonstrate the experimental results of three-class, four-class, and five-class MCLP models in Linux version on the same real credit database.[13]

In the three-class MCLP model, the criterion of defining classes is the number of over-limits done by each credit card account during the previous two years. Class 1 (G1) represents "Bad" for all accounts with over-limits > 6; Class 2 (G2) represents "Normal," for all accounts with 1 < over-limits ≤ 6; and Class 3 (G3) represents "Good," for all accounts with over-limits ≤ 1. Accounting to this definition, we first chose 300 samples with 100 accounts in each class as the training set. We used 5,000 records where 218 were in G1, 557 were in G2, and 4,225 were in G3 as the verifying set. After several times of learning, we found that G1 has been correctly identified 83 percent (83/100), G2 72 percent (72/100), and G3 91 percent (91/100) of the time. In addition to these absolute classifications, the KS scores are 60 for G1 versus G2, and 80 for G2 versus G3 (see Figure 9.9). Note that normally a commercial practice requires KS values of 45 and above. Suppose this model is found as the better classifier. Then we can use it to predict the verifying set as G1 for 64.7 percent (141/218), G2 for 64.1 percent (357/557) and G3 for 59.6 percent (2,516/4,225). The predicted KS values are 29.31 for G1 versus G2, and 59.82 for G2 versus G3 (see Figure 9.10). As you can see, the predicted classification rates are stable around 60 percent, but the predicted KS value for G1 versus G2 isn't good.

In the four-class MCLP model, we define four classes as Bankrupt charge-off accounts (the number of over-limits ≥ 13), Non-bankrupt charge-off accounts (7 ≤ the number of over-limits ≤ 12) , Delinquent accounts (2 ≤ the number of over-limits ≤ 6), and Current accounts (0 ≤ the number of over-limits ≤ 2). In this case, we selected 160 samples with 40 accounts in each class as the training set. We used the same 5,000 records with 53 in G1, 165 in G2, 557 in G3, and 4,225 in G4 as the verifying set. The better learning provided that G1 has been correctly identified

FIGURE 9.10
A Three-Class
Verifying Data Set

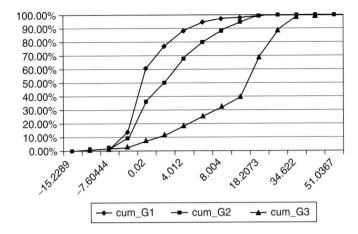

FIGURE 9.10
A Three-Class
Verifying Data Set

FIGURE 9.11
Four-Class Training
Data Set

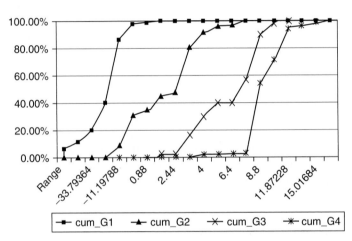

FIGURE 9.12
Four-Class
Verifying Data Set

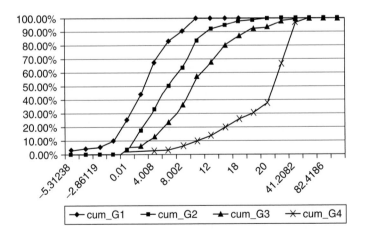

85 percent (34/40), G2 70 percent (28/40), G3 62.5 percent (25/40), and G4 70 percent (28/40), while KS values are 70.5 for G1 versus G2, 65 for G2 versus G3, and 52.5 for G3 versus G4 in Figure 9.11. Using this model as the better classifier, we can predict the verifying set as G1 for 32 percent (17/53), G2 for 83.6 percent (138/165), G3 for 41.4 percent (231/557), and G4 for 63.5 percent (2,682/4,225). The predicted KS values are 35.8 for G1 versus G2, 28.23 for G2 versus G3, and

FIGURE 9.13
Five-Class Training Data Set

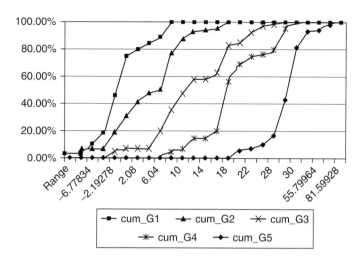

61.86 for G3 versus G4 in Figure 9.12. These results show that the predicted separation between G3 and G4 is better than others.

In the five-class MCLP model, we define five classes as Bankrupt charge-off accounts (the number of over-limits $\geq$ 13), Non-bankrupt charge-off accounts (7 $\leq$ the number of over-limits $\leq$ 12), Delinquent accounts (3 $\leq$ the number of over-limits $\leq$ 6), Current accounts (1 $\leq$ the number of over-limits $\leq$ 2), and Outstanding accounts (no over-limit). This time we selected 200 samples with 40 accounts in each class as the training set. The same 5,000 records with 53 in G1, 165 in G2, 379 in G3, 482 in G4, and 3,921 in G5 is used as the verifying set. We found in the training process that G1 has been correctly identified as 47.5 percent (19/40), G2 as 55 percent (22/40), G3 as 47.5 percent (19/40), G4 as 42.5 percent (17/40), with KS values of 42.5 for G1 versus G2, G2 versus G3, and G3 versus G4, but 67.5 for G4 versus G5 in Figure 9.13. When we used this as the better classifier, we predicted the verifying set as G1 for 50.9 percent (27/53), G2 for 49.7 percent (82/165), G3 for 40 percent (150/379), G4 for 31.1 percent (150/482), and G5 for 54.6 percent (2,139/3,921). The predicted KS values are 36.08 for G1 versus G2, 23.3 for G2 versus G3, 27.82 for G3 versus G4, and 42.17 for G4 versus G5 in Figure 9.14. This indicates that the separation between G4

FIGURE 9.14
Five-Class Verifying Data Set

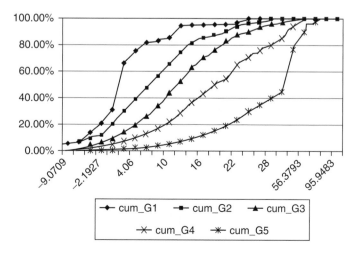

and G5 is better than other situations. In other words, the classifier is favorable to G4 versus G5.

Note that although the MCLP models can be theoretically applied to classify any number of classes of data, finding a better classifier to efficiently handle the real-life problems is not easy. Besides, many real-life applications do not require more than five class separations. This claim is partially supported by psychological studies. Based on the fact that the human attention span is "seven plus or minus two," for the practical purpose of classification in data mining, classifying five interesting classes in a terabyte database can be very meaningful.[14]

Linear Programming–Based Software Support

Because linear programming–based classification can be viewed as an application of regular linear programming, any available software dealing with linear programming could be adapted to conduct such data mining projects. For small scale problems, either MS Excel Solver (www.microsoft.com) or What'sBest in the Excel version of Lindo System Inc. (www.lindo.com) can be used. For large-scale problems, LINDO and Matlab (www.mathworks.com) can be readily applied. The Data Mining Lab at the University of Nebraska at Omaha also developed a knowledge management software based on LP, MCLP, and FLP that runs on both Linux and SAS platforms (http://dm.ist.unomaha.edu/). This system can effectively and efficiently handle the entire process of classification, including finding a solution, calculating scores, and predicting unknown data patterns.

Appendix

Data Mining Linear Programming Formulations

The following contains the formulations of linear programming–based data mining used in this chapter.

MULTIPLE-CLASS SEPARATION

Given the m-class of data C_j, $j = 1, \ldots, m$, let θ_j be the overlapping between the jth class and $j + 1th$ class, and p_i be the penalties for θ_i (a "cost" of misclassification). Then, two versions of multiple-class separation models can be set up as follows:[2]

Version 1
Minimize $p_1\theta_1 + \cdots + p_r\theta_r$
Subject to:

$$b^{Lj} \leq A_{i1} x_1 + \cdots + A_{ir} x_r \leq b^{Uj}, A_i \in C_j \ \ j = 1, \ldots, m,$$

$$b^{Uj} + \varepsilon \leq b^{Lj+1}, + \theta_j, \ \ j = 1, \ldots, m - 1,$$

where A_i and ε are given, X, b^{Lj} (lower bound), and b^{Uj} (upper bound) are unrestricted, and $\theta_j \geq 0$.

Version 2
Minimize $p_1 \theta_1 + \cdots + p_r \theta_r$
Subject to:

$$b^{Lj} \leq A_{i1} x_1 + \cdots + A_{ir} x_r \leq b^{Uj}, \mathbf{A_i} \in C_j \quad j = 1, \dots, m,$$

$$b^{Uj} \leq b^{Lj+1}, \quad j = 1, \dots, m - 1,$$

where A_i is given, X, b^{Lj} (lower bound), and b^{Uj} (upper bound) are unrestricted, and $\theta_j \geq 0$.

MULTIPLE CRITERIA LINEAR PROGRAMMING SEPARATION

To use the commercial software for linear programming to solve the two-class MCLP problem, we assume the "ideal value" of $-(\alpha_1 + \cdots + \alpha_r)$ be $\alpha^* > 0$ and the "ideal value" of $\beta_1 + \cdots + \beta_r$ be $\beta^* > 0$. Then, if $-(\alpha_1 + \cdots + \alpha_r) > \alpha^*$, we define the regret measure as $-d_\alpha^+ = (\alpha_1 + \cdots + \alpha_r) + \alpha^*$; otherwise, it is 0. If $-(\alpha_1 + \cdots + \alpha_r) < \alpha^*$, the regret measure is defined as $d_\alpha^- = \alpha^* + (\alpha_1 + \cdots + \alpha_r)$; otherwise, it is 0. Thus, we have (i) $\alpha^* + (\alpha_1 + \cdots + \alpha_r) = d_\alpha^- - d_\alpha^+$, (ii) $|\alpha^* + (\alpha_1 + \cdots + \alpha_r)| = d_\alpha^- + d_\alpha^+$, and (iii) $d_\alpha^-, d_\alpha^+ \geq 0$. Similarly, we derive $\beta^* - (\beta_1 + \cdots + \beta_r) = d_\beta^- - d_\beta^+$, $|\beta^* - (\beta_1 + \cdots + \beta_r)| = d_\beta^- + d_\beta^+$, and $d_\beta^-, d_\beta^+ \geq 0$ (see Figure 9.4). An MCLP formula (3) has evolved as:

Revised Two-Class MCLP
Minimize $d_\alpha^- + d_\alpha^+ + d_\beta^- + d_\beta^+$
Subject to:

$$\alpha^* + (\alpha_1 + \cdots + \alpha_r) = d_\alpha^- - d_\alpha^+$$

$$\beta^* + (\beta_1 + \cdots + \beta_r) = d_\beta^- - d_\beta^+$$

$$A_{11} x_1 + \cdots + A_{1r} x_r = b + \alpha_1 - \beta_1, \quad \text{for } \mathbf{A_1} \in B,$$

$$\cdots\cdots\cdots\cdots$$

$$A_{n1} x_1 + \cdots + A_{nr} x_r = b - \alpha_r + \beta_r, \quad \text{for } \mathbf{A_n} \in G,$$

$$\alpha_1, \dots, \alpha_r, \beta_1, \dots, \beta_r, d_\alpha^-, d_\alpha^+, d_\beta^-, d_\beta^+ \geq 0.$$

A three-class MCLP model, similar to a two-class model, can be written by:

Revised Three-Class MCLP
Minimize $d_{\alpha 1}^- + d_{\alpha 1}^+ + d_{\beta 1}^- + d_{\beta 1}^+ + d_{\alpha 2}^- + d_{\alpha 2}^+ + d_{\beta 2}^- + d_{\beta 2}^+$
Subject to:

$$\alpha_*^1 + \Sigma_i \alpha_i^1 = d_{\alpha 1}^- - d_{\alpha 1}^+,$$

$$\beta_*^1 - \Sigma_i \beta_i^1 = d_{\beta 1}^- - d_{\beta 1}^+,$$

$$\alpha_*^2 + \Sigma_i \alpha_i^2 = d_{\alpha 2}^- - d_{\alpha 2}^+,$$

$$\beta_*^2 - \Sigma_i \beta_i^2 = d_{\beta 2}^- - d_{\beta 2}^+,$$

$$b_1 + \alpha_i^1 \leq b_2 - \alpha_i^2,$$

Class 1: $\mathbf{A}_i X = b_1 - \alpha_i^1 + \beta_i^1, \quad \mathbf{A}_i \in C_1,$

Class 2: $\mathbf{A}_i X = b_1 + \alpha_i^1 - \beta_i^1, \quad \mathbf{A}_i \in C_2,$

                $\mathbf{A}_i X = b_2 - \alpha_i^2 + \beta_i^2, \quad \mathbf{A}_i \in C_2,$

Class 3: $\mathbf{A}_i X = b_2 + \alpha_i^2 - \beta_i^2, \quad \mathbf{A}_i \in C_3,$

where $\mathbf{A}_i$ is given, $b_1 \leq b_2$, X, b_1, and b_2 are unrestricted, and $\alpha_i^1, \alpha_i^2, \beta_i^1,$ and $\beta_i^2 \geq 0$.

FUZZY LINEAR PROGRAMMING SEPARATION

Let y_{1L} be the objective value of MSD and y_{2U} be that of MMD, then we can assume that the objective value of Maximize $\Sigma_i \alpha_i$ to be y_{1U} and that of Minimize $\Sigma_i \beta_i$ to be y_{2L}. Normally, such an "upper bound" y_{1U} related to model (1) and a "lower bound" y_{2L} related to model (2) do not exist for the formulations. Let $F_1 = \{x: y_{1L} \leq \Sigma_i \alpha_i \leq y_{1U}\}$ and $F_2 = \{x: y_{2L} \leq \Sigma_i \beta_i \leq y_{2U}\}$ and their membership functions can be expressed respectively by:

$$\mu_{F_1}(x) = \begin{cases} 1, & \text{if } \Sigma_i \alpha_i \geq y_{1U} \\ \dfrac{\Sigma_i \alpha_i - y_{1L}}{y_{1U} - y_{1L}}, & \text{if } y_{1L} < \Sigma_i \alpha_i < y_{1U} \\ 0, & \text{if } \Sigma_i \alpha_i \leq y_{1L} \end{cases}$$

and

$$\mu_{F_2}(x) = \begin{cases} 1, & \text{if } \Sigma_i \beta_i \geq y_{2U} \\ \dfrac{\Sigma_i \beta_i - y_{2L}}{y_{2U} - y_{2L}}, & \text{if } y_{2L} \geq \Sigma_i \beta_i < y_{2U} \\ 0, & \text{if } \Sigma_i \beta_i \leq y_{2L} \end{cases}$$

Then the fuzzy linear programming based on these membership functions can be built as follows:

Fuzzy Linear Program
Maximize ξ
Subject to:

$$\xi \leq \frac{\Sigma_i \alpha_i - y_{1L}}{y_{1U} - y_{1L}}$$

$$\xi \leq \frac{\Sigma_i \beta_i - y_{2L}}{y_{2U} - y_{2L}}$$

$$A_i X = b + \alpha_i - \beta_i, A_i \in G,$$

$$A_i X = b - \alpha_i + \beta_i, A_i \in B,$$

where $A_i, y_{1L}, y_{1U}, y_{2L},$ and y_{2U} are known, X and b are unrestricted, and $\alpha_i, \beta_i, \xi \geq 0$.

The preceding formulation will produce a value of ξ with $1 > \xi \geq 0$. To avoid a trivial solution, one can set up $\xi > \varepsilon \geq 0$, for a given ε.

Summary

Since Freed and Glover (1981) published the original formulation of linear programming (LP)–based classification (linear discriminant analysis), a number of researchers have contributed to this approach with tests of small data samples. However, LP approaches to classification problems were not reported in real business applications until Shi et al. (2001). There are two possible reasons for this. The first is that since LP requires extensive computation time, most computers were not adequate to solve the large-scale LP classification problems in a reasonable time before 1995. The second is that the previous researchers using LP classification may not have had access to real financial data. LP approaches have a great potential for being alternative classification tools to decision trees, neural networks, rough sets, and fuzzy sets in business decision making.

Glossary

compromise solution   A best trade-off in terms of the shortest norm-distance between the ideal value and trade-off points.

constraints   Linear equalities or inequalities that represent the limitation condition in linear programming.

infeasible solution   The value exceeds the limitation conditions by the constraints.

maximize the minimum distances (MMD)   First finding the shortest distance of each data segment from its adjusted boundary, and then finding the largest value of the resulting shortest data distance.

minimize the sum of the deviations (MSD)   Finding the smallest deviation (overlapping) over the summation of deviations of all data in terms of the different class boundary.

multiple criteria linear programming   A generalization of linear programming with multiple conflict objective functions, instead of a single objective function.

near optimal solution   A solution that is feasible to all constraints in a linear program and close to the value of the optimal solution.

objective function   A mathematical representation of a target or goal in mathematical programming. In linear programming, it can be a linear combination of decision (or attribute) variables.

optimal coefficients   The optimal solution for the coefficients of attributes among the data observations. They are used to determine the score for classification.

optimal solution   The best decision values obtained by solving a linear programming.

threshold   An acceptable (or cutting) value given by the decision maker for the desirable data mining results.

trade-offs   Variations of different combinations on multiple conflict objective functions.

unbounded solution   An unlimited objective case that occurs while finding the optimal solution.

Exercises

1. Apply the model (1) MSD and model (2) MMD to the Job Applicant data file, using the first 20 "adequate" observations and 20 "unacceptable" observations as the training set. Note that "adequate" and "unacceptable" become the labels of two predetermined classes and the numerical transformation of categorical attributes "degree" and "major" can be subjective. Use data mining software in Excel if available.

2. Take all data considered "adequate" and "unacceptable" and form a two-class data set from the Job Applicant data file. Use the first 50 observations as the training set, and apply it to the rest of the observations as test observations. Apply models (1) MSD, (2) MMD, and (3) MCLP for the data mining by adapting available linear programming software. Develop a comparison table for these results.

3. The Insurance Fraud data set is a two-class data set (outcome: yes or no) with six attributes (Age, Gender, Claim, Prior Claim, Tickets, and Attorney). Use the first 50 observations as the training set, and apply to the practice Insurance Fraud data set for classification by using Excel or the linear programming package.

4. The Business Loan data set can be regarded as a three-class data set with the class label Risk (high, medium, and low) and seven attributes (Age, Income, Assets, Debts, Wanted-amount, Credit, and Online). Try to apply the MCLP model (7) for classification on the first 100 observations as a training set. Then predict the risk patterns for the rest of the 550 records.

5. Use the first 100 observations as the training set, and then apply it to test the rest of the 550 observations in the Business Loan data set. Employ available classification software, such as decision tree, neural networks, rough set, fuzzy set, and others to the Business Loan data set. Compare these results with that of Exercise 4.

Endnotes

1. G. B. Dantzig, *Linear Programming and Extensions*, Princeton Press, Princeton, New Jersey, 1963.

2. N. Freed and F. Glover, "Simple but Powerful Goal Programming Models for Discriminant Problems," *European Journal of Operational Research*, v: 7, 1981, pp. 44–60.

3. Y. Shi, M. Wise, M. Luo, and Y. Lin, "Data Mining in Credit Card Portfolio Management: A Multiple Criteria Decision Making Approach," *Advance in Multiple Criteria Decision Making in the New Millennium*, Springer, Berlin, 2001, pp. 427–436.

4. Y. Shi and P. L. Yu, "Goal Setting and Compromise Solutions," *Multiple Criteria Decision Making and Risk Analysis and Applications*, Springer-Verlag, Berlin, 1989, pp. 165–203.

5. Y. Shi, Y. Peng, W. Xu, and X. Tang, "Data Mining via Multiple Criteria Linear Programming: Applications in Credit Card Portfolio Management," *International Journal of Information Technology and Decision Making*, v: 1, 2002, pp. 131–151.

6. H. J. Zimmermann, "Fuzzy Programming and Linear Programming with Several Objective Functions," *Fuzzy Sets and Systems*, v: 1, 1978, pp. 45–55.

7. N. Freed and F. Glover, "A Linear Programming Approach to the Discriminant Problem," *Decision Science*, v: 12, 1981, pp. 68–74.

8. www.fairisaac.com

9. www.firstdata.com

10. R. Rymon, "Search Through Systematic Set Enumeration," Proceedings of the Third International Conference on the Principle of Knowledge Representation and Reasoning, Cambridge, MA, pp. 539–550, 1993.

11. W. J. Conover, *Practical Nonparametric Statistics*, Wiley, New York, 1999.

12. www.rulequest.com/see5-info.html

13. G. Kou, X. Liu, Y. Peng, Y. Shi, M. Wise, and W. Xu, "Multiple Criteria Linear Programming to Data Mining: Models, Algorithm Designs, and Software Developments," *Optimization Methods and Software*, v: 18, 2003, pp. 453–473.

14. G. A. Miller, "The Magical Number Seven, Plus or Minus Two: Some Limits on Our Capacity for Processing Information," *The Psychological Review*, v: 63, 1956, pp. 81–97.

PART THREE

Business Applications

CHAPTER TEN

Business Data Mining Applications

This chapter:

Reviews data mining applications in business

Provides real examples of applications

Describes the concept of lift

Discusses customer relationship management, credit scoring, and other business applications

Compares data mining methods in terms of relative advantages

Have you ever wondered why your spouse gets all of these strange catalogs for obscure products in the mail? Have you also wondered at his or her strong interest in these things, and thought that the spouse was overly responsive to advertising of this sort? For that matter, have you ever wondered why 90 percent of your telephone calls, especially during meals, involve opportunities to purchase products? (Or for that matter, why calls assuming you are a certain type of customer occur over and over, even though you continue to tell them that their database is wrong?)

One of the earliest and most effective business applications of data mining has to do with customer segmentation. This insidious application utilizes massive databases (obtained from a variety of sources) to segment the market into categories, which are studied with data mining tools to predict responses to particular advertising campaigns. It has proven highly effective. It also represents the probabilistic nature of data mining, in that it is not perfect. The idea is to send catalogs to (or call) a group of target customers with a 5-percent probability of purchase rather than waste these expensive marketing resources on customers with a 0.05-percent probability of purchase. The same principle has been used in election campaigns by party organizations—give free rides to the voting booth to those in your party; minimize giving free rides to voting booths to those likely to vote for your opponents. Some call this bias. Others call it sound business.

Data mining offers the opportunity to apply technology to improve many aspects of business. Some standard applications are presented in this chapter. The value of this education is to present you with past applications so you can use your imagination in order to extend these application ideas to new environments.

As discussed in Chapter 1, data mining can be classified into two general functions: hypothesis testing and knowledge discovery. Data mining technology is used increasingly by many companies to analyze large databases in order to discover previously unknown and actionable information that is then used to make crucial business decisions. This is the basis for the term "knowledge discovery." Data mining can be performed through a number of techniques, such as association, classification, clustering, prediction, sequential patterns, and similar time sequences. Modifications to these are developed all the time. Data mining algorithms are implemented from various fields such as statistics, decision trees, neural networks, fuzzy logic, and linear programming. Many data mining software product suites exist, including Enterprise Miner (SAS), Intelligent Miner (IBM), Clementine (SPSS), and PolyAnalyst (Megaputer). There are also specialty software products for specific algorithms, such as CART and See5 for decision trees, and other products for various phases of the data mining process.

Applications

Data mining has proven valuable in almost every academic discipline. Understanding the business applications of data mining is necessary to expose business college students to current analytic information technology. Data mining has been instrumental in customer relationship management,[1] financial analysis,[2] credit card management,[3] banking,[4] insurance,[5] telecommunications, and many other areas of statistical support to business. Business data mining is made possible by the generation of masses of data from computer information systems. Understanding this information generation system and the tools available that assist in analysis should be fundamental for business students in the 21st Century. There are many highly useful applications in practically every field of scientific study. Data mining support is required to make sense of the masses of business data generated by computer technology.

This chapter presents examples of some of the major applications of data mining. By doing so, there will also be opportunities to demonstrate various techniques that have proven useful. Table 10.1 presents several aspects of these applications.

A wide variety of business functions are supported by data mining. Those applications listed in Table 10.1 represent only some of these applications, but all are based on very recent reports. The underlying statistical techniques are relatively

TABLE 10.1
Applications
Presented

Application	Sources[6]	Function	Statistical Technique	Data Mining Method
Catalog sales	Various	Customer segmentation	Cluster analysis	k-means
		Mailstream optimization		Neural network
CRM (telecom)	Drew et al. (2000)	Customer scoring Churn analysis	Cluster analysis	Neural network
Credit scoring	Adams et al. (2001)	Loan applications	Cluster analysis Pattern search	k-means
Banking (loans)	Sung et al. (1999) (1999)	Bankruptcy prediction	Prediction Discriminant analysis	Decision tree
Investment risk	Becerra-Fernandez et al. (2002)	Risk prediction	Prediction	Neural network
Insurance	Smith et al. (2000)	Customer retention (churn) Pricing	Prediction Logistic regression	Decision tree Neural network

simple: to predict, to identify the case closest to past instances, or to identify some pattern.

We begin with probably the most spectacular example of business data mining. Fingerhut Inc. was a pioneer in developing methods to improve business. In this case, they sought to identify the small subset of the populace that was most likely to purchase items from their specialty catalogs. They were so successful in this endeavor that they were later purchased by Federated Stores. Ultimately, Fingerhut operations were a victim to the general malaise in IT business in 2001 and 2002. But they still represent a pioneering development of data mining application in business.

Mailstream Optimization at Fingerhut

Fingerhut's use of data mining was initially reported in Chapter 1. Their segmentation model enabled the creation of new mailings to targeted customers. IBM joined Fingerhut in a project to consider thousands of customer attributes in determining which customers would receive each catalog.[7] The IBM application was called Advanced Targeted Marketing for Single Events (ATM-SE), and was designed to construct customer-profitability and likelihood-of-response models for retail targeted marketing. Specifically, the purpose was to identify and eliminate unproductive mailings without harming revenues. This led to the mailstream optimization system, which considers saturation, advertising limits, and catalog preferences. The mailstream optimization system has a planning horizon of about 12 weeks. Its system components are shown in Table 10.2.

This system was run weekly, given six months of catalogs. The program is massive, running up to 12 hours on parallel computing systems. A second mailstream optimization program, also run weekly, generated mailstreams for 1,000,000 new customers. The goal of this second system was to control advertising and risk while boosting catalog response. Fingerhut estimated savings of near $3 million per year through mailstream optimizing.[8] This system enabled Fingerhut to go against the trend of the catalog sales industry in 1998 and reduce mailings by 20 percent while increasing net earnings to over $37 million.[9]

Retailers and manufacturers know they are wasting a lot of money on mass marketing. The concept of lift is critical to marketing promotion. **Lift** is the difference between the average probability of positive response and the response obtained. Neural network models were used to identify overlaps in mailing patterns and order-filling telephone-call orders. This enabled Fingerhut to more efficiently staff their telephones and enable them to handle heavy order loads.

TABLE 10.2
The Fingerhut Mailstream Optimization System

Phase	Operation	Function
Data Extraction	Segment customers	Assign appropriate advertising levels by customer
	Advertising allocation	Assign budgets by micro-class
	Profit score customers	Predict profit by customer
	Determine saturation	Identify interactions
	Reduce scores	Discount profit scores by interactions
Optimization	Cluster	Reduce problem size
	Generate mailstreams	Generate candidate mailstreams
	Select mailstreams	Identify best mailstream by cluster
	Assign mailstreams	Assign customers to clusters
Mail	Send catalogs	Contact customers

Extracted from Campbell et al. (2001)[10]

TABLE 10.3
Fingerhut
Mailstream
Optimization
System Response
by Segment

Ordered Segment	Proportion (Expected Responses)	Cumulative Proportion	Random Average Proportion	Lift
Origin	0	0	0	0
1	0.0987	0.0987	0.05	0.0487
2	0.0923	0.1910	0.10	0.0910
3	0.0873	0.2783	0.15	0.1283
4	0.0823	0.3606	0.20	0.1606
5	0.0773	0.4379	0.25	0.1879
6	0.0723	0.5102	0.30	0.2102
7	0.0673	0.5775	0.35	0.2275
8	0.0623	0.6398	0.40	0.2398
9	0.0573	0.6971	0.45	0.2471
10	0.0523	0.7494	0.50	0.2494
11	0.0473	0.7967	0.55	0.2467
12	0.0423	0.8390	0.60	0.2390
13	0.0373	0.8763	0.65	0.2263
14	0.0323	0.9086	0.70	0.2086
15	0.0273	0.9359	0.75	0.1859
16	0.0223	0.9582	0.80	0.1582
17	0.0173	0.9755	0.85	0.1255
18	0.0125	0.9880	0.90	0.0880
19	0.0080	0.9960	0.95	0.0460
20	0.0040	1.0000	1.00	0

Calculations based on original data from Campbell et al. (2001)

Lift

This section demonstrates the concept of lift used in customer segmentation models. We can divide the data into groups as fine as we want (here we divide them into 20 equal portions of the population, or groups of 5 percent each). These groups have some identifiable feature, such as a ZIP code, income level, and so on. We can then sample and identify the portion of sales for each group. The idea behind lift is to send promotional material (which has a unit cost) to those groups that have the greatest probability of positive response first. We can visualize lift by plotting responses against the proportion of the total population of potential customers, as shown in Table 10.3.

Both the cumulative responses and the cumulative proportion of the population are graphed to identify lift. Lift is the difference between the two lines in Figure 10.1.

The purpose of lift analysis is to identify the most responsive segments. Here, the greatest lift is obtained from the first 10 segments. We are probably more interested in profit, however. We can identify the most profitable policy, but what really needs to be done is identify the portion of the population to send promotional materials to. For instance, if an average profit of $80 is expected for each positive response, and a cost of $5 is expected for each set of promotional materials sent out, it obviously would be more profitable to send to the first segment containing an expected 0.0987 of the total responses ($80 times 0.0987 equals an expected revenue of $7.896, which covers the cost of $5 plus an extra $2.896 profit). But it still might be possible to improve overall profit by sending to other segments as well (always selecting the segment with the larger response rates in order). The plot of cumulative profit is shown in Figure 10.2 for this set of data. The second most responsive segment would also be profitable, collecting $80 times 0.0923 or $7.384 per $5 mailing for a

FIGURE 10.1
Lift Identified by
Mail Optimization
System

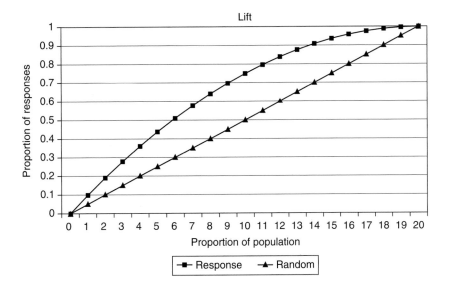

net profit of $2.384. It turns out that the seventh most responsive segment collects 0.0673 times $80 ($5.384), while the eighth most responsive segment collects $80 times 0.0623 ($4.984). Table 10.4 shows the calculation of the expected payoff.

The profit function in Figure 10.2 reaches its maximum with the seventh segment.

It's clear that the maximum profit is found by sending to the eight most responsive segments of the 20 in the population. The implication is that in this case, promotional materials should be sent to the six segments expected to have the largest response rates. If there was a promotional budget, it would be applied to as many segments as the budget would support, in order of expected response rate, up to the 15th segment.

It is possible to focus on the wrong measure, however. The basic objective of lift analysis in marketing is to identify those customers whose decisions will be influenced by marketing in a positive way.[11] In short, the methodology described earlier identifies those segments of the customer base that we would expect to make

FIGURE 10.2
Profit Impact
of Lift

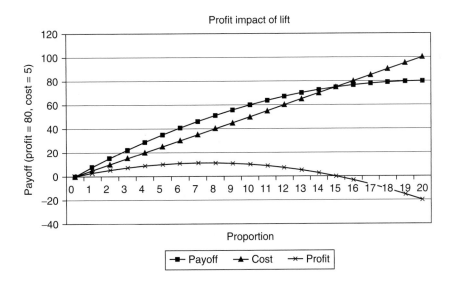

TABLE 10.4
Calculation of
Expected Payoff

Expected Segment Revenue = $80 × P	Cumulative Expected Payoff	Random Cumulative Cost = $5 × i	Expected Payoff
$0.000	$ 0.000	$ 0	$ 0.000
$7.896	$ 7.896	$ 5	$ 2.896
$7.384	$15.280	$ 10	$ 5.280
$6.984	$22.264	$ 15	$ 7.264
$6.584	$28.848	$ 20	$ 8.848
$6.184	$35.032	$ 25	$10.032
$5.784	$40.816	$ 30	$10.816
$5.384	$46.200	$ 35	$11.200
$4.984	$51.184	$ 40	$11.184
$4.184	$59.952	$ 50	$ 9.952
$3.784	$63.736	$ 55	$ 8.736
$3.384	$67.120	$ 60	$ 7.120
$2.984	$70.104	$ 65	$ 5.104
$2.584	$72.688	$ 70	$ 2.688
$2.184	$74.872	$ 75	−$ 0.128
$1.784	$76.656	$ 80	−$ 3.344
$1.384	$78.040	$ 85	−$ 6.960
$1.000	$79.040	$ 90	−$10.960
$0.640	$79.680	$ 95	−$15.320
$0.320	$80.000	$100	−$20/000

a purchase. This may or may not be due to the marketing campaign effort though. The same methodology can be applied, but more detailed data is needed to identify those whose decisions would have been changed by the marketing campaign rather than simply those who would purchase.

Another method that considers multiple factors is Recency, Frequency, and Monetary (RFM) analysis. As with lift analysis, the purpose of RFM is to identify customers who are more likely to respond to new offers. While lift looks at the static measure of response to a particular campaign, RFM keeps track of customer transactions by time, frequency, and amount. Time is important since some customers may not have responded to the last campaign, but might now be ready to purchase the product being marketed. Customers can also be sorted by frequency of responses, and by the dollar amount of sales. Subjects are coded on each of the three dimensions (one approach is to have five cells for each of the three measures, yielding a total of 125 combinations, every one of which can be associated with a positive response to the marketing campaign). RFM still has limitations in that there are usually more than three attributes important to a successful marketing program, such as product variation, customer age, customer income, customer lifestyle, and so on.[12] The approach is the basis for a continuing stream of techniques to improve customer segmentation marketing.[13]

Understanding lift enables an understanding of the value of specific types of customers. This allows more intelligent customer management, which is discussed in the next section.

Customer Relationship Management (CRM)

The idea of **customer relationship management** is to target customers for special treatment based on their anticipated future value to the firm. This requires an estimation of where in the customer life cycle each subject is, as well as a lifetime customer value based on expected tenure with the company, monthly transactions by that customer, and the cost of providing them service. The lifetime value of a customer is the discounted expected stream of cash flow generated by them.

Many companies applying CRM score each individual customer by their estimated lifetime value (LTV), which is stored in the firm's customer database.[14] This concept has been widely used in catalog marketing, newspaper publishing, retailing, insurance, and credit cards. LTV has been the basis for many marketing programs offering special treatment such as favorable pricing, better customer service, and equipment upgrades.

A problem with using LTV in this manner is that it assumes a common tenure distribution over all customers. However, company actions (and competitor actions) can change customer tenure. Customer evaluation can be based on dynamic relationships, reflecting the hazard of customer **churn.** Large customers often are targets of intense competition, and thus are high risks for churn. Loyal customers, even with lower volumes of business, are more valuable to the firm than high-volume customers whom are likely to take their business to competitors. Therefore, LTV can be multiplied by the probability of customer retention. Artificial neural network models were proposed to estimate these probabilities by customer class rather than regression, due to covariations across customer classes and a limited knowledge of these relationships.

To model each customer's target hazard, tenure and a binary churn flag variable were used. For every customer in a given month, the neural network model can provide a prediction of churn and tenure. This was argued to be superior to ordinary least squares regression or logarithmic regression, because statistical assumptions were not required for the neural network model. In this example, negative features of the neural network approach were that no formula was available for analysis, and the relative importance of model covariates could not be identified. The neural network model also was subject to data problems such as sample bias or correlated observations just as much as regression analysis.

The model was applied to data from a cellular telephone division of a major U.S. telecommunications firm. Data was available on billing, usage, and demographics, as shown in Table 10.5.

The model was tested on a small market of 21,500 subscribers in April 1998. Tenure predictions up to 36 months ahead were predicted. Only a small percentage of customers left the firm during this month, giving yet another example of biased data. The sample also predominately consisted of customers with short tenures. By basing the neural network models on churn proportions by month of tenure, both biases were avoided. The training set was based on 15,000 subscribers, leaving a holdout sample of 6,500 for testing. There were 36 customer tenure classes.

The model enabled clustering customers into four segments. Those least likely to churn were left alone, assuming that contact might trigger churn. A second cluster consisted of those with a small increase in churn propensity at the end of a contract. Marketing treatment for this second group was a moderate pre-expiration effort. For the third segment, which involved a large spike in churn at expiration, concentrated marketing efforts prior to expiration were applied. For the highest risk segment, continued competitive offers to designated customers were suggested.

While CRM is very promising, it has often been found to be less effective than hoped. Patton (2001) found that up to 70 percent of CRM projects had not produced measurable business benefits.[15] CRM systems can cost up to $70 million to develop, with additional expenses incurred during implementation. Patton cited

TABLE 10.5
CRM Data

Data Category	Specific Variables
Billing	Previous balance
	Charges for access
	Minutes used
	Toll
	Roaming
	Optional Features
Usage	Total calls
	Minutes of local use
	Toll minutes
	Peak minutes
	Off-peak calls
Subscription	**Months in service (prediction variable)**
	Rate plan
	Contract type
	Date
	Duration
Churn	**0–1 flag of cancellation (prediction variable)**
Other	Age
	Current profitability
	Historical profitability
	Optional features

problems with applications at Monster.com, Mshow, and CopperCom. One reason cited for problems in implementing CRM was that its users, marketing personnel for the most part, were not as computer familiar as were accounting and production personnel. At Mshow, the sales force refused to use a new CRM system. At CopperCom, a $500,000 CRM project was reduced in size due to lack of support from an applications service provider. On the other hand, Siebel Systems, the largest provider of CRM software, reported that the vast majority of its customers were happy with their product. Even Fingerhut, a pioneer in using data mining for business, has seen their operations shut down after being absorbed by a large sales organization.

Many of the problems in CRM expectations have been blamed on overzealous sales pitches. CRM offers a lot of opportunities to operate more efficiently. However, they are not silver bullets, and benefits are not unlimited. As with any system, a prior evaluation of benefits is very difficult, and investment in CRM systems needs to be based on sound analysis and judgment.

Credit Scoring

Data mining can involve model building (extension of conventional statistical model building to very large data sets) and pattern recognition. Pattern recognition aims to identify groups of interesting observations. Often, experts are used to assist in pattern recognition. The Adams et al. paper compared data mining used for model building and pattern recognition to the behavior of customers over a one-year period. The data set involved bank accounts at a large British credit card company, which were observed monthly. These accounts were revolving loans with credit limits. Borrowers were required to repay at least some minimum amount each month. Account holders who paid in full were charged no interest, and thus not attractive to the lender.

We have seen that clustering and pattern search are typically the first activities in data analysis. Then appropriate models are built. Credit scoring is a means to use the results of data mining modeling for two purposes. Application scoring was applied in this example to new cases, continuing an activity that was done manually for half a century in this organization. Behavioral scoring monitors revolving credit accounts with the intent of gaining early warnings about accounts facing difficulties.

Data was collected concerning the state of accounts by month. The state variable could take on integer values between 0 and 8, indicating the cumulative number of missed monthly repayments. There were over 90,000 customers. Data quality was maintained by removing observations that increased by more than 1 in any month, or that included missing values.

For the study, a biased sample of 10,000 observations was selected. The bias arose from requiring all observations to have an initial state of 0, as most observations did. Over 70 percent of the customers never left state 0.

Clustering

Two **clustering** methods were studied. One unsupervised clustering technique is partitioning, the process of examining a set of data to define a new categorical variable that divides the space into a fixed number of regions. This amounts to segmenting the data into clusters. The most widely known partitioning algorithm is k-means, where k center points are defined, and each observation is classified to the closest of these center points. The k-means algorithm attempts to position the centers to minimize the sum of distances. Centroids are used as centers, and the most commonly used distance metric is Euclidean. Seeking a more stable procedure in this study, the partitioning method used was k-median. A function converting the 12 state values for each customer into a single value was used. Partitioning the range of these values into groups required a threshold. The arbitrary threshold value used yielded 8,261 class 0 profiles and 1,739 class 1 profiles.

Pattern Search

The study sought patterns formed from object grouping. In this case, a pattern was defined as an unexpectedly large number of similar objects. The algorithm estimated the probability in the profile space of each of the 10,000 data points. Then each point was examined to identify those with estimated probabilities that are the maximum among nearby points. This identified peaks. Euclidean distance was used to yield the local comparison set through a fast algorithm. This approach identifies profile neighborhoods of observations with similar characteristics larger than expected.

Comparison

Both methods sought to group objects. Clustering partitions the entire data sample, assigning each observation to exactly one group. **Pattern search** seeks to identify local clusterings since there are more objects with similar characteristics than one would expect. Pattern search does not partition the entire data set, but identifies a few groups exhibiting unusual behavior.

In the application on real data, clustering was useful for describing broad behavioral classes of customers. Pattern search, on the other hand, was useful in identifying groups of people behaving in an anomalous way.

Bankruptcy Prediction

Corporate bankruptcy prediction is very important to management, stockholders, employees, customers, and other stakeholders. A number of data mining techniques have been applied to this problem, including multivariate **discriminant analysis,** logistical regression, probit, genetic algorithms, neural networks, and decision trees.

Late in the 20th century, East Asian corporate bankruptcy was at a critical stage. A number of firms that would have been assessed as economically strong under normal conditions failed during the crisis period in the late 1990s. Bankruptcy prediction models have been developed for both normal and crisis conditions.[16] This study also sought explanations for predictions. Therefore, a decision tree approach was adopted since that method provides a set of rules explaining model predictions. Conversely, neural network models, which tend to be very good at prediction in this environment, were not applied due to their lack of explanatory ability. Discriminant analysis was applied to benchmark the resulting decision tree prediction models.

Korean corporate bankruptcy was studied with the intent of comparing bankruptcy prediction models under normal conditions, and under crisis conditions. The Korean economy was stable throughout most of the 1990s, until an economic crisis began in the fourth quarter of 1997. Despite International Monetary Fund (IMF) assistance, an unprecedented number of Korean corporations went bankrupt as banks charged high interest rates and labor unions hindered downsizing. Data for all bankrupt corporations on the Korea Stock Exchange list from the second quarter of 1997 to the first quarter of 1998 were obtained. Seventy-five such companies existed. Full data was not available for some firms, resulting in 30 firms retained for analysis. For the normal period from the second quarter of 1991 until the first quarter of 1995, 56 firms went bankrupt. After eliminating those firms for which full data was not available, 29 bankrupt firms from the normal period were included in the study. Each selected bankrupt firm was matched with one or two nonbankrupt firms that had similar assets and a comparable number of employees. The control sample included 49 nonbankrupt firms in the normal period, and 54 from the crisis period.

Fifty-six financial ratios were identified from a comprehensive literature review. Sixteen of these ratios were eliminated to eliminate duplication. This resulted in 40 financial ratios, including growth (5), profitability (13), leverage (9), efficiency (6), and productivity (7). The dependent variable was a zero-one variable of bankruptcy or nonbankruptcy.

Multivariate discriminant analysis was applied. The stepwise procedure (where variables are entered one at a time based on their ability to contribute a new explanatory power of changes in the dependent variable) identified three variables for the normal period:

Discriminant score = 0.058 B9 + 0.0623 E6 − 0.006 D42

where

B9 = Cash flow to total assets
E6 = Productivity of capital, and
D4 = Average inventory turnover period

Bankrupt firms showed lower cash flow to total assets, lower productivity of capital, and longer inventory turnover periods.

The model for the crisis period was the following:

Discriminant score = 0.053 C8 + 0.056 E6 + 0.014 C3

where

C8 = Cash flow to liabilities ratio
E6 = Productivity of capital, and
C3 = Ratio of fixed assets to stockholders' equity and long-term liabilities.

Bankrupt firms showed lower cash flow ratios, lower capital productivity, and lower asset ratios.

Jackknife Validation

The original data sets were very small. Therefore, **jackknifing** (also known as the "leave one out" method since data is manipulated in order to use most of it to predict the left-out observation in the sequence) was used for validation. This excluded one data point from the original sample, training on the remaining observations. Then, the trained model predicted the excluded case. This was repeated, excluding each observation in turn.

Decision Tree Model

The **decision tree model** requires a training set of data. The software package C4.5 was used. Pruning significantly increased overall prediction accuracy in the crisis period, indicating that data collected in the crisis period was more influenced by noise than data from the period with normal conditions. Prediction accuracy nearing 80 percent was obtained for the normal period regardless of the minimum number of cases. For the period of crisis conditions, minimum cases of 7 were needed to obtain this level of accuracy.

The technical procedure of **boosting** was used to improve predictive power. This involved the construction of several classifiers rather than one. Those cases misclassified in the training set were given greater emphasis in the next iteration. The boosting came from adding ratio variables to improve prediction rates. The rules obtained were as shown in Table 10.6.

where

C3 = Ratio of fixed assets to equity and long-term liabilities
C8 = Ratio of cash flow to liabilities
C9 = Ratio of cash flow to total assets, and
E6 = Productivity of capital

Predictive validity was measured by percent accuracy, chi-square, and sensitivity. Boosting improved predictive accuracy a great deal. The prediction of the

TABLE 10.6
Rules

Condition	Rule	Prediction	Confidence Level
Normal	E6 > 19.65	Nonbankrupt	0.86
Normal	C9 > 5.64	Nonbankrupt	0.95
Normal	C9 ≤ 5.64 and E6 ≤ 19.65	Bankrupt	0.84
Crisis	E6 > 20.61	Nonbankrupt	0.91
Crisis	C8 > 2.64	Nonbankrupt	0.85
Crisis	C3 > 87.23	Nonbankrupt	0.86
Crisis	C8 ≤ 2.64, E6 ≤ 20.61, and C3 ≤ 87.23	Bankrupt	0.82

Based on Sung et al. (1999).

TABLE 10.7
Discriminant
Analysis and
Decision Tree
Prediction Rates

Condition	Correct Bankrupt	Correct Nonbankrupt	Overall	Key Variables
DA-Normal	69%	90%	82%	C9, E6, D4
DA-Crisis	53%	85%	74%	C8, E6, C3
DT-Normal	72%	90%	83%	C9, E6, A1, B1, B12, C1, C3, D3
DT-Crisis	67%	89%	81%	C8, E6, C3, B2, B8, C2

Based on Sung et al. (1999)

discriminant analysis models (DA) and decision trees (DT) were as shown in Table 10.7.

where

DA = Discriminant analysis
DT = Decision tree
A1 = Growth rate of total assets
B1 = Ratio of gross profit to net sales
B2 = Ratio of operating income to net sales
B8 = Ratio of ordinary income to stockholders' equity
B12 = Earnings per share
C1 = Ratio of stockholders' equity to total assets
C2 = Fixed ratio
C3 = Ratio of fixed assets to equity and long-term liabilities
C8 = Ratio of cash flow to liabilities
C9 = Ratio of cash flow to total assets
D3 = Inventory turnover ratio
D4 = Average turnover period for inventories, and
E6 = Productivity of capital

The decision tree models proved to be better at predicting bankrupt firms under either normal or crisis conditions. Chi-squared tests indicated that the normal and crisis models were significantly different. Sensitivity was defined as the proportion of correctly predicted cases among actual bankruptcies. The crisis model was proved significantly superior at predicting bankruptcy over the range of interest than the normal model.

Investment Risk Analysis

Data mining has been applied in the form of knowledge discovery supporting classification of investment risk by country.[17] This application applied decision tree and neural network models to data using 27 variables with 52 countries. Expert assessment of risk was available for each of the countries.

A great deal of research has been applied to assess financial risks. Each country's economic performance and financial market features impact investment risk. Beginning in 2001, widespread increases in risk have appeared, due to political unrest in Africa, worker unrest in South America, separatism in Asia, and the states arising from the breakup of communism. The motivation for data mining rather than statistical classification was the desire to capture expert knowledge, and to avoid restrictive statistical assumptions.

The Wall Street Journal classified 52 countries into these five risk categories in mid-1997. The set of 27 variables demonstrates the complexity of this knowledge discovery task. Six variables were deleted due to weak correlating with investing risk. The 21 variables selected are given in Table 10.8. The data was analyzed with decision tree and neural network models.

TABLE 10.8
Country Investing
Variables

Variable Class	Variable	Abbreviation
Economic indicators	GNP per capita	GNPc
	GDP real growth rate	GDPg
	Inflation rate projected	INFL
	Interest rate—short-term	INTER
Depth and liquidity	Market capitalization	MARKcap
	Turnover percent of capitalization	TURNOVER
	Public ADRs	ADRs
	Country fund available in U.S.	FUNDS
Performance and value	Return in three years	RET3Yr$
	P/E ratio	PE
	P/E forward ratio	PEforw
	Projected earnings growth	EARNproj
	Dividend yield	YIELD
Economic and market risk	S&P long-term For. Curr. Credit	SandP
	Moody's For. Curr. Rating	MOODY
	Volatility (standard deviation)	VOLATILITY
	Correlation with U.S.	CORREL
Regulation and efficiency	Settlement efficiency rating	SETTLE
	Safekeeping efficiency rating	SAFEKEEP
	Operational costs	OPERCOST
	Year stock exchange started	YEAR

Based on Becerra-Fernandez et al. (2002)

There were five risk classifications:

1. Most safe
2. Developed
3. Mature emerging markets
4. New emerging markets
5. Frontier

Only 52 samples using 21 variables were found, making it difficult to separate data into a training set and a testing set. Bootstrapping was therefore used, with jackknifing. **Bootstrapping** selects K members of the population for the hold-out sample. Jackknifing uses a hold-out sample of size one, which is repeated for each member of the population.

Another data problem was missing observations. The C5.0 algorithm did not need the missing observations. For the neural network analysis, an entropy measure (discussed in Chapter 8) approach was used to transform quantitative variables into categorical variables. Missing values were identified as not belonging to any of the categories defined.

The classification decision tree obtained is displayed in Figure 10.3.

Two decision tree models were applied. The first had a pruning rate of 50 percent, while the second had a pruning rate of 75 percent. A higher pruning rate yields a smaller, more concise tree, while a lower pruning rate will be more accurate.

Three neural network learning algorithms were applied (backpropagation, a fuzzy model-ARTMAP, and learning vector quantization). Backpropagation is a common neural network learning algorithm. The fuzzy model combined the unsupervised learning of adaptive resonance theory with the generalization capabilities of supervised learning. The fuzzy model approach was expected to

FIGURE 10.3 The Investment Risk Decision Tree

Extracted from Becerra-Fernandez et al. (2000)

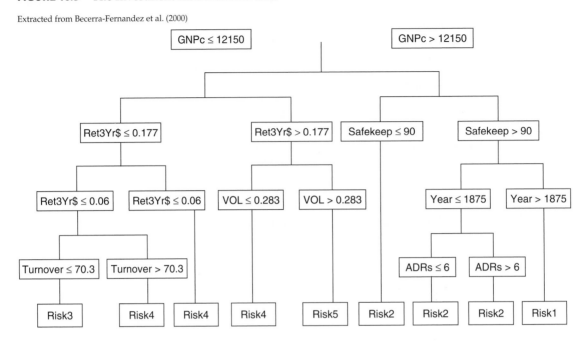

be useful when dealing with noisy or missing data, which was the case here. Learning vector quantization neural networks exploit the presence of unique decision criteria for disjoint sets. A total of 18 different neural network architectures were implemented.

Results from the models are shown in Table 10.9, comparing model predictions with expert assessments.

The decision tree algorithms were more accurate in this case. The decision tree model with the lower prune rate had the lower error rate, as expected. The different neural network models had different errors, as can be seen in Table 10.9. Neural networks are at a relative disadvantage in data sets as small as this. However, the decision tree models were consistently optimistic in their risk classifications relative to expert ratings.

Data Mining Applications in Insurance

Data mining has successfully supported many aspects of the insurance business, including fraud detection, underwriting, insolvency prediction, and customer segmentation. For instance, an insurance firm had a large data warehouse system recording details on every transaction and claim.[18] An aim of the analysis was to accurately predict average claim costs and frequency, and to examine the impact of pricing on profitability.

The specific decision was to set the price for insurance products with the aim of increasing market share, retaining existing customers, and increasing profitability. Successful pricing in the insurance industry requires understanding how many customers are likely to renew their policy, their level of risk, and comprehending customer sensitivity to price increases. This makes it necessary to consider the interactions among these objectives.

The application involved the discovery of information from a database in a four-step process.

TABLE 10.9
Classification
Results by Model

Actual	1	2	3	4	5	Accuracy	Missed
C5P50							
1	12	0	0	0	0	1.000	
2	0	9	0	0	0	1.000	
3	0	0	10	1	0	0.909	Korea
4	0	1	0	10	0	0.909	Israel
5	0	0	0	1	8	0.889	Jordan
C5P75							
1	12	0	0	0	0	1.000	
2	3	6	0	0	0	0.667	Belgium, Japan, Spain
3	0	0	10	1	0	0.909	Korea
4	0	1	0	10	0	0.909	Israel
5	0	0	0	1	8	0.889	Jordan
Backpro							
1	11	0	1	0	0	0.917	Ireland
2	1	8	0	0	0	0.889	Belgium
3	0	1	8	2	0	0.727	Brazil, Chile, Portugal
4	0	1	1	8	1	0.727	Indonesia, Taiwan
5	0	0	2	2	5	0.556	Pakistan, Peru
ARTMAP							
1	12	0	0	0	0	1.000	
2	0	9	0	0	0	1.000	
3	0	0	9	2	0	0.818	Brazil, Mexico
4	0	1	1	8	1	0.727	China, Indonesia, Taiwan
5	0	0	2	2	5	0.556	Jordan, Morocco, Peru, Russia
LVQ							
1	10	1	1	0	0	0.833	Ireland, Germany
2	0	9	0	0	0	1.000	
3	0	1	8	1	1	0.727	Brazil, Greece, Portugal
4	0	0	1	8	2	0.727	China, Indonesia, Taiwan
5	0	0	1	0	8	0.889	Peru

Extracted from Becerra-Fernandez et al. (2002)

1. Identification of the business problem
2. Data analysis
3. Action
4. Measure of outcomes

Within data analysis, the process steps of data preparation, initial descriptive statistics, hypothesis testing, and knowledge discovery are undertaken. This holistic approach to data mining seeks to ensure the integration of results with existing business knowledge and procedures. Initial descriptive statistics allow orientation with the data, identification and treatment of outliers, and the opportunity to formulate initial hypotheses that can be tested early. Once initial data analysis is completed, knowledge discovery can be applied.

The data mining tool was developed to evaluate the impact of changes to insurance policy details, including premium rates. The system predicted termination prediction, and the enabled analysis of proposals for marketing initiatives.

Customer Retention Analysis

The first set of data mining models dealt with customer retention. The ability to predict customer response to price change is, of course, fundamentally important. Data mining can provide a better prediction of customer response to changes.

Data Collection and Preprocessing

The sample set included over 20,000 motor vehicle policies due for renewal in a particular month. All policy holders were contacted by letter in the months prior to their policy lapse date, and notified that their policy was due for renewal, giving the premium for the next year. Slightly over 7 percent of this sample did not renew their policy, thus terminating. Details on each policy holder were gathered, including demographic information, policy premiums, insurance amounts, policy holder history, and information about the differences in the premium and the sum insured between the current policy and the renewal policy.

The analysts met with management to discuss reasons for policy termination. Three primary factors were identified: pricing, service, and the insured value of the vehicle. Preliminary statistical analysis was conducted to investigate the likely impact of each of these factors, validating opinions about pricing and the sum insured. The insured value of the vehicle turned out to not be important. Other factors, such as age, new business, and policy duration were not found to improve predictability.

Data Mining

SAS Enterprise Miner was used, enabling the construction of a process flow diagram connecting data, variable selection, transformation, partitioning, and modeling. Data exploration tools identified a number of variables as having low relationships with the dependent variable. Three binary variables, two categorical variables, and eight continuous variables were used in the study, as shown in Table 10.10.

Log transformations were used when data was highly skewed, and variables grouped into bins were converted to binary variables representing each bin. The dependent variable was "Terminated." After representing grouped data by binary variables, there were 29 independent variables.

The data was divided into a training set and a test set through the Data Partitioning node. Data in the training set was analyzed in the assessment node by logistic regression, decision trees, and neural networks.

The test set revealed that for this data, the neural network model had the best fit. The top ten percent of the list of test observations for the neural network model

TABLE 10.10
Variables for
Customer Retention
Analysis

Variable	Type	Transformation
New business	Binary	
Gender	Binary	
Terminated	Binary (dependent variable)	
Postal code	Categorical	Grouped into 10 bins
Rating	Categorical	Grouped into two bins
Vehicle age	Continuous	Grouped into four bins
Years on rating	Continuous	
Policy holder age	Continuous	Grouped into five bins
Premium	Continuous	Log transformation
Premium difference	Continuous	
Sum insured	Continuous	Log transformation
Sum insured difference	Continuous	
Years on policy	Continuous	

Extracted from Smith et al. (2000)

identified 50 percent of all terminations. The corresponding top ten percent of the regression model identified only 40 percent, and the decision tree model only 28 percent. However, the neural network had a low proportion of cases classified as probable terminations. The system allowed moderating model parameters to improve this feature.

Action

The results of the preceding analysis were used to create a unified pricing methodology, based on the interactions of growth, claims, and profitability. The data warehouse contained data about current pricing and profitability, as well as growth patterns and claim patterns. Knowledge gained from the data mining exercise was used to balance the portfolio of policies to obtain greater profitability and continued growth and retention.

Claims Analysis

Claims analysis is more unstructured than customer retention analysis, and requires a more undirected approach. Thus, data analysis for hidden trends and patterns is needed. In this case, recent growth in the number of policy holders led to lower profitability for the company. Understanding the relationships between cause and effect is fundamental to understanding what business decisions would be appropriate.

Policy rates are based on statistical analysis assuming various distributions for claims and claim size. In this case, clustering was used to better model the performance of specific groups of those insured.

Key Performance Indicators

Profitability in insurance is often expressed by the cost ratio—the sum of claim costs divided by the sum of premiums. The claim frequency ratio is the number of claims divided by the number of policy units of risk (possible claims). Profitability would be improved by lowering the frequency of claims, or the costs of claims relative to premiums.

Data Collection and Preprocessing

Data was extracted from the data warehouse for policies for which premiums were paid in the first quarter over a three-year period. This meant that policies were followed during that time, augmented by new policies, and diminished by terminations. Data on each policy holder was available as well as claim behavior over the preceding year. The key variables of cost ratio and claim frequency ratio were calculated for each observation. Sample sizes for each quarter were well above 100,000.

Analysis and Impact of Growth

Descriptive statistics found exceptional growth in policies over the past two years for young people (under 22), and with cars insured for over $40,000.

Clustering

Predicting the claim cost of each individual policy holder would be pointless, as the vast majority of claims cannot be predicted. Therefore, directed data mining is inappropriate. The goal is rather to predict group policy claims behavior. Clustering requires a definition of the number of clusters. Too few clusters give no discriminating ability, while too many clusters lead to clusters with too few observations. After experimentation, the study was based on 50 clusters. A basic k-means algorithm was used. This identified several clusters as having abnormal cost ratios or frequency sizes. By testing over a two-year gap, stability for each group was determined.

Comparisons of Data Mining Methods

Most of the primary business data mining methods were referred to in the previous example applications. Sung et al. compared a number of these methods with respect to advantages and disadvantages, while Table 10.11 draws upon their analysis and expands it to include the other techniques covered.

Cluster analysis is attractive, in that it can be applied automatically (although ample computational time needs to be available). It can be applied to all types of data, as demonstrated in our example. Cluster analysis is also easy to apply. However, its use requires selecting from among alternative distance measures, and weights may be needed to reflect variable importance. Results are sensitive to these measures. Cluster analysis is appropriate when dealing with large, complex data sets with many variables and specifically identifiable outcomes. It is often used as an initial form of analysis. Once different clusters are identified, pattern search methods are often used to discover rules and patterns.

Discriminant analysis has been the most widely used data mining technique in bankruptcy prediction. Neural network algorithms can prove highly accurate, but are difficult to apply to new data, or when used for model interpretation. Neural networks work well unless there are many input features. An overabundance of features makes it difficult for the network to find patterns, thus resulting in long training phases, with lower probabilities of convergence. Genetic algorithms have also been applied to data mining, usually to bolster operations of other algorithms.

Decision tree analysis requires only the last assumption that groups are discrete, non-overlapping, and identifiable. They provide the ability to generate understandable rules, can perform classifications with minimal computation, and their calculations are easy. Decision tree analysis can deal with both continuous and categorical variables, and provide a clear indication of variable importance in prediction and classification. Given the disadvantages of the decision tree method, it's a good option when the data mining task concerns classification of records or prediction of outcomes.

Regression is probably the most widely used analytic tool historically. A main benefit of regression is the broad understanding people have about regression models and tests of their output. Logistic regression is highly appropriate in data mining, due to the categorical nature of resultant variables that are usually present. While regression is an excellent tool for statistical analysis, it does require assumptions about parameters. Errors are assumed to be normally distributed, without autocorrelation (errors are not related to prior errors), without heteroskedasticity (errors don't grow with time, for instance), and without multicollinearity (independent variables don't contain high degrees of overlapping information content). Regression can deal with nonlinear data, but only if the modeler understands the underlying nonlinearity and develops appropriate variable transformations. There usually is a trade-off—if the data fit well with a linear model, regression tends to be better than with neural network models. However, if there is nonlinearity or complexity in the data, neural networks (and often genetic algorithms) tend to do better than

TABLE 10.11 Comparison of Data Mining Methods Features[19]

Method	Advantages	Disadvantages	Assumptions
Cluster analysis	Can generate understandable formula Can be applied automatically	Computation time increases with data set size Requires identification of parameters, with results sensitive to choices	
Discriminant analysis	Able to incorporate multiple financial ratios simultaneously Includes coefficients for combining independent variables Can be applied to new data	Violates normality and independence assumptions Reduces dimensionality issues Offers a varied interpretation of the relative importance of variables Can prove difficult in specifying classification algorithms Can prove difficult in interpreting time-series prediction tests	Assume multivariate normality within groups Assume group covariances are equal across all groups Groups are discrete, nonoverlapping, and identifiable
Neural Network models	Can deal with a wide range of problems Produces good results in complicated domains (nonlinear) Can deal with both continuous and categorical variables Has many software packages available	Requires inputs in the range of 0 to 1 Does not explain results May prematurely converge upon an inferior solution	Groups are discrete, nonoverlapping, and identifiable
Genetic algorithms	Produce explainable results Easy to apply results Can deal with wide range of data Allow optimization Can be integrated with neural networks	Has difficulty encoding many problems Offers no guarantee of optimality Is computationally expensive if multiple functions are present Has limited commercial package availability	Groups are discrete, non-overlapping, and identifiable
Decision trees	Can generate understandable rules Can classify with minimal computation Uses easy calculations Can deal with continuous and categorical variables Provides clear indication of variable importance	Some algorithms can only deal with binary-valued target classes Most algorithms only examine a single field at a time Can be computationally expensive	Groups are discrete, non-overlapping, and identifiable
Regression	Can generate understandable formula Is widely understood Is founded in a strong body of theory	Computation time increases with data set size Not very good with nonlinear data	A normality of errors exist No error autocorrelation, heteroskedasticity, or multicollinearity

regression. A major relative advantage of regression relative to neural networks is that regression provides an easily understood formula, while neural network models have a very complex model.

Summary

Data mining applications are widespread. This chapter sought to give concrete examples of some of the major business applications of data mining. We began with a review of Fingerhut data mining to support catalog sales. That application was an excellent demonstration of the concept of lift applied to retail business. We also covered five other major business applications, intentionally trying to demonstrate a variety of different functions, statistical techniques, and data mining methods. Most of those studies applied multiple algorithms (data mining methods). Software such as Enterprise Miner has a variety of algorithms available, encouraging data miners to find the method that works best for a specific set of data.

The second portion of the book seeks to demonstrate these methods with small demonstration examples. The small examples can be run on Excel or other simple spreadsheet packages with statistical support. Businesses can often conduct data mining without purchasing large scale data mining software. Therefore, our philosophy is that it is useful to understand what the methods are doing, which also provides users with a better understanding of what they are doing when applying data mining.

Glossary

boosting Procedure applying multiple models and using selections of each model as votes for a predicted category.

bootstrapping Sampling technique to generate greater understanding from small data sets.

churn Turnover in customers, especially loss of customers in the telephone industry.

cluster analysis Statistical technique to group data into discrete sets.

clustering Dividing data into groups.

customer relationship management (CRM) Use of data mining to identify details about a customer, including the customer's value to the organization and the characteristics that the customer is looking for in products.

decision tree model Set of rules to classify data into a finite number of possible conclusions.

discriminant analysis Statistical technique using regression scores to assign observations to categories.

jackknifing The use of advanced statistical sampling to generate greater understanding from small data sets.

lift The marginal difference in a segment's proportion of response to a promotion and the average rate of response.

micromarketing Focused marketing directed at a small subset of the total population. This subset is expected to contain a much higher proportion of product purchasers than the general population.

pattern search Identification of relationships in data.

Exercises

1. Visit the library and/or Internet to find updates on the Fingerhut case or other related customer segmentation businesses.

2. Describe the concept of lift. How is this useful to marketing organizations?
3. What does the RFM method do differently from lift?
4. You have the following data for ten types of customer profiles, each providing your company profit at the stated rates. Calculate and plot lift.

Customer Profile	Profit Rate	Customer Profile	Profit Rate	Customer Profile	Profit Rate
A	12	E	10	I	18
B	15	F	6	J	11
C	8	G	4		
D	7	H	9		

5. Your firm mails credit card solicitations to people. It costs the firm $6 for each mailing. You have gathered data and are able to profile people into the following 10 groups, with the stated expected response. Your firm expects to make $100 in net present profit for each positive response. Identify the optimal policy.

Customer Profile	Response Rate	Customer Profile	Response Rate	Customer Profile	Response Rate
A	0.05	E	0.08	I	0.03
B	0.12	F	0.04	J	0.13
C	0.15	G	0.11		
D	0.10	H	0.09		

6. What is the correlation between customer relationship management and data mining?
7. Discuss ethical issues involved in customer relationship management. How can CRM negatively impact society?
8. What sources of inaccuracy exist in calculating the lifetime value of a customer?
9. Describe credit scoring. Are there any ethical concerns involved in its application?
10. Casinos have been heavy users of data mining. What do they use data mining for? Are there any ethical considerations?
11. In the country-investing example, classification results were given in Table 10.8. Calculate the aggregate accuracy rates for each of the five methods.
12. If one method was more accurate than another in Table 10.8, why might those methods whose measurements were less accurate still be attractive?
13. Elaborate upon the relative attraction of discriminant analysis, neural network models, genetic algorithms, decision tree models, regression, and cluster analysis relative to each other.

Endnotes

1. J. H. Drew, D. R. Mani, A. L. Betz, and P. Datta, "Targeting Customers with Statistical and Data-Mining Techniques," *Journal of Service Research*, volume 3, number 3, 2001, pp. 205–219; M. S. Garver, "Using Data Mining for Customer Satisfaction Research," *Marketing Research*, volume 14, number 1, 2002, pp. 8–17.
2. A. M. Cowan, "Data Mining in Finance: Advances in Relational and Hybrid Methods," *International Journal of Forecasting*, volume 18, number 1, 2002, pp. 155–156.
3. N. M. Adams, D. J. Hand, and R. J. Till, "Mining for Classes and Patterns in Behavioural Data," *The Journal of the Operational Research Society*, volume 52, number 9, 2001, pp. 1017–1024.

4. T. K. Sung, N. Chang, and G. Lee, "Dynamics of Modeling in Data Mining: Interpretive Approach to Bankruptcy Prediction," *Journal of Management Information Systems*, volume 16, number 1, 1999, pp. 63–85.

5. K. A. Smith, R. J. Willis, and M. Brooks, "An Analysis of Customer Retention and Insurance Claim Patterns Using Data Mining: A Case Study," *The Journal of the Operational Research Society*, volume 51, number 5, 2000, pp. 532–541.

6. Drew, Mani, Betz, and Datta, op. cit.; Garver, op. cit.; Adams, Hand, and Till, op. cit.; Sung, Chang, and Lee, op. cit.; I. Becerra-Fernandez, S. H. Zanakis, and S. Walczak, "Knowledge Discovery Techniques for Predicting Country Investment Risk," *Computers and Industrial Engineering*, volume 43, 2002, pp. 787–800; Smith, Willis, and Brooks, op. cit.

7. C. Apte, B. Liu, E. P. D. Pednault, and P. Smyth, "Business Applications of Data Mining," *Communications of the ACM*, volume 45, number 8, 2002, pp. 49–53.

8. S. Deck, "Mining Your Business," *Computerworld*, volume 33, number 20, May 17, 1999, pp. 94–98.

9. S. Chiger, "Bragging Rights," *Catalog Age*, volume 15, number 9, August 1998, pp. 1, 66+.

10. D. Campbell, R. Erdahl, D. Johnson, E. Bibelnieks, M. Haydock, M. Bullock, and H. Crowder, "Optimizing Customer Mail Streams at Fingerhut," *Interfaces*, volume 31, number 1, 2001, pp. 77–90.

11. V. S. Y. Lo, "The True Lift Model—A Novel Data Mining Approach to Response Modeling in Database Marketing," *ACM SIGKDD*, volume 4, issue 2, 2003, pp. 78–86.

12. M. Fitzpatrick, "Statistical Analysis for Direct Marketers—In Plain English," *Direct Marketing*, volume 64, issue 4, 2001, pp. 54–56.

13. R. Elsner, M. Krafft, and A. Huchzermeier, "Optimizing Rhenania's Mail-Order business Through Dynamic Multilevel Modeling (DMLM)," *Interfaces*, volume 33, number 1, 2003, pp. 50–66.

14. Drew, Mani, Betz, and Datta, op. cit.; Garver, op. cit.

15. S. Patton, "The Truth about CRM," CIO *Magazine*, May 1, 2001, http://www.cio.com/archive/050101/truth_content.html.

16. Sung, Chang, and Lee, op. cit.

17. Becerra-Fernandez, Zanakis, and Walczak, op. cit.

18. Smith, Willis, and Brooks, op. cit.

19. Sung, Chang, and Lee, op. cit.

CHAPTER ELEVEN

Market-Basket Analysis

This chapter:

- Defines market-basket analysis
- Presents market-basket terminology
- Demonstrates concepts with examples
- Reviews market-basket software products
- Demonstrates market-basket procedure in the appendix

When you go to the grocery store on Mondays in the fall, have you ever noticed how easy it is to obtain the beer and potato chips you need for your friends coming over to watch the football game? Have you ever noticed that in order to get milk for your kids, you have to pass through the entire store? Have you noticed people in the uniforms of particular products, such as popular beverages, carefully stacking their products in a grocery store with no known ownership connection to the beverage? These are only some of many symptoms of product positioning, critically important to grocery store success. Obviously, one important factor is that you sell more if customers can see the product. Another important principle is that customers that purchase one type of product are likely to be interested in other particular products.

Market-basket analysis is interested in identifying which products tend to be purchased together. This information enables stores to make intelligent positioning decisions. The Monday night kiosks of beer and potato chips are obvious, due to the propensity of the American public to watch Monday Night Football. But things like orange juice, cold medicine, and tissues might be less apparent.

Market-basket analysis refers to methodologies studying the composition of a shopping basket of products purchased during a single shopping event. This technique has been widely applied to grocery store operations (as well as other retailing operations, including restaurants). Market-basket data in its rawest form would be the transactional list of purchases by customer, indicating only the items purchased together (with their prices). This data is challenging because of a number of aspects:[1]

- A very large number of records (often millions of transactions per day)
- Sparseness (each market basket contains only a small portion of items carried)
- Heterogeneity (those with different tastes tend to purchase a specific subset of items)

The aim of market-basket analysis is to identify what products tend to be purchased together. Analyzing transaction-level data can identify purchase patterns, such as which frozen vegetables and side dishes are purchased with steak during barbecue season. This information can then be used in determining where to place products in the store, as well as aid inventory management. Product presentations and staffing can be more intelligently planned for specific times of day, days of the week, or holidays. Another commercial application is electronic couponing, tailoring coupon face value and distribution timing using information obtained from market-baskets.[2]

Definitions

Market-basket analysis examines the tendencies of customers to purchase items together. This can include buying products at the same time, such as milk and cookies, or bread, butter, and jam. It also can involve sequential relationships, such as purchasing a house followed by purchases of furniture, or purchasing a car one year and purchasing new tires two years later. Knowledge of customer tendencies is very valuable to retail organizations, as well as information about purchase timing. For instance, Monday night football purchases can be expected to motivate Monday afternoon sales, so stores would be wise to ensure that ample supplies of beer and potato chips line their shelves. Other information may not be useful, such as hypothesized relationships between new hardware store openings and toilet ring sales.[3] Information of this type has no **actionable** content. While hardware stores may wish to make sure they have toilet rings on hand when they open, market-basket information offers no real value unless it contains information that can be explained. In other words, the conclusions drawn must make sense.

Market-basket analysis (along with clustering) is an undirected data mining operation, seeking patterns that were previously unknown. This makes it a form of knowledge discovery. Market-basket analysis begins with categorizing customer purchase behavior. The next step is to identify actionable information that improves profit according to purchase profile. Once profitability by purchase profile is known, retailers then have factual data that can be used for key decision making. Laying out retail stores by purchase categories is referred to as **affinity positioning.** An example of this is including coffee and coffee makers in the office products area. Affinity is measured a number of different ways, the simplest of which is **correlation.** This information is often applied two ways.[4] If product positioning matters, a store choice model assumes that a change in the mix of customers due to marketing activities leads to correlations. If product positioning doesn't matter, global utility models view cross-category dependence as a result of consumer choice. Either view finds value in knowing which products tend to be sold together. **Cross-selling** refers to the propensity for the purchaser of a specific item to purchase a different item. Retail outlets can maximize cross-selling by locating those products that tend to be purchased by the same consumer in places where both products can be seen. A good example of cross-selling is orange juice, cold medicine, and tissues, which are all attractive to consumers with colds.

TABLE 11.1
Possible Grocery Market Baskets

Customer #1:	beer, pretzels, potato chips, aspirin
Customer #2:	diapers, baby lotion, grapefruit juice, baby food, milk
Customer #3:	soda, potato chips, milk
Customer #4:	soup, beer, milk, ice cream
Customer #5:	soda, coffee, milk, bread
Customer #6:	beer, potato chips

TABLE 11.2
A Co-occurrence
Table

	Beer	Potato Chips	Milk	Diapers	Soda
Beer	3	2	1	0	0
Potato chips	2	3	1	0	1
Milk	1	1	4	1	2
Diapers	0	0	1	1	0
Soda	0	1	2	0	2

Market-basket analysis leads to the identification of which products are being purchased together. Such information can be useful in more effectively laying out stores or catalogs, as well as in selecting products for promotion. This information is typically employed in advertising and promotion planning, space allocation, product placement, and personal customer relations.

Steve Schmidt, president of ACNielsen-US, described some of the benefits of market-basket analysis.[5] Market-basket analysis can be vitally important in the effective selection of promotions and merchandising strategies. Analysis can uncover buried consumer spending patterns, and identify lucrative opportunities to promote products together. Schmidt reported that Italian entrees, pizzas, bakery pies, Asian entrees, and orange juice as products that are most sensitive to price promotion. Analysis has revealed a high correlation between orange juice and waffle sales. Data mining analysis includes the entire process of not only identifying such correlations, but also in deriving a reason for such relationships, and more important, creating ways to increase overall profit.

Simple market-basket analysis can be applied beginning with a **co-occurrence table** that lists the number of incidents from a given sample size in which products are purchased together. For instance, six customers may have products in their grocery market baskets as shown in Table 11.1.

The co-occurrence table for five selected products would be as shown in Table 11.2.

In this example, the strongest correlation is between beer and potato chips. This is an expected relationship, because the two products go well together. The correlation matrix for this data is given in Table 11.3.

While the correlation between diapers and milk is low, every instance of diaper purchase in this small sample included milk (and for that matter, other baby products), things that would be expected. It appears that it would not make sense to seek cross-sales of milk or soda to beer drinkers. This information could be actionable in a negative sense to advertisers (or maybe beer drinkers just haven't thought of the value of milk in combination with beer). On the other hand, it would make sense to push potato chips to beer drinkers. Some combinations, such as that between milk and soda, may not include any actionable content, even though the statistical relationship may be quite strong.

TABLE 11.3
A Correlation
Matrix for the
Co-occurrence Table

	Beer	Potato Chips	Milk	Diapers	Soda
Beer	1				
Potato chips	0.773574	1			
Milk	−0.264706	−0.269069	1		
Diapers	−0.490098	−0.720577	0.490098	1	
Soda	−0.383482	0	0.766965	0	1

TABLE 11.4
Jaccard Coefficients
for Co-occurrence
Table

	Beer	Potato Chips	Milk	Diapers	Soda
Beer					
Potato chips	0.333				
Milk	0.143	0.143			
Diapers	0	0	0.200		
Soda	0	0.200	0.333	0	

There are basic ways to identify which products in a market basket go together.[6] Correlation was just demonstrated. However, correlation is not particularly good when dealing with binary data (and raw market basket data is binary). The product-moment **correlation coefficient** standardizes for mean and standard deviation. Distance measures identify some metric of similarity. A third method, Jaccard's coefficient, is very simple but effective, often more effective than either correlation or distance measures. The Jaccard coefficient is the ratio of the number of cases where two products were purchased together to the total number of cases where each product was purchased.

To demonstrate using the example previously given, Table 11.2 informs us that beer and potato chips were purchased together twice. The total number of beer purchases was 3, and the total number of potato chip purchases was also 3. Thus, the Jaccard coefficient for beer and potato chips would be {2/(3+3)} = 0.333. The Jaccard coefficients for the other products relative to beer are 0.143 for milk, 0 for diapers, and 0 for soda. Table 11.4 gives the Jaccard coefficients corresponding to the correlation coefficients shown in Table 11.3.

The correlation coefficients infer relationships of cross-references, while the Jaccard coefficients focus on the pairs of items directly. Both measures are easily obtained (correlation coefficients from widely available software; Jaccard coefficients from simple formulas). The primary issue is the relative accuracy in identifying relationships. The simpler Jaccard coefficient could well be more accurate, but requires a significant amount of representative data before results are reliable. (For instance, in our simple example, there were many zeroes, which are not reliable on a large scale. However, in real retail establishments with a great deal of turnover, such data would be widely available.)

Setting up market-basket analysis requires significant investment and effort. Retail organizations can take over 18 months to implement this type of analysis. However, it provides a tool to compete in an increasingly competitive environment.

Demonstration

The magazine *Chain Store Age Executive* conducted an in-depth study of one market-basket analysis.[7] The first step was to associate products by category. The next step was to determine what percentage of each of these categories was in each market basket. Market baskets were assigned to the profile based on greatest dollar value. These profiles were then viewed as capturing the reason the shopper was in the store. Market-basket analysis reveals that customers do not shop based on product groupings, but rather on personal needs. The 30 **purchase profiles** for this discounter are shown in Table 11.5.

The consumer orientation helps in understanding combinations in product purchases. For instance, cotton balls, hair dye, and cologne are four different products,

TABLE 11.5
Purchase Profiles for Market-Basket Analysis

Based on anonymous, *Chain Store Age Executive*, 1995.

Beauty conscious	Home handyman	Photographer
Women's fashion	Health conscious	Men's image conscious
TV/Stereo enthusiast	Kids' fashion	Sports conscious
Sentimental	Seasonal/traditional	Hobbyist
Smoker	Kids' play	Homemaker
Student/Home office	Casual drinker	Pet lover
Home comfort	Illness (prescription)	New family
Gardener	Fashion footwear	Men's fashion
Illness over-the-counter	Automotive	
Casual reader	Convenience foods/drinks	

but all are part of the beauty-conscious purchase profile. Particular customers may buy a market basket in one profile during one visit, and another profile later. The focus is on the market basket, not customers as individuals.

Retailers typically determine the profitability of each purchase profile. The returns for 27 of the purchase profiles for the retailer in dollars per market basket are shown in Table 11.6.

This information can assist in promotion decision making. Often retailers find that their past advertising has been for products in purchase profiles with low profitability returns. The same approach can be applied to other promotional efforts, although promotions often cross profiles. The effect of promotions can be estimated by measuring the profitability by market basket.

Space allocation and product placement is another important retailing decision supported by market-basket analysis. In Table 11.6, Kids' Fashion represents 3 percent of total profits, while the casual drinker purchase profile represents 0.3 percent.[8] Yet both may have equal floor space. If so, it may be wise for retailers to reallocate greater floor space to more profitable products. Beauty-conscious market baskets included greeting cards 25 percent of the time, and seasonal candy 16 percent of the time. This indicated that overall sales might be increased by moving greeting cards and seasonal candies to areas adjacent to the primary beauty care area.

Market-basket analysis can also uncover items frequently purchased together. As you might expect, cold medicines are often found in the same market baskets as Kleenex. Market-basket analysis also found that over 30 percent of these market baskets included bottled juice. By locating a selection of bottled juice near cold remedies, cross-selling can be increased.

Promotional events can be designed based upon product affinities. The grocery chain identified 16 purchase profiles representing unique shopping occasions, such as summer barbecues and Monday night football airings, as shown in Table 11.7.

TABLE 11.6
Purchase Profile Returns

Based on anonymous, *Chain Store Age Executive*, 1995.

Kid's fashion	$15.24	Illness (OTC)	$6.64	Seasonal/traditional	$4.79
Men's fashion	$13.41	Fashion footwear	$6.48	Automotive	$4.63
Women's fashion	$11.84	TV/Stereo enthusiast	$4.36	Gardener	$4.36
Home comfort	$9.37	Men's image cons.	$5.79	New family	$3.98
Health conscious	$8.11	Sentimental	$5.79	Convenience food/dr.	$3.82
Hobbyist	$7.99	Casual reader	$5.78	Pet lover	$3.00
Photographer	$7.81	Beauty conscious	$5.36	Casual drinker	$2.96
Home handyman	$7.70	Kids' play	$5.30	Smoker	$2.88
Sports conscious	$7.45	Homemaker	$5.21	Student/home office	$2.55

TABLE 11.7
Purchase Profiles:
Grocery Chain

Based on anonymous, *Chain Store Age Executive*, 1995.

Weekly stock-up	Meal for one	Household cleaning	Weekend trip
Dinner party/entertainment	Healthy eating	Convenience meal	Monday night football
Backyard barbecue	Cold and flu	Snack attack	Personal care/needs
Bake from scratch	Baby needs	Pet needs	Family needs/club pack

If a healthy-eating market basket was worth $17 in margin and a pet-needs market basket was worth $4, this information could be used as the basis for advertising and promotion. Advertising budgets could then be directed toward health foods rather than pet foods.

There are noted variations from store to store for purchase profiles. Therefore, market-basket analysis needs to focus on the store level. For instance, the Gardener market basket was found to have marginal profitability of $4.36 in one store, but $8.90 in another.

Market-basket analysis can involve three categories of relationships:[9]

1. Complementary relationships, such as beer and pretzels
2. Relationships with similar purchase cycles, such as milk and fruit
3. Relationships reflecting household preferences or household demographics

Not accounting for these three motivations can lead to the erroneous analysis of market baskets.

Market-Basket Limitations

Anne Milley of SAS Business Solutions warned of the limitations of market-basket analysis.[10] Identifying relationships among product sales is no good unless it is used. Measurement of effects is critical to sound data mining. One of the most commonly cited examples of market-basket analysis was the hypothesized tendency for men to purchase beer and diapers together. If this were true, the knowledge would only be valuable if action could be taken that would increase sales. For instance, one theory is that retailers should locate beer and diapers close to each other, encouraging sales of both. An alternative theory would be to locate the two products as far apart as possible, forcing customers to see the maximum number of products available in the store. In either case, a measurement of impact is required to gain useful knowledge. Milley contended that market-basket analysis, an exploratory algorithm, can only generate hypotheses. Once hypotheses are generated, they need to be tested.

Market-basket analysis is often an initial study intended to identify patterns. Once a pattern is detected, it can be explored more thoroughly through other methods, such as neural networks, regression, or decision trees.[11] The same analytic approaches can be used in applications outside of retail. Telecommunications companies and banks often bundle products together, and market-basket analysis has been applied in those fields. The insurance industry has been a major user of link analysis to detect fraud rings. In the medical field, combinations of symptoms can be analyzed to gain a deeper understanding of a patient's condition.

The overall strengths of market-basket analysis include clear results through simple computations. Market-basket analysis can be undirected, in that hypothetical relationships do not need to be specified prior to analysis. Different data forms can be used as well. Weaknesses of the method are (1) that the complexity of the analysis grows exponentially with the volume of products considered, and (2) that it is difficult to identify an appropriate number of product groupings. The 30 groupings demonstrated earlier is a good workable, actionable number. Too few product groupings provide no benefit, while too many will hamper attempts to make sense of the analysis. Market-basket analysis is a technique that's good for undirected, or unstructured, problems with well-defined items. It's very suitable for cash register data.

Market-Basket Analysis Software

Market-basket analysis is more qualitative than most other forms of data mining. Recent reports of market-basket analysis include use of neural network approaches combined with visualization[12] as well as the use of collaborative filtering algorithms for prediction of choices or preferences.[13] The primary analytic tool is correlation analysis, which can easily be accomplished on a spreadsheet. In fact, many firms that use data mining employ simple internal software to perform their analyses. A major problem for market-basket analysis is the magnitude of the data-set size. This problem can often be coped with by grouping products into product types or categories (as long as crucial knowledge about the decisions to be made aren't then lost). Often, data manipulation tools such as Visual Basic and Standard Query Language (SQL) are applied.

Most major data mining tools are not designed for market-basket analysis. Exceptions are Clementine (by SPSS) and PolyAnalyst (by Megaputer). (The appendix to this chapter shows an example of market-basket analysis using PolyAnalyst.) Currently, a line of software products are devoted specifically to market-basket analysis. One of these is DataSage Inc.'s DataSage Customer Analyst, which is designed to link point-of-sale output from an enterprise system to enable the analysis of customer buying patterns, pricing patterns, and other data.[14] Another product is Xaffinity, which offers unique association and sequence-pattern detection and analysis.[15]

Not only is software available to support market-basket analysis, but there are data sets that have been cited in the literature as well. Manchanda et al. used a market-basket data set generated by A.C. Nielsen, including multiple categories of products available in groceries.[16] Heilman et al. used a Stanford University set of data (Information Resources Inc.'s Market Basket Data) that was created in 1994, containing two years' worth of purchases by over 1,000 consumers in 10 grocery stores across 24 product categories.[17]

Appendix

Market-Basket Procedure

In this appendix, we'll describe the process of market-basket analysis used by PolyAnalyst, one of the data mining software products discussed in the prior section. For this product, market-basket analysis can be conducted on binary data or on data reflecting the volume of products (say, four of the same item in one basket). Both are intended to identify which products tend to be sold together, which can be the basis for the product positioning or cross-selling applications described earlier. Once the data is processed, the analyst needs to set a minimum support level. If binary data is used, minimum support is expressed in terms of percentage. The default is 10 percent, meaning that if fig newtons and apples are purchased together in 8 percent of the market baskets analyzed, this relationship will be skipped. Conversely, if chicken soup and crackers are sold together in 15 percent of

FIGURE 11A.1
PolyAnalyst Binary
Market-Basket
Data Set

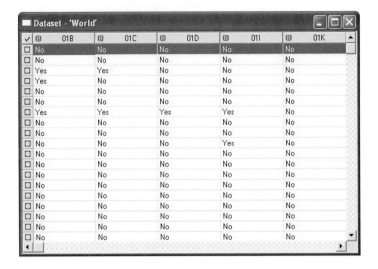

the baskets in the data set, this relationship will be grouped in a product cluster. The lower this minimum, the more clusters (and the greater the risk of a sea of output that is more difficult to analyze). Of course, too high a minimum can yield zero product clusters. The system is designed to be interactive, allowing the analyst to use sliders to change parameters such as minimum support, yielding the desired number of product clusters. If numeric data is used, the number of units sold becomes the basis for the minimum support level. Figure 11A.1 (taken from PolyAnalyst help) shows a binary data set in PolyAnalyst.

Over all market baskets, including chicken soup, the proportion containing each of the other products is easily identifiable (although there clearly are a lot of combinations to count). The software reports minimum improvement, indicating

FIGURE 11A.2
A Product Cluster
Report from
PolyAnalyst

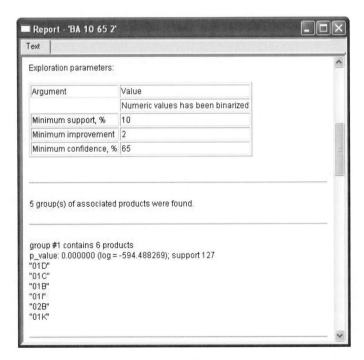

FIGURE 11A.3
PolyAnalyst
Market-Basket Rule
Example

	Filter:	Support < 10.90	Confidence > 65.00	Improvement > 3.30
"01C", "01B", "01I", -> "01D" "02B", "01K"		10.81%	95.49%	3.484
"01D", "01C", "01B", -> "02B" "01I", "01K"		10.81%	78.88%	3.737
"01D", "01C", "01B", -> "01K" "01I", "02B"		10.81%	88.19%	3.611
"02C", "02D" -> "06K"		10.72%	78.26%	4.971
"06K", "02D" -> "02C"		10.72%	91.97%	4.618
"06K", "02C" -> "02D"		10.72%	84.56%	4.358

how much better the confidence of the association rule generated is better than random. The minimum confidence reported is the probability that if a customer purchased a particular product cluster, that customer would purchase the item under consideration. Association rules are based upon minimum improvement or minimum confidence. The software reports whatever product clusters were found, as in Figure 11A.2.

The output of market-basket analysis (binary data) or transaction-basket analysis (continuous data) is a list of products in clusters, and association rules relating to each cluster. The association rules are stated in terms of:

IF "chicken soup" THEN "crackers," with the proportion of transactions supporting this relationship, and the probability of purchasing crackers if chicken soup were in a basket. An example output is displayed in Figure 11A.3. This relationship is unidirectional (it doesn't imply anything about the likelihood of chicken soup being found in market baskets where there are crackers). The report also shows the number of times this relationship occurs relative to random chance.

In Figure 11A.3, products are expressed by codes. The second-to-last rule indicates that:

IF product "02L" is present, THEN product "01X" is present

This is an association rule. This relationship was found in 0.1260 of the total market baskets in the data set. Of those baskets, including product "02L," 71.50 percent of them included product "01X." The last column displayed provides the multiple of random chance that was detected. Here, products "02L" and "01X" were found together 3.231 times more than random. The first three rules shown display more complex product clusters (the existence of multiple products in a cluster).

Summary

Market-basket analysis is fundamental data mining, relying upon simple statistical analysis to deal with high volumes of data. This information can provide highly useful data about product affinity, and has been used to increase sales revenues through product positioning and cross-selling. The concept has proved useful for many market sellers, not just grocery chains.

Many retailing organizations have supplemented market-basket data with more information. Grocery stores often provide item price reductions in return for use of a small identifier that enables the grocery to not only track sales by single consumer, but also to identify the personal characteristics of each buyer. This additional information can include the category of income, marital status, and a variety of other personal information (obtained through filling out an application for the price-reduction mechanism) that can enable targeted marketing.

Glossary

actionable Information that can be used to make more effective business decisions (and thus more profit).

affinity positioning Laying out retail stores to place complementary products together.

co-occurrence table A listing of products that have been purchased together.

correlation A measure of the linear relationship between two variables.

correlation coefficient Covariance divided by the standard deviation of each variable.

covariance The degree to which variables change together.

cross-selling Marketing products to a customer that are related to other products the customer has purchased.

market basket analysis Analysis of the tendency for purchase of items by the same consumer at the same time.

purchase profile A prototypical type of customer.

Exercises

1. Why is market-basket analysis less structured than other forms of data mining?
2. What do grocers often do to gain more structured data?
3. Identify the correlation among a firm's advertising and sales of three of its car products.

Month	Advertising	Sedans	SUVs	Sports cars
1	500,000	50	812	30
2	600,000	61	798	32
3	700,000	68	821	33
4	600,000	57	815	35
5	500,000	48	817	36
6	600,000	58	815	37
7	600,000	59	806	39
8	600,000	60	805	41

4. What is the correlation between time (variable Month) and sales of the three types of automobiles in problem 3?
5. How can correlation analysis aid market-basket analysis? What is the difference between a co-occurrence table and a correlation table?
6. Describe the term "actionable."
7. What is the difference between affinity positioning and cross-selling?
8. What is the relationship between a purchase profile and a market basket?
9. How does knowing the average store profit for each profile help the store?

10. What type of customer profiles would you assign for the following co-occurrence table of hardware store market-basket sales? Obtain the correlation coefficients and calculate Jaccard coefficients. How can each be interpreted to assist in identifying customer profiles?

	Flowers	Softball	Glove	Peat	Fertilizer	Spade	Bat
Flowers	32	3	0	12	18	6	1
Softball	3	25	6	0	3	2	12
Glove	0	6	8	0	1	0	5
Peat	12	0	0	15	8	10	0
Fertilizer	18	3	1	8	21	15	2
Spade	6	2	0	10	15	16	1
Bat	1	12	5	0	2	1	14

11. What type of customer profiles would you assign for the following co-occurrence table of fast-food market baskets? Obtain the correlation coefficients and calculate Jaccard coefficients. How can each be interpreted to assist in identifying customer profiles?

FOOD	Oatmeal	Oranges	Yogurt	Carrots	Potato Chips	Hamburger
Oatmeal	10	3	5	4	2	1
Oranges	3	8	4	3	1	2
Yogurt	5	4	6	2	0	0
Carrots	4	3	2	7	1	1
Potato chips	2	1	0	1	12	5
Hamburger	1	2	0	1	5	6

12. What type of customer profiles would you assign for the following co-occurrence table of movie rentals over a year? Obtain the correlation coefficients and calculate Jaccard coefficients. How can each be interpreted to assist in identifying customer profiles?

MOVIES	Western	Romance	Action	Foreign	Classic
Western	20	3	18	0	1
Romance	3	30	2	5	1
Action	18	2	80	6	2
Foreign	0	5	6	10	3
Classic	1	1	2	3	5

Endnotes

1. C. Apte, B. Liu, E. P. D. Pednault, and P. Smyth, "Business Applications of Data Mining," *Communications of the ACM*, volume 45, number 8, 2002, pp. 49–53.

2. G. J. Russell and A. Petersen, "Analysis of Cross Category Dependence in Market Basket Selection," *Journal of Retailing*, volume 78, number 3, 2000, pp. 367–392.

3. M. J. A. Berry and G. Linoff, *Data Mining Techniques* (New York: John Wiley & Sons, 1997).

4. Russell and Petersen (2000), op. cit.

5. Anonymous, "New Data on 'Frozen' Consumers Can Improve Promos: ACNielsen," *Frozen Food Age*, volume 45, number 11, June 1997, pp. 6, 42.

6. D. Iacobucci, P. Arabie, and A. Bodapati, "Recommendation Agents on the Internet," *Journal of Interactive Marketing*, volume 14, number 3, Summer 2000, pp. 2–11.

7. Anonymous, "Every Transaction Tells a Story," *Chain Store Age Executive*, volume 71, number 3, March 1995, pp. 50–62.

8. Ibid.

9. P. Manchanda, A. Ansari, and S. Gupta, "The 'Shopping Basket': A Model for Multicategory Purchase Incidence Decisions," *Marketing Science*, volume 18, number 2, 1999, pp. 95–114.

10. Anonymous, "Data Mining Is More than Beer and Diapers," *Chain Store Age Executive,* volume 74, number 6, June 1998, pp. 64–68.

11. G. Linoff, "Which Way to the Mine?" *As/400 Systems Management*, volume 26, number 1, January 1998, pp. 42–44.

12. R. Decker and K. Monien, "Market-Basket Analysis with Neural Networks and Self-Organising Maps," *Journal of Targeting, Measurement & Analysis for Marketing*, volume 11, issue 4, June 2003, pp. 373–386.

13. A. Mild and T. Reutterer, "An Improved Collaborative Filtering Approach for Predicting Cross-Category Purchases Based on Binary Market Basket Data," *Journal of Retailing & Consumer Services*, volume 10, Issue 3, May 2003, pp. 123–133.

14. E. F. Moltzen, *Computer Reseller News*, volume 834, Mar 22, 1999, p. 111.

15. Anonymous, "ANGOSS Mines Exclusive Ore Technology for Basket Analysis," *Computergram Weekly*, Issue 4408, May 2, 2002, p. 6.

16. P. Manchanda, A. Ansari, and S. Gupta, op. cit.

17. C. M. Heilman, K. Nakamoto, and A. G. Rao, "Pleasant Surprises: Consumer Response to Unexpected In-Store Coupons," *Journal of Marketing Research*, volume 39, number 2, 2002, pp. 242–252.

PART FOUR

Developing Issues

CHAPTER TWELVE

Text and Web Mining

This chapter:

- Describes text mining and web mining
- Demonstrates the use of link analysis in text mining
- Describes applications of both web mining and text mining
- Reviews some of the many software products available
- Shows semantic text analysis in the appendix

Our culture generates more and more text in electronic form. As students, you're served by electronic library services that offer links to millions of articles over the Web. You have library search engines that enable you to search for articles with particular keywords, or that use selected terms in the abstract, or possibly even in the article.

This demonstrates the existence of documents in electronic form. There are many domains where large quantities of electronic documents exist. One example is police reports, which 50 years ago were all written by hand, and thus were very difficult to decipher in some cases. Forms were developed to make the gathering of specific items of information easier, like the time of an incident that was investigated by the police. In the 21st century, almost all police reports are entered on computers, making them quickly accessible through such technology.

Text mining is the data mining of textual data. It has been used by the airline industry to detect patterns in commercial airline incident reports, similar to how police departments analyze trends detected in police reports. In the airline industry, particular airports might experience a heavy incidence of a particular type of mechanical problem, which further analysis might identify as due to some fixable defective arrangement or procedure. Police reports might identify areas where particular types of crime might occur, and provide useful information for when scheduling patrols.

Text mining is a developing area, with a great deal of potential to business. It requires that text be analyzed in electronic form. Afterward, a great deal of processing is needed to eliminate words that provide no value in the particular analysis. Once these steps are accomplished, data mining tools can be applied to great use.

Data mining operates using numerical data. The same concept can be, and has been, applied to symbolic data, such as text. Text mining provides a means to wade through the massive glut of data that is generated by our computer-driven society. Text mining can involve analysis to distill meaning, summarize content through text processing, explore texts through the analysis of keywords, cluster themes and documents, and retrieve information through semantically important words and relevant sentences. Often semantic networks are used to support text mining. **Semantic networks** connect the most important concepts from a set of text and

225

establish relationships between those concepts. The most developed form of text mining is **web mining.** Web mining obviously implies use of the World Wide Web. But there are a number of different ways in which that can be done.

Text Mining

Text mining is the process of analyzing words or other non-numeric data. The first step typically used in text mining is to uncover individual pieces of information, such as synonyms, that are hidden in the text. Text mining software often includes a library of synonyms, and can make associations based upon this synonym library. It's claimed that this software has the ability to identify key terms, understand context, and identify interrelationships.[1] Then, the text mining algorithm recombines information to discover general patterns or relationships.

SAS text mining software is designed to analyze text from a variety of sources, such as e-mail, which could be used to block **spam** more effectively or to help detect patterns in customer complaints. It also could be useful in the **link analysis** needed to analyze potential fraudulent insurance or warranty claims.[2] For example, analysis of customer verbal responses to quality surveys could be mined to identify key concepts such as "too expensive" or "poor service."

Back in 1996, the Dow Chemical Company began text mining by accessing hundreds of thousands of documents from a variety of sources, including the Internet. Their goal was to discover knowledge and patterns of information that couldn't be found using conventional database or search-engine tools. Dow was thus able to search for new customers, technologies, and business partners through text mining. They also were able to identify market trends that couldn't be detected by other means.

Other types of text mining can also be used for human resource applications, such as filtering and matching résumés to particular job postings. Another application would be to have text mining identify documents of interest to users with specific profiles. Portals can automatically push out specifically identified text documents to these users.[3] Text mining can also be used to monitor operations such as help desks, to ensure better quality control. It can be employed as well to monitor volumes of data in order to gain competitive intelligence, or used by insurance companies and others that provide warranties to detect fraud.[4]

Identification of Key Terms

Text mining requires processing a document to define interesting words as variables. Once this challenging task is completed, the analysis is much like market-basket analysis, where words (or phrases) are associated with other words (or phrases). Take, for example, the sample document in the box.

Ethics are important in all aspects of business, but the development of digital technology has created new ethical business practice issues. While information technology provides powerful tools, these tools can be used for unethical purposes. In fact, the terrorist events of the past three years emphasize the difficulty in clearly seeing what is ethical or not, balancing societal needs for monitoring against personal rights. Data mining is clearly involved in such issues, as it provides the ability to scan and analyze vast masses of electronic data to identify previously unseen patterns. Unfortunately, this is a double-edged sword, having two types of traditional errors (failing to catch cases being sought, and identifying too many false positive cases). This presents a difficult ethical trade-off with the value

TABLE 12.1
Key Term List

Ability	Data mining	Failing	Olivier	Tavani
Analyze	Difficult	False positive		Terrorist events
	Difficulty		Patterns	Thuraisinghani
Balancing	Digital technology	Individual rights	Past three	Tools
Brankovic	Double-edged sword	Information	years	Trade-off
Business		technology		Traditional errors
Business	Electronic data	Involved	Scan	
practice	Errors	Issues	Society	Unethical purposes
	Estivill-Castro		Societal needs	
Cases	Ethics	Masses	Sword	Value
Catch	Ethical			

to society being pitted against individual rights (Brankovic and Estivill-Castro, 1999; Olivier, 1999; Tavani, 1999a; Thuraisinghani, 2002).

Manually reading this short document we come up with the list of interesting terms shown in Table 12.1.

Some root words have multiple forms (difficult; difficulty), while a few interesting terms are actually phrases consisting of multiple words (past three years). There are also synonyms (errors; false positives—which is a specific type of error). There might be other synonyms not found in this document that would be interesting if applied to larger documents (ability; capability; skill). Developing a list of interesting terms is a challenge.

Text mining software comes in various forms, some with the ability to aid this text data processing stage. PolyAnalyst has a semantic dictionary, which includes many synonyms that recognize different words meaning the same thing. It also has the ability to identify different forms of the same root word. For any particular application, the analyst has the ability to define words, or key terms, or to discard words generated by the software (see the appendix to this chapter for an example of semantic text analysis).

Text Mining Demonstration

Assume that a firm is placing a bid to take over a small competitor (for purposes of demonstration, let's call it JDE). Top management is concerned that two other industry competitors (let's call them Delphi and ZAP) may make similar offers. The IT department of the firm has recently acquired text mining software, and top management would like to apply it to whatever data they can acquire to gain a better understanding of the intentions of Delphi and ZAP with respect to this deal.

The first activity in this analysis is to gather data. Two sources came to the mind of the people in charge of the study: trade publications and e-mail. While not all trade publications are available in electronic form, many are, and any article referring to Delphi or ZAP in conjunction with JDE could be flagged by the text mining software. This would yield many hits, most of which were probably not pertinent. But these hits could be further analyzed for clues as to the intentions of Delphi and ZAP. Searching on keywords and phrases would be an effective tool, given electronic access to this source.

E-mail is another source. If access could be obtained to the e-mail of top management at Delphi or ZAP (or JDE), these could be excellent sources of information. This activity, when performed by the CIA, is called spying. When security firewalls are breached by computer people, it's called hacking. We certainly would not condone illegal or immoral activity. But technological data is available in many forms. Once e-mail data is obtained, it's a formidable task to identify knowledge from the many messages sent back and forth. Again, keyword or phrase searches are the best starting point.

This initial search would amass a great deal of data. Once all the sources containing the selected key phrases are obtained, they should be filtered through other keywords or phrases to focus on the hopefully much smaller subset containing information related to takeover proposals and intentions. The safest way to draw inferences from such information would be through human reading and interpretation. If the volume of filtered sources was still very large, however, machine inference would be attractive. This is the area of cutting edge research, where artificial intelligence products are being developed to do more and more of the interpretation of information gathered in electronic form.

Link Analysis

Text mining can be used for many applications. One such application is to analyze a series of text messages, such as customer complaints. Let's assume a distributor of printers deals with three products: inkjet black-and-white printers, inkjet color printers, and laser black-and-white printers. Table 12.2 gives five such messages, providing product, a quality rating on a 1 (bad) to 5 (best) scale, the name of the representative involved, and comments.

This set of comments involves some variety of comments. In order to apply text mining, the first step is to generate a set of keywords. Some software products, such as PolyAnalyst by Megaputer, provide text analyst capabilities that focus on words that appear at a high rate. The user of the system can delete words which are not pertinent, and develop a file that will include the sentences where these selected keywords appear. One use of such files is to condense large documents to some percentage of their original size, focusing on sentences containing words of interest to the user. Another use is to identify those terms of interest to the user. For instance, in Table 12.2, words such as those in bold could be selected for link

TABLE 12.2
Printer Complaints

Printer Product	Quality Rating	Rep	Comments
Inkjet	1	Ben	This printer is a piece of **junk.** It is so **cheap** that it constantly **clogs.** In futile attempts to fix it, it **breaks** regularly.
Color	3	Abner	I wish to commend your representative, who was very **understanding** of my lack of **knowledge,** and **kindly** provided every guidance to help me learn about this printer.
Inkjet	2	Chuck	The printer works most of the time, but jams **paper** and involves expensive **service.** Furthermore, your representative was highly **abusive** on some occasions, and I won't be bothering you with future business once I settle this difficult matter.
Inkjet	2	Abner	I am not happy with your printer. It **smears paper** when it is in **service,** which is not all that often.
Laser	4	Dennis	Your representative was very **knowledgeable** about your product, and enabled me to get it to function.

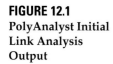

FIGURE 12.1
PolyAnalyst Initial
Link Analysis
Output

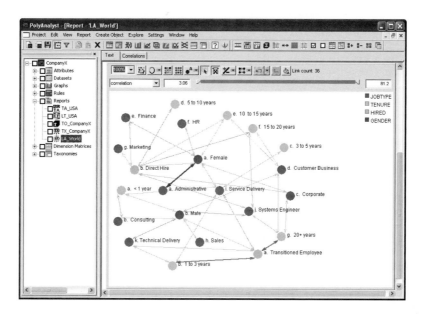

analysis. Note the ability to pick up different variants of the key terms (knowledge and knowledgeable, break and breaks (or broken), kind and kindly). Then a data file can be constructed using each of the key terms as a binary (yes/no, Boolean, 0/1) variable reflecting the presence or absence of the key term in each message. The file containing these key-term variables can include any other variables, such as the categorical variables from a text file relating to different job types, time with company (tenure), how they obtained their current position, and gender. Figure 12.1 shows the screen from PolyAnalyst. This is an initial output, where all variables are displayed in which any of the variables had common entries.

The link analysis utilizes all categorical and binary data (not the numeric quality rating). While it doesn't show up in Figure 12.1, positive and negative correlations are color-coded. The user has the option of deleting either. The system uses a minimum value to include relationships. The link analysis indicates strong relationships between female employees and administrative positions, as well as between transitioned employees (those who changed jobs during their time with the company) and tenure times of 1 to 3 years, and 20 or more years. The analyst would now be challenged to explain the identified relationship. Possibly the company historically (20 years ago) had done very little outside hiring, but switched to a policy hiring directly. The more recent period may have been due to a hiring freeze.

Since Figure 12.1 was very cluttered, the analyst has the ability to reset the minimum count necessary to show in the link analysis display. Figure 12.2 gives such an output for a minimum setting of 6.5 occurrences.

This makes relationships much clearer. By clicking on the heaviest line in this clearer link analysis, the software provides the degree of correlation (over 0.81, or 81.1503% as shown) and support (130 instances). Transitional employees are seen to be most commonly found in service delivery, and in technical delivery. In the corporate office, most employees are seen to be direct hire. Systems engineers are also direct hires for the most part, and also are male and have been with the firm a long time (15 to 20 years). Possibly the firm might now identify areas where

FIGURE 12.2
The PolyAnalyst
Initial Link
Analysis Output
at a Minimum
Correlation
Setting of 6.5

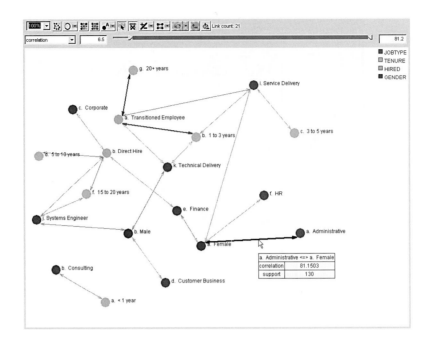

gender equity action should be considered. It also is seen that the firm's consulting personnel tend to be new hires, indicating that that position is an entry-level position. A positive indicator is that these new hires seem to be equitably balanced by gender.

Text Mining Applied to Legal Databases

Association techniques are intended to discover ways in which data elements are associated. This is useful in many fields, including law. Data mining association techniques have been applied to the legal field, in a way demonstrating the transition from pure numbers to concepts expressed in words.[5] The study used association rule generation on a set of records for knowledge discovery. This effort involved a great deal of work in order to generate many rules, and then filter these down to a set of relationships that were interesting, in the sense that they were not expected before the study.

One way to generate association rules is to simply count the number of times events occurred together, divided by the total number of the base event. For instance, if analysis were to uncover the fact that there were 30,052 assault cases tried in Texas in a given year, and that in 9,843 of these cases the complainant was related to the person charged, the support for the hypothesis that those charged with assault were family members would be 9,843 divided by 30,052, or 0.316. Interestingness refers to the degree to which a pattern identified matters to the system user, based on novelty (it wasn't obvious) and usefulness (it mattered).

The Ivkovic et al.[6] study applied data mining to generate association rules from over 380,000 applications for legal aid. The intent was to provide legal aid in the most effective, economic, and efficient manner. The degree of relationship between entities required for generation of a rule was based on expert input prior to data analysis. Web access was used to allow users to express the level of confidence they expected from rules such as:

Variable	Possible Values
Sex	M, F, Both
Age	Eight categories
Occupation	Seven categories
Reason for refusal	Codes
Law Type	Categories, including civil law, family law, and so on
Decision	Granted, Not Granted
Dealing Type	Advice, Court Appearance, and so on

IF age = 35–40, THEN decision = APPROVED

IF occupation = X, THEN law type = CRIMINAL LAW

IF sex = F, THEN reason for refusal = INSUFFICIENT FUNDS

There were a great many of these rules that could potentially be supported by the data. Web access provided a means to identify the expected relationships.

Data selection involved selecting a target set of variables for consideration. Data was available on over 300 variables, too much data for available resources. Experts from the legal aid organization selected seven variables as important and interesting, shown in Table 12.3.

Data pre-processing checked for missing or irrelevant data. The data set was maintained in a manner that included integrity checks on all input data. Data transformation modified continuous data (such as date of birth) to a reasonable number of intervals.

There were over 226,000 possible associated rules that could have been generated from the transformed data set. A web tool was used to generate rules, allowing one antecedent and one consequent, and the entry of levels of support and confidence. Potential rules were presented to users who gave their expected confidence in terms of expected correlation. For instance, a user might select the antecedent "IF age = over 50 THEN law type = CIVIL LAW" and assign a confidence of 0.90. Once all of the expected relationships were identified, the system analyzed the cases and identified support, measured as the correlation of the actual data. These results were compared in a plot that allowed the identification of interestingness. If the difference between confidence and support was less than 0.1, this was considered "not interesting." In order to be interesting, rules also had to be useful in that they could suggest hypotheses.

The Web tool was tested on three experts using 144 different rules. The system identified rules that were not expected, which were then discussed by the panel of experts. Surprising associations prompted the creation of hypotheses to explain the discovered phenomena. This then led to further research to more solidly establish relationships.

This application dealt with data that was available in verbal form. It also needed web tools to be implemented, but the focus was more on data mining in general. Text mining applies because the data concerned concepts expressed with words. The case demonstrates that text mining involves the transformation of verbal data into counts that can be dealt with through tools such as memory-based reasoning.

Text Mining Products

There is an active growth in text mining software. Table 12.4 provides a brief description of some of these products.

TABLE 12.4 **Text Mining Products**

Extracted from M. Biggs, "Resurgent Text-Mining Technology Can Greatly Increase Your Firm's 'intelligence' factor," *Infoworld*, Jan. 10, 2000, www.infoworld.com; B. Grushkin and S. S. Simmel, "Taming Text: Unstructured Data Mining," *IntelligentEnterprise.com*, January 1, 2003, p. 38; T. Sullivan, "SAS Uncovers Text-Mining Deal," *Infoworld*, January 28, 2002, p. 28, www.infoworld.com.

Company	Application	Contact
Attensity Corp.	Text recognition of objects with reasons	www.attensity.com
Blossom Software	Web robots monitoring site changes, real-time index	www.blossom.com
Cricket Technologies LLC	Data extraction from hundreds of media	www.crickettechnologies.com
IBM	Intelligent Mining for Text	www.ibm.com/software/data/iminer/for_text
Megaputer	PolyAnalyst	www.megaputer.com
Metacarta Inc.	Feature recognition tied to location via GPS	www.metacarta.com
Neuro-Technology Solutions	Search literature based on the graphic of a brain	sbeardsl@bu.edu
Sageware Inc.	Classifies items based on ontologies	www.sageware.com
SAS	Text Miner—Basic text mining added to Enterprise Miner	www.sas.com
SAS	LinguistX Platform—natural language text mining to analyze words, phrases, and sentences.	
SAS	Inxight's Thing Finder—identify and extract key content such as names, products, addresses, and dates	
SemenTx Life Sciences Inc.	Identify articles based on synonyms as well as grammatical and functional relations	www.semantxls.com
Semio	SemioMap—extract and index text, cluster concepts, visual tools	www.semio.com
SPSS Inc.	LexiQuest Mine—linguistics-based text mining, identifying key concepts and relationships	
TEXTANALYST	PolyAnalyst from Megaputer provides semantic network access to text	info

Web Mining

Web mining is a bit more general than text mining. The U.S. Internet economy purportedly involved $523 billion in revenues in 1999.[7] Such business-to-business activity was expected to expand rapidly.[8] The online travel market did $5 billion in business in 1999, and was predicted to hit $30 billion in 2001.[9] It probably didn't reach that figure, but there clearly has been extensive growth. Online stock investing in the U.S. began in 1994, and has grown to cover over 33 percent of U.S. retail stock trades. In 2001, there were supposedly over 110 million World Wide Web servers, with over 89 million home users in the U.S., and 33 million Europeans.[10] These numbers are unimportant with regard to their specificity, but e-commerce and e-business have grown rapidly.

Cinergy Marketing and Trading LP is an example of web mining potential.[11] They needed fuel price, availability, production volume, industry developments, and weather predictions in order to make their predictions of supply, demand, and price. This important activity of data collection was done manually, which limited Cinergy to visit about 30 web sites. Cinergy obtained a web mining server, which enabled them to monitor about 100 web sites, demonstrating their ability to cover a greater area in a more thorough and efficient manner. Web mining also provided Cinergy with the ability to apply automatic monitoring and alerting. Furthermore, collected information can be made available in a variety of requested formats, such as XML, Excel, or another specified database.

The exponential growth of the World Wide Web has swamped us with material. We are currently drowning in information, but starving for knowledge.[12] Web mining can aid in the location of documents and services on the Web. Search engines are fundamental to this type of operation, and provide the initial act needed to conduct more complex forms of web mining. Web mining can also involve information extraction, including numerical (or text) data found during search activities. Web mining can be applied to servers, to clients (through **cookies**), and to databases. Data obtained can include numbers, text, image, audio, and any other medium in which data is stored. Web mining can involve the focused activity of monitoring user behavior on a web site, with the intent of detecting user behavior patterns that can be used to not only predict potential customer behavior, but also to trigger action to improve the prospects of that potential customer buying from the site.

Web Mining Taxonomy

A common taxonomy for web mining research includes three primary focuses: web content mining, web structure mining, and web usage (web log) mining.[13]

Web content mining concerns the discovery of useful information (and accessing information) from web sources. Within a web business operation, a great deal of customer information is available, as has been demonstrated by Amazon.com and its competitors. It has been useful to keep track of what each customer purchases, and perform cluster analysis on this very large database to enable the prediction of other items that a particular type of customer might want. In the case of books, the customer is more likely to purchase a book they have never purchased before, requiring **imputation** of what a particular customer with a given profile might be interested in.[14] Dealing with such data is challenging, due to the massive size of a data matrix, which contains information on both customers and books. Web content also comes in many forms, including text, image, audio, video, and other media. The Web itself can be queried. Web-based data collection has been found to be unobtrusive, experimentally based, externally valid, and easily capable of obtaining large sample sizes.

Web structure mining seeks to discover the underlying link structures of the Web, or the relationships between web pages. Web links between sites are identified, and their strength measured, thus allowing clustering and the classification of web pages. Measures can be obtained concerning how easy it is to find related documents on different web sites. Data sources include HTML documents and link information.

Web usage mining (or web log mining) analyzes secondary data resulting from human use of the web. Nagivational patterns are usually obtained from web logs, and may include both patterns and visitor profiles. Information obtained may concern what pages were accessed and in what sequence. Web log mining falls within this category, along with web site visitor profile analysis. Web usage mining in marketing consists of three broad types of application:[15]

1. Data acquisition
2. Cost and quality measures
3. Assessment of user/owner satisfaction

Data acquisition can be invasive, actively contacting the user through questionnaires or other methods, or it can be non-invasive and involve the recording of user behavior without their interaction. **Web server logs** are the primary means of obtaining this information, which is often stored in web data warehouses for deep analysis. Once data on customer web behavior is gathered, it can be used to estimate customer satisfaction in various ways.

Web User Behavior

The Internet offers businesses the opportunity of having one-on-one interactions with their customers. This has resulted in a large amount of research on ways to increase the profitability of Internet shopping sites. First, many sites have been found to benefit from considering the importance of the web content's psychological effects on customers. Personalized web content that targets specific customer preferences has led to a second level of web competition. Third, dynamic web content and personal discount offers can also be used by site managers. However, this third level of sophistication requires additional resources. Plus, high-traffic sites may end up losing customers due to slower response time.

Web usage mining has grown in importance, as has the ability to conduct web measurement. Products like that of **Clickstream Technologies** (www.clickstream. com) provide a means of measuring web activity, much like how ACNielsen measures television set activity. Data collected can include page hit-counts (the frequency of page visits during a session), the sequence of page accesses, and page viewing time. The most important uses of this type of measurement have been in advertising statistics, checking web site audience growth, monitoring the behavior of those visiting web pages, and monitoring web site operational management. The two basic methods of web measurement are to ask what users are doing, or to monitor what web servers are doing. Asking users is a form of panel-based research. Monitoring servers is **server log analysis. Event logging,** meanwhile, is the process of recording user-initiated activities (see www.netconversions.com). This practice has been widely developed. Event logs capture how web site users are using the interface. Table 12.5 provides comparisons of the type of data captured by each method.[16]

It's clear that a great deal of information can be obtained through web monitoring. This information has been widely used to analyze the effectiveness and weaknesses of web sites. Such information has been used to analyze web site visitor interests as well.[17] By recording operations that users perform on a web site, results can be statistically analyzed using objective data. Survey results or user comments can also be a source of subjective data about web site use.

Web personalization involves custom tailoring sites for specific users. This is a very widely used practice in e-commerce since many firms seek to identify profitable market segments and to track web user activity in order to remind users of

TABLE 12.5
Web Monitoring Data Captured

Adapted from Kangas & Chiu (2001)

Server Logs	Event Logs
Date/time data	Path analysis
Entry/exit pages	Page abandonment
Requested pages	Field completion times
Downloaded files	Drop-down box selections
Types of browsers	Scrolling
Level of server activity	Click density by link, non-link
IP address	Mouse movements
Number of page views	Browser controls
Referring sites	Error occurrence

the availability of products that they are likely to be interested in. This allows businesses such as Amazon.com to present information that is likely to be of interest to a specific user. Customers are profiled, enabling predictions of products interesting to them, using the same techniques applied in customer segmentation applications discussed in prior chapters. Web personalization is made possible through a number of computer tools, to include collaborative filtering, agents, intelligent interfaces, and bots.[18] Cluster analysis is often used for this application.[19] These same tools make web mining possible.

Web Mining Examples

Three SAS operatives reported the use of web-enabled software in a number of real applications.[20] One general application is to monitor web use. Data obtained from the web is characterized by a number of features. On the positive side, it's very easy to obtain this data through automatic means. On the negative side, it's very dynamic. Other uses of web-related data involve access to data mining by users. These are demonstrated by the following three example applications.

United Sugars Corporation is a grower-owned cooperative, one of the largest marketers of sugar in the U.S. In 1998, United Sugars developed a multitiered architecture to drive web applications for optimization of their supply chain. This system was used to optimize packaging, inventory, and distribution as well as for decision support to analyze a number of operational decisions. This architecture included optimization of inventory replenishment, and of portfolios of suppliers to improve company purchasing leverage. The major source of data was the firm's ERP system. The system was used monthly for planning about 85 percent of its operations. A network optimization model planned about 80 plants in the United Sugars supply chain over a 13-month horizon, with 250 sugar products and over 2,000 customers. The optimization routine generated a minimum-cost schedule for packaging, distribution, and inventory. This schedule was used for budgeting freight and warehousing. The system included web access to monitor product quality. Extensions to the system included additional graphical reports of summary information, and drill-down capabilities distributed over the Web for multiple users.

Cameron and Barkley Company is a distributor of industrial, electrical, and electronic supplies. They inventoried almost 500,000 products. Cameron and Barkley sought data mining as a way to reduce inventory while maintaining high levels of customer service. Their process involved a team of buyers who watched to assure that minimum levels of customer service were maintained, using their intuition, and their knowledge of the market and simple demand forecasts. This process was automated to free buyer time for more strategic decisions. The automated system included a web interface that captured user interactions and that built a model approximating lead-time demand to minimize ordering and fixed costs.

Lockheed Martin Astronautics Division is responsible for design, fabrication, and delivery of the Titan and Atlas missile space transportation systems. There was a need for management to monitor production systems telling top management where missiles were in the production cycle, when they would be completed, how changes would affect the schedule, and where improvements to the schedule could be made. Reports were published to the Web, allowing management real-time access to this information.

The last application reported in this article involved general web mining. Web-log analysis summarizes raw web-log data using descriptive statistics, reports, and charts. This is followed by click-stream analysis, which identifies user navigation

TABLE 12.6
Web Mining
Products

Extracted from Pal et al.
(2002)

System	Application	Contact
Aptronix	A fuzzy inference system to build Java applets, C, MatLab, and assembly code	www.aptronix.com
DNS search	A fuzzy logic system to find the closest string	www.amnesi.com/dnssearch
Finder	Uses multidimensional optimization to display most suitable matches to a query	www.finder.co.uk
Nzsearch	Fuzzy logic search engine	www.searchnz.co.nz

paths through the web site. The third and final stage is data mining the summarized web-log data, possibly supplemented by data from other sources. This type of process involves massive volumes of data, often incomplete and difficult to identify by user. At an extreme, a web site may get 2 million visits per day, producing a correspondingly massive web log. However, this source of data can be used to more intelligently design and operate web sites.

Web Mining Systems

A number of commercially available systems are currently on the market, some of which are shown in Table 12.6. Since the field of web mining involves development of new technology, this is expected to be a very dynamic market.

Web Usage Mining Demonstration

To show how clickstream data can be obtained, we can use visits to an e-commerce site selling some product. The following detectable locations are on page 1 of the web site:

- A: URL line
- B: Button to search for product line I, leading to page 2
- C: Button to search for product line J, leading to page 3
- D: Link to competitor X products and prices
- E: Link to competitor Y products and prices
- F: Shopping cart to place a purchase order.

Data consists of the sequence of clicks that the user makes during a site visit, as well as the outcome (the amount of purchase, which most often is zero). Table 12.7 provides a set of data for hypothetical site visitors.

These few visits have some detectable patterns. In all cases where site visitors went to the URL line (A), they departed (to another web site) without purchasing anything at this site. This could be actionable if the site manager were to insert a pop-up offer of a discount or some other premium whenever an entry was made

TABLE 12.7
Web Usage
Example Data

Visitor							Outcome
1	B	D	E	A to exit			0
2	B	F	exit				200
3	B	D	F	exit			150
4	C	E	A to exit				0
5	C	E	A to exit				0
6	B	D	E	B	D	A to exit	0
7	C	E	C	A to exit			0

to the URL (with no purchase). Another pattern is that whenever the site visitor clicked button E (competitor Y's link), no purchase was made. A site management action might be to remove the link to competitor Y. (More realistically, it might be wiser to see why competitor Y was so competitive, and ideally redesign products to match these features.)

This very cursory example demonstrates the type of data involved in web usage analysis. It consists of a very large number of potential data elements, and the sequence of site elements activated from a chain of links that can be quantified with some effort.

Appendix

Semantic Text Analysis

Text mining tools provide the ability to take unstructured data in the form of digitized text, and translate this data into useful knowledge. Semantic text analysis combines quantitative computer support with expert experience to process text data qualitatively. This can give new views of data that can lead to human insight. This paper demonstrates the process by which PolyAnalyst can take employee survey data and develop business taxonomies showing the logical organization of responses, making it easier to see the views held on each issue along with their relative support.

The data context in this case is employee survey data, an extract of which is shown in Figure 12A.1.

The data set includes 105 attributes reflecting profile characteristics of respondents, demographic data, time data, and both structured and open-ended responses for 6,476 entries. The window on the lower left indicates some of these 105 attributes. One of these attributes, "Job Function," is displayed in a histogram. For example, the

FIGURE 12A.1
Employee
Survey Data

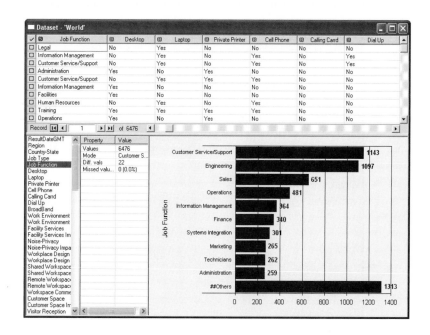

Customer Service/Support group submitted 1,143 responses. Structured responses can be dealt with by traditional data mining techniques. There is a great deal of information, however, available in the unstructured text data. PolyAnalyst software tools provide the ability to tap into this useful source of knowledge.

SEMANTIC TEXT ANALYSIS

The aim of this appendix is to demonstrate the process through which unstructured text data is converted to useful knowledge. PolyAnalyst Text Mining software includes user dictionaries, which can be edited for each specific study. Figure 12A.2 shows the primary window to access a user dictionary.

An important step is to enter items to be ignored, eliminating common terms that are not interesting in this particular study. The semantic dictionary keeps track of important terms in a variety of forms, classifying them by different root words and synonyms. A basic semantic lexicon is part of the system, but the user can enhance this resource for particular studies. Once dictionary settings are made, the system can count the number of occurrences of key words. Figure 12A.3 shows text analysis results for workspace comments in the employee survey database.

It can be seen that workspace comments here include semantic variants of noise in 335 records. That's almost one-half of the almost 700 records that have workspace comments. This list guides the analyst to identify workspace features that triggered comment by those surveyed. Some comments addressed the workspace (or the office) in general. The next most common term related to people. Specifics for any particular phrase among workspace comments can be selected, allowing the user to drill down to more details. Those comments relating to workspace distractions can be gathered in a subset of the data. There were 163 such records. The analyst labeled this data subset "Workspace Distraction." Figure 12A.4 shows the drill-down results for the phrase "workspace" in the workspace comment attribute.

The second line in Figure 12A.4 concerns a comment made relating to noise in the environment, which blamed the high number of cubicles in the room. However, this employee has coped with the noise problem through the use of headphones. Thus, the conclusion of this subject is that the workspace would be

FIGURE 12A.2
A User Dictionary

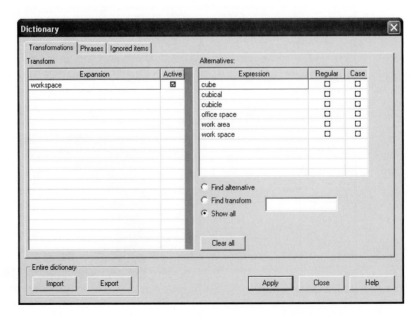

FIGURE 12A.3
Text Analysis
Results

Rule name	Rec Count	%
Workspace Comment_noise	335	50.99
Workspace Comment_workspace	163	24.81
Workspace Comment_office	156	23.74
Workspace Comment_people	144	21.92
Workspace Comment_area	103	15.68
Workspace Comment_privacy	131	19.94
Workspace Comment_phone	136	20.7
Workspace Comment_noise level	74	11.26
Workspace Comment_desk	75	11.42
Workspace Comment_meeting room	76	11.57
Workspace Comment_space	95	14.46
Workspace Comment_environment	116	17.66
Workspace Comment_meeting	92	14
Workspace Comment_room	126	19.18
Workspace Comment_conversation	72	10.96
Workspace Comment_due	47	7.154
Workspace Comment_cubicle	42	6.393
Workspace Comment_customer	39	5.936
Workspace Comment_meeting call	37	5.632
Workspace Comment_cube	34	5.175
Workspace Comment_wall	48	7.306
Workspace Comment_employee	32	4.871
Workspace Comment_work environment	31	4.718
Workspace Comment_problem	30	4.566
Workspace Comment_storage	34	5.175

FIGURE 12A.4
Distraction
Drill-Down
Results

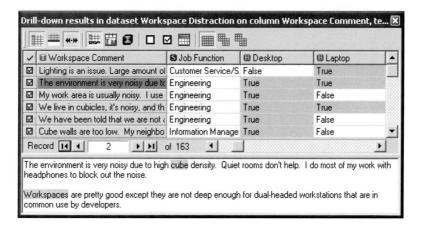

FIGURE 12A.5
A Distribution Chart

acceptable, given sufficient depth to allow dual-headed workstations. The ability to drill-down enables the analyst to make more sense of what subjects are trying to say relative to the noise or any other workspace comment keyword.

QUANTITATIVE MODELS

PolyAnalyst includes a number of data mining tools that can be used to quantitatively analyze data. For instance, Figure 12A.1 shows a distribution chart, while Figure 12A.5 shows a distribution chart for the attribute "Work Environment," which includes five possible values as well as "Don't know" and "Not applicable."

FIGURE 12A.6
A Trend Chart

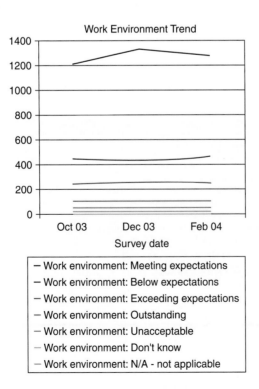

FIGURE 12A.7 **Link Chart Across Attributes**

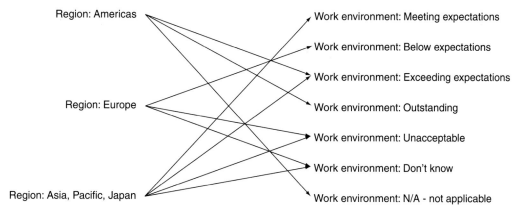

The distribution chart provides a quick view of the number of responses for each attribute value. Most survey responses were satisfied with current conditions, but about 1,250 felt that the work environment was below expectations. Work environment opinions in this database can be evaluated longitudinally, as survey data is available over the period October 2003 to February 2004. Figure 12A.6 shows trends for the attribute "Work Environment" over time.

Link charts enable analysts to view the correlation among attribute values. Figure 12A.7 shows those combinations of attribute values for "Region" and "Work Environment" that have strong correlations. The boldness of the arcs linking attribute values also provides a representation of the strength of the correlation.

The PolyAnalyst software includes the ability to generate decision trees of association rules. Figure 12A.8 shows such a decision tree.

In this case, if "Workplace Design" has an attribute value of "Meeting expectations," there are 3,664 records (56.7 percent of the 6,476 total), among which 0.71 percent are rated as unacceptable on attribute "Facility Services," 14 percent are below expectations, 74.3 percent meet expectations, 8.82 percent exceeded expectations, and 1.99 percent are rated as outstanding. The analyst here selected the subgroup with the Facility Services rating "Meeting expectations," and those

FIGURE 12A.8
The Decision
Tree of a Work
Eenvironment

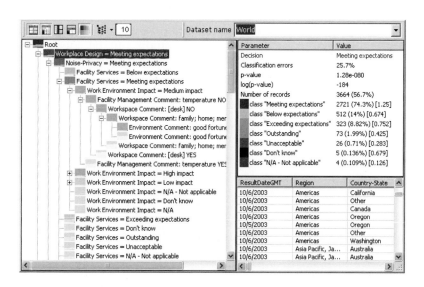

FIGURE 12A.9
Keywords

Term	Record Count	% of Records
noise	234	56.521740
office	98	23.671497
people	86	20.772947
room	79	19.082127
phone	77	18.599035
privacy	76	18.357489
environment	71	17.149759
workspace	61	14.734300
area	55	13.285025
noise level	52	12.560387
space	52	12.560387
meeting room	40	9.661836
conversation	34	8.212561
meeting	34	8.212561

records are displayed in the lower right window. The user can view these records in detail.

UNSTRUCTURED TEXT ANALYSIS

Text mining software's value in dealing with unstructured text can be demonstrated here. First, keywords are identified. Figure 12A.9 shows the count of records with those keywords displayed.

Of those keywords displayed that involved workplace distractions, "office" showed up in 98. The software can display a tree of these keywords, as exhibited in the left window of Figure 12A.10.

Here, there were 178 occurrences of the keyword "noise." The first five of these records are shown in the upper right window. The third of these is selected, and the lower right window displays the survey response, with keywords highlighted in coded color. Figure 12A.11 shows further drill-down results for ten records.

This is also color-coded to quickly guide the user to key terms.

TAXONOMY CLASSIFICATION

A taxonomy classification can be developed through a general process. Those terms important to a specific study can be identified, based upon survey responses. In Figure 12A.12, the left window displays a set of well-defined categories used to group terms defining subsets.

FIGURE 12A.10
Category
Development

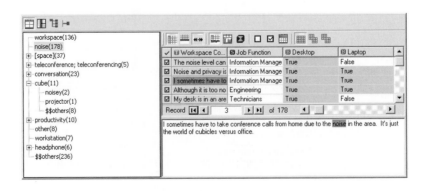

FIGURE 12A.11
Drill-Down
on a Keyword

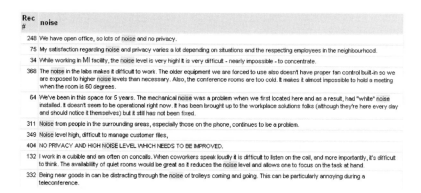

The analyst has selected the term "Laptop," a subset of workspace comments involving "Equipment." There are a total of 53 such records, the first 12 of which are displayed in the upper right window. The eighth is selected, and the full comment displayed in the lower right window. Key terms are highlighted by color. Development of this taxonomy can guide the analyst to identify key issues.

This process can focus on key issues. For instance, 414 of the total 6,476 comments involved workspace distractions. These 414 records were exported for detailed analysis. Figure 12A.13 displays the first seven of these comments.

Noise is apparent in these three comments, and analysis can look at other factors related to distractions. Figure 12A.14 displays a link chart showing key terms related to workspace comments.

This link chart is also color-coded, with a key at the upper right. Two regions show up. In the Americas, comments relate to noise in cubicles, conversations, and the workspace in general. Other strong correlations show up for cubes and walls. In the area Europe, comments relate to noise associated with desks, offices, and open space. Figure 12A.15 shows key correlations among this subset of data.

Strongest correlations displayed in the Americas are with the workspace and productivity, while the strongest correlations in the Europe region are with facilities, furniture, and meeting rooms. Figure 12A.16 shows an additional quantitative tool: a snake chart.

The snake chart displays correlations visually on multiple (here 13) dimensions, with stronger correlations graphed at greater distances from the center. Two attributes were selected for display on this snake chart (distractions reported by

FIGURE 12A.12
Taxonomy
Classification

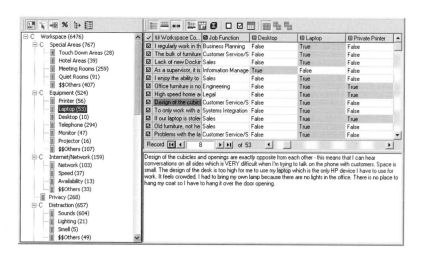

FIGURE 12A.13
An Export of
Records Focusing
on Distractions

Distractions	
Project:	Employee Survey Analysis
Join Type:	n/a
Number of Records:	414
Export Date:	04/22/05 15:45:13
Generator:	PolyAnalyst 5.0

Job Function	Workspace Comment
Information Management	The noise level can get bad because there are 2 loud speakers in the group next to me on the phone all the time. In one person's case some form of amplified headset would help greatly and the other quite often uses the speakerphone. One other option that could help would be a noise reduction headset that I could wear during phone meetings to help block out the other people's conversations.
Sales	The layout that we have at the office is not helping us to have privacy for phone calls,audioconference,neither employee interview,etc.It doesn't mean that the office is very noisy,it is about privacy.
Sales	The office area has been remodelled 3 times, each with minor improvements. The noise level however in all designs has been totally unacceptable.
Information Management	I sometimes have to take conference calls from home due to the noise in the area. It's just the world of cubicles versus office.
Engineering	Although it is too noisy because people around me may be on conference calls, I alway have options to work from home to be more productive.
Engineering	My work area is usually noisy. I use ear muffs to mitigate noise. My storage is good, but I've requested keys three times for my overhead cabinet and have yet to get any.
Sales	very noisy; no privacy; workstations very small

individuals, and distractions reported by managers). Managers had fairly equal correlations with all 13 distractions graphed. Individuals had lower correlations with storage and workspace, and a less reported impact on productivity and distractions than did managers. The analyst can drill-down to reports such as that shown in Figure 12A.17.

FIGURE 12A.14
A Link Chart of
Distraction
Comments

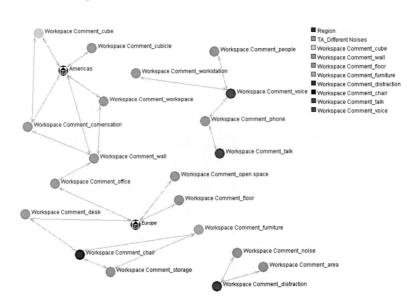

FIGURE 12A.15
Correlation Links

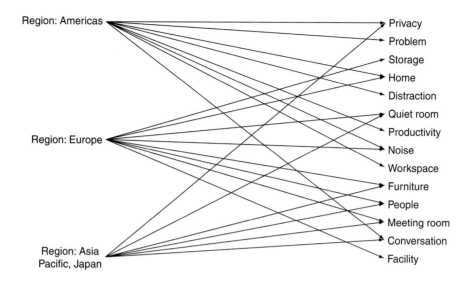

FIGURE 12A.16
A Snake Chart

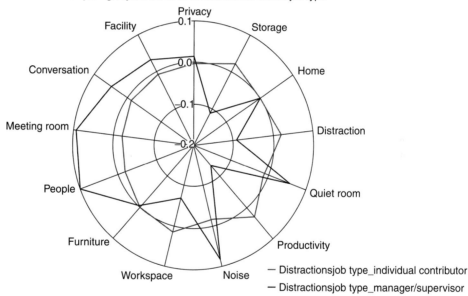

Comparing objects involved in distractions across job type

— Distractionsjob type_individual contributor
— Distractionsjob type_manager/supervisor

FIGURE 12A.17
A Drill-Down Report for Distractions by Managers

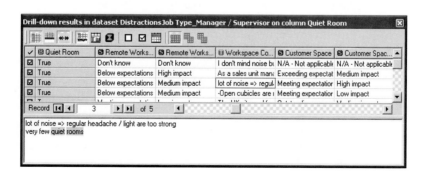

Drill-down results in dataset DistractionsJob Type_Manager / Supervisor on column Quiet Room

✓	▦ Quiet Room	⑤ Remote Works...	⑤ Remote Works...	⑪ Workspace Co...	⑤ Customer Space	⑤ Customer Spac...
☒	True	Don't know	Don't know	I don't mind noise bu	N/A - Not applicable	N/A - Not applicable
☒	True	Below expectations	High impact	As a sales unit mana	Exceeding expectat	Medium impact
☒	True	Below expectations	Medium impact	lot of noise => regul	Meeting expectation	High impact
☒	True	Below expectations	Medium impact	-Open cubicles are i	Meeting expectation	Low impact

Record ◄◄ ◄ 3 ► ►◄ of 5

lot of noise => regular headache / light are too strong
very few quiet rooms

FIGURE 12A.18
An OLAP Chart

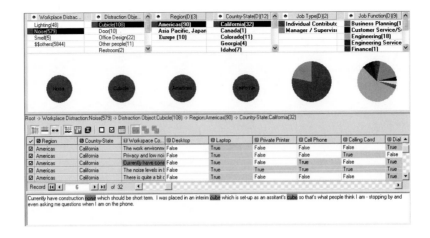

The snake chart, supplemented by specific reports obtained by drilling down, indicates that managers complain about difficulties in meetings, while individual employees complain more about lost productivity due to noise.

OLAP CHARTS

The text analysis of generated key terms can then be used to sort out the data by selected attributes. This is demonstrated in Figure 12A.18, which shows who is affected by noise, how they are affected, and where.

The analyst can select the header attributes. In this case, of the 6,476 comments in the database, 579 related to noise (48 to lighting, and five to smell). The analyst here has selected "Noise" for further analysis by job function. Of the 576 comments relating to noise, 108 involved cubicles. Of those 108, 90 involved the Americas region. Of those 90, 32 were from California. The analyst could search by group, but here those 32 records are available for detailed review. The first is displayed in the bottom window, with key terms highlighted by color.

In this case, the data indicates that engineers in California want better cubicle dividers to reduce noise. This is a demonstration of discovered knowledge, something that the user or analyst would not have known to expect without going through the process of text analysis.

SUMMARY

Text mining using PolyAnalyst software is supported by quantitative and qualitative tools. Quantitative support begins with visualization, providing histograms, pie charts, bar charts, and snake diagrams to show the relative density of key terms. Other quantitative support is provided by correlation models, through link charts, and decision trees sorting key terms. Qualitative support is provided by the process of identifying key words, which are categorized by the software, and a series of reports of subsets of data selected by the analyst. This leads to the development of business taxonomies, which can lead to a better understanding of survey data than would be possible by traditional methods where all variables have to be set up prior to analysis. In this example, a focus on the concept of distraction led to identification by region and job category. Analysis of the OLAP dimension matrix revealed support for issues such as the inadequate cubicle walls, which mostly affected engineering and customer service staff.

Summary

Text mining is much more challenging than quantitative data mining since numbers are much easier to process by computer than text. However, many useful tools have been developed to find patterns in text that divulge knowledge of human behavior. This can include learning about the intentions of competitors, as well as studying general customer actions.

Web mining has grown rapidly. It is characterized by at least three broad categories of application. First, the Web is a source of quantitative data that can be used along with other sources of data in data mining. Second, the behavior of web users at e-commerce or e-business web sites can be monitored with the intent of improving the profitability of such web sites. Third, the Web includes massive quantities of text, which can be used in text mining. Tools for searching the Web were among the first applications of technology to web analysis. There have been many artificial intelligence tools that have provided support to web mining. In the future, these tools may lead to the mining of multimedia data as well as text.

Glossary

clickstream technology Measurement of a web user's path through a web site.

cookie Very small file deposited on a web site visitor's hard drive, which is used to identify the visitor and track visits.

event logging The process of recording user-initiated activities.

imputation Inference of prediction for missing data.

link analysis Analytic technique graphically displaying the relationship among variables.

semantic networks (webs) Changing human language found in documents into a form that computers can process.

server log analysis Data analysis of data on server activity.

spam Junk messages obtained from e-mail (the term comes from an economical near-meat product).

text mining The application of large scale analysis of non-numeric data, symbols, or text.

web mining Use of data mining on the Web.

web server log A log of web site visitor activity, recording visitor clicks and entries.

wrapper Shell to integrate software into user applications

Exercises

1. Identify terms of interest in text mining in the following document:

   "There also is an issue related to **privacy.** Electronic technology provides ample opportunities for businesses to intrude on customers who use the Internet to do business (Brankovic and Estivill-Castro, 1999; Tavani, 1999b; Cary et al., 2003). The issue of prior permission is important, as well as third-party use of data. Data mining is a very valuable tool, but requires detailed data about customers. The more details gathered, the more understanding of consumer preferences. Maury and Kleiner (2002) stated that a major revenue stream for web-based businesses is to sell such information. Sama and Shoaf (2002) also discussed the privacy dilemma of e-business. Pragmatic accommodation of the needs of both consumers and e-business data miners is possible. But if care is not taken, we can expect improper invasion of the privacy of e-business customers."

2. Report on a search of the Web for 10 applications of text mining, all current to the last 12 months.

3. Report on five library articles within the past three years for applications of text mining.

4. Search the www.kdnuggets.org web site for text mining products.

5. Search the Web for 10 applications of web mining, all current to the last 12 months. Classify these applications as to the type of data they used.

6. Find five library articles within the past three years for applications of web mining. Classify these applications as to the type of data they used.

7. Search the www.kdnuggets.org web site for web mining products. Identify the type of data that they deal with (to the extent possible).

Endnotes

1. G. Du Bois, "Three Tuning Up Their Search Engines," *eWEEK*, 23, October 2000, p. 45.

2. W. M. Grossman, "E-Mail Lie Spy," *Smartbusinessmag.com*, June 2002, p. 34.

3. T. Sullivan, "SAS Uncovers Text-mining Deal," *Infoworld*, January 28, 2002, p. 28, www.infoworld.com.

4. R. Craig, "Tapping Text Resources," *ENT*, volume 5, issue 12, July 19, 2000, pp. 28–29.

5. S. Ivkovic, J. Yearwood, and A. Stanieri, "Discovering Interesting Association Rules from Legal Databases," *Information & Communication Technology Law*, volume 11, number 1, 2002, pp. 35–47.

6. Ibid.

7. M. D. Maury and D. S. Kleiner, "E-commerce, Ethical Commerce?" *Journal of Business Ethics*, volume 36, 2002, pp. 21–31.

8. A. G. Peace, J. Weber, K. S. Hartzel, and J. Nightingale, "Ethical Issues in ebusiness: A Proposal for Creating the ebusiness Principles," *Business and Society Review*, volume 107, number 1, 2002, pp. 41–60.

9. Ibid.

10. Z. Pabarskaite and A. Long, "Decision Trees for Web Log Mining," *Intelligent Data Analysis*, volume 7, 2003, pp. 141–154.

11. Anonymous, "Cinergy Marketing and Trading Mines Information Gems," *American Gas*, June 2003, pp. 10–11.

12. S. K. Pal, V. Talwar, and P. Mitra, "Web Mining in Soft Computing Frameworks: Relevance, State of the Art, and Future Directions," *IEEE Transactions on Neural Networks*, volume 13, number 5, 2002, pp. 1163–1177.

13. Pabarskaite and Long, op. cit.; R. Kosala and H. Blockeel, "Web Mining Research: A Survey," *ACM SIGKDD*, volume 2, issue 1, 2000, pp. 1–15.

14. D. Iacobucci, P. Arabie, and A. Bodapati, "Recommendation Agents on the Internet," *Journal of Interactive Marketing*, volume 14, number 3, 2000, pp. 2–11.

15. M. Spiliopoulou, "Web Usage Mining for Web Site Evaluation," *Communications of the ACM*, volume 43, number 8, 2000, pp. 127–134.

16. S. Kangas and A. Chiu, "Learning from Event Logging," www.netconversions.com, 2001.

17. B. Mobasher, R. Cooley, and J. Srivastava, "Automatic Personalization Based on Web Usage Mining," *Communications of the ACM*, volume 43, number 8, 2000, pp. 142–151.

18. C. Shahabi and F. Banaei-Kashani, "Efficient and Anonymous Web-Usage Mining for Web Personalization," *Journal on Computing*, volume 15, number 2, 2003, pp. 123–147.

19. M. Anandarajan, "Profiling Web Usage in the Workplace: A Behavior-Based Artificial Intelligence Approach," *Journal of Management Information Systems*, volume 19, number 1, 2002, pp. 243–266; R. Bapna, P. Goes, A. Gupta, and Y. Jin, "User Heterogeneity and Its Impact on Electronic Auction Market Design: An Empirical Exploration," *MIS Quarterly*, volume 28, number 1, 2004, pp. 21–43.

20. M.-D. Cohen, C. B. Kelly, and A. L. Medaglia, "Decision Support with Web-Enabled Software," *Interfaces*, volume 31, number 2, March-April 2001, pp. 109–129.

CHAPTER THIRTEEN

Ethical Aspects of Data Mining

This chapter:

- Presents issues in the use of sensitive data
- Gives examples of canceled data access applications
- Gives examples of threats to personal privacy and discrimination
- Discusses the effectiveness of publicity, litigation, and proactive action

The large amount of data generated by our global culture creates four major concerns:

1. We collect a great deal of information, much of which can be used for negative purposes.
2. There are often errors in this data.
3. Access to this data is not always as controlled as we would like.
4. It is tempting to use data that was collected for one purpose for other data mining studies.

The tools of data generation, data storage, and data mining are not immoral in themselves. This book has sought to demonstrate how data mining can be applied to benefit organizations. However, it is critically important to consider the negative possibilities of these tools as well. Every natural resource and artifact can be used for good or evil. The same is true for data mining. The ethical aspects of data mining are crucially important.

This importance is demonstrated by the example of the Matrix (Multistate Anti-Terrorism Information Exchange), a federally funded crime and terrorism database project to share information across agencies.[1] State records are combined with 20 billion pieces of data held by a private company. However, some states are concerned about privacy. In fact, the Governor of Utah halted that state's participation in January 2004, initiating a panel to examine security and privacy issues. Georgia also stated it was pulling out after Associated Press confrontation. In addition, other states have decided not to participate, some due to costs (each state might have to spend up to $1.8 million per year to participate). Proponents of the system argue that Matrix is an efficient use of information technology, but privacy advocates fear that law enforcement will gain too much access to details on millions of people.

This very real and current issue demonstrates the first and fourth points listed at the beginning of this chapter extremely well. We collect a great deal of information. It can be used for virtuous purposes, but there are usually disputes about just how virtuous or beneficial those particular purposes are. Furthermore, it's hard to adequately control data use when it's readily available. A consideration of the ethics of data mining is a very important issue.

The Hazards of Data Access

This book has concentrated on what can be done with data mining, and how it is done. But human systems have proven over and over to be highly nonlinear, with many unintended consequences.[2] Data mining technology is no different in that respect. Massive data storage facilities and software (statistical and artificially intelligent) that are capable of visualizing relationships and identifying patterns from large scale data sets give us many useful tools. However, as with almost everything complex, these technologies can create problems as well as solve them.[3]

There has long been a concern with the risks of concentrating too much data into one location. Simson Garfinkel relates a series of governmental projects proposing centralized data.[4]

- In 1965, there was a proposal to combine records from the Bureau of the Census, the Bureau of Labor Statistics, the Internal Revenue Service, and the Social Security Administration. Such a combined database was expected to reduce costs, and also lead to greater accuracy due to greater use and thus better identification of errors. It was also argued that such a centralized database would be easier to secure (although this point is debatable). In addition, it was envisioned that extra sources of data might be consolidated into this massive repository. However, concerns about ensuring privacy led to the project being canceled in 1968. A poll conducted by Harvard University in 1969 found that 56 percent of the populace opposed the project.

- In the private sector in the 1960s, credit bureaus were widely used to identify cases where loans were not repaid, payments were late, individuals were found to have changed addresses multiple times to evade creditors, and so on in an effort to measure the likelihood of bad credit risk. Consumers were rarely aware of the existence of these services, and credit bureau policies forbade consumers from seeing these files. Some consumers would note that their applications for loans were being denied regularly. Congressional action was taken, leading to the 1971 Fair Credit Reporting Act. This act allowed credit bureaus to use computers to track credit, but gave consumers rights to review their records, challenge them, and to insert their own version of events.

- In 1990, Lotus and Equifax jointly created a database entitled "Lotus Marketplace: Households," which was intended to include the names, addresses, and demographic information on every U.S. household. The intent of this database was to offer small businesses the ability to conduct market segmentation analysis as applied by larger organizations (see Chapter 4). While this might seem a noble effort to serve small business, there was strong negative reaction, with over 30,000 requests to Lotus to delete names. This negative reaction led to the cancellation of the proposed database.

- Lexis-Nexis is one of the most powerful database services in the market. Lexis provides attorneys the ability to search for related legal cases, while Nexis offers a search ability for news publications. In 1996, Lexis-Nexis started a project to develop the P-TRAK database, which would publish the social security numbers of most U.S. residents. When this project became public knowledge, thousands called Lexis-Nexis to complain, shutting down their telephone switchboard. Within 11 days, Lexis-Nexis discontinued the project.

- In 1997, the Social Security Administration publicized a service offered over the Internet that would enable taxpayers to obtain their detailed tax history. Security was considered, with personal information needed to access the system, similar to that used by credit card companies. This wasn't regarded as sufficient by tens of thousands who complained, leading to a Senate investigation and ultimately cancellation of the service.

While data mining offers the ability to learn many useful things, it is a powerful tool which can be used for bad as well as good. In fact, what is good for General Motors is not necessarily good for the consumers of General Motors products. Better information can lead to the design of products more useful to consumers, but which can also be used to extract more money for the same product. **Yield management** is designed to do just that for American Airlines and other carriers. Yield management is very similar to data mining—identifying the probability of last-minute cancellations to allow overbooking, and develop price schedules that maximize revenue obtained from customers. For most people, this is good business, and is to be commended. In fact, some would like to see similar tools available to consumers to help in competing with the airlines.

There are threats inherent in the use of large-scale databases. One threat is the process of **inference,** where acquisition of various pieces of information that are not threatening or intrusive in themselves can be put together to learn more than was initially authorized. Inference can have negative ramifications with respect to privacy and civil liberties.[5] For instance, the amount of sales for a particular organization may be protected by regulation. Sales tax information is collected and used for other purposes, such as monitoring the value of particular industries by SIC code. But if a particular organization is the only distributor of a specific product in a given geographic area by which the data is organized, one can infer that organization's sales of that product from the data. This can be protected against by not reporting data when there are fewer than three organizations with sales activity. Another sensitive issue might be insurance data. There are legitimate reasons for insurance companies to collect data on traffic violations, and insurance claims. However, this information, when tied to a specific individual identifier (such as a Social Security number), can yield more information than intended.

Other nuisances created by data mining exist. Some of us don't appreciate all of the sales opportunities offered to us over the telephone at meal-time. Marketing sometimes seems to be out of control. Recent regulations have been imposed to offer us the ability to take our names off of telephone lists, but the news media emphasizes the many loopholes that still exist. Organizations in these trying economic times have found alternative sources of income through sales of membership data. Personal information has become a commodity. Furthermore, just because data is recorded on a computer database doesn't make it correct. There also is the danger that while controls may be emplaced, dramatic events could lead to use of the data they were intended to protect. After September 11, 2001, the American public placed a much higher emphasis upon the ability to track potentially dangerous individuals than it did on protecting individual data. Data mining has been credited with tracing those responsible for the bombing of the Oklahoma City Federal Building. There have been a number of instances where pressure has been placed on law enforcement agencies to access data that was previously considered to be protected. Garfinkel cited a case of the Drug Enforcement Agency (DEA) demanding access to drug chain frequent-buyer inventories.[6] Most of us would support the DEA's efforts to better enforce our drug laws. However, this is an example of a governmental agency using data gathered for one purpose and then implementing it in an entirely different fashion without the authorization of those affected.

In the field of personal identification, fingerprints have long been a mainstay. Each of us has fingerprints that consist of over 90 elements, providing a characteristic that's unique to each of us. The FBI has long gathered a database on fingerprints. In fact, they were so effective in this endeavor that in 1987 they needed computers to do more than simply match prints with names. Another biological characteristic that recently has become extremely helpful in the realms of identification is DNA. A database of DNA is being gathered that would be useful to many. Not only does DNA provide an identifier that is highly unique for individuals (except for identical twins), it also can be used to predict health characteristics. Insurance companies, for instance, could mine DNA data in order to possibly predict future health risks. This would enable them to offer lower rates to those with low genetic propensities toward certain maladies, such as heart attack, stroke, or cancer. However, those less fortunate from a genetic perspective would be placed in great jeopardy. Should their histories be left simply to market interpretation and follow-through, they would likely pay medical insurance rates that are extremely high. In such cases, should the government instead step in and pay such high-risk premiums? Would it be better not to know **risk propensities,** and to pool insurance risks with those more fortunate? This knowledge could be carried even further, with DNA testing conducted at (or before) birth, opening up the possibility of policy options most of us would find abhorrent. An even more drastic step would be the Orwellian imposition of government policies that allow or bar marriage (or parenting) by individuals based upon an evaluation of their DNA.

Web Data Mining Issues

The masses of data available on the Web make some forms of data mining highly attractive in that they can access information critical to one's domain of decision making. This type of web mining can take a number of different forms. Web access has been used to better control operations and to monitor customers. The web makes data mining easier through access to large volumes of data, either from external sources or through internal sources such as enterprise resource planning systems. There also is an opportunity to data mine web log activity.

Like almost every other good thing, this opportunity comes with potential problems. First is the issue of privacy. The open nature of the Web makes almost everything we place on it available to the world, including competitors, adversaries, or governmental agencies. Technology makes it easy to monitor the web usage of others, and has created an industry out of selling such data, much of it obtained through web mining, and usually without the subject's permission. Web mining also can lead to new forms of discrimination.

Where technology meets opportunity, heavy use can be expected. Spiliopoulou identified three broad applications of web mining in regards to marketing: data acquisition, measurement of cost and quality, and assessment of user/owner satisfaction.[7] This is much faster and less expensive than mail surveys. Invasive data acquisition methods actively contact users through questionnaires or other methods. Data acquisition can be non-invasive by recording user behavior without their interaction. **Web server logs** are the primary means of obtaining this information. Web-based data collection has been found to be unobtrusive, experimentally based, externally valid, and easily capable of obtaining large sample sizes. See Chapter 11 for more on the various applications of web mining.

The Problem

The World Wide Web has grown exponentially. Web-based tracking has a number of positive features, such as **user profiling,** which is intended to be helpful to customers (in the sense that businesses try to sell things that customers need). The same is true for market research, with profile data being used to design products that will theoretically have a greater value to consumers. Portal support to ease transactions is also positive, making it more convenient to do business. Web access for businesses to reach customers and to cooperate with other businesses in various chains has proven invaluable. There is, however, the potential for web linkage to cause damage through privacy invasion and discrimination. Web monitoring can easily extend itself to the Big Brother presence that Aldous Huxley and George Orwell warned us about. More threatening at the moment is theft of identity, a growing criminal activity. Table 13.1 compares the pros of web mining with its cons.

In short, the Web itself is a tool that provides many benefits to business. It reaches much broader markets much faster. It allows business organizations to communicate with each other thus enhancing coordination and cooperation, and permits businesses to exchange information within the organization much faster and more efficiently as well. Consumers benefit by being able to comparison shop at their convenience. However, as with any tool, abuse is possible. Web ethics are important because the potential for abuse needs to be considered.

Web Ethics

There are a number of ethical issues involved in web mining. Privacy is an obvious issue. But there are other concerns, including the price discrimination inherent in yield management types of marketing. The **utilitarian view** (greatest good for the greatest number)[8] is the basis for most logical positivist philosophies shared by many business decision makers. Web mining practitioners realize that

TABLE 13.1
Web Mining Benefits and Negative Aspects

Benefits	Benefit Elements	Negative Features	Instances of Negative Impact
Business freedom	Make more profit	Discrimination	Use of Web to profile customers illegally
Make more profit	CRM Statistics: insurance, banking ERP: use of generated data	Privacy abuse	Identity theft
Consumer gets better deals	Intelligent marketing *could* lower prices Consumers see more opportunities	Telemarketing	Nuisance

some damage to particular individuals may be possible, but their primary focus is on getting a good job done for their organization. The **Rawlsian view** places much more emphasis on individual protection.[9] This view is more conservative (in the sense of protecting individual interests). This approach is held by many, although it can lead to the extreme of paralyzing business. The **pragmatic view** (decisions are best that lead to the best outcomes) provides a compromise.[10] (There are an endless number of other philosophical refinements which we're not in a position to relate.) Web mining is a technology with the potential to do a lot of good, but it can also impact individuals negatively.

Privacy Issues

Mason (a well-published MIS researcher) was a very early predictor of the danger of computer infringement on personal privacy.[11] He warned that the twin drivers of ability and value would make it likely that someone would take advantage of the access to personal systems. Data mining is a very valuable tool, but requires detailed data about customers. The more details that can be gathered, the more understanding of consumer preferences is gained. Two studies recently published in the *Journal of Business Ethics* cited problems with this opportunity. Maury and Kleiner stated that a major revenue stream for web-based businesses is to sell such information.[12] Sama and Shoaf also discussed the privacy dilemma of e-business.[13] Pragmatic accommodation of the needs of both consumers and e-business data miners is possible. But if care is not taken, we can expect the improper invasion of the privacy of e-business customers. Levine[14] reviewed a number of privacy factors, shown in Table 13.2.

It's important that personal information be protected through aggregation. Even then, it is dangerous to make it easy to identify the specific profile of each individual (which after all is a necessary condition for effective use of data mining results).

There are a number of technical tools developed to support web mining (as well as other functions).[15] **Portals** regulate the distribution of information given to users, and can generate actions to enhance sales volume. **Site trackers** collect information, often without the knowledge of the customer. **Profilers** are sets of data about individual web surfing and buying habits. This data is obtained through trackers, which can be placed on a web page to monitor visitor time and keywords. The existence of profilers is given as an icon appearing on the user's screen. **Search bots** gather information on Internet users and take actions such as sending advertisements. In addition to having agent capabilities, search bots are covert, with no introduction given on the user's screen. There's also the ability to

TABLE 13.2
Web Privacy Factors

Factor	Function	Utilitarian	Rawlsian
Freedom	Protection from social ostracism, punishment, discrimination, and criticism	More focus on society than individual	Individual is the focus
Informed consent	Permission required	Not central	Strong importance
Personality development	Private reflection and experimentation for growth	Not central	Individual focus
Avoidance of discrimination	Laws insufficient for personal protection	Hinders society	Individual protection
Separation	Market, family, religion, politics, other relationships separated	Complete data access helps planning	Individual protection over full disclosure

establish hyperlinks to customer web sites, including **deep-linking** (which allows web site providers to link to other sites, without crediting those other sites for their content), **meta-tagging** (posting keywords on their web site to falsely lure search engines), framing, and in-line linking.[16]

Cookies provide web site owners with the ability to gather detailed data, and enter into data mining, which can be viewed as a service to the customer, although cynics might be more impressed by the service to the web retailer's bottom line. The Rawlsian philosophy of distributive justice would argue for giving the customer a fair opportunity to veto the presence of the cookie. A more pragmatic view would allow web retailers to do what their competitors do (or what the legal system allows them to do).

The extent of Internet privacy invasion through portals is impressive. Peace, et al. reported a survey of the 100 web sites with the most volume.[17] Of these 100 sites, 86 used cookie technology, while 35 of them allowed advertisers to set cookies. Of these, 18 did not provide a privacy policy.

Discrimination

Discrimination can occur through use of consumer profiles that exclude classes of consumers from market participation, or that limit access to essential information.[18] A key concept in customer segmentation, a fundamental data mining practice, is to separate customers into groups, treating each group differently. After identifying price sensitivity by group through data mining, the seller may offer special prices to specific customer groups. Implementation of price discrimination is often applied by banks, which charge extra for services that they would prefer customers didn't use (such as encouraging the use of ATMs rather than more expensive human tellers).

A variant form of price discrimination would be product versioning, implemented by airlines that offer different priced tickets depending upon the degree of restrictions. In this case, customers can self-select, by paying more for the removal of various restrictions, such as allowing weekend travel or the ability to change itineraries. The film industry applies windowing, another form of price discrimination. Through windowing, the same film can be sold in many different channels, such as theaters, DVDs, cable TV, network TV, or syndication. Usually versioning is implemented by staggering release times of the film in various media to maximize revenue. Since consumers can select the form of goods they want (at different prices), these forms of discrimination are deemed acceptable by most.

Yet another form of technologically enabled discrimination has been labeled web-lining by Danna and Gandy. One example cited was Kozmo.com, an Internet-based home-delivery service. Kozmo.com defined its service area on the basis of Internet usage. This was considered a form of **web-lining,** because classes of customers were excluded based on neighborhood characteristics rather than individual characteristics. Kozmo thus did not make its services available to predominately African-American neighborhoods. As a result, Kozmo was forced out of business in litigation based on the identification of patterns of discrimination.

Methods of Control

Alternative philosophies would suggest different means of controlling web mining (and data mining in general). The World Wide Web was designed as an uncontrolled entity, encouraging the exchange of information. It does that fairly well, and it would be a shame to lose the many benefits it offers of being able to communicate freely throughout the world. These benefits include the positive outcomes of web mining, such as broader exposure to products, the ability to tailor products for individual tastes, and the potential for lower marketing costs (which in theory could be passed on to consumers).

However, totally unrestricted web mining can infringe upon the rights of others. Telemarketing is a benefit that many of us would rather forego, for instance. There's also a great potential for the abuse of privacy—more serious forms of privacy invasion including malicious identity theft. Obviously, some aspects of our lives (such as medical histories, tax records, and court dockets) we would rather not have shared with the rest of the world in an uncontrolled manner.

The final issue involves the potential for harmful discrimination. Web mining offers its users the opportunity to select their customers. The primary idea behind bank loan analysis (and insurance) through data mining is to avoid giving loans (or policies) to those less likely to pay (or less likely to make claims). Thus, there's a fine gray line between identification of bad credit risks and fair treatment—a line which has been defined by litigation over many years.

More rigid control of web mining is risky, though. First, there's the problem of who has authority over the Internet. The Web's international nature probably provides it some assurance of freedom; however, each country still imposes some control over internal traffic (with varying degrees of thoroughness). Second, granting the ability to any agency to more rigidly control the Web would impose the type of access consumers wish to avoid in the first place. After all, who would police the police?

The way in which control is currently imposed is systemic and market-driven. Publicity is the most effective way to modify behavior that steps over the line. This approach usually works since businesses operate in a climate where there is perceived value in avoiding unhappy customers. Pressure from watchdog organizations modified the behavior of DoubleClick cited earlier. If publicity doesn't work, litigation is a more severe (and expensive) resort. For example, litigation worked to modify the behavior of Kozmo.com. Publicity is the market-driven element, and litigation the systemic corrective for more involved cases. In a pragmatic sense, these control devices seem to work.

Summary

Data mining is a potentially useful tool, capable of doing a lot of good, not only for business but also for the medical field and for government. It does, however, bring with it some dangers. So, how can we best protect ourselves, especially in the area of business data mining?

A number of options exist. Strict control of data usage through governmental regulation was proposed by Garfinkel.[19] This chapter began with a review of a number of large database projects that were ultimately stopped. Those involving government agencies were successfully stopped due to public exposure, the negative outcry leading to cancellation of the National Data Center and the Social Security Administration projects. A system with closely held information by credit bureaus in the 1960s was only stopped after governmental intervention, which included the passage of new laws. Times have changed, with business adopting a more responsive attitude toward consumers. Innovative data mining efforts by Lotus/Equifax and by Lexis-Nexis were quickly stopped by public pressure alone.

Public pressure seems to be quite effective in providing some control over potential data mining abuses. If that fails, litigation is available (although slow in effect). It is necessary for us to realize what businesses can do with data. There never will be a perfect system to protect us, and we need to be vigilant. However, too much control can be dangerous, too, inhibiting the ability of business to provide better products and services through data mining. Garfinkel prefers more governmental intervention, while we would prefer less governmental intervention and more reliance on publicity and, if necessary, the legal system.

Web mining is a natural extension of the use of technology. The vast majority of web-site content is predominately not of interest to any one individual. Search engines display a great deal of intelligence and cunning in their ability to identify content related to specific keys. But we all have used keywords yielding thousands of contacts that we did not want, and sometimes have difficulty finding useful content. Web mining provides a more efficient ability to identify relevant content, but with this technological ability comes the risk of abuse.

Control would be best accomplished if it were naturally encouraged by systemic relationships. The first systemic means of control is publicity. Should those adopting questionable practices persist, litigation is a slow, costly, but ultimately effective means of system correction. However, before taking drastic action, a good rule is that if the system works, it's best not to fix it. The best measure that electronic retailers can take is probably the pragmatic Calpurnian solution: don't do anything that will cause customers to suspect that their rights are being violated. Editor: I like "best" better—it isn't necessarily efficient.

Glossary

cookie   Software attached to a web site visitor's computer to identify personal characteristics or preferences for future reference.

deep-linking   The ability to link one's own web site to other sites.

inference   The process of posing queries and deducing unauthorized information from legitimate responses.

meta-tagging   The posting of keywords on others' web sites with the intent of attracting search engines.

portals   Gateways to network systems that are usually capable of being tailored to individual preferences.

pragmatic view   View that decisions are best that lead to the best outcomes.

profiler   Sets of data about buying habits of a class of customer.

Rawlsian view   Emphasis on preservation of the rights of the weakest member.

risk propensity   Likelihood of an event for a particular group.

search bot   Software that gathers information on Internet users, and that's capable of taking action, such as sending advertisements.

site trackers   Software that gathers information about a web site visitor.

user profiling   Identification of a subgroup of a population with unique characteristics relative to product demand.

utilitarian view   View that decisions are best that provide the greatest sum of good over all members of society.

web-lining   Using web facilities to illegally discriminate against a particular group.

web server log   A log of web site visitor activity that records visitor clicks and entries.

yield management   Using statistics, probability analysis, and industry plane seat reservation systems as a basis for dynamic ticket pricing.

Exercises

1. Discuss the major concerns people have regarding the mining of large databases.
2. What means of resistance to the use of large databases have been used, and how effective have they been?
3. Find articles (or references on the Web) to cases where data mining efforts were halted. Try to determine the role of (1) publicity, (2) litigation, and (3) governmental regulation in the cancellation.
4. Identify and report on instances of governmental use of information that was gathered for the purpose of controlling some problem (for instance, drug control, terrorist threats, and so on).
5. Discuss the conflicting issues regarding the need for greater information sharing by law enforcement in the light of privacy needs.
6. Outline possible privacy infringement that may be caused by data mining.

Endnotes

1. B. Bergstein, "Some States Plug Into Matrix," *Lincoln Journal Star*, 1 February 2004, p. 3A.
2. The unintended consequences of technology are thoroughly described by C. Perrow, *Normal Accidents: Living with High-Risk Technologies*, Princeton, NJ: Princeton University Press, 1999; E. Tenner, *Why Things Bite Back: Technology and the Revenge of Unintended Consequences*, New York: Vintage Books, 1996; and D. Dörner, *The Logic of Failure: Recognizing and Avoiding Error in Complex Situations*, New York: Metropolitan Books, 1996.
3. J. S. Brown and P. Duguid, *The Social Life of Information*, Boston: Harvard Business School Press, 2000.
4. S. Garfinkel, Database Nation: *The Death of Privacy in the 21st Century*, Cambridge, MA: O'Reilly & Associates, 2000.
5. B. Thuraisingham, "Data Mining, National Security, Privacy, and Civil Liberties," *SIGKDD Explorations*, volume 4, number 2, 2002, pp. 1–15.
6. Ibid.
7. M. Spiliopoulou, "Web Usage Mining for Web Site Evaluation," *Communications of the ACM*, volume 43, number 8, 2000, pp. 127–134.
8. J. S. Mill, *Utilitarianism*, New York: Prometheus Books, 1987 (original 1863).
9. J. Rawls, *A Theory of Justice, revised edition*, Cambridge, MA: Harvard University Press, 1999 (original 1971); J. Rawls, *Justice as Fairness: A Restatement*, Cambridge, MA: The Belknap Press, 2001.
10. W. James, *Pragmatism*, New York, Prometheus Books, 1991 (original 1907).
11. R. Mason, "Four Ethical Issues of the Information Age," *MIS Quarterly*, volume 10, number 1, 1986, pp. 5–12.
12. M. D. Maury and D. S. Kleiner, "E-Commerce, Ethical Commerce?" *Journal of Business Ethics*, volume 36, 2002, pp. 21–31.
13. L. M. Sama and V. Shoaf, "Ethics on the Web: Applying Moral Decision-Making to the New Media," *Journal of Business Ethics*, volume 36, numbers 1–2, 2002, pp. 93–103.

14. P. Levine, "Information Technology and the Social Construction of Information Privacy: Comment," *Journal of Accounting and Public Policy*, volume 22, 2003, pp. 281–285.

15. M. Calkins, "Rippers, Portal Users, and Profilers: Three Web-Based Issues for Business Ethicists," *Business and Society Review*, volume 107, number 1, 2002, pp. 61–75.

16. Maury and Kleiner, op. cit.

17. A. G. Peace, J. Weber, K. S. Hartzel, and J. Nightingale, "Ethical Issues in Ebusiness: A Proposal for Creating the Ebusiness Principles," *Business and Society Review*, volume 107, number 1, 2002, pp. 41–60.

18. A. Danna and O. H. Gandy, Jr., "All that Glitters Is Not Gold: Digging Beneath the Surface of Data Mining," *Journal of Business Ethics*, volume 40, 2002, pp. 373–386.

19. S. Garfinkel, *Database Nation: The Death of Privacy in the 21st Century*, Cambridge, MA: O'Reilly & Associates, 2000.

GLOSSARY

A

actionable Information that can be used to make more effective business decisions (make more profit). 8

affinity positioning Laying out retail stores to place complementary products together. 8

analysis of variance (ANOVA) Analysis of model errors (specifically, the differences among group means).

artificial intelligence Use of machine learning to reach conclusions; in the context of data mining, use of neural networks, case-based reasoning, genetic algorithms, and other AI tools. 54

association Data mining function identifying correlation patterns; set of rules used to express relationships among data. 25

B

backpropogation Commonly used learning rule in neural networks, where results of prior iterations are used to guide model adjustments in future iterations. 124

boosting Procedure applying multiple models and using selections of each model as votes for a predicted category. 199

bootstrapping Sampling technique to generate greater understanding from small data sets. 201

branches The subcategories on a decision tree. 136

C

churn Turnover in customers; especially the loss of customers in the telephone industry. 5

classification Analysis that assigns cases to different classes. 25

clickstream technology Measurement of a Web user's path through a Web site. 234

cluster Group of related objects, often defined by shared characteristics.

clustering Analysis that groups data into classes; an initial analytic tool that identifies general groupings in data. 26

cluster analysis Statistical technique to group data into discrete sets. 206

coincidence matrix Table displaying actual counts with model predictions. 29

compromise solution A best tradeoff in terms of the shortest norm-distance between the ideal value and tradeoff points. 169

confidence level The number of events where items that were associated are divided by the total number of events for the base item. 138

constraints Linear equalities or inequalities that represent a limitation condition in linear programming. 165

co-occurrence table A list of products purchased together. 213

cookie Very small file deposited on a web site visitor's hard drive, which is then used to identify the visitor and track their visits. 233

correct classification rate Ratio of correct assignments of test cases to total opportunities. 29

correlation A measure of the linear relationship between two variables. 212

correlation coefficient Covariance divided by the standard deviation of each variable. 214

cost function The sum of test case errors multiplied by expected cost by type of error. 29

covariance Average of the products of deviations of each observation from its respective mean.

cross-selling Marketing products to a customer that are related to other products the customer has purchased. 8

customer profile Description of a case by values or categories for selected variables. 84

customer profiling Identification of good customers. 5

customer relationship management (CRM) Use of data mining to identify details about a customer, including the customer's value to the organization, and the characteristics that the customer is looking for in products. 9

D

data integrity Elimination of meaningless, corrupt, or redundant data. 44

data management Retrieving information from the data warehouse. 35

data mart A database system used to extract a subset of data from a data warehouse so it can be used for a data mining application. 12

data standardization Process of developing unique variable values. 44

261

data warehouse   A large-scale data storage system designed to contain complete and clean data that can be accessed efficiently. 35

data warehouse generation   The process of extracting data from sources, transforming and cleansing this data, and then loading the data into the data warehouse. 39

decision trees   Logical branching on variables that enumerates cases with outputs. 135

deep-linking   The ability to link one's own web site with other sites. 256

demographic data   Data relating to population characteristics. 22

detection   Identification of anomalies and irregularities, as in fraud detection. 56

discriminant analysis   Identifies which category an observation most likely belongs to. 109

E

entropy   Measure of information, or more specifically, the degree of randomness in data. Lower scores indicate more of an ability to discriminate outcome categories. 139

estimation   Method used to predict an outcome. 53

event logging   The process of recording user-initiated activities. 234

expert system   Artificial intelligence system designed to replicate the behavior of an expert. Usually implemented through a series of production rules (IF-THEN). 146

G

goal driven   Method of generating rules through induction based on improved successful performance.

granularity   The level of data detail. 36

H

heuristic   Method of reaching conclusions that works fairly successfully, but does not guarantee optimality. 136

hypercube   Term used to describe the multidimensional capabilities of OLAP systems. 37

hypothesis testing   Developing a theory and then conducting a test to statistically validate or reject the theory. 5

I

imputation   Inference of prediction for missing data; filling in missing data with values consistent with adjacent data. 22

infeasible solution   A solution which exceeds the limitation conditions of the constraints. 176

inference   The process of posing queries and deducing unauthorized information from legitimate responses. 252

interestingness   Characteristic of rules that are recognized as important and unexpected. 138

J

jackknifing   The use of advanced statistical sampling to generate greater understanding from small data sets. 199

K

k-means clustering   Clustering technique where the number of clusters is predefined. 75

knowledge discovery   Looking for patterns in data without relying on preconceived theories. 4

L

lift   The marginal difference in a segment's proportion of response to a promotion and the average rate of response. 191

linear discriminant analysis   Discriminant analysis based upon a discriminant function identified through linear regression. 109

link analysis   Analytic technique graphically displaying the relationship among variables. 226

logistic regression   Regression based upon the probability of membership in one of two or more groups. 100

M

machine learning   A system to develop rules automatically. 138

market-basket analysis   Analysis of the tendency for purchase of items by the same consumer at the same time. 211

matching   Associating variables. 45

maximize the minimum distances (MMD) Finding the shortest distance from data to an adjusted boundary, and then finding the largest value of the resulting shortest data distances. 165

median Average based on the midpoint value for each variable. 84

metadata A set of references to keep track of data. 40

meta-tagging Posting of keywords on others' web sites with the intent of attracting search engines. 256

micromarketing Focused marketing directed at a small subset of the total population. This subset is expected to contain a much higher proportion of product purchasers than the general population. 4

minimize the sum of the deviations (MSD) Finding the model with the smallest sum of deviations from actual observations. 165

multilayered feedforward neural networks Common structure of a neural network model, with multiple hidden layers connecting arcs with data inputs that lead through the hidden layers to output. 124

multiple criteria linear programming A generalization of linear programming with multiple conflict objective functions instead of a single objective function. 169

N

near optimal solution A solution which is feasible to all constraints in a linear program and close to the value of the optimal solution. 172

neural network Artificial intelligence model based upon fitting data with a network of arcs that consist of weights which have been adjusted to optimize fit. 123

node A decision tree element where branching takes place. 136

normalize Statistical operation to subtract the mean and divide by the standard deviation in order to put data on a scale where dispersion is easy to detect. 85

O

objective function A mathematical representation of a target or goal in mathematical programming. In linear programming, it can be a linear combination of decision (or attribute) variables. 165

online analytic processing (OLAP) Tools for accessing databases with the intent of providing

users with a multidimensional display of information. 35

optimal coefficients The optimal solution for the coefficients of attributes among the data observations. They are used to determine the score for classification. 165

optimal solution The best decision values obtained by solving a linear programming. 172

outlier Statistical observation with variable values quite different from the majority of other observations. 85

P

pattern search Mathematical procedure to analyze data using a systematic pattern. 84

portals Gateways to network systems, which are usually capable of being tailored to individual preferences. 255

pragmatic view View that decisions are best that lead to the best outcomes. 255

prediction Model used to take explanatory variable inputs and convert them through a formula to predict an outcome variable. 26

profiler Sets of data about the buying habits of a class of customer. 255

purchase profile A prototypical type of customer. 214

Q

qualitative data Data not measured numerically. 22

quantitative data Data measured numerically. 22

R

Rawlsian view View with an emphasis on the preservation of the rights of the weakest member. 255

regression Mathematical model to fit data based upon the minimization of one of many possible error metrics. 100

regression tree Decision tree based upon continuous outcomes. 137

risk propensity Likelihood of an event occurring for a particular group. 253

rule induction Algorithms capable of generating sets of rules based upon the analysis of data. 138

rule-based system   Algorithm that classifies cases based upon a set of association rules developed from a training set. 136

S

scalable   The ability to efficiently analyze very large data sets. 6

search bot   Software that gathers information on Internet users, and which is capable of taking action such as sending advertisements. 255

self-organizing map   Clustering algorithm based on neural network technology. 85

self-organizing neural networks   Neural networks capable of adjusting the number of clusters. 124

semantic networks (webs)   Changes human language found in documents into a form which computers can process. 225

sequential pattern analysis   A search for patterns of similarity. 26

server log analysis   Data analysis of data on server activity. 234

similar time sequences   A search for sequences in data. 26

site trackers   Software used to gather information about a web site visitor. 255

socio-graphical data   Data related to cultural activities. 22

spam   Junk messages obtained from e-mail (the term comes from an economical near-meat product). 226

statistics   In the context of data mining tools, the use of algorithms based on traditional statistical methods, such as regression. 55

sum of squared errors (SSE)   Model error squared and added. 103

summarization   Descriptive statistical and graphical analysis that shows variable features to data mining analysts. 54

support   The proportion of records covered by a set of attributes. 138

T

targeting   Determination of the characteristics of customers who have left for competitors. 5

test set   Portion of the data available that's used to test the data mining model. 25

text mining   Application of large-scale analysis of non-numeric data, symbols, or text. 25

threshold   An acceptable (or cutting) value given by the decision maker for the desirable data mining results. 172

time intelligence   The ability to specify a variety of time dimensions for reporting. 37

time series   Data set of a variable measured over time. 100

trade-offs   The variations of different combinations regarding multiple and conflicting objective functions. 169

training set   Portion of the data available that's used to build the data mining model. 25

transactional data   Data related to business activities at the basic level. 22

U

unbounded solution   An unlimited objective case that occurs while searching for the optimal solution. 175

undirected knowledge discovery   Automatic data mining analysis where the computer software identifies relationships without user guidance. 85

user profiling   Identification of a subgroup of a population with unique characteristics relative to product demand. 254

utilitarian view   View in which decisions are best that provide the greatest sum of good for all members of society. 254

V

versatile   Providing a wide variety of data mining tools. 6

W

web-lining   Using web facilities to illegally discriminate against a particular group. 256

web mining   Use of data mining on the web. 226

web server log   Log of web site visitor activity that records visitor clicks and entries. 234

wrapper   Shell to integrate software into user applications.

Y

yield management   Using statistics, probability analysis, and industry plane seat reservation systems as a basis for dynamic ticket pricing. 252

Index

software
  clustering methods used in, 85–86
  for market-basket analysis, 217
software development quality as a
    decision tree application, 144–146
software products
  for data mining, 13
  decision trees, 153
  including neural network
    technology, 130–131
  for text mining, 231–232
SOM. *See* Kohonen self-organizing
    maps; self-organizing maps
space allocation, 215
spam, 247, 264
sparseness of market-based data, 211
spreadsheet approach to shared data
    storage, 37
squared distance, 75
SSE (sum of squared errors), 103, 104
SST (sum of squared deviations of the
    dependent variable), 104
standardized data, 114, 128–129
standardized form, 86
stars, cluster analysis of, 74, 75
statistical approaches to
    classification, 26
statistical classification, compared to
    data mining, 200
statistical estimation, 25
statistical methods
  preprocessing data, 23
  systematic exploration through
    classical, 5
statistical techniques, 54
statistics, 71, 264
stepwise regression, 113–114, 119
stochastic search, algorithms using, 153
stratified method in Enterprise
    Miner, 65
string data type in PolyAnalyst, 23
subclusters, 85
subscription fraud in
    telecommunications, 11
sum of squared distances, 109
sum of squared errors (SSE), 103, 104
sum of squared residuals (SSE), 120, 264
summarization, 71, 264
Summers Rubber Company, 34, 46–48
supervised approach to data mining, 4
support, 138, 160, 264
support factor, 25
survey results, adding to a data
    mart, 42
Symbolic Knowledge Acquisition
    Technology (SKAT), 91
synaptic connections in the human
    brain, 123
synonyms, 226, 227
SYSTAT, 127
System for Information Delivery, 14

T

target hazard, modeling, 195
target variable, selecting, 63–64
targeted marketing programs, 8
targeting, 5, 15, 264
taxonomy
  classification, 242–246
  for web mining research, 233–234
technical metadata, 40, 41
technical tools, supporting web
    mining, 255
telecommunications, 11–12
telemarketing, 12
telephone companies, 99
telephone customer problems, 11
tenure. *See* customer tenure
test set, 25, 32, 125, 264
text data, 237, 238
text data type in PolyAnalyst, 23
Text Miner, 232
text mining, 225–226, 247, 264
  applied to legal databases,
    230–231
  demonstration of, 227–228
  identification of key terms,
    226–227
  software, 227, 231–232
  uses of, 226
Text Mining software from
    PolyAnalyst, 238
textual data, data mining of, 225
theft of identity, 254
three-class MCLP model, 170–171,
    179, 183
threshold, 185, 264
  levels in machine learning
    systems, 138
  value in FLP, 172
time intelligence, 37, 49, 264
time series, 120, 132, 264
time series data, 101
  forecasts from the regression
    model, 102
  graph of, 101
  graph with forecasts, 102–103
  regression output of, 102
tolerance level, 123, 125
Toyota, 4
tradeoffs, 185, 264
traditional lifetime value, 127–128
training set, 25, 32, 264
transaction processing systems, 46
transactional data, 22, 32, 264
transformation of data warehouse data,
    33–34
transformation programs, 39
Tree Statistics box in Enterprise
    Miner, 69
trend chart in PolyAnalyst, 240, 241
trend line, extending, 100–103

trends
  analyzing, 42
  spotting, 12
T-scores in Enterprise Miner, 66, 67
two-class MCLP model, 169–170
two-class MCLP problem, 183
TwoStep Clementine model, 87, 88
two-step clustering, 85, 86
TwoStep method, 85
TYPELESS data type in Clementine, 23

U

UCI Machine Learning Repository, 14
unbounded solution, 175, 185, 264
undirected knowledge discovery, 85,
    96, 264
undirected market-basket analysis, 216
United Sugars Corporation, 235
unstructured text analysis, 242, 243
unsupervised approach to data
    mining, 4
U.S. Army, 74, 75
user dictionaries in PolyAnalyst, 238
user profiling, 254, 258, 264
user-initiated activities, 234
utilitarian view, 254, 258, 264

V

validation
  during data warehouse
    implementation, 45
  jackknife, 199, 201, 208
variables
  associating, 45
  coding as ordinal, 107
  describing cardholders'
    behavior, 176
  developing unique values, 44
  emphasizing using weights in cluster
    analysis, 79
  independence of, 22
  interactions considered by artificial
    neural network models, 126
vendors by product category, 45–46
VeriComp software, 11
versatility, 15, 264
versioning, 256
visualization, 20, 23

W

Wall Street Journal, classifying
    countries, 200–201
Wal-Mart, 34, 46
warehouse generation. *See* data
    warehouses